Christianity and
Social Systems

Christianity and Social Systems

Historical Constructions and Ethical Challenges

Rosemary Radford Ruether

ROWMAN & LITTLEFIELD PUBLISHERS, INC.
Lanham • Boulder • New York • Plymouth, UK

ROWMAN & LITTLEFIELD PUBLISHERS, INC.

Published in the United States of America
by Rowman & Littlefield Publishers, Inc.
A wholly owned subsidiary of The Rowman & Littlefield Publishing Group, Inc.
4501 Forbes Boulevard, Suite 200, Lanham, Maryland 20706
www.rowmanlittlefield.com

Estover Road
Plymouth PL6 7PY
United Kingdom

Copyright © 2009 by Rowman & Littlefield Publishers, Inc.

All rights reserved. No part of this publication may be reproduced, stored in a retrieval system, or transmitted in any form or by any means, electronic, mechanical, photocopying, recording, or otherwise, without the prior permission of the publisher.

British Library Cataloguing in Publication Information Available

Library of Congress Cataloging-in-Publication Data:

Ruether, Rosemary Radford.
  Christianity and social systems : historical constructions and ethical challenges / Rosemary Radford Ruether.
    p. cm.
  Includes bibliographical references (p.   ) and index.
  ISBN-13: 978-0-7425-4642-4 (cloth : alk. paper)
  ISBN-10: 0-7425-4642-X (cloth : alk. paper)
  ISBN-13: 978-0-7425-4643-1 (pbk. : alk. paper)
  ISBN-10: 0-7425-4643-8 (pbk. : alk. paper)
  eISBN-13: 978-0-7425-6554-8
  eISBN-10: 0-7425-6554-8
  1. Christian sociology. 2. Social systems. I. Title.
BT738.R84 2009
261.8—dc22
                                                    2008014936

Printed in the United States of America

∞™ The paper used in this publication meets the minimum requirements of American National Standard for Information Sciences—Permanence of Paper for Printed Library Materials, ANSI/NISO Z39.48-1992.

Contents

Acknowledgments		vii
Introduction		ix
1	Social Systems: Orders of Creation or Demonic Powers?	1
2	Models of Church and State: Historical and Theological	11
3	Patriarchy as a Social System	25
4	Modernizing Patriarchy: Women, Children, and Slaves	41
5	Anti-Semitism, European Nationalism, and Zionism	59
6	Racism in the United States: White, Black, Red, Brown, and Yellow	75
7	Social Ideologies: Sexism, Slavery, and Racism	91
8	Political-Economic Ideologies: Liberalism, Socialism, and Fascism	105
9	Economic Class in the United States	121
10	European Colonialism, 1492–1965	135
11	The Global Economy: Neocolonialism and Neoliberalism	155
12	U.S. and Global Militarism	167
13	Nicaragua in the Caribbean and Central American Context	183
14	The Two Koreas: Divergent Systems, Hope for Reunification?	199
15	South Africa: Constructing and Deconstructing Apartheid	213
16	Ecology: The Context for All Social Systems	227
17	Social Systems and the Church's Mission	243

Appendix: The Earth Charter 257
Bibliography 267
Index 281

Acknowledgments

The material in this book was taught for many years as a foundational social ethics course at Garrett-Evangelical Theological Seminary in Evanston, Illinois. It was taught again in spring 2007 to students at the Claremont School of Theology and Claremont Graduate University in Claremont, California. I thank the students who have helped to develop this course over the years. I particularly thank Marirose Lescher, Diane Ward, and Theresa Yugar, doctoral students at Claremont Graduate University, who read and critiqued all the draft chapters in a reading seminar on the book. I also thank Pat Hynds, who read the chapter on Nicaragua, and Dwight and Linda Vogel and the progressive Christians writing seminar at Pilgrim Place, who read the concluding chapter on social systems and the church's mission. I thank Ward McAfee for scanning the maps and graphs and putting them on CD and Rebecca Dornon for scanning these maps to send to the publisher. I especially thank Herman J. Ruether, who read the whole manuscript and gave me meticulous feedback on every chapter.

Introduction

The purpose of this book is to provide an introductory analysis of the history, social structures, and ideologies connected with the basic social systems that have shaped Western Christian and post-Christian societies, with a focus on the U.S. context. The book is designed as a text for social ethics courses at an undergraduate level or for Master of Divinity or Master of Arts programs in either theological education or social-historical studies. The book would be useful for those with a particular interest in understanding social systems and how the church should relate to them. The book would also be useful to those who have no special interest in being part of the Christian church's struggle to understand its role in social systems but who want to understand these systems and the ethical challenge they pose for humans today in a broad ethical-humanist perspective.

The Christian churches have been in a relationship or conflict with various economic and political systems through the centuries. Politically, the church has related to such systems as Roman imperialism, medieval kingdoms, and city-states and national states as monarchies, constitutional democracies, fascist national security states, and the colonial empires of nation-states. Economically, the church has related to such systems as the Roman slave economy, feudalism with a serf economy, mercantilism, early and advanced capitalism, various forms of socialism and communism, and multinational corporations. Militarism can be seen as the armed defense and aggressive expansion of any of these political and economic systems.

Various forms of social organization have set up the relationship of men and women in terms of gender, race, and class hierarchies. Patriarchy, as both the subjugation of women and generational relations, is one basic system that was shaped in the ancient Near East several millennia before Christianity. It has been modified through the centuries but still exists in many of its basic assumptions in modern societies. Various forms of class hierarchy—masters over slaves, nobles over serfs, and owners over workers—have divided the laboring classes from property-owning and ruling elites. Religious and racial discrimination, such as anti-Semitism and racism against Africans, American Indians, Asians, and Hispanics, has separated ethnic groups and subjugated them to a ruling "white" European group in U.S. society.

The Christian churches have related in various ways to these political, economic, and social systems and their justifying ideologies both as an institution and in its teaching messages. At various times and contexts over its 2,000-year history, Christian churches have sought to separate themselves from and to form an alternative community over against the state and the dominant social and economic system, assuming either a nonviolent pacifist or a revolutionary confrontational relationship to the surrounding society. At other times, Christian churches have sought to become a force for reform or transformation of society from within. At yet other times, Christian churches have identified with the dominant political system and sacralized it as a manifestation of God's reign on earth.

These various options of relationship of church and state/society are traced in their historical development in chapter 2. In the concluding chapter, this question of the relationship of church, state, and society is posed in terms of norms for Christian ethics. How should Christians concerned with creating a just society relate the church or Christian community to the social, economic, and political systems in the world of the twenty-first century? Can and should the church become a force for justice in an unjust world?

This book also seeks to help readers understand and critique the cultural dimensions of social systems. It asks, How do various social systems legitimate themselves culturally by the use of religious, philosophical, psychological, and/or social/scientific norms? How have the ideologies of social legitimation changed? Where religious and philosophical norms once prevailed, in modern times the languages of psychology and social science have come to dominate. In discussing ideologies, it is also important to distinguish between systems of ideas used to legitimate existing social relations and systems of ideas used to criticize social relations, to denounce them as unjust, and to call for their transformation.

A further problem is the way in which ideological patterns once used in a critical, transformative way have shifted in a later context to be used to legitimate new social relations. For example, how was Christianity used to criticize the Roman Empire when it was a persecuted sect but later adapted to sacralize a Christianized Roman Empire? Or how has Marxism, once used to denounce capitalist class hierarchy, been adapted to legitimize a new class hierarchy in a state economy that claims to be "building" a communist classless society?

The book is divided into seventeen chapters. Chapter 1 discusses the theological understanding of social systems. Are they a part of God's "orders of creation" and hence to be accepted as an expression of God's creational ordinances? Or are they expressions of distorted relations between humans that must be judged as sinful—as manifestations of the "powers and principalities" that the church is called to struggle against and to change? Or are they both?

Chapter 2 outlines the changing relation of the church to the state through the centuries, from the New Testament period; to the Constantinian establishment of Christian empire in the late fourth century C.E.; to medieval Catholicism, the Reformation era, and the development of European nation-states; and to the religiously plural societies of the modern world, particularly the United States. In this chapter, we see the variations of three strategies of relationship of church and state—separation, amalgamation, and transformation—through the centuries. New versions of these strategies often divide churches not only on denominational lines but within denominations today as well.

The next two chapters focus on patriarchy as a social system in ancient and then in modern times. Chapter 3 begins by exploring the question of prepatriarchal societies. Have significant alternatives to patriarchy existed in earlier human history? How did patriarchy develop within the ancient Near East? The discussion then focuses on the Roman family. In Roman law, the *familia* referred to all persons and things under the *potestas*, or power, of the *paterfamilias*, or male head of the family. Thus, patriarchy here refers to the legal, social, and economic ways of positioning male heads of families over women, children, and slaves. The chapter also shows how the churches resisted aspects of this patriarchal order but ultimately incorporated it into its understanding of church hierarchy.

Chapter 4 turns to the question of "modernizing patriarchy" in relation to women, children, and slaves. The chapter first discusses the changing relations of work to the members of the family, especially women and children, from the late Middle Ages into the early twentieth century. Work, originally centered in the family, gradually moved out of the family into corporate institutions, such as factories, changing the relation of work to the family and the work roles of women and children. By the twentieth century, the idea that children should not work but should be full-time students came to prevail.

Feminism also changed the legal status and rights of women and their access to higher education and professional work, reshaping the relation of men and women in the family and in the social hierarchies of public society. The chapter then turns to the issue of slavery and its revival in the fifteenth century and its expansion in the era of colonization, when slaves became a major source of labor in European colonies, and then to the struggle to abolish slavery in the nineteenth century. The question of lingering remnants of slavery in the contemporary world is also addressed.

The next three chapters focus on various kinds of prejudice and discrimination in Western history, based on religious or racial ideology. Chapter 5 addresses the question of anti-Semitism in Christian society rooted originally in religious conflicts of Christians and Jews but gradually shifting to a "racial" construct of this discrimination against Jews in modern Christian society. How this racial construction of anti-Semitism was related to modern European nationalisms and to Zionism as a response to anti-Semitic nationalism is also explored.

Chapter 6 turns to the question of racism against the two main groups of "others" excluded from U.S. citizenship in the Constitution: enslaved Africans and Indigenous Americans. It also discusses how the forms of racist ideology and practice developed in the United States against Africans and Indians were extended in the conflicts with Mexicans and "Orientals," especially Chinese and Japanese, in nineteenth- and twentieth-century U.S. history.

Chapter 7 focuses on the ideological aspect of these social prejudices in relation to sexism and racism. The mandates justifying gender and racial discrimination have changed from antiquity to modern times, with religious and philosophical mandates dominating in antiquity, while modern prejudice seeks to buttress itself by references to science, whether psychological or social sciences.

Chapter 8 turns to a second arena of ideology: economic and political ideologies. In the nineteenth and twentieth centuries, two ideologies have been in fierce competition in Europe globally: liberalism and socialism. A third ideology, fascism, briefly flourished in Europe in the 1930s and 1940s but has been the basis of deformations of both capitalist and socialist systems as well as accusations by their opponents who decry one or another system as "becoming fascist." The chapter seeks to sort out the varieties of liberalism and socialism and the reasons for confusion in discussing the meaning of these terms, especially in the United States. What fascism means and what it should refer to and not refer to are also clarified.

After this discussion of conflicting economic ideologies, the discussion turns in chapter 9 to the realities of economic class in the United States. What economic class is and whether the United States is a "class" society is discussed. There is a brief history of the relation of the wealthy to political power in the United States. Is the wealthy class the ruling class in America? The hierarchy of wealth and poverty in late twentieth-century and early twenty-first-century America is laid out. This chapter makes clear that the

United States is a highly stratified society economically with the very rich holding vastly more wealth than the middle and poorer classes. Yet ideologically, class analysis is resisted in American culture as "un-American."

Chapter 10 shifts from an American to a global focus, discussing the development of colonialism in successive waves from the sixteenth through the twentieth centuries and how colonialism shaped the global economy to the present. The chapter also discusses the struggles of Latin American, Asian, and African peoples in the nineteenth and twentieth centuries to free themselves from European colonial domination and the ways in which these struggles for emancipation were undermined to create new or neocolonial forms of European and U.S. domination of these formerly colonized regions.

Chapter 11 addresses the global economy: the international economic system that has emerged especially after World War II in the context of neocolonialism. It shows how this global economy has been shaped by both global corporations and the Bretton Woods institutions, the World Bank, the International Monetary Fund, and the World Trade Organization. Chapter 12 turns to the discussion of the military aspect of this pattern of global domination by the West, especially by the United States, since World War II.

Chapters 13 to 15 present "case studies" of these issues of colonialism, decolonialism, neocolonialism, conflicts over racism, and conflicting economic systems in the global system of nations. These three chapters discuss the countries of Nicaragua, the two Koreas, and South Africa as examples of how these conflicts have played out in specific nations in three "Third World" continents. How the Christian churches have related to these conflicts in these three regions is also mentioned.

Nicaragua, within the Caribbean and Central American context, exemplifies a small country that the United States has long sought to dominate and control. Its effort to break free of this domination by overthrowing the U.S.-sponsored dictator and creating a revolutionary democratic-socialist system in the 1980s was undermined by concerted U.S. pressure, resulting in exacerbated impoverishment and almost but not complete defeat for ongoing struggles for reform.

Chapter 14 on the two Koreas tells the story of a historically unified people, divided by the United States and the Soviet Union at the advent of the Cold War in 1945. The Koreas have developed into two widely divergent systems, capitalist and communist, that seem to defy the continuing aspirations of the Korean people for reunification. Chapter 15 on South Africa tells the story of an effort by white settlers to create a comprehensive system of racial segregation and apartheid and then the painful process of dismantling it, with mixed results for economic justice for the still mostly black poor.

Chapter 16 addresses ecology as the planetary context for all social systems. The chapter details the dimensions of the ecological crisis created by the interlocking trajectories of rapid population expansion; the pollution of air, water, and soil created by the reliance on the burning of fossil fuels, pesticides, and petroleum-based fertilizers in agriculture; threats of climate change; and the rapid deforestation and extinction of species. But the chapter also addresses what steps are necessary to reverse these trends in terms of population, energy use, agriculture, pollution, and protecting biodiversity.

Actual organizing efforts for change on the local, bioregional, national, and international levels are discussed, culminating in the comprehensive vision of the Earth Charter, which seeks to bring together the issues of economic and social justice and the environment. The Earth Charter is seen as a possible model for a comprehensive vision of a just, peaceful, and sustainable global society that touches on all the social systems discussed in this book. The text of this charter is included in an appendix.

The final chapter addresses the question, Can the Christian churches be a force for justice in an unjust world? What are the constraints that limit the ability of the Christian churches to critique and change societies? How should the church relate to the state and to wealth and political power? The chapter shows the deep schisms that divide the churches in the United States over questions of social mission in the nation and internationally. The chapter also examines the challenges posed for the Christian church by the ideological claims of the United States to a messianic, redemptive mission as a nation.

How does the church's understanding of its mission relate to this "mission" of the United States, particularly as it has emerged as a claim to rule the globe as an empire in the twenty-first century? Is the church to see itself as an auxiliary to this American national mission, or should it see itself as deeply opposing it as the contrary of its true mission? Can the Christian churches continue to see themselves as having an exclusive mission that is the center of world history, or must it revise this view to take account of many world religions and redemptive hopes in human culture? These are the deep questions that vex any effort to discuss the church's mission in the context of the global challenges to humanity in the first decade of the twenty-first century.

• *1* •

Social Systems: Orders of Creation or Demonic Powers?

In this chapter, I address the question of the theological status of social systems. Are political configurations, such as nations and empire; economic systems, such as capitalism and socialism; and social systems, such as patriarchy, essentially benign organizations that express God's intention to order society? Or are they demonic patterns of oppression that distort God's intended will for society and bring sinful, destructive modes of relationship? Or are they, in some way, both? Do social systems have a metaphysical status as part of God's original cosmic order to be ultimately redeemed? Or are they merely ephemeral human constructs that endlessly change, coming together and passing away? Or are they, in some way, both?

New Testament scholar Walter Wink has made these questions central to his exegetical and theological work in his trilogy *Naming the Powers, Unmasking the Powers,* and *Engaging the Powers*.[1] In his first volume on the language of power in the New Testament, Wink argues that "the powers" or social systems are both spiritual and material and are both good and evil. Created in the original order of things, they have become fallen, alienated, and demonic yet are to be redeemed at the end when Christ "delivers the Kingdom to the Father after *destroying* every rule and every authority and power" (1 Cor. 15:24). Wink argues that this term should be translated as "neutralize" rather than as "destroy" since Christ overcomes what is evil in the powers but redeems the powers themselves as good instruments of God's will. But most translations say "destroy" or "abolish."[2] Contra Wink, the New Testament view of the final status of the powers is unclear.

Christians have seen each human being as having both body and soul or being an embodied soul. The soul cannot exist without the body, nor can the body cannot exist without the soul. The soul is the inward life and person of the body and cannot exist without being embodied. Wink understands institutions and social systems as having a similar combination of inwardness and outwardness. He sees this combination as accounting for the peculiar language of the New Testament toward institutional structures, such as the state, the governing authorities, and even empires, nations, and churches. Each are concrete embodiments of human organization with their physical structures and human representatives. But these "powers" and "authorities" also have a "heavenly" identity. They can be spoken of as being "angels" or "demons" or spiritual "rulers," "powers," and "principalities."

By using an analogy to a Greek dualistic anthropology of soul and body in which souls are believed to be able to exist independently of bodies, Wink confuses his argument. He seems to want to argue that this "spiritual" aspect of the powers should be understood today not as something that exists apart from their material existence but as the inwardness or corporate "spirit" of institutions. This corporate "spirit" encompasses all that holds the institution together, its historical memory, the vision of its identity and meaning, and all that commands allegiance and brings people together in community.

Every corporate group, however ephemeral, exists as a group through some corporate spirit. Thus, even a mob exists as a mob through taking on some "mob spirit." Through exhortations of leaders and other galvanizing events, a group of people cohere as a mob, even if only for an hour, with a collective spirit that can cause a group to do things together that each individual might find impossible to imagine doing alone, such as tearing down an offending wall or building or massacring another group of people. The mob and the mob spirit coexist. The mob spirit disappears as the mob disperses.

But many group entities take on a much longer lasting life. They institutionalize and reproduce their group spirit through laws that seek to codify its rules of life, structures for enforcing these rules, educational systems that socialize people into its identity, and rituals that celebrate its vision of itself. Thus, the "spirit" of an institution lives beyond its particular human embodiments, reproducing its corporate body and spirit even as its human leaders and members change. One thinks, for example, of universities, such as Oxford and Cambridge in England and Harvard and Yale in the United States. Although not static but continually adapting to new times, nevertheless there is a conscious perpetuation of a continuous historical identity, sometimes actual buildings that remain although continually maintained. But most of all, what is maintained is a sense of "who we are" and also "who we are not," reproduced through a variety of cultural means.

These are "great" universities that have lasted for many centuries, but even small and recent schools, colleges, high schools, and even elementary schools want to create a "school spirit." They compose a school song, write a mission statement, develop rituals and "traditions" to open classes, celebrate graduations and festivals, and in other ways bond faculty, administration, students, and alumni together with a sense of corporate identity and loyalty. Accreditation agencies set standards that each school must meet, and the law demands certain forms of incorporation to be recognized as a school.

While we accept the idea that cultural institutions, such as schools, have and should express a school spirit, it is more surprising when business corporations also claim a corporate persona. Unfortunately today, this often means very little loyalty to workers, who are readily fired in "downsizing," even as such businesses pretend to demand total loyalty from workers. But the most important expression of this is the way in which business corporations, since the late nineteenth century, have assumed the legal status, rights, and privileges of "persons" even while shielding themselves from the responsibility for harm done to the public. The expansion of the constitutional rights of persons under the law to corporations has allowed corporations to continue to exist in perpetuity even while exempting them from democratic control by state and local governments.[3]

Nations are another corporate human construct that have not simply taken on legal and cultural identities but often also claimed a kind of biological essentialism as a people united by common ancestry, land, and even "blood." Thinkers in the ancient Mediterranean world—Jews, Greeks, and Romans—were struck by the existence of different tribal groups (gens) with their distinct languages, cultures, social organizations, and identities. As they came in contact with various peoples different from themselves, they sought to place them in their theological universe. Jewish tradition saw itself as an elect nation with a special identity as the chosen people of God against other "nations," seen as both enemies of God and those to be finally positioned in relation to God and God's people.

One way of doing this was to claim that God had given an "angel" to each nation. "When the most High gave the nations their inheritance, when he separated the sons of God, he fixed the bounds of the peoples according to the number of the sons of God" (Deut. 32:8). This number was fixed symbolically as seventy, each of the seventy nations having their distinct ruling angel. Patristic Christianity, in thinkers such as Origen, picked up the idea of each nation having its distinct angel, but this was reinterpreted as different demonic powers, as distinct from Israel, which alone worshipped the true God. This claim was taken over by the Christian church, which saw itself as the universal people that gathers "all nations" into itself, a universal identity that Christians would later identify with a Christianized Roman empire.

Notions of universal Christian empire continued through the medieval world as well as the eastern Christian empire. But in the sixteenth and seventeenth centuries there emerged distinct national monarchies in Europe, Spain, France, and England in particular, each claiming to be heirs of Israel as God's new elect nation and each claiming an expanding empire in the "new world" of the Americas. The United States inherited this claim to be God's elect nation from its mother nation, England. It developed its own claims to an imperial extension across the continent and then across the seas in the nineteenth and twentieth centuries as a "light to the nations" with a messianic mission to bring "freedom and democracy" to the world.[4]

With the end of World War I and the breakup of the Austro-Hungarian Empire, which had brought together many ethnic groups in Eastern Europe, the political formula for legitimate statehood became the "nation-state." Theoretically, this was supposed to mean that every ethnic community with a distinct language and culture should be an independent political entity or state. With the breakup of the British, French, Belgian, and Dutch colonial empires after World War II, this formula was applied to the colonized peoples of Asia and Africa. There thus emerged a host of new nation-states. International relations between nations were to be arbitrated by a League of Nations and then a United Nations, in which all nations were supposedly equal to one another.

But this formula of the nation-state and an international order made up of equal nation-states has always been something of a fiction, with conflicting realities of power and identity both below and above the level of the nation. Most nations that have emerged in the modern world are composed not so much of one ethnic group with one culture and language as of a variety of ethnic groups and often distinct languages and cultures that have been forged into one state by a dominant ethnic group subduing the others, often imposing its language and culture on them. This is obvious in Great Britain, or the United Kingdom, where the distinct peoples of Scotland, Wales, and Ireland have often been brutally subdued to create the appearance of one nation.

Many of the new nations in Africa, Asia, and the Middle East that emerged from colonialism also were not unities of single ethnic groups but rather a collection of ethnic groups, languages, and ethnic territories carved into composite political entities by the different colonial powers. When the dominant ethnic group loses control, this poses the possibility of the whole national construct dissolving into civil war, with each of its component ethnicities seeking to become an independent nation-state, as has been the tragic story of the breakup of the former Yugoslavia in the post–Cold War era. The nation of Iraq, pasted together by Britain in 1922 from three distinct regions and ethnic communities—Kurdish, Sunni Muslim, and Shiite Muslim—is collapsing into civil war under the misrule of U.S. military occupation after 2003.

On the international level, it is evident that large nations, often with a heritage of empire, by no means intend smaller nations to be equals in power with themselves within a United Nations. The imperial nations that emerged victorious from World War II—the United States, Great Britain, France, Russia, and China—claimed the role of the permanent members of the Security Council with the power of collective veto of all the others. As the United States has increasingly claimed a kind of global hegemony over the world, it has also sought to either make the United Nations its subservient tool or marginalize it altogether.

Empires, by contrast to nations, seek to subdue many peoples under one ruling group that imposes its language, culture, and institutions on the rest. Christianity was born with a hostility to empire from its first three centuries of struggle with the Roman Empire. But in the late fourth century, the emperor Constantine declared Christianity the state religion of the Roman Empire. In the sixteenth and seventeenth centuries, Spain, France, and England each sought empires in the Americas as rivals of each other. The Spanish broke up two empires in the Americas—the Aztec and the Incan—in order to impose its empire on the entire region of Central and South America. Britain, having lost much of its empire in North America, created a vast empire in Asia, Africa, and the Middle East in the nineteenth century lasting to 1950s.

The United States was born with a negative view of empire from its revolution against Britain but has gradually adapted to become an imperial nation in the subsequent two centuries. Those who claim to be an empire often seek a kind of messianic status for themselves as a world power whose superiority gives them the right to rule others. But the contrary tradition of the struggle of subjugated ethnic peoples for liberation against empire means that both Christianity and democratic political traditions have identified empire as evil, as the bearer of the demonic.

How, then, do we sort out these conflicting claims of the ethical status of institutions? Are nations "angelic" and empires "demonic"? Are large corporations demonic, while small, self-owned businesses are "good"? Are some social systems embedded in God's created order and others in violation of that order? Can the church become demonic? What are the criteria for distinguishing what is of God and what is not?

The Christian tradition in the West, especially Calvinism, distinguished between the "orders of Creation" and the "orders of redemption." The orders of redemption had to do with the sacraments, the dispensation of redemption given by Christ to the church, while the orders of creation were understood as systems of social order created by God that dictated the rule of men over women, parents over children, and masters over servants within history. These orders of creation were summed up in the New Testament household codes: "wives obey your husbands, children obey your parents, servants [slaves] obey your masters."[5] These hierarchical relationships were assumed to include obedience of subjects to their political rulers. In short, patriarchy as a system of social relations was seen as written into the laws of the universe as divine ordinances that were inviolable and unchangeable.

Although modern Calvinists have generally dropped the ordinances having to do with slavery, this concept of the subjugation of women as an ordinance of creation is still used by conservative Protestant churches to insist that women cannot exercise authority over men, and thus women can be neither political officials in society nor ordained pastors of the church.[6] Such traditionalist Christians would also see these orders of Creation as ruling out any form of marriage other than the union of a heterosexual couple. Other Christians, by contrast, would see this use of the orders of Creation to make patriarchal relations sacred and unchangeable as itself idolatrous, a confusion of unjust and oppressive human systems with divine ordinances.

Wink, drawing from his New Testament exegesis, argues that "the powers" were created good in the beginning, have fallen and become demonic, but will be redeemed in the end. Let us examine each of these claims in turn. Colossians 1:16–17 is central to his argument for the appearance of the powers as part of God's original creation. Speaking of Christ, through whom we have been "delivered from the dominion of darkness and transferred to the kingdom of his beloved son in whom we have redemption, the forgiveness of sins," the author refers back to Christ's role as Logos creator: "He is the image of the invisible God, the first born of all creation, for in him all things were created in heaven and on earth, visible and invisible, whether thrones or dominions or principalities or authorities—all things were created through him and for him. He is before all things and in him all things hold together."

What we see in this passage is the conviction that Christ, the redeemer at the end, is the principle of creation at the beginning, and in him all the powers cohere and hold together. Assuming Wink's view that these "thrones, dominions, principalities and authorities" are the inner being of all created systems of power, does this mean that actual systems of rule that we encounter in history, such as patriarchy, class hierarchy, monarchy, and empire, are sacred? Wink argues that all these ways of organizing power are, in fact, historically demonic, parts of a "dominator system," so how are they created originally through and for Christ?

Wink argues that some kind of political, social, and economic systems of power are necessary to created existence. It is not that these particular ways of organizing power that have developed in history are good and intended by God but rather that some ways of relating humans to each other are needed, just as the "elements" of the cosmos are interrelated to each other to make a whole. I understand this to mean that both creation and society consist not of a series of isolated individual "atoms" but rather of systems of relationship. From atoms to galaxies, nature consists of systems of interconnection. Each part exists through its connection with the whole. Natural systems carry built-in patterns of sustainability. Planets, plants, cosmic, and earth systems cohere in orders of relationship.

In the Islamic tradition, nature is seen as naturally in harmony with God's rule.[7] Christians are more ambiguous about whether nature is "fallen" because of human sin, but for Christians as well as Muslims, it is humans alone who can revolt against God and distort relationships in sinful and destructive ways. It is through human apostasy from God that power relationships become demonic. It is in this context of distorted power relationships that "the powers" become the enemy of human and other forms of created life and the enemy of God, their creator. According to Paul's letter to the Colossians, in order to deliver us from our bondage to these powers, Christ has "nailed it to the cross. He disarmed the principalities and powers and made public example of them, triumphing over them in it," that is, in the cross (Col. 2:15).

What distinguishes power relations as divinely created and power relations as demonic? Ecofeminist philosopher Starhawk has characterized this as the difference between "power with" and "power over." "Power with" interconnects humans with each other, humans with animals, with plants, and with the soil, in a way that is mutually enhancing. Power is communicated in a way that enhances both sides of the relationship. "Power over," by contrast, is competitive, exploitative power. It is a relationship of domination and oppression in which one side grows wealthy by impoverishing the other side and one side gains power by disempowering and subjugating the other side. This is how power is understood in dominator systems, which have ruled public society for most of recorded history even though life is still carried on in livable ways because many people in their daily lives understand other, more mutual ways of relating to each other.

In her own teaching in permaculture, Starhawk demonstrates the difference between "power with" and "power over" as two different ways of human cultivation of the soil. Permaculture communicates with and learns to understand the soil as its living system. It learns "how to feed the life of the soil, how to encourage and nurture the worms and the beneficial bacteria and fungi and other soil organisms. How a healthy soil will grow healthy plants, that can resist pests."[8]

Industrial agriculture, by contrast, is based on violence, on power over. It sees pests as "enemies" to be killed and forces the soil to produce. "So if corn borers are attacking your crop, blast it with insecticides. Kill the bastards! Are there weeds among the fields? Zap them with Roundup. Root-feeding nematodes, perchance, below the ground? Blanket the whole thing in plastic and gas it with methyl bromide."[9] This way of treating the soil as a war against enemies appears to work for a while, but it "breeds resistance. And so the insects that survive the onslaught of the pesticides breed young that are not affected. We up the doses and breed more and more resistant pests, which require more insecticides to kill, in another self-reinforcing cycle. The helpful insects, the predators that might have kept the pests in balance, are wiped out. And the residues of poison remain, in the soil and in the crops themselves."[10]

Commenting on the cycle of violence that engulfs the Middle East, manifested in the summer of 2006 in the Israeli war against Hizbollah in Lebanon, Starhawk sees the system of force and violence in human relations as working in the same self-defeating way, creating more and more violence that simply breeds more resistance. Unlike bacteria in the soil, "the human resistance that force breeds are not in the genes, but in hearts and minds. And so the bombing of Beirut breeds rockets falling on Haifa and airplane bombers in London, and all the assaults on South Lebanon, the bombs and blown-up bridges and armed teenaged boys in uniform on the ground will breed more rockets, yet more suicide bombs of the future, more death in retaliation."[11]

Those who try to force the other side to submit are also corrupted by the use of more and more force. Thus, in the case of Israel, "the devotion to force is itself a toxin, poisoning the soil of Israeli society, starving its own social programs, warping the very soul and ethics of the religion it purports to defend."[12] Starhawk then asks how we break this cycle of force and violence, how we can discover a different way of relating to each other that generates mutual flourishing. "What would a regenerative paradigm look like? If compost, worm castings and plants that feed beneficial bugs are the gardening alternative to chemical warfare, what would be the political parallel."[13] This is the question we need to ask when we turn to the question of how the "powers" can be redeemed.

Wink believes that the dominator system has ruled in public affairs in most world societies for a long time. It came to power about 5,000 years ago with the rise of military, imperial societies in the ancient Near East. Although he does not rule out that there may have been oppressive violence in human relations before that, such patterns became institutionalized as the primary mode of relationships at that time. This dominator system permeates all public institutions, political systems of government, the economic system of production and exchange, and social relations, organized in terms of slavery, class and gender hierarchy, an educational system that socializes the young into this manner of relating, and a religion that sacralizes it. All social institutions become a system that works together to maintain the power and wealth of the few by exploiting the many.[14]

Yet I would argue that this pattern of domination has never been the only way of relating to each other. People have farmed the soil in a renewable way, raised families lovingly, built good friendships and community ties, and exchanged goods and services in a way that was mutually enhancing and life giving. It is these positive experiences of relationship that have made life tolerable and worth living on a daily basis. Beneath the drumbeat of domination, people have maintained and constantly rediscovered good relationality.

Religious prophets, such as Jesus, have critiqued the dominator society, predicted its coming demise, and taught nonviolence and love of neighbor. Despite the corruption of the church by the dominator society that structured its public system along patriarchal lines, the message of mutual love and care has constantly broken through. Despite the fact that the dominator system seems to have grown steadily worse, until today it threatens human survival and the sustainability of the planet, Christians claim that it is already defeated in principle. What does this mean? If it is very much in power, how can it be said that it is already defeated in principle?

I would say that this means that it lacks moral legitimacy. Those who awaken to the path of mutual care know that the way of domination should not finally win, for it only breeds more and more violence and destruction. It reflects not the authentic "way of life" built into creation but an apostasy from authentic life. We can survive and begin to flourish on earth only by rediscovering the permaculture way in relation to the earth and to each other and by finding how to make this way of relating prevail. This is the meaning of the "redemption of the powers." This is the authentic message and mission of the Christian church, along with many other parallel movements for redemptive life relations from other religions and from social movements, such as feminism, environmental justice, and liberation.

In conclusion, I would say that Wink's argument is confusing because he continues to use a hierarchical dualism of soul and body and a triune sequence of creation, fall, and redemption from New Testament mythology that sounds like it is intended to be literal. This needs to be translated into two basic affirmations. First, social systems are necessary. Humans always exist in relationships, not as isolated individuals. Second, social systems exist along a spectrum of good and bad forms of relationality, dominating, oppressive relationality, and mutual, life-enhancing relationality. We need to reject oppressive relations and their claims of legitimacy. But we also need to have hope that good forms of relationality are possible and continually struggle to create ways of relating to each other, politically, economically, and socially, that are life enhancing.

NOTES

1. Walter Wink, *Naming the Powers: The Language of Power in the New Testament* (Philadelphia: Fortress, 1984); *Unmasking the Powers: The Invisible Forces That Determine Human Existence* (Philadelphia: Fortress, 1986); *Engaging the Powers: Discernment and Resistance in a World of Domination* (Minneapolis: Fortress, 1992).
2. The term *katargese* can mean "abolish" or "nullify."
3. See Richard L. Grossman and Frank T. Adams, *Taking Care of Business: Citizenship and the Charter of Incorporation* (Cambridge, Mass.: Charter, Ink., 1993); see also David C. Korten, *When Corporations Rule the World* (San Francisco: Berrett-Koehler, 1995), 57–60.
4. See Rosemary Ruether, *America, Amerikkka: Elect Nation and Imperial Violence* (London: Equinox, 2007).
5. See, for example, Ephesians 5:21; 6:1, and 5.
6. See, for example, the argument of the moderate Lutheran theologian against the conservatives in the Missouri Synod Lutheran Church who use this idea of the "orders of Creation" against the possibility of women's ordination: Edward H. Schroeder, "The Orders of Creation—Some Reflection on the History and the Place of the Term in Systematic Theology," *Concordia Theological Monthly*, no. 43, March 1972, 165–78.
7. Ibrahim Ozdemir, "Toward an Understanding of Environmental Ethics from a Qur'anic Perspective," in *Islam and Ecology: A Bestowed Trust*, ed. Richard C. Foltz, Frederick M. Denny, and Azizian Baharuddin (Cambridge, Mass.: Harvard University Press, 2003), 16–20.
8. Starhawk, "Lebanon: While the Bombs Fall," www.Starhawk.org.
9. Starhawk, "Lebanon."
10. Starhawk, "Lebanon."
11. Starhawk, "Lebanon."
12. Starhawk, "Lebanon."
13. Starhawk, "Lebanon."
14. See Walter Wink, *The Powers That Be: Theology for a New Millennium* (New York: Doubleday, 1998), 37–62.

· 2 ·

Models of Church and State: Historical and Theological

As I noted in the introduction, the Christian churches have found themselves in various relationships to a variety of types of states through their 2,000-year history. Christianity was born at the time of the consolidation of the Roman Empire over much of the Mediterranean world, with its northwestern boundary stretching to Britain and its eastern boundary to Persia. This empire sought to unify the various religious cults of the diverse peoples under its rule in a common veneration of the emperor, through whom the power of the imperial state would be blessed by the gods and assured of prosperity and power. Christianity resisted any gesture of emperor worship as idolatry and so came under state persecution as a subversive force. Thus, Christianity developed its initial views of church and state in relation to the Roman Empire and its quest for divine favor.

The New Testament reflects two markedly different views of church and state among first-century Christians. For the author of the book of Revelation, following in the tradition of Jewish revolutionary apocalyptic, the church is God's messianic people engaged in spiritual warfare against the forces of evil represented by the Roman Empire. Although the church as God's elect is suffering under imperial power, that power is destined to fall, and all those who worshipped it will drink the "wine of God's wrath" (Rev. 14:10). God's people are called to exit from "her" dominion, "lest you take part in her sins, lest you share in her plagues" (Rev. 18:4). With the fall of "Babylon the great" (the Roman Empire), her leaders will be thrown into a lake of fire, while God's true messianic people will rejoice and inherit the earth.

Paul, in his letter to the Romans, lays out a different view of the "governing authorities." For Paul, all authority is from God, including the authority of the Roman state and its representatives. All must obey them as they would obey God, give them due respect, and honor and pay their taxes (Rom. 13:1–9). The role of rulers is to keep order and repress evil conduct. They are a terror only to those who do wrong, not to those who are good. However, the power of the state, although divinely founded, is temporal, and the time for ultimate salvation, represented by the church, is close at hand. "For salvation is nearer to us now than when we first believed" (Rom. 13:11).

Thus, Paul enunciates the basis of what will become a dual theory of church and state. The state represses evil and keeps order and is to be obeyed as representative of God in all that falls under its proper jurisdiction. Outwardly, Christians should live as good, obedient servants of the state, but inwardly, they belong to another order of salvation that is about to dawn, when all earthly powers will be subjected to the reign of Christ, who then submits all to God (1 Cor. 15:28). Paul also operates with an imminent apocalyptic view of world history but with a very different view from Revelation, that is, of the theological status and juridical authority of the Roman state in the interim.

In the years between the late first and the early third centuries, Christianity operated with versions of these two views, although the view of the Roman Empire as an incarnation of demonic evil became marginalized as a stance of heretical radicals. What would become orthodox Christianity sought to assure the emperor and his representatives that Christians were quiet, good citizens who obeyed the law and prayed for the emperor's welfare although declining to participate in any gesture of actual worship of him as a deity.[1] When forced into such a gesture to prove their loyalty, they must be ready for a martyr's death. But only radical apocalypticists courted such death as a contest with the Devil.

A variant of this view of the empire as demonic developed among Gnostics who took a spiritualist rather than a militant view of the demonic nature of the empire. For Gnostics, the whole material world devolved from a fall in the heavens in which evil "aeons" and "archons" arose to spin out a lower world of oppressive ignorance. Although the Gnostics saw the Roman Empire as the key manifestation of this fallen demonic world, their stance toward it seemed to have been one of quiet withdrawal into an inner world of spiritual community while awaiting their liberation from the flesh and the return of their souls to the higher heavenly world of the divine pleroma.[2]

But these various stances—quiet coexistence, while accepting or rejecting the divine authority of the empire, or active resistance—were changed in the third century when the emperor Constantine adopted Christianity as the official religion of the empire. Constantine continued the basic stance of Roman emperors toward religion, namely, that the continued power and prosperity of the empire depended on the favor of the gods who are to be placated through prayer and sacrifice offered in the official cult. He simply changed his view about who was the "true" God through whose worship this favor and prosperity were to be won. At first, pagan worship was not banned but continued side by side with the rituals of the church. But as the Christian emperors transferred their allegiance and hopes of divine favor from the pagan gods to the Christian God, imperial subsidies would be withdrawn from pagan cults and finally, by the late fourth century, banned altogether.

But the Christian emperors had a more difficult problem with the theological disputes and divisions among Christians. For Constantine, for the church to be the new vehicle of divine favor for the empire, it was necessary to decide which church group represented the true church teaching correct orthodoxy in order to know which church the empire should subsidize. This problem drew Constantine into establishing and presiding over church councils where such decisions about right teaching would be hammered out. Soon Constantine began to think of himself as a "bishop among bishops," even a presiding imperial bishop who could himself offer a suggestion as to the orthodox theological formula for the relation of the Son of God to the Father.[3]

At first, all groups of Christians, even the apocalyptic Donatists, were content to allow the emperor to arbitrate between warring parties. However, during the reigns of Constantine's sons, Constantius and Constans, powerful bishops who favored the Nicaean "homoousian" formula (the Father and the Son are of the same substance) found themselves losing out in imperial favor to the "semi-Arians," who favored the formula "homoiousian" (of like substance). Christians who found themselves in disfavor soon reverted to the view that the emperor, as a heretic, was demonic and even the forerunner of the Antichrist. Bishops, such as Ambrose of Milan, redeveloped the dualistic view of church and state in which the "things that belong to Caesar" must remain separate from the "things that belong to God." The emperor's role is to keep order in the temporal realm but not meddle in matters of the church.[4]

But dualistic separation of the spheres of church and state in the thinking and practice of Bishop Ambrose soon veered in the direction of the superiority of church over the state. Constantine's claim to be a kind of superbishop was rejected in favor of an insistence that the emperor, as a mere layman, was under the authority of the bishop when it came to religious and moral matters. In a series of confrontations with emperors and political leaders, Ambrose refused to hand over a church in Milan to Arians favored by the Western emperor Gelasius; he opposed the "pagan party" in the senate over the restoration of the pagan Altar of Victory in the Senate, and he went toe-to-toe with the emperor Theodosius when he ordered a bishop to rebuild a synagogue destroyed by riotous monks. The culminating confrontation took place when Theodosius, who ordered a punitive massacre of rioting citizens of Thessalonica, was refused communion by Ambrose until he had repented.[5]

Greenslade makes clear that all these Christian views of church and state across this spectrum assumed that the state as well as the church were derived from God and under divine authority. A purely secular view of the state was unthinkable until modern times. The question was how the two spheres were interrelated.[6] Constantine favored a union of political and religious authority in which the emperor was both king and priest, with the church as a department of state. Those who found themselves on the losing side in theopolitical contests with imperial authority veered to a separation of powers, moving in the direction of the superiority of church to state. Both Byzantine and Western or Latin views of church and state would continue to navigate across this spectrum for the next 1,400 years.

The Byzantine world and its heirs in the Russian Orthodox Church, favored a vision of a unified and harmonious *corpus Christianum* in which the state was the body and the church the animating soul of the body. The Christian emperor governed the political and ecclesiastical body as priest-king, although there remained an independent role for the monastic community as prophetic critics who could denounce corruption of state and church. Charlemagne and his heirs made similar claims as emperors of a "Holy Roman Empire" of the Latin West. As both king and priest, both church and state stood under the emperor's power.

However, in practice, a unified state in the western half of the Roman Empire disintegrated in the fifth century. Although Charlemagne reestablished a larger sphere of power by 800, when he was crowned Holy Roman emperor by the pope in Rome, this soon disintegrated under his heirs. In the ninth century, the pope in Rome fell largely under the control of local Roman noble families and the German Holy Roman emperor. The pope had little jurisdiction over the church beyond central Italy, while the claimants to the title of Holy Roman emperor held a precarious sway over warring feudal nobles of Germany. Political power was exercised primarily on the local level of cities and feudal territories; the lines between the religious and the political were thoroughly blurred. Bishops held power as lords over feudal territories, while nobles invested bishops with the insignia of both religious and political office.

In the eleventh century, a reform movement arose in the church that sought to clearly separate these spheres of power. Investiture of bishops with the insignia of religious office by lay nobles was rejected, along with married priests and bishops who could pass on religious office and property to family heirs. This struggle to separate the spheres of church and state, the unification of jurisdiction over ecclesiastic office under the pope, and the subordination of the emperor to the pope in matters of religion and moral conduct would be fought out between a strong-willed reforming pope, Gregory VII, and a Holy Roman emperor, Henry IV, who sought to continue the tradition of Charlemagne that the pope was the handmaiden of the emperor. The two traded anathemas, with the emperor seeking to depose the pope and the pope declaring the emperor excommunicated. When the papal excommunication threatened to justify the rebellion of German nobles against the emperor, Henry IV had to bow to the spiritual power of the pope and stand as a penitent in the snow at Canossa in 1077.

In 1077, Gregory issued a *Dictate* that expressed the far-reaching power not simply of spiritual superiority but also of legal jurisdiction over church and state being envisioned by the pope. The *Dictate* claimed,

> That the Roman Pontiff alone can be rightly called universal.
> That he alone can depose or reinstate bishops.
> That he alone may use the imperial insignia.
> That he himself may be judged by no one.
> That of the pope alone all princes shall kiss the feet.
> That the Roman church has never erred nor shall ever err.
> That it may be permitted to him to depose emperors.
> That he may absolve subjects from their fealty to wicked men.[7]

The pope here is claiming not to run the functions of government for all states (except for his own Papal States) but to have the final moral judgment over all political leaders, with the right to depose them and release their subjects from fealty to them.

This reform vision of a universal church under the pope, with direct jurisdiction over the church and final rights to judge and depose princes, would triumph under Innocent III, who ruled from 1198 to 1216. Christian Europeans accepted a vision of themselves as a unified Christendom under the final moral and religious authority of the pope. But the legitimacy of this papal power began to disintegrate a century later under Boniface VIII (1294–1303). The decentralized political world in which the pope could claim a higher jurisdiction over all princes by playing one against another was giving way to emerging nation-states under the centralized power of national kings, especially in England, France, and Spain. The pope would prove unequal to best these new national kings, particularly those of France, even though and in part because the kings of France had previously been protectors of the papacy in its contests with German emperors.

In 1295, Boniface VIII sought to stop a war between England and France by denying the right of the two kings to tax bishops to pay for their wars without papal consent. Philip the Fair, king of France, responded by stopping the transport of gold and valuables to Rome. In further contests with Philip, Boniface sought to reaffirm papal supremacy with the bull "Unam

Sanctam" (1302). Boniface's vision is that the two "swords" of church and state are under the final authority of the pope, declaring that "it is altogether necessary for salvation for every human creature to be subject to the Roman pontiff." Philip responded to these universal religious claims with a show of superior brute force. When Boniface prepared to excommunicate Philip, Philip simply sent an army to take him prisoner. Although released three days later, the pope died shortly thereafter of broken health.[8]

The emerging nation-states of the fourteenth to fifteenth centuries, expanded by their colonial empires of the sixteenth to seventeenth centuries, would soon make their own claims to unify religious with political authority. The French, Spanish, and English would each claim to be divinely elected people, heirs of God's chosen Israel, uniting throne and altar.[9] New national priest-kings would make themselves the head of the church within their nations and their colonial empires, appointing both bishops and governors.

Henry VIII became the "head of the church" in England only by breaking with the pope, who refused to accept his divorce and remarriage (1529–1535), while France effectively subordinated the national church to the king despite the protests of the pope. Both Spain and Portugal would be granted the royal Patronato (rule over their national church, including its colonial extensions) by the pope in return for keeping "heretics" out of their territories. Henceforth, the struggle of church and state among Western Christians would be fought on the level of nations and principalities, between national churches and dissenters, rather than on the level of a European Christendom between pope and Holy Roman emperor.

In the sixteenth century, there arose what Catholics call "the Great Schism" and Protestants "the Reformation." Substantial sections of the European Christian churches in Germany, France, Scandinavia, Switzerland, and England broke from communion with the pope. Most of the leaders of the Reformation, such as Luther and Calvin, as well as Henry VIII in England, did not seek separatist churches independent of the state but wanted to continue established churches funded and protected by the state. Henry had no idea of reform of the church but simply wanted to nationalize the Catholic Church in England under his headship. But under his successors in the sixteenth and seventeenth centuries, a protracted struggle would break out between an English Catholic (Anglican) view of the church and one reformed along Calvinist lines.

Although both Luther and Calvin continued to support an established relationship between church and state that excluded those they saw as heretics (both Catholics and Anabaptists), their version of this relationship differed. For Luther, there was a sharp division between the roles of church and state qua the "two kingdoms." Both are from God, but their theological functions differ, as law to gospel. The state represents the law, which keeps order and punishes wrongdoers, but it has no capacity to redeem in the sense of bringing about converted lives in its citizens. Only the church can convey the redeeming grace of Christ through its preaching and sacraments. The state also governs the external material structure of the church, including appointment of pastors and funding churches, while pastors should keep out of politics.[10] For Luther, this meant the Lutheran princes who protected the Lutheran churches from the political power of pope and Catholic princes. But later, Lutheranism would counsel obedience to state authorities of any kind as long as they left the church free to preach the gospel. This would create a crisis in the mid-twentieth century, when it appeared that this concept of the "two kingdoms" gave little space for resistance to an anti-Christian state, such as that promoted by Nazism.[11]

Calvinism also demanded a separation of roles of church and state, but ideally there should be a more dynamic relation between the two. Pastors alone preach, announcing the saving grace of Christ to the elect. God alone chooses these elect from all eternity, but it is in the context of hearing the word of God in the church that this grace becomes evident through convicted and converted lives of Christian persons. Magistrates, by contrast, not only keep order and punish wrongdoers but also see that all citizens under their power attend church and behave according to the moral law. Thus, civil and moral law coincide. Blaspheming or dissenting from the teachings of the pastors becomes as much an infraction punishable by the magistrates as stealing or not paying taxes.

Ideally, magistrates should be selected from converted, baptized, leading laymen of the church. Thus, the two powers of church and state coincide as two forms of leadership within the same Christian community. While the state cannot redeem in the sense of conveying redeeming grace, it can enforce morals in such a way as to create an outwardly reformed society that testifies to God's glory, a foretaste of the kingdom of God, where "God's will is done on earth as it is in heaven."[12] Unlike Lutheranism, reformed churches were more open to tyrannicide or rebellion against evil princes.[13] It was under a Puritan parliament that an English king, Charles I, was executed in 1649 for leaning too far toward a Catholic pattern of the church.

Presbyterianism also wanted an established church but one that conformed to their understandings of a reformed church in a reformed state. But more radical dissenters also arose in England and, with the Reformation, on the Continent. Some Puritan dissenters became separatists who came to believe that it was impossible to reform the English state along Calvinist lines, so a true church must become independent of the state. It was a group of such Puritan dissenters that were the settlers who left from England to form the

Plymouth community in New England in 1620. By contrast, the Puritans who settled the neighboring Massachusetts Bay Colony in 1630 were of the establishment variety that sought a reformed church and state in one community. For them, magistrates could be elected from only full members of the church.[14]

Roger Williams, a more radical Puritan separatist, not only demanded separation from the state but also gave up on the possibility of a truly reformed church, demanding instead small covenanted communities that would await the redeeming return of Christ while demanding from the state toleration of religious differences.[15] He was thrown out of the Massachusetts Bay Colony and made his way to Rhode Island to found settlements where separation of church and state would allow toleration for various dissenters. He would be revered in American history as a precursor of religious toleration and the disestablishment of all religions.

But the separation of church and state that separatist Puritans sought was very different from the American idea of a "wall" between church and state. Puritans sought to separate from the state in order to create the true reformed church as the sole sphere of God's redeeming truth, while rationalist proponents of separation of church and state of the eighteenth- and early nineteenth-century Enlightenment saw religion as a reactionary force to be privatized in order to form a secular enlightened state. The first seeks separation from the state for a better church, the second separation of the state from the church for a better political order.

Establishment Puritans warred not only with separatists, such as Williams, but also with other dissenters, such as Anabaptists and Quakers. Anabaptists were also anathema to Luther and Calvin. These dissenters sought separation of church and state in order to create a truly converted and holy church. Anabaptists of various types were united in rejecting infant baptism. Only believer's baptism, which coincided with personal conversion, was a valid entrance into the redeeming grace of God.[16] Establishment churches, both Catholic and Protestant, accepted infant baptism as conveying an objective grace available through the sacramental church. This means that in some state churches in Europe even today, a baptismal certification becomes effectively equivalent to the registration of one's birth.

Anabaptists saw believer's baptism as an entrance into an alternative lifestyle that signaled one's converted life in a converted community. For some, this meant eschewing luxury for simple dress and lifestyle. War and violence were incompatible with the Christian life, so believers should not accept positions as magistrates or soldiers where it would be necessary to take life. Thus, Anabaptists saw the true church as a transformed Christian community subsisting within but spiritually over against both the state and the state church, both of which represent a fallen, worldly, unredeemed humanity. Quakers took a similar view of the dominant state and state church, although they were more spiritualists than communitarians. They saw themselves as living a quiet, holy life in the inner spirit but generally did not seek to form separate self-subsistent agrarian communities, like some forms of Mennonites, such as the Amish and the Hutterites.

In the mid-eighteenth century, beginning in France and spreading to other areas, such as Germany and North and South America, there arose a very different concept of separation of church and state, primarily for the sake of an enlightened, rational state rather than for the sake of a holy, converted church. This takes milder or more radical forms, generally depending on the extent to which the church exists as a strong coercive power in society. In the more militant form, the church (and the Christian religion generally) is seen as a retrograde, irrational force in society that should be disestablished, its properties confiscated. It should be deprived of influence in areas such as education so that it will fade away, to be replaced by a rational society and culture.

At the time of the French Revolution in 1887, a lay state sought to subject a nationalized French church as a department of state in the "Civil Constitution of the Clergy." This was resisted by about half the French clergy, although many of the lower-order priests accepted it. But this soon gave way to a radical stage in which all Christian religion was abolished, and there was an effort to turn the churches into "temples of Reason." The chaos of this period led to a reaction, namely, a takeover of the state by Napoleon, who restored a more traditional Catholic Church through a concordat between the French state and the Catholic Church in communion with the pope.[17]

Marxism arose in the mid-nineteenth century and became an inspiration for efforts to transform whole societies into communist utopias. This also led to a militant form of separation of church and state in which the state adopts an ideology of political and socioeconomic redemption that demands the "withering away" of the church. Persecuting communist states arose in several areas, such as the Soviet Union,[18] China,[19] Albania, and Cuba,[20] which not only privatized the church and deprived it of all public functions but also sought to prevent it from evangelizing. Those who continue to go to church are made second-class citizens who cannot belong to the governing Communist Party. Religion is ridiculed in the official culture and educational system. Although not Marxist, some aspects of the militant separation of state from church in Mexico, especially in the 1930s, also sought to virtually ban the Catholic Church from public life.[21]

The United States has represented a milder version of separation of state from church. The First Amendment to the U.S. Constitution (ratified December 15, 1791) stated that "Congress shall make no law respecting the establishment of religion or prohibiting the free exercise thereof." Thus, no established church is to be allowed on the federal level, although this did not prevent established churches from existing on the state level. In the colonial period, the Church of England was the established church in most of the thirteen colonies, although a Congregationalist established church existed in Massachusetts and Connecticut. But their ability to coerce dissenters had largely disappeared by the eighteenth century, and such relations of church and state faded with the new Constitution. The last church to be disestablished (the Congregational Church) was that of Massachusetts in 1833.[22]

The American disestablishment of the churches, however, did not reflect an anticlerical hostility to Christianity, such as was found in France, Mexico, or communist states. Rather Christianity, although legally disestablished, remains very much a part of the dominant culture, valued as a means of creating a disciplined, moral citizenry. America itself assumed a sacral identity as an elect people chosen by God to spread its message of freedom and democracy throughout the world and to subjugate or eliminate lesser races and cultures, such as American Indians, Catholic Mexicans, and Filipinos.[23] These sacral claims for the "American way" as a culture and political-military system continue into the twenty-first century, as "born-again" Christians, such as George W. Bush, come to rule the United States. Protestant Christianity was thought of as a privatized but nevertheless potent and indispensable cultural force in shaping this "holy" people.

However, by the twentieth century and especially toward the end of that century, Protestant Christianity began to lose its monopoly on American life. Catholics, formerly despised as un-American, grew in numbers to rival Protestants. Jews also grew in numbers and became an important political and social presence. For a while, Americans flirted with a kind of "holy triumvirate" of American religions, "Protestant–Catholic–Jew," who together bless American values.[24] But this construction became more questionable by the late twentieth century as other religious options grew, such as Buddhism and Islam, not only through immigration but also by gaining American converts. At the same time, a renewed form of Protestant Christian fundamentalism has grown that not only seeks close political alliance with the American state but also, among some thinkers, seeks to reestablish the Puritan alliance of church and state in which only (born-again) Christians should hold political office.[25]

These new Protestant fundamentalist "dominionists" are worrisome in several ways, but they are unlikely to prevail, even among conservative evangelicals. The legal formula of separation of church and state American style is unlikely to be radically changed, although minor shifts in the neutrality of the American school might be conceded, such as the right of evangelicals (and all religious groups) to have released time to study their religions during school hours or to have officially recognized school clubs. A principle firmly established in American law is that any concession given to one religion is given to all. Thus, even despised Wiccan or nature-worshipping religions are being allowed their chaplains in prisons and in the U.S. military,[26] while "faith-based" contracts with religious groups for state-funded social services might be claimed by Muslim mosques as well as by evangelical Christian churches.[27]

Thus, in the twentieth century, a new situation of unlimited religious pluralism in relation to the state—in a nation that itself claims sacral, moral identity—had arisen in the United States. While theoretically all religions, unless outright criminal, are to be tolerated as private choices, the dominant American assumption is that all make themselves American by accepting the American "way of life" as an economic and political system. As in the early years of the reign of the emperor Constantine, all religions are tolerated as long as all pray to their various gods in their various tongues for the prosperity and power of the American empire and its global redemptive mission.

However, disestablishment within the various nations has not necessarily made the churches impotent in relation to powerful nation-states with redemptive claims. Rather, both Protestantism and Catholicism began to realize in the twentieth century that disestablishment of the church from the state also freed the churches from domination by the state to organize its own sphere as an institution. Catholicism, deprived of its landed properties, schools, and hospitals, could rebuild its cultural and social presence through privately owned Catholic institutions. Freed from national kings and states, it could reorganize internationally under the pope, who reclaimed jurisdiction over the Catholic ecclesiastic hierarchy in all nations of the world. A far more powerful papacy and world Catholic Church arose as a global system, separate and parallel to a political world divided into warring nation-states. Through its status as a permanent observer at the United Nations (thanks to its residual status as a state based on its ownership of Vatican City), the Holy See makes its voice heard in international meetings of the United Nations, especially in matters of family and sexual ethics.[28]

Protestants also built their own denominational institutions. Although functioning more on the national level, many denominations developed global interconnections that united one or several denominations, such as the World Council of Churches (for most of mainstream Protestantism and Eastern Orthodoxy), the World Alliance of Reformed Churches (WARC) for the reformed tradition, and the Anglican communion for world Anglicanism. At times, these global bodies, as well as their national hierarchies, assert a prophetic voice, questioning the economic, social, and military policies of nation-states. Thus, the WARC in 1982 excommunicated the reform churches of South Africa on the grounds that the state theology of apartheid was a heresy. In 2005–2006, the WARC called for a similar condemnation of the economic and military systems of power being promoted by an American state with imperial claims.[29]

In the beginning of the twenty-first century, tensions between church and state are by no means over. Residual state churches continue to exist, such as the Church of England; the Lutheran state churches in Sweden, Norway, Finland, Denmark, and Iceland; and Roman Catholicism in some Latin American countries, such as Argentina and Costa Rica. But the principle of freedom of religion is generally acknowledged in these mainly Christian areas so that the established church no longer prevents the presence of other religions. In some cases, membership in the established church has grown nominal, with its members seldom coming to the church save for life cycle rituals, baptism, marriage, and burial. State patronage of the established church functions to maintain church buildings and pay salaries of pastors.

But the churches, often more potently when they are independent of the state, continue to see themselves as mandated to judge the state on moral grounds. But this judgment itself becomes conflicted as Christians split along liberal–conservative lines that often lead them to focus on different understandings of desirable public morality. Conservative Christian churches seek political influence to enforce what they see as the key issues of public morality, such as banning abortion and marriage between homosexuals and mandating school prayer. Liberal churches, by contrast, focus on the rights of racial and sexual minorities, supporting equal rights for blacks, women, and homosexuals. Militarism and economic injustice become their key issues for criticism of national and international systems.

This division among Christians as to what public morality is advocated weakens the collective Christian voice, as states patronize those Christian bodies that support their policies and dismiss and even disparage those that do not. Christians seeking a social ethics for the relation of church and society function within these deeply divided churches with their sharply differing views of what public morality the churches should advocate. This issue is taken up again in chapter 17.

NOTES

1. This is generally the stance of the second-century apologists, such as Justin Martyr.

2. Hans Jonas's *The Gnostic Religion: The Message of the Alien God and the Beginnings of Christianity* (Boston: Beacon Press, 1963) is important as an interpretation of Gnostic cosmological dualism as metaphor for resistance to Hellenistic and Roman imperial power.

3. During the Council of Nicaea, it was Constantine who proposed the formula "homoousian" (the same substance) for the relation of Son to Father, which became the winning definition at the Council; see S. L. Greenslade, *Church and State from Constantine to Theodosius* (London: SCM Press, 1954), 18.

4. Greenslade, *Church and State from Constantine to Theodosius*, 54–63.

5. Greenslade, *Church and State from Constantine to Theodosius*, 71–79.

6. Greenslade, *Church and State from Constantine to Theodosius*, 79–85.

7. See Thomas J. Renna, *Church and State in Medieval Europe, 1050–1314* (Dubuque, Iowa: Kendall/Hunt, 1974), 12.

8. Renna, *Church and State in Medieval Europe*, 162–186.

9. For French claims of divine election of the nation, see Joseph P. Strayer, "France: The Holy Land, the Chosen People and the Most Christian King," in *Action and Conviction in Early Modern Europe*, ed. Theodore K. Rabb and Jerrold E. Sergel (Princeton, N.J.: Princeton University Press, 1969), 6–10. See also Colette Beaume, *The Birth of an Ideology: Myths and Symbols of Nation in Late Medieval France*, trans. Susan Ross Huston (Berkeley: University of California Press, 1991), 96–125. Similar ideas of an elect nation for sixteenth-century Spain can be found in John Leddy Phelan, *The Millennial Kingdom of the Franciscans in the New World* (Berkeley: University of California Press, 1970). A major source for this idea of an elect nation for England is William Haller, *The Elect Nation: The Meaning and Relevance of Foxe's Book of Martyrs* (New York: Harper and Row, 1963).

10. For a good summary of Luther's view of church and state, see Thomas G. Sanders, *Protestant Concepts of Church and State: Historical Backgrounds and Approaches for the Future* (New York: Holt, Rinehart and Winston, 1970), 23–48.

11. Sanders, *Protestant Concepts of Church and State*, 52–59.

12. Sanders, *Protestant Concepts of Church and State*, 225–34.

13. Sanders, *Protestant Concepts of Church and State*, 231.

14. See Francis J. Bremer, *The Puritan Experiment: New England Society from Bradford to Edwards* (Hanover, N.H.: University Press of New England, 1995).

15. See Edmund Morgan, *Roger Williams: Church and State* (New York: Harcourt, Brace and World, 1967).

16. A classic treatment of the Anabaptist view of the church is Franklin H. Littell, *The Anabaptist View of the Church: An Introduction to Sectarian Protestantism* (Hartford, Conn.: American Society for Church History, 1952).

17. See Luigi Sturzo, *Church and State* (Notre Dame, Ind.: University of Notre Dame Press, 1962), 375–83. Sturzo's book is a comprehensive overview of the history of church–state relations from a traditionalist Roman Catholic perspective. For the Civil Constitution of the Clergy and other key documents of the French revolutionary period and subsequent Napoleonic concordat with Rome, see J. F. Maclear, *Church and State in the Modern Era* (New York: Oxford University Press, 1995), 77–97.

18. For the key document disestablishing the Orthodox Church in Russia after the Bolshevik Revolution, depriving the church of all property and legal status, see "The Separation Decree," February 5, 1918, printed in Maclear, *Church and State in the Modern Era*, 331–33.

24   Chapter 2

19. For key documents for the Christian church's status in communist China, see Maclear, *Church and State in the Modern Era*, 428–32.

20. In the first two decades of the Cuban Revolution, the churches were discriminated against as a reactionary force, but in the 1990s much of this was changed to declare Cuba simply a "lay" state (secular). For the earlier period, see John M. Kirk, *God and the Party: Religion and Politics in Revolutionary Cuba* (Tampa: University Press of Florida, 1989).

21. For the Cristero War, in which Catholics battled a militantly anticlerical state, see "Cristero War," *Wikipedia, the Free Encyclopedia*, http://en.wikipedia.org/wiki/Cristero.

22. For the disestablishment of Congregationalism in Massachusetts, see Maclear, *Church and State in the Modern Era*, 201–2. For key documents in American church–state relations in 1820–1860 in which the mainline Protestant leaders adjusted themselves to a strategy of voluntary church membership together with the building of independent Protestant institutions, see "The Era of Republican Protestantism," in *Church and State in American History: Key Documents, Decisions and Commentary from the Past Three Centuries*, ed. John F. Wilson and Donald L. Drakeman (Boulder, Colo.: Westview Press, 2003), 83–119.

23. See Conrad Cherry, ed., *God's New Israel: Religious Interpretation of American Destiny* (Chapel Hill: University of North Carolina Press, 1998); see also Rosemary R. Ruether, *America, Amerikkka: Elect Nation and Imperial Violence* (London: Equinox Press, 2007).

24. The classic essay on this is Will Herberg, *Protestant, Catholic, Jew: An Essay on American Religious Sociology* (Garden City, N.Y.: Anchor Books, 1960).

25. For Protestant "dominionists," see Bruce Barron, *Heaven on Earth: The Social and Political Agendas of Dominion Theology* (Grand Rapids, Mich.: Zondervan, 1992).

26. See Catherine Cookson, "Report from the Trenches: A Case Study of Religious Freedom Faced by Wiccans Practicing in the United States," *Journal of Church and State* 39 (autumn 1997): 723–48.

27. For a thoughtful consideration of church–state relations in the United States and government funding of faith-based social service, see Ronald J. Sider and Heidi Rolland Unruh, "'No Aid to Religion'? Charitable Choice and the First Amendment," *Brookings Review*, spring 1999, 46–49, taken from Ronald Sider and Heidi Rolland Unruh, "An (Ana)baptist Theological Perspective on Church-State Cooperation," in *Welfare Reform and Faith-Based Operations*, ed. Derek Davies and Barry Hankins (Baylor, Tex.: J. M. Dawson Institute of Church-State Studies, 1999), 89–138.

28. See Thomas J. Reese, "The Catholic Church as a Global Actor," paper delivered May 4, 2006, University of California at Santa Barbara, http://uctv.ucsb.edu/2006/voices/4332reese.html.

29. See "An Ecumenical Faith Stance against Global Empire for a Liberated Earth Community," Manila, July 13–15, 2006, http://warc.jalb.de.

· 3 ·

Patriarchy as a Social System

*T*heories in Western anthropology about gender relations in the prehistoric human family have varied. In the late nineteenth century, it was widely assumed that there were fixed stages of the evolution of the family, starting with chaotic promiscuity, then proceeding to a stage of matriarchy, or female domination, that was then succeeded by patriarchy, or male domination. These stages were correlated with a theory of progress from more primitive and disordered to more rational and ordered cultures, culminating in Roman patriarchy as the highest pattern and the basis of Western civilization.[1]

In the 1920s, these theories of fixed stages were rejected by most Western anthropologists. Anthropologists adopted more empirical methods, studying different societies case by case. In the 1960s, anthropologists generally insisted that there had never been a matriarchal society where women ruled. The few cases of matrilineal societies (descent from the mother) were aberrant and unstable. Human societies from the origins of humanity had been overwhelmingly patrilineal and patrilocal (descent from the father, with the family located in the father's household). It was assumed that this meant a patriarchal (male-ruled) society, with women dependent on men for food and protection.

But in the 1970s and 1980s, more women entered the field of anthropology. They were able to demonstrate that this thesis of near universal patriarchy was based on biased assumptions and information. Male anthropologists observed and conversed only with men of the groups they studied and were precluded by their gender from contact with the women. When women anthropologists observed the activities and viewpoints of the women, they found a much more complex picture.

BEFORE PATRIARCHY

The earliest form of human economy, lasting from the earliest hominids to the development of horticulture and domestication of animals (about 9000 B.C.E. in the ancient Near East and later in other regions of the world), is foraging (i.e., hunting animals, fishing, and gathering dead animals, plants, nuts, and berries). These societies did not plant or control herds of animals but depended for their food supply on existing wild animals and plants. Foraging societies are generally composed of small groups that range over large territory. Although foraging societies have today been pushed to the margins of fertile lands by settled societies, originally they were highly successful and provided an adequate and in some regions abundant diet without long hours of work.[2]

Contemporary foraging societies generally reckon descent bilaterally (both mother and father), and two-thirds tend toward a matrilocal household.[3] Even those that are patrilocal and patrilineal are mostly egalitarian. Although there is usually a sexual division of labor, with women concentrating on gathering plants and small animals and men on hunting larger animals, the contribution of men and women to food is equally important. In many foraging societies, women actually provide the predominant amount of food, while male hunting is seen as more prestigious but also more occasional. Status is based less on gender than on individual skills.[4]

Gardening societies in which seeds were planted and harvested seem to have been pioneered by women, who had dominated in plant gathering. Men in such societies often help women by clearing fields, but women do the actual planting and harvesting by hand. Male hunting may continue alongside female gardening. It is significant that among contemporary ethnic groups, eighty-four out of 565 are matrilineal (15 percent). Thirty-six percent are bilateral and 44 percent patrilineal.[5] It is likely that matrilocal patterns with matrilineal or bilateral descent were much more widespread among horticulturalists in earlier times before the development of dominant patriarchal colonial systems of power. But it has not been proven that this was a universal stage.

Matriliny does not mean exclusive female rule. Both men and women have spheres of power, with the mother's brothers holding key governing roles. The tendency to dismiss matrilineal societies and give them insufficient study is based on the assumption of male anthropologists that men still rule in these societies, and therefore they do not present an alternative to the universality of male dominance. This assumption is based on the false equation of patriliny with patriarchy (male rule). Hence, any real alternative to patriarchy must be matriarchy or female rule, which is claimed to have never existed. What has been missed is that matrilineal societies may present not a reversal of patriarchy, qua matriarchy, but an alternative to rule by one or another gender, that is, balanced societies where both genders have equal, complementary areas of power.

Before discussing the development of patriarchy in agricultural societies in the ancient Near East and its expression in the Roman family, it is helpful to discuss some examples of matrilineal societies to demonstrate the possibility of alternative patterns of gender relations. I discuss two such cases of matrilineal societies: the Iroquois of the North American plains and the Minangkabau of central Sumatra.

Matrilineal matrilocal societies likely developed from a core family consisting of a mother and her daughters remaining together and forming a collective work group with their young children. In horticultural societies, this means not only that descent is reckoned through the mother but also that landownership or usufruct (rights to use of land) is passed down from mothers to daughters, with women working together in cultivating gardens, usually controlling the storage and distribution of food. Matrilineally descended men (i.e., mother's brothers) play important governing roles, but men also marry out, joining other female-centered households. Thus, a key difference between matrilineal/matrilocal societies and patrilineal/patrilocal ones is that the women stay together in matrilineal/local ones, and men are dispersed or "exchanged," while men stay together and women are dispersed (exchanged) in patrilineal/local ones.

Among the Iroquois, women of the same matrilineage remained together for life. Men were imported from other matrilineal households and joined their wives in the matrilocal longhouse but also continued to have responsibilities toward their own matrilineal kin. The women as a group determined who would enter the longhouse as husbands and who could remain. Any husband behaving badly could be asked to leave the longhouse, effectively being divorced.

Women were the exclusive cultivators of the land, working together and controlling seeds and the storage and distribution of food. The cultivated land belonged to the women by common kinship. This power over food production and distribution also rebounded to considerable political power of women, particularly the senior women as a group. In the Iroquois Confederacy, the male council of chiefs held power through female approval. Eligibility was determined matrilineally. Senior women of the matriclans nominated chiefs who were then approved or vetoed by the chiefs. If a nominee was vetoed, the women nominated another until one was approved.

The matrons monitored the performance of chiefs and could initiate impeachment proceedings against an unsatisfactory chief. Women also had their own representatives in council meetings to represent their position on all important issues. They held the power to veto war declarations and to introduce peacemaking. Women provided the dried food carried by war parties, so men could not go to war without these provisions from women. In religious life, women had a voice in the selection of sacred practitioners, half of whom were female. Thus, female power based on matrilineal kinship penetrated all parts of traditional Iroquoian society. What we have here is not female "dominance" but a system of checks and balances in which male power roles in war and governance are balanced by female economic power and monitoring of men's roles.[6]

The Minangkabau of the highlands of central Sumatra, Indonesia, today number about 4 million people. They are significant because they have maintained and strengthened their matrilineal social system through both Islamization in the seventeenth century and colonialism by the Dutch (1750–1949), both conditions that are assumed to cause matriliny to cede to patrilineal, male-dominant societies.[7] The Minangkabau are not a "primitive tribe" but a modern ethnic group with elegant houses and successful businesses.[8]

Here matrilineally related women stay together lifelong in a cluster of houses. Farming continues to be the main source of food, both for immediate consumption and for exchange, with both women and men working in the fields. But small shops, businesses, and banks have also developed. Some work as state employees, teachers, or civil servants. Property is handed down matrilineally in perpetuity as long as there are female descendants of the matrilineage. Men are "exchanged" or marry into the matrilineages but continue to have responsibilities for their own matrilineage. Men hold official governing power, whose chief function is to protect the passing on of the lands of their sisters and to settle disputes over land and office.[9] Matrilineally related men are appointed to these offices. Men have power as brothers, not as fathers.

Ceremonial exchange of food is very important. This occurs during the life cycle ceremonies, such as birth, marriage, house building, death, and installation of men who hold the Penghulu title, the matrilineal title of office that oversees the *adat*, or customary law. Women are in charge of these ceremonies, organizing them and producing the food for exchange, while men give the flowery speeches. For the Minangkabau, maternity provides more than a system of kinship and law. It is the central value of the society. "All are born from the mother."

Maternity as nurture of the weak into health and strength and the interdependence of all things are seen as the central principle of nature. Women are seen as naturally adept at nurture, while men, particularly young men, have to be socialized into nurturing, curbing their tendencies to chaotic behavior, war, and violence. Nature is seen in continuity with culture rather than as transcended by culture, as in patriarchal cultures.[10] Minaugkabau societies are markedly free of domestic violence or rape. If a husband beats his wife, he is summarily divorced and sent back to his mother. Thus, the Minaugkabau offer a strikingly different system of social relations and worldview from that which developed under Western patriarchy.

THE DEVELOPMENT OF PATRIARCHY

Gardening societies, where women dominate as food producers, often are characterized by a strong female sphere of power as long as women control the storage and distribution of food. Pastoral herding societies where men control the animal herds generally have favored a dominant male role, with women reduced to marginal roles in cooking, cleaning, child care, and control of small animals, such as chickens. The most important shift in women's status seems to have happened with the development of plow agriculture, between 6000 and 3000 B.C.E. in the ancient Near East. When men developed plows yoked and pulled by oxen, this innovation allowed men to redefine the land and its products as belonging to them.[11] The plow united male dominance over both cattle and land.

With the plow, land becomes defined as private property to be passed down from the male head of family to his heirs rather than usufruct shared by the community. Settled agricultural societies allow for the accumulation and storage of food and goods. Rivalries developed with other settled societies as well as with nomadic societies on the edges of settled areas. The weapons of hunting are reshaped into the weapons of war to attack and to defend settled areas. Conquered groups are enslaved, often killing the warrior-age males and enslaving women and children.[12]

At the same time, class hierarchy begins to develop, with farming households reduced to semiserf status who owe regular contribution of goods and labor to an elite who monopolize control over land, slaves and serfs, and war.[13] Legal codes are written that canonize this system of hierarchical ordering of wealth and power, and organized religion validates this order by seeing it as handed down by the gods. Walled cities develop, with temples and palaces as the centers of government, to control the nearby land and labor and the storage of wealth by these elites.[14] Elites ruling through city centers reach out to form alliances with other city centers and then to seek to subdue many cities in empires ruled from one dominant city.

Gender hierarchy is integrated into this developing class hierarchy with women as secondary members of each class. The whole system becomes defined from the perspective of the males of the ruling class. Women of the ruling class may exercise considerable power through their relations to men of their families as wives, mothers, or daughters. Thus, a wife or queen mother may rule the labor of a palace complex. A daughter might be given the governance of a temple, seen as priestess of its god or goddess and ruling over the attached land and labor. Occasionally, when there is a lack of an adult male heir, a woman may rule as queen mother on behalf of an underage male heir or even as the heir. Some patrilineal systems developed legal fictions when a man lacked a male heir by which a daughter might be appointed as her father's "son," ruling over her father's inheritance and counting her children in her father's lineage.[15] Or daughters of the elite might be appointed as cloistered priestesses, administering the temple compound and its lands and workforce and engaging in trade. This seems to have developed as a way to prevent lands given to daughters from passing out of the control of the patrilineal family through marriage. The daughters thus endowed by land by their fathers could not officially marry but could adopt a son who then belonged to her father's paternal line.[16]

This hierarchy of power and value is made evident in ancient law codes. For example, in the section on personal injuries in the Code of Hammurabi (1727 B.C.E.), we have the following laws, dealing with violence by a member of the nobility toward women of different classes:[17]

> If a seignior (nobleman) struck another seignior's daughter and has caused her to have a miscarriage, he shall pay ten shekels for her fetus.
> If that woman has died, they shall put his daughter to death.
> If by a blow he has caused a commoner's daughter to have a miscarriage, he shall pay five shekels of silver.
> If that woman has died, he shall pay one-half a mina of silver.
> If he struck a seignior's female slave and has caused her to have a miscarriage, he shall pay two shekels of silver.
> If that female slave has died, he shall pay one-third mina of silver.[18]

The presuppositions of these laws are clear. The females are always referred to in terms of their relation to their "owners," father, or slave master. Presumably the payment goes to this father or slave master, not to the daughter or mother of the daughter. There is a hierarchical value of fetal and adult female life in terms of their social class. The fetus of a seignior's daughter is worth ten shekels, of a commoner five shekels, and of a seignior's female slave two shekels. The life of the first daughter is invaluable. It can be paid only by killing the other seignior's daughter. The life of the commoner's daughter is worth half a mina of silver and the slave one-third a mina of silver.

As the patriarchal system develops, the females of the male ruling class increasingly lose public roles as producers or managers of goods and property and become secluded within privatized space within home, even as that home may have expanded into a palace complex. The male elite also expand their access to women, marrying many wives as well as having unlimited access to slave women and boys. Within this privatized space, the elite daughters and wives may do some ornamental spinning and weaving, personal nurture of children, or supervision of household work, but they are no longer valued for their work. Any heavy work, even in the home, such as cooking and cleaning, including more regular child care and nursing of children, would become the work of slaves. Rather, their primary values are their sexuality, fertility, and beauty. Since patriarchy demands that a man be assured that his wife or wives produce only his own children, seclusion prevents other men from having sexual access to them and thus causing children to be born whose paternity is in doubt.

The practice of seclusion of women applied first to the nobility and eventually to the upper class.[19] There also have been various other ways of circumscribing the bodies of the elite man's females, such as veiling and the practice of foot binding in China. Peasant women are still needed to work in the fields, and artisan-class women are expected to work as producers in family workshops and in trade. Thus, seclusion of women is applied to those women who can be valued solely as ornaments and as means of sexual pleasure and reproduction, not as workers. These women become heavily veiled or carried in curtained vehicles when they do venture out in public. Such a seclusion of elite women in the female or back part of the house was characteristic of classical Athens.[20]

THE ROMAN FAMILY

The focus of this chapter now turns to the patrician Roman family as an exemplar of classical patriarchy and one that has been key in the development of Western law. In Roman law, the word *familia* meant something different from the English word *family*.[21] In Roman law, *familia* referred to all the persons and things under the *potestas*, or sovereign power, of the male head, or *paterfamilias*. This meant his slaves as well as any ex-slaves who owed him service. It included nonhuman property, land, houses, and animals. It included children, even grown sons, who remained under his paternal power until his death unless the father emancipated them, at which point they became *sui iuris*, or under their own rule. It included married daughters if they had been married under a form of marriage that did not put them under their husband's power (*sine manu*). Such married daughters remained under their father's power, unless they had been granted autonomy (*sui iuris*).

The *familia* did not include the wife of the *paterfamilias* unless she had been married *cum manu*, that is, in a form of marriage that handed over her father's power to her husband. If she was married *sine manu*, she remained under her father's power unless she had been granted autonomy from her father and gained autonomous control of property that has been inherited or given to her (*sui iuris*). The *familia* was distinguished from the *domus*, or kin network, which consisted of the male lineage of blood descendants through the generations.[22]

By contrast, when Americans speak of their family, they mean a nuclear family, particularly a married couple and their children, usually living in a neolocal household (a household separate from that of their parents), and also their parents, siblings, and cousins on both their mother's and their father's side. Thus, even though most Americans are officially patrilineal, passing the family name down through the male side, they are affectively bilineal, counting their relatives on both the father's and the mother's side.

Roman patrician society was concerned with maintaining and reproducing the *domus*, or male lineage, from generation to generation with all its rights of power and privilege. To this end, females needed to be exchanged between male lineages for the purpose of producing legitimate sons. If a man failed to produce a son, he might adopt a son from another lineage, gaining full paternal power over such an adopted son who thereby gained the same rights as a blood son.[23]

In earlier Roman law (i.e., third to second centuries B.C.E.), most women exchanged between Roman male lineages were married *cum manu*; that is, her father's *manus* (hand) or power over her was passed over to her husband, who thereby had full paternal power over his wife. But by the first century C.E., the legal practice had developed of not passing this power to the husband over his wife at marriage, which would have meant that any property she had inherited or been given would have become the property of her husband. By marrying *sine manu*, the wife retained control over her own property as a member of her own paternal family, thus keeping family property from being alienated into other male lineages.[24]

The upper-class Roman woman thus might have considerable economic power and personal prestige while at the same time suffering sharp limitations. If she was married *sine manu* and particularly if she had been emancipated by her father, she might enjoy control of vast properties that she could manage as she wished. Such wealthy women were important to the developing church since by the third and fourth centuries they were using their control of property to give vast endowments to the church.[25]

Educationally, upper-class Roman women were treated very differently from their brothers. Their brothers were expected to enter into a career of military and political service (*cursus honorum*). To this end, they were intensely schooled in Latin rhetoric and literature into their twenties to give them facility in eloquent public speech. Daughters of the same class, by contrast, got only the equivalent of primary school to give them the basic ability to read and keep accounts for their future role as wives in which they were expected to manage all the internal affairs of the house, including oversight of the household labor of slaves.

An unusual father might secure a private tutor for a daughter, giving her a higher level of literary education. Some women studied philosophy with philosophical mentors. Later, educated women attracted to the Christian church might study Scripture and the church fathers with a Christian teacher. St. Jerome played such a role with upper-class women in Rome in the late fourth century.[26] But such educated women were not especially appreciated in Roman society, which saw them as deviants from the normal development of daughters into wives, and Roman mothers were expected to nurture their sons toward public service and their daughters to become proper matrons.

Most important, the literary work of Roman women was not circulated publicly and so only accidentally has survived. This continued to be the case with Christian literati women. Jerome believed that the studies and writings of the women he taught should remain strictly private. They might mentor other women and exchange letters and other writings with himself and other male teachers, but such female work was not to be published as a part of the public corpus of church writings.[27]

Politically, elite Roman women remained private citizens. They could not pursue the public career expected of their brothers. They could not speak or vote in public assemblies. Thus, Roman women never gained public political status. This did not mean that women of well-connected Roman families did not seek to manipulate power behind the scenes for themselves or a favorite child, using skills of persuasion, including sexual charms. Women in all patriarchal societies have used such informal power. But such use of manipulative power by women was seen as illegitimate in Roman society. The good Roman *matrona* kept to managing her household, producing sons for her husband, and even emulating women of earlier centuries who did their own spinning at home. They kept out of politics.

When it came to marriage, the upper-class Roman woman was largely a tool of her father. This of course did not mean that a mother or a daughter might not scheme and manipulate, seeking an alliance to their liking, but the choice was that of the father. The Roman girl was usually married shortly after puberty to a man twice her age, chosen by her father to cement his political alliances.[28] Some girls and boys were engaged to be married even as children to confirm an alliance of their fathers. Moreover, if the father and the husband of his daughter had a political falling out, the woman could be summarily divorced, returning to her father's house, where she might then be married to a different ally of her father.

The Roman child of the wealthy upper class grew up in a very different household from the American nuclear family. The household might consist of dozens or even hundreds of slaves, not to mention the thousands of slaves who labored on estates owned by the *pater*. While the child's mother might supervise his or her early childhood development, the male or female infant was usually nursed by a slave wet nurse and later cared for by slave child minders, often in the company of slave children who might be half siblings.[29] As the boy grew up, he would be handed over to slave tutors (*paedagogi*) who accompanied him to school and supervised his lessons. Sometimes the master who taught him in school was also a slave. The boy would be expected to continue his education into the secondary and advanced levels, sometimes traveling to other cities to learn from an elite teacher of rhetoric. The girl, as we have seen, was not expected to go on to these secondary and advanced levels of education.

The *potestas*, or power of the father, gave him theoretically unlimited power over all those under his paternal power, including his children and his slaves. He could flog a son or daughter, sell them into slavery, or even kill them, although such treatment was not approved.[30] Flogging boys at school was regarded as normal treatment. St. Augustine remembered with horror the constant flogging he received as a schoolboy.[31] Slaves could be flogged even to death, executed, or sold at the whim of the master. The interrogation of slaves always took place under torture. By contrast, the adult male Roman citizen was not to be tortured and when sentenced to death was given the prerogative of taking his own life. A Roman woman, lacking political status, could not be publicly sentenced to death but could be privately executed by her father. A woman of an elite family who made herself politically undesirable could be quietly murdered by whatever male took charge of the situation, be that a son or a husband. The alternative to death for Roman citizens, male and female, was to be banished.

SLAVERY IN ROMAN ANTIQUITY

Slavery was not racial in antiquity, and slaves were acquired in various ways. Many were produced by natural reproduction in the household. Slaves could not legally marry but did, in fact, form relationships that were deeply felt and produced children in those relationships. But the offspring of such relationships belonged to the slave master, not the child's father. The slave's body was sexually accessible to the master or other males in the household, such as sons, so children were produced from such relationships with slave women. Slave children followed the status of their mother, so a slave child fathered by the master remained a slave. A freed woman could not be married by a master of senatorial rank, nor could a freed slave be adopted, thus preventing children of slaves from passing into the patrician lineage.

A second source of slaves was through war in which conquered peoples were sold into slavery, the adult males often being sent to do the most arduous work, such as in mines, where few survived long. A third source was capture, in which slave hunters grabbed travelers on roads or on ships and sold them as slaves. Infant exposure was also a major source of slaves. An infant did not have a "right to life" until it had been acknowledged by its father. If a family already had too many children, especially daughters, the infant could be set out in a public place, where it was often picked up by others and raised as a slave. People thus enslaved might be freed if they could prove they were of free birth, but this was difficult, particularly for one exposed as an infant. A man could also sell dependent members of his family or even himself into slavery, and this happened primarily when a family fell into poverty and debt.[32]

Slaves did most of the physical labor in Roman society. Greek society had seen manual labor as inherently "servile" and hence degrading to the elite man. The Romans, who originally valued hard work as landowning farmers, adopted this same negative view of work as they developed the empire. The Roman citizen belonged to an elite of leisure and public service, including military leadership. Thus, in elite households, slaves did all household labor. They did the agricultural labor on larger estates, although small farms where the householder and his wife did most of the work, with help from children and perhaps one or two slaves, still existed in rural areas.

Slaves also did much of the productive work in factories and artisan shops. They managed estates and factories and served as financial agents of their masters. Educated slaves were tutors of children and could become teachers in schools. Slaves could be rented out as workers, even as prostitutes, their wages being shared between their masters and those who managed their work. Slaves ran errands and were at their master's or his wife's beck and call for any services he or she desired. They could be figures of conspicuous consumption, with wealthy men surrounding themselves with a retinue of slaves and clients. At banquets, an elegant slave boy might serve exclusively as cupbearer for his master. Thus, slaves were ubiquitous in Roman antiquity, making up as much as a third of the population of Roman Italy in the first century C.E.[33]

The human status of slaves was ambiguous in classical antiquity. Aristotle saw slaves, along with barbarians and women, as inherently lesser humans, suited to be used as instruments, lacking capacity for autonomous life.[34] The Stoics saw slavery as an accident of fortune and insisted that a man (it is not clear if this included women) remained the "captain of their soul" even as a slave. A true philosopher could ignore the indignities to their bodies and maintain the freedom of their soul even in slavery. But this view was based on the ability to divorce the mind from its bodily experiences.[35]

The legal status of the slave was that of an owned body. Thus, although Romans did not deny that slaves were human persons, as owned bodies they could be used any way the master wanted. They had no "rights" as persons. Thus, slaves could be flogged (even to death), tortured, executed, and forced into any kind of work. Both female and male slaves were accessible to the sexual demands of their masters or other owning-class males of the household, such as sons of the master. They could be used as prostitutes. Exposed infants raised as slaves were typically made into prostitutes.

Emancipation was relatively common in Roman antiquity. As a skilled manager, a slave could become wealthy and be able to pay his master for his emancipation. Slaves could also be freed in wills as well as passed on as slaves to a person's heirs. Ultimately, it was the decision of the owner to free a slave by officially "turning him (or her) around" before a magistrate. The freed slave, however, often owed some continuing service to the master as a client. Freed slaves became a kind of nouveau riche in the early Roman Empire, dominating the imperial bureaucracy. In the first-century C.E., Roman satire the *Satyricon*, the freedman Trimalchio holds a banquet in which he makes a vulgar display of his wealth for his guests. The purpose of this satire was to show that, no matter how wealthy, a freedman could never attain *dignitas* as a true Roman.[36]

It is sometimes assumed that early Christianity opposed slavery and thus was an important force for ending ancient slavery. But this is doubtful. Although St. Paul affirms that in Christ "there is no more slave and free," just as there is no more Jew and Greek, and neither male nor female" (Gal. 3:28), Christians in the first five centuries did not oppose slavery as an institution. In fact, slavery is affirmed in the New Testament household codes where slaves are repeatedly told to "obey their masters," not only the kind and gentle ones but even the abusive ones (1 Pet. 2:18–20). Some churches may have helped buy people out of slavery, especially freeborn people who had been unjustly captured, but church authorities cautioned against using church funds in this way.[37] Patriarchy as a social system thus was confirmed by the developing church despite some initial challenges.

Moreover, slaves were not fully equal to freeborn people in Christian congregations. The fact that a slave man or woman could not protect his or her body from sexual use probably precluded a slave from being able to qualify for the sexual code promoted by Christian communities that demanded that their members be free of all "fornication."[38] By the fifth century, the economic collapse of the Western Roman Empire meant that slavery began to decrease for economic reasons. But there was never a real abolitionist movement in antiquity. That would have to wait until the nineteenth century.[39]

NOTES

1. See, for example, Johann Jakob Bakhofen, *Myth, Religion and Mother Right: Selected Writings*, trans. Ralph Manheim (Princeton, N.J.: Princeton University Press, 1967).

2. Richard E. Leakey, *The Making of Mankind* (New York: E. P. Dutton, 1981), 98–109.

3. M. Kay Martin and Barbara Voorhies, *Female of the Species* (New York: Columbia University Press, 1975), 184–89.

4. Martin and Voorhies, *Female of the Species*, 190.

5. David F. Aberle, "Matrilineal Descent in Cross-Cultural Perspective," citing the 1957 work of George Peter Murdock, *World Ethnographic Sample*, in *Matrilineal Kinship*, ed. David M. Schneider and Katheleen Gough (Berkeley: University of California Press, 1961), 663.

6. Martin and Voorhees, *Female of the Species*, 225–28; see also Judith K. Brown, "Economic Organization and the Position of Women among the Iroquois," *Ethnohistory* 17: 151–67.

7. See Katheleen Gouch, "The Modern Disappearance of Matrilineal Descent Groups," in Schneider and Gough, *Matrilineal Kinship*, 631–52.

8. The major study of the contemporary Minangkabau is Peggy Sanday, *Women at the Center: Life in a Modern Matriarchy* (Ithaca, N.Y.: Cornell University Press, 2002).

9. Sanday, *Women at the Center*, 173–87.

10. See "Adat Matriarchaat as a World View," in Sanday, *Women at the Center*, 15–31.

11. See Margaret Ehrenberg, *Women in Prehistory* (London: British Museum Publications, 1989), 99–107.

12. Gerda Lerner's stresses the relation of the creation of slavery and the development of patriarchy. See her *The Creation of Patriarchy* (New York: Oxford University Press, 1986).

13. See Susan Pollock, *Ancient Mesopotamia: The Eden That Never Was* (Cambridge: Cambridge University Press, 1999), 45–116.

14. For the development of cities in the Ancient Near East around 3000 B.C.E., see Gwendolyn Leick, *Mesopotamia: The Invention of the City* (London: Penguin, 2001).

15. This custom persists in Africa; see Ifi Amadiume, *Male Daughters, Female Husbands: Gender and Sex in an African Society* (New York: Zed Books, 1987).

16. For this practice in ancient Mesopotamia, see Rivkah Harris, "Independent Women in Ancient Mesopotamia," in *Women's Earliest Records: From Egypt and Western Asia*, ed. Barbara S. Lesko (Atlanta: Scholars Press, 1989), 150–56.

17. "The Code of Hammurabi, Laws from Mesopotamia and Asia Minor," in *Ancient Near Eastern Texts Relating to the Old Testament*, ed. James B. Pritchard (Princeton, N.J.: Princeton University Press, 1969), 175.

18. The pattern of the laws is that when a nobleman injures another nobleman, he suffers the same injury; that is, if he destroys the eye of another member of the aristocracy, he loses his eye, but if he injures a commoner or slave, he pays a fee. See Pritchard, *Ancient Near Eastern Texts Relating to the Old Testament*.

19. For the development of the seclusion of women in agricultural societies, see Martin and Voorhees, *The Female of the Species*, 290–96.

20. See W. K. Lacey, *The Family in Classical Greece* (Ithaca, N.Y.: Cornell University Press, 1986).

21. See Jane Gardner, *Family and "Familia" in Roman Law and Life* (New York: Clarendon Press, 1998).

22. See Richard P. Saller, "*Familia, Domus* and the Roman Concept of the Family," *Phoenix* 38 (1984): 336–55. see also Richard P. Saller, *Patriarchy, Property and Death in the Roman Family* (Cambridge: Cambridge University Press, 1994), 74–101.

23. On adoption into the Roman family, see Gardner, *Family and "Familia,"* 114–208.

24. See Susan Treggiari, *Roman Marriage: "Iusto Coniuges" from the Times of Cicero to Ulpian* (Oxford: Clarendon Press, 1991), 32–36.

25. See Rosemary R. Ruether, "Mothers of the Church: Ascetic Women in the Late Patristic Age," in *Women of Spirit: Female Leadership in the Jewish and Christian Traditions*, ed. Rosemary R. Ruether and Eleanor McLaughlin (New York: Simon and Schuster, 1979), 75–94.

26. Ruether and McLaughlin, *Women of Spirit*, 75–79.

27. Ruether and McLaughlin, *Women of Spirit*, 75–76. See also Rosemary Ruether, *Women and Redemption: A Theological History* (Minneapolis: Fortress, 1998), 79–80. For women's writing in patristic and medieval Christianity, see Andrew Kadel, *Matrology: A Bibliography of Writings by Christian Women from the First to the Fifteenth Centuries* (New York: Continuum, 1995).

28. See Treggiari, *Roman Marriage*, 39–43.

29. See "Children in the Roman Family," in Suzanne Dixon, *The Roman Family* (Baltimore: Johns Hopkins University Press, 1992), 98–132.

30. See "Whips and Words: Discipline and Punishment in the Roman Household," in Saller, *Patriarchy, Property and Death in the Roman Family*, 133–53.

31. Augustine, *Confessions*, bk. I, 19–23.

32. On sources of slaves, including the question of self-sale, see Jennifer A. Glancy, *Slavery in Early Christianity* (Oxford: Oxford University Press, 2002), 73–85.

33. Two major studies of slavery in the Roman era are Keith Bradley, *Slavery and Society at Rome* (Cambridge: Cambridge University Press, 1994), and *Slaves and Masters in the Roman Empire* (New York: Oxford University Press, 1987).
34. Aristotle, *Politics*, 124a-b.
35. For Stoic views of slavery, particularly Epictetus, see Glancy, *Slavery in Early Christianity*, 30–34.
36. Petronius, *Satyricon*, trans. J. P. Sullivan (New York: Penguin, 1986), 51–91.
37. See Glancy, *Slavery in Early Christianity*, 96, 151–52.
38. Glancy, *Slavery in Early Christianity*, 58–67.
39. Glancy, *Slavery in Early Christianity*, 150.

· 4 ·

Modernizing Patriarchy: Women, Children, and Slaves

This chapter traces the changing patterns of work and legal status of women, children, and slaves in Western Europe and the United States from the Reformation era (1500 C.E.) until the twenty-first century, with some attention to the continuing reality of slavery, subjugation of women, and exploitation of children's labor in the world economy today. The status and work of these three groups of subjugated people within the patriarchal family—women and children (across class) and slaves—are interconnected. So it is problematic to trace these changes of women's status and work, children's status and work, and the revival and gradual abolition of slavery as parallel trajectories. In this chapter, I intertwine the issues of women and children while treating slavery and its abolition (and de facto continuation) separately.

The basic context for the changing roles of women, children, and slaves in the past 500 years in the West is the gradual reduction of the household economy. The household economy was the traditional preindustrial economy in which the male-headed household was largely self-sufficient, producing and processing its own food and spinning, weaving, and making its own clothes, tools, and other artifacts of daily life. This household might own or manage larger or smaller areas of land. For those with a small amount of land, the householder himself, with his wife and children, were the basic workforce. Those with a larger amount of land could use slaves for most agricultural and household labor, including specialized factories for textiles and other goods, freeing the wife of the householder from productive labor for household management and social roles, male children for education for elite leadership, and females to prepare for marriage.

Trade in surplus food and goods were early a part of the household economy, but this surplus of food and goods was produced by households. It is the elimination of the household economy through industrialization (i.e., the organization of economic production in factories no longer owned by the family, however extended) that gradually made slavery redundant and eliminated the roles of women and children as producers within the household economy.

The year 1500 C.E. represents an important turning point in this development of the relation of work, family, and religion in Western Europe. In Protestant areas, the ideal of celibacy that had dominated Christianity for a millennium and a half was rejected. This meant that monasteries for both men and women were dismantled and their lands bought up by wealthy laypeople.[1] Priests were now married; thus, the male clerical caste was integrated into householder society. This had the effect of depriving women of an alternative vocation to marriage and abolishing areas of production and trade that were related to the Catholic liturgy, such as making candles.[2]

In Catholic areas, the celibate clerical caste, monastic vocations for women, as well as employment in making sacramental objects remained, but in both Catholic and Protestant areas of Europe, there was a renewal of Roman law that dictated stricter economic and legal subordination of women.[3] As a result, women were marginalized from skilled, paid work. They were removed from membership in guilds or craft unions in their own right. Single women who were not part of patriarchal households (or nunneries) were looked on with suspicion, and in Catholic areas the subordination of nuns to the male episcopal hierarchy was tightened up. Strict cloister and separation from the "world" was enforced.[4]

The guild system had based artisan production of all kinds in workshops attached to the household, but women's labor was more strictly separated from men's labor. Women no longer could participate in skilled work that would allow them to inherit their husband's guild membership should he die. Rather, women were allowed only unskilled supportive work to male skilled work, such as preparing thread for weavers. They were directed toward unpaid domestic work or the marketing of small items, such as dishcloths or hairbrushes, in the informal economy. The ability of women to be a self-supporting householder was thus becoming more difficult.[5]

Protestantism continued the tradition of banning public teaching, preaching, or ministerial roles for women. Its concern that the whole lay community, men and women, be literate in order to read the Bible had the effect of including young girls in expanded grammar schools, but the priority was on education for boys. Advanced education for girls was not encouraged by Protestants or Catholics. Women were shut out of universities, although humanist scholars did promote some higher education for elite women in the context of tutors and libraries in their fathers' homes.[6]

Children were an integral part of the artisan household economy, but boys were quickly separated from girls. Boys from the age of twelve became apprentices either to their father's trade or were sent to another household to learn a trade, thus preparing them to become journeymen and eventually master craftsmen with their own guild membership. Young boys from other families joined the household as apprentices.[7] The housewife's chores included feeding this workforce and cleaning their clothes. Girls assisted their mothers in supportive roles in the family trade and domestic work, with older girls pressed into service to care for younger children. Their future was to marry and become a housewife in another household.

The seventeenth to nineteenth centuries saw a series of economic developments in Western Europe that reshaped this artisan household economy. These shifts are sometimes called "protoindustrialism," followed by full-fledged industrialism. In the protoindustrial developments, an entrepreneur secures the materials and contracts for them to be assembled in workshops in or connected to the household. But the artisan household no longer controls its own materials and marketing of goods. It simply becomes the low-paid assembly place for making material into clothes, hats, and so on. It receives the material and is paid per piece for the finished product, which is marketed by the entrepreneur.[8]

The whole family—women, men, and children—may work together on such assembly of products, or such work might be combined with agricultural labor on land that provides part of the family's subsistence. Women and girls often did much of this work, while the men and boys worked in agriculture. This pattern would continue in an even more exploitative form in sweatshops under more advanced industrialization where women and girl children worked together to assemble flowers and other products in their tenement apartments. Usually the man of the family and older boys were employed outside the home.[9]

The next stage in this development is full-fledged industrialization in which the entrepreneur builds the building, supplies the tools and machinery and raw material, and markets the finished goods. The artisan has thus been reduced to a wage earner. He no longer owns the workshop, the tools, and machinery; obtains the materials; or markets the finished product but simply sells his labor to the factory owner. Factories in the nineteenth century drew whole families into their workforce—men, women, and children—depending on the work. Some factories, such as textiles, particularly employed young women as well as even younger girls and boys, with the older girls running the spinning and weaving machines and younger children assisting in support jobs, such as repairing broken threads.[10]

These factories depended on the low-paid labor of teenage girls and even lower-paid labor of children as young as four or five to make a profit. Work hours were greatly extended, with workers typically working from dawn to late in the evening. In this factory economy, no one worker made anything close to a "living wage." Thus, families depended for survival on putting together a "family income" from the wages of multiple workers—husband and wife and older and younger girls and boys. Home-based production for consumption also helped families eke out a living, such as gardening, keeping chickens, preserving food, making soap, and so on, much of this in the hands of women.

The poorest girls were sent away as early as eight years old as domestic servants in wealthier households. Domestic workers were expected to work long hours but often got no wages, being paid in kind (e.g., food, cast-off clothing, or a place to sleep). Such domestic work differed little from slavery, and indeed this is a major arena where slavery continues today, drawing on either poor rural girls or girls from Third World countries.[11]

As industrialism develops in the nineteenth and into the twentieth centuries in Western Europe and the United States, its different functions become more specialized. In earlier factories, the entrepreneur might live in a "big house," adjacent to the factory and to the cottages or dormitories of the workers. The goods produced might be sold in a shop nearby run by the entrepreneur's wife, who also kept the account books. Later, all these functions become separated and specialized. The entrepreneur moved to a separate elite part of town, distinct from where the workers lived and worked. Marketing and finance become lodged in an elite downtown of shops and banks, also removed from where work is done and where workers live. The entrepreneur's wife is removed from partnership in marketing or accounts and becomes the full-time "housewife" presiding over the consumption of the private household, usually assisted by domestic servants. The garden is now purely ornamental and a place of play; families no longer rely on it for food. The children of this elite household no longer work. School and leisure time social life occupy their hours.[12]

With these sharper divisions of class and gendered work and life, a new ideal of the "family" arises in the middle class of the nineteenth century. The Victorian middle-class family ideology is based on a series of dichotomized spheres—public and private, work and home, and masculine and feminine. Both women and children in this ideal family are segregated in the privatized home, separated from the adult male sphere of "work." It is assumed that the work of the male head of household should provide fully for the needs of the whole family, thus relieving both his wife and their children of work. The nonworking full-time housewife and mother thus becomes the family ideal, supported by the income of her husband.[13]

But this high income of the middle-class head of family conceals the toiling masses whose low wages support it: low-paid men and women and children working in factories and shops. The leisure of the wife and her children also conceals the low-paid domestic labor that cooks and cleans in the home, not to mention the cooks and cleaners of public institutions, restaurants, banks, stores, and streets. Thus, the middle-class ideal of the family with its division of work and home, public and private, and male and female was always unattainable by most working-class families in nineteenth- and twentieth-century Europe and America. They remained dependent on multiple incomes from the work of a husband, older and younger children, and the wife. Although the wife might be able to stay "at home" thanks to several incomes from husband and children, she was not a leisured wife but performed vital home-based production of the sort mentioned previously that supplemented the income brought by husband and children.

The middle-class housewife ideal with its dependent children was even less available to the black family after slavery in the post–Civil War era. Black women always had to work to support the family. But only the poorest-paid work, such as sharecropping, domestic service, and laundry, was available to them. They typically had to leave their own children unattended to work as child carers, cleaners, and cooks in rich (usually white) women's households. Black women, men, and children, moreover, were shut out of factory work. They were allowed only the "outside" work, such as unloading goods for the factory or cleaning the premises. Thus, black families were also dependent on putting together several incomes but with much poorer possibilities of employment even than low-waged white workers.[14]

These divisions of gender and social class and growing disparities of wealth and poverty sparked several reform movements in late nineteenth-century United States. One of these was the union movement, which sought better wages, working conditions, shorter hours, health benefits, and pensions for workers. But the major unions sought only to organize white adult males. They wanted to raise the adult male wage so that children and women could be sent home. They shared the middle-class family ideal and believed that women should be full-time housewives and mothers and that children should be in school. They also had no interest in organizing black workers or helping them gain access to broader and better-paid areas of work. Better-paid factory work should remain a prerogative of white males.[15]

A second important reform movement of the late nineteenth century was feminism, with its beginning going back to the 1850s. Feminism sought to change the historic legal status of women under patriarchy. They sought equal legal status as autonomous citizens with men to vote, hold political office and own property in their own name. They sought access to higher education, admission to professional schools, and acceptance in elite professions, such as law, medicine, and college teaching. The leaders of the feminist movement came largely from the white middle class. They were the daughters of the white middle class stifled by its "family ideal." They wanted the same access to public life as their brothers.

Most feminists ignored the plight of poor women toiling in factories or sweatshops, although a few, notably the settlement house movement under leaders such as Jane Addams in Chicago, addressed these issues of poor women and their children. But even the settlement house leaders focused on white immigrant families in urban areas, such as Chicago, ignoring the even greater disadvantages of blacks.[16] At the very time when white women sought the vote, black men were being shut out of the vote supposedly won for them by the Fourteenth Amendment of the U.S. Constitution. Some feminists even suggested that the vote for (white middle-class) women would ensure the dominance of the "better" class of Americans over blacks and immigrants.[17]

Nevertheless, the feminist movement would succeed in changing the legal status of all women. With the Nineteenth Amendment to the U.S. Constitution ratified in August 1920, women gained the right to vote. But not all women had access to this new right. Jim Crow laws in the South effectively prevented black women and men from voting. Other disabilities also remained for women in general. Financial institutions usually did not lend money to women or allow them to make major purchases, such as a car or a house, without the signature of their fathers or husbands. Elite universities instituted quotas limiting the admission of women to a third or less. Elite professions, such as law, medicine, and college teaching, allowed few women in their upper ranks.[18]

In the 1920s, an ideological campaign decried women seeking professions as "unnatural viragos" who had rejected true "femininity." Laws condemned public promotion of birth control as "pornography." Margaret Sanger, the leading crusader for contraceptives, was jailed for founding clinics that provided them.[19] Protestants would not change their views of contraception until the 1950s, and officially Catholicism still forbids it. In the 1930s, during the American Depression, there was an attack on working wives led by the federal government and by business, claiming that working wives caused male unemployment (even though there was little connection between the two). Married women found themselves shut out of jobs in government, public school teaching, business, and finance. But women with unemployed husbands needed all the more to work, so the effect of this ban was to push women out of better-paid into lower-paid work. Men took over the upper level of what had been female professions, such as public school teaching and librarians.[20]

Public works projects during the Depression aimed at employing white men. Women were included in only a few of these projects, mainly to do cooking and sewing for male workers. Wage differentials for men and women were ratified under New Deal legislation. The National Industrial Recovery Act of 1933 enshrined minimum wages ranging from 14 to 30 percent lower for women than for men doing the same job. Some jobs were excluded from minimum-wage requirements, work described as "light and repetitive" (i.e., female labor). Agricultural and domestic work, where poor black and Hispanic women and men dominated, was exempt from the minimum wage. The same pattern of sex (and de facto race) discrimination continued in the Full Labor Standards Act of 1938.[21]

The Social Security Act of 1935 inscribed in law several important social reforms for workers, making provision for unemployment benefits, old-age insurance, and stipends for the disabled. It also awarded stipends for dependent children in families lacking an employed breadwinner. This would be expanded into Aid for Dependent Children in the 1939 revision of this act. The Fair Labor Relations Act banned employment of children under the age of sixteen. This New Deal legislation laid the basis for the American Social Security system. Most important for most Americans is the federally guaranteed old-age pension, which workers pay into through their years of work to receive a pension in retirement. Working wives were discriminated against in this legislation, receiving less for their own earned Social Security pension than they would as a widow of an insured husband.[22] Many jobs filled by women, such as domestic work, were not covered by Social Security.

The law forbidding child labor under the age of sixteen was controversial in many parts of the United States. Southern textile factories still depended on employing children at low wages. Immigrant families still depended on children's wages to contribute to the family income. Agriculture particularly depended on employing whole families—men, women, and children—as seasonal workers. Enforcement of child labor laws often ignored these cases and continues to do so, particularly in agriculture.[23]

But the victory of laws against child labor reshaped the historic economic role of nonelite children from economic assets to economic liabilities. Instead of workers in training and contributors to family income, children became consumers wholly dependent on parents. Their primary role is to be educated through the school. This was buttressed by laws making school attendance mandatory to the age of sixteen and punishing children and their parents for failure to attend (truancy).[24]

This economic dependency on parents lengthens for those with high educational and professional expectations for their children. Children of such parents may not become economically self-sufficient until their mid-twenties as they pursue college and graduate school. Even when young adults are employed, it is no longer an expectation that they contribute to family income. The teenager may get an after-school job, but this is seen as going into his or her own pocket money for consumer items, not into the family budget. When adult children secure a full-time job, parents hope only that their offspring are on their way to economic independence, not that they will pay back their parents for their twenty or more years of investment in his or her development. Most American parents do not expect to live with their children in old age but intend to provide for themselves in their own homes or in retirement homes. Thus, the pattern of child–parent relations of working-class preindustrial Europe has been decisively changed in modern America.

World War II temporarily changed the U.S. government's discrimination against female employment. With the men away at war, women's work was valued. Women were encouraged by national campaigns funded by the government to take up employment in various kind of war work, including making planes and ships. Official propaganda portrayed this new "Rosie the Riveter" as a single young white woman waiting for her boyfriend to come home from the war so that she could turn to her true vocation as his wife and mother of his children. However, most women war workers were married women who had worked before. Some black women were able to gain a step up in employment through war work. Many such women had children. For the first and only time in U.S. history, the federal government recognized that such women needed day care for their children in order to work and funded an (inadequate) system of day care for some of these women's children.[25]

However, at the end of the war, with the return of the veterans, there was a quick and total reversal of this policy. Women were summarily laid off to make room for jobs for the vets. The federal government subsidized higher education and the purchase of homes for these vets, while working women were again attacked as pathological. The 1950s became the apogee of the ideal of the suburban (white) family with full-time wife and mother. Women's level of education actually fell for a decade or two, with women marrying earlier (in their late teens) and having three, four, and more children. Working-class and black women continued to combine work and family, but they were invisible in this national culture.[26]

The years 1953–1968 saw a concerted revolt of black Americans against racism and Jim Crow laws that had prevailed in American society since the 1890s. Voting, political office, and broader opportunities for education and jobs opened up for the "talented tenth" of American blacks, including black women, although the prevailing culture of the black civil rights movement focused primarily on the black male.[27] The decade of 1965–1975 also saw a new feminist movement as middle-class white women revolted against their domestication in the 1950s.

This new feminist movement had two wings that gradually merged. One wing was white (and some black) professional women in government and law concerned to complete the emancipation of women, legally, economically, and educationally. A second wing was younger women who had joined the civil rights and New Left movements of the 1960s and then were dismayed by its sexism. The first wing was typified by leaders such as Betty Friedan, founder of the National Organization for Women. The second wing was more radical cultural revolutionaries who promoted a broad agenda of "women liberation," including acceptance of lesbian relations and women's reproductive rights. The two gradually accommodated each other by the 1970s.[28]

Feminism won several legislative victories that increased the number of women in higher education and professional employment. The capstone of this effort was the passing of the Equal Rights Amendment by the 1972 Congress (which had been stalled in Congress since it was first proposed in 1923). In 1973, the Supreme Court approved the *Roe v. Wade* case, legalizing abortion through the second trimester. The feminist movement had not actually been involved in bringing this case, but the issue of abortion was quickly identified with feminism.[29]

The decade of 1975–1985 saw a major antifeminist backlash led by the rise of right-wing Christians, both Protestant and Catholic, in political power. The Equal Rights Amendment was blocked from passage by the states.[30] There was a continual effort to roll back reproductive rights and legal, political, and economic gains made by women. Feminists were vilified as "antifamily lesbians." Welfare rights from the New Deal era were also attacked, claiming that it allowed black women to live in luxury with their many children as "welfare queens." In reality, black women had gained only some access to welfare in the 1960s, while at the same time the actual welfare stipends had sunk to an average of $6,000 a year, or about half of the federally defined "poverty" level for a family of four.[31] In 1996, under President Clinton, the system of Aid to Families with Dependent Children was effectively abolished for a limited system of income support for poor women with children aimed at getting them off welfare for waged labor, typically low-paying jobs that sometimes paid less than welfare stipends.[32]

Thus, the situation for women in the United States has greatly changed in one way yet remains discriminatory toward women in other ways. Although the Equal Rights Amendment was blocked from passage, the Supreme Court effectively abolished laws that overtly discriminated against women, such as lower pay for the same work or lack of access to financial transactions in their own name. Women legally have equal rights with men. But culturally there remains great hostility to women overtly claiming this equality in public life. A "strong" woman in business or politics has to mask this equality with a show of cultural "femininity" although not in a way that would interfere with her actually efficiency. Thus, women in American public life walk a cultural tightrope between the need to be equally if not more effective in their jobs than men and not appearing too "masculine."

On the economic front, it has become almost impossible for all but the richest families to live the American upper-middle-class lifestyle without a double income. Since the 1980s (and as of this writing), there has been a continual increase in the two-earner household as well as working single women and female-headed households. Roughly a quarter of American households are single men or women living alone. Female-headed households, either alone or with dependent children, are at a distinct disadvantage compared to the two-earner family or even the male-headed household, with white women earning an average of $22,000 and black women an average of $15,000. The two-earner white family, by contrast, averages $56,500 and black two-earner households $48,533. The white male averages $33,000 and the black male $25,500.

White Americans generally marry in their middle to late twenties and bear an average of 1.85 children, with blacks only slightly more (2.02 children). Sixty percent of women are in the labor force, 78.1 percent between the ages of thirty and fifty. Thus, the "full-time housewife" of the Victorian family ideal has greatly diminished, although it is doubtful that this was ever available to more than a small minority. Half of white Americans live in two-earner households, 32 percent in male-earner households, and 14.1 percent in female-headed households, while 46.8 percent of black families are female headed.[33]

Most notably, there is a widening economic polarization in American society, with well-paid manufacturing jobs disappearing, to be replaced by service jobs, some in the high tech areas being well paid but mostly low paid. Thus, lawyers average $99,000 and computer programmers $63,420, while fast-food cooks average $15,000 and cashiers $16,260. The top 5 percent make $200 million a year to the billions, while the bottom 50 percent earns less than $30,000.[34] Thus, for most American women, a full-time paid job has little to do with "liberation" and mostly to do with survival.

THE REVIVAL AND ABOLITION OF SLAVERY

Having surveyed the changing patterns of life for free women and their children, I turn to an account of the revival of slavery in the fifteenth century and its gradual legal abolition by the late nineteenth century in Western and global society. The persistence of de facto slavery in some sectors of society worldwide is also noted.

Slavery never completely disappeared from Europe during the Middle Ages. It faded from agriculture, being replaced by serfdom. Some slaves continued to be used in household service. Captives taken in war were sometimes sold into the slave trade in the eastern Mediterranean. The Children's Crusade of 1212 brought thousands of children under the age of twelve to Marseilles who were mostly kidnapped by slave traders and sold to Egypt.[35] But the major renewal of the slave trade by Europeans took place in the mid-fifteenth century with the Portuguese trading ventures into the western coast of Africa.

In 1441, a Portuguese ship captured twelve Africans in a raid on the Atlantic coast of Africa and brought them back to Portugal as gifts to Prince Henry the Navigator (1394–1460). Prince Henry sought approval for more slave raids from the pope, who in 1455 authorized Portugal to reduce to servitude all heathen people.[36] Prince Henry led Portugal in a vast overseas trading expansion down the coast of Africa around Cape Horn to India. Slaves were brought back to work in the sugar plantations in the Canary, Madeira, and Cape Verde islands. With Columbus's "discovery" of America in 1492, the Spanish took sugar to the Caribbean islands and Mexico.

By this time, slaving raids had grown into an organized slave trade that connected Europe, Africa, and the Americas. Slaves taken from Africa were shipped to Cuba, where they were dispersed to sugar plantations in the Americas, and sugar and other raw materials were brought to Europe. By 1600, 900,000 slaves had crossed the Atlantic and by 1700 another 2,750,000.[37] It is estimated that 15 million slaves landed in America between the fifteenth century and the ending of the slave trade in the nineteeenth. Since a third to a half of the African slaves died on the "middle passage" voyage and others died in the process of being taken from their villages and marched to the African coast to be shipped, Africa lost at least 30 million of its population to slavery in these years.[38] On sugar plantations and in mines, slaves were often worked to death within three years since it was seen as cheaper to buy slaves than to preserve their lives through adequate care.[39]

By 1640, the Portuguese no longer had a monopoly of the slave trade. The Dutch took over much of the Gold Coast trade by 1642, and the English and the French surpassed the Dutch as the leading slave traders by 1700. In the eighteenth century, the British would dominate more than half the trade.[40]

Black Africans were not the only ethnic group enslaved. The Spanish and Portuguese saw American Indians as slave labor for agriculture, mines, and household service. When outright enslavement of Indians was forbidden by Spanish law (as a result of the interventions of defenders of the Indians, such as Bartolomeo de las Casas[41]), Indians were reduced to de facto serfdom through the *encomienda* system (i.e., large tracts of land given to Spanish settlers that brought with it the resident Indians whom the settler was obliged to "Christianize" in return for their labor[42]). English settlers in North America were more interested in getting rid of Indians than in enslaving or Christianizing them. Boatloads of Indians conquered in war were shipped from North America into slavery in the West Indies.[43]

Europeans also saw slavery as a way of getting rid of enemies among other Europeans. During the English Civil War in the mid-seventeenth century, Oliver Cromwell put many Royalist prisoners up for sale in Bristol. When Cromwell forcibly subjugated Ireland, many Irish were shipped to the West Indies as slaves.[44] As in Roman times, pirates roamed the Mediterranean capturing boatloads of Europeans and selling them into slavery in Egypt.[45] The enslavement of Europeans was a major reason for Britain and other European countries to turn against slavery in the nineteenth century. But the overwhelming majority of slaves in the European slave trade were black Africans, whom the Europeans generally saw as racially inferior and fit only for slave labor.[46]

In the period of the American Revolution, the existence of slavery caused some of the "founding fathers," such as Jefferson, a crisis of conscience. Although Jefferson hated slavery as corrupting to whites (its effects on slaves seemed less interesting to him) and wished to abolish it, he also believed the African inferior to the white and could not imagine them as equal citizens in the new American nation. In addition, the task of bringing the southern colonies together with the North into one "union" seemed to necessitate a "compromise" in which blacks slaves were counted as three-fifths of a person for purposes of (white) representation (article 1, section 2, of the U.S. Constitution).

This compromise strengthened the political power of the South, where most of the slaves resided. In 1775, there were 2.5 million whites and 750,000 black slaves. Northerners believed that slavery would soon die out. They sought to abolish the slave trade, compromising in 1787 by allowing it to exist for another twenty years, until 1808. Many northern states passed laws in which slavery would gradually die out by providing for the emancipation of children born of slaves. But the invention of the cotton gin allowed cotton to become "king" in southern states, greatly increasing the use of slaves. By 1860, three-quarters of world cotton came from the American southern states. Slaves had grown to over 4 million and in South Carolina and Mississippi were the majority of the population. The slave trade continued within the United States, where many "homegrown" slaves were traded to the developing western and southern states. Moreover, the slave trade from Africa continued covertly, with New England slavers actively involved in shipping goods, particularly rum, to Africa in return for slaves whom they traded to the West Indies.[47]

It would take the Civil War to abolish slavery in the United States. In January 1863, President Lincoln issued the Emancipation Proclamation, which freed all slaves in areas of rebellion against the U.S. government. The Thirteenth, Fourteenth, and Fifteenth Amendments to the U.S. Constitution (1865, 1868, and 1870, respectively) abolished all involuntary servitude (except for those imprisoned for crime) within the United States and gave freed blacks citizenship rights and the vote. However, by the 1890s, Jim Crow laws effectively disenfranchised blacks in the South. It would take the civil rights movement of 1953–1968 to abolish these laws of racial segregation and give American blacks equal citizenship, at least according to law.

The British, spurred by a strong abolitionist movement led by Evangelicals, abolished the slave trade by British citizens in 1807 and emancipated slaves in British colonies in 1834. These moves were not totally altruistic. The British had come to see free trade as economically superior to slave labor and also sought to ruin their rivals in the sugar trade in the Caribbean by forbidding slave labor.[48] But slavery continued in Cuba until 1886 and in Brazil until 1888. Although the Atlantic slave trade was legally dead by 1841, smuggling of slaves from Africa also continued, with slave traders evading the laws of their countries by hoisting a Spanish flag when they encountered the Royal Navy charged to prevent this trade. Merchants from areas such as Salem, Massachusetts, continued to be involved in this illegal trade.[49]

Moreover, the slave trade did not disappear in Africa and the Arab world. Slaves continued to be seized in Africa and marched to the east coast of the continent, where they were marketed through a lively slave trade run by the sultan of Zanzibar.[50] In 1884, the major European nations gathered in Berlin to divide Africa into colonies among themselves, claiming as one of their intentions to abolish slavery in Africa and substitute "Christianity and commerce."[51]

In the twenty-first century, most Americans believe that slavery is a thing of the past, put to rest at the end of the Civil War. In 1958, the UN Supplementary Convention on the Abolition of Slavery declared the slave trade, slavery, and similar forms of forced servitude illegal. Most countries have signed on to this convention and have made slavery illegal. But this hardly means that all de facto slavery disappeared in the twentieth century.

One of the major ways it has continued has been through forced labor in totalitarian societies. The Soviet Union, Nazi Germany, imperial Japan, and communist China rounded millions of political prisoners and sent them to forced labor camps. In Asia and Africa children, especially girls, continue to be major victims of enslavement. Impoverished parents sell their girls to recruiters who promise them that they will receive education and employment. However, these young girls find themselves imprisoned in brothels as prostitutes or sold as household servants. Claiming that they owe their owner for their transportation, these girls are saddled with debts and forced to work to pay these debts, which prove to be unpayable. Children—male and female—are also sold by parents to work in the carpet industry in India, Pakistan, and Nepal.[52]

The European world and the United States are not innocent of these forms of de facto slave labor. Women sold into servitude as domestic servants occasionally escape elegant households in London and Paris to tell their stories of imprisonment and abuse. Groups of Asians or Latin Americans desperate for work have been smuggled into the United States to find themselves imprisoned as prostitutes or forced to work in locked factories in areas such as Los Angeles.[53] Thus, the struggle to fully abolish servile labor continues into the twenty-first century. It will continue to exist as long as the vast gap between rich and poor continues and as long as it remains profitable to exploit impoverished people and their children in various forms of unpaid exploitative labor.

NOTES

1. Rosemary Ruether, *Christianity and the Making of the Modern Family: Ruling Ideologies and Diverse Realities* (Boston: Beacon Press, 2000), 67.

2. See Merry E. Wiesner, "Women's Reponses to the Reformation," in *The German People and the Reformation*, ed. R. P. Chi Hsia (Ithaca, N.Y.: Cornell University Press, 1988), 148–71.

3. See Merry E. Wiesner, *Women and Gender in Early Modern Europe* (Cambridge: Cambridge University Press, 1993), 30–34; see also Thomas Kuehn, *Law, Family and Women: Toward a Legal Anthropology of Renaissance Italy* (Chicago: Chicago University Press, 1991).

4. On enforcement of cloister for women and their resistance to it, see Ruth P. Liebowitz, "Virgins in the Service of Christ: The Dispute over the Active Apostolate for Women during the Counter-Reformation," in *Women of Spirit: Female Leadership in the Jewish and Christian Traditions*, ed. Rosemary R. Ruether and Eleanor McLaughlin (New York: Simon and Schuster, 1979), 131–52.

5. See Merry E. Wiesner, *Working Women in Renaissance Germany* (New Brunswick, N.J.: Rutgers University Press, 1986), 168–85.

6. On educated women in the Renaissance and seventeenth-century England, see Hildah L. Smith, *Reason's Disciples: Seventeenth Century English Feminists* (Chicago: University of Illinois Press, 1982), xi–xii.

7. See Hugh Cunningham, *Children and Childhood in Western Society since 1500* (Harlow: Pearson, 2005), 56.

8. Cunningham, *Children and Childhood in Western Society since 1500*, 86–87; see also see Franklin F. Mendels, "Proto-Industrialization: The First Phase of Industrialization," *Journal of Economic History* 31 (March 1972): 241–61, and Hans Medich, "The Proto-Industrial Family Economy: The Structural Function of Household and Family during the Transition from Peasant Society to Industrial Capitalism," *Social History* 3 (1976): 291–311.

9. See Hugh D. Hindman, "Tenement Homework: The Birth of the Sweatshop," in *Child Labor: An American History* (New York: M.E. Sharpe, 2002), 187–212.

10. See Cunningham, *Children and Childhood in Western Society since 1500*, 88–89; see also Ruether, *Christianity and the Making of the Modern Family*, 87–90, and Louise A. Tilly and Joan W. Scott, *Women, Work and Family* (New York: Holt, Rinehart and Winston, 1978), 60–75.

11. Domestic service was referred to as "slavery." In 1881 in England, 45.3 percent of girls under age fifteen were in domestic service; see Colin Heywood, *A History of Childhood* (Cambridge: Polity Press, 2001), 127–28.

12. Ruether, *Christianity and the Making of the Modern Family*, 101–2; see also Mary P. Ryan, *The Cradle of the Middle Class: The Family in Oneida County, New York, 1790–1865* (Cambridge: Cambridge University Press, 1981), 145–55.

13. Ruether, *Christianity and the Making of the Modern Family*, 102–4.

14. Ruether, *Christianity and the Making of the Modern Family*, 100–101; see also Jacqueline Jones, *Labor of Love, Labor of Sorrow: Black Women, Work and Family from Slavery to the Present* (New York: Basic Books, 1985), 80–95, 113–14, 127–31.

15. Eleanor Flexner, *Century of Struggle: The Women's Rights Movement in the U.S.* (New York: Atheneum, 1972), 193–202, 240–47.

16. Ruether, *Christianity and the Making of the Modern Family*, 108–13.

17. Ruether, *Christianity and the Making of the Modern Family*, 113–14; see also Eileen S. Kraditor, *The Ideas of the Women's Suffrage Movement, 1890–1920* (Garden City, N.Y.: Anchor Books, 1971), esp. 31–44, 105–71.

18. Ruether, *Christianity and the Making of the Modern Family*, 118–26.

19. See David M. Kennedy, *Birth Control in America: The Career of Margaret Sanger* (New Haven, Conn.: Yale University Press, 1970).

20. Ruether, *Christianity and the Making of the Modern Family*, 126–28; see also Lois Scharf, *To Work and to Wed: Female Employment, Feminism and the Great Depression* (Westport, Conn.: Greenwood Press, 1980), 91.

21. Ruether, *Christianity and the Making of the Modern Family*, 129; Scharf, *To Work and to Wed*, 110–13.

22. Scharf, *To Work and to Wed*, 128–29.

23. Hindman, *Child Labor*, 47–85, 152–86, 248–90.

24. Cunningham, *Children and Childhood in Western Society since 1500*, 157–61.

25. Ruether, *Christianity and the Making of the Modern Family*, 132–36; see also Sherma Berger Gluck, *Rosie the Riveter Revisited: Women, the War and Social Change* (Boston: Twayne, 1987).

26. Ruether, *Christianity and the Making of the Modern Family*, 136–39.

27. Ruether, *Christianity and the Making of the Modern Family*, 139–41.
28. Ruether, *Christianity and the Making of the Modern Family*, 141–49; see also Sara Evans, *Personal Politics: The Roots of Women's Liberation in the Civil Rights Movement and the New Left* (New York: Vintage, 1970).
29. See Marion Faux, *"Roe v. Wade": The Untold Story of the Landmark Supreme Court Decision That Made Abortion Legal* (New York: Macmillan, 1988).
30. See Ruether, *Christianity and the Making of the Modern Family*, 158–63.
31. Ruether, *Christianity and the Making of the Modern Family*, 198–99; see also Guida West, *The National Welfare Rights Movement: The Social Protest of Poor Women* (New York: Praeger, 1981).
32. Ruether, *Christianity and the Making of the Modern Family*, 200–203; see also Christina Cobourn Herman, *Poverty amid Plenty: The Unfinished Business of Welfare Reform* (Washington, D.C.: Network, 1999).
33. Ruether, *Christianity and the Making of the Modern Family*, 190–96.
34. Ruether, *Christianity and the Making of the Modern Family*, 196–205; see also "Special Report: America at 300 Million," *Time*, October 30, 2006, 48–49.
35. See Milton Meltzer, *Slavery: A World History* (New York: Da Capo Press, 1993), pt. 1, 209–22.
36. Meltzer, *Slavery*, pt. 2, 1.
37. Meltzer, *Slavery*, pt. 2, 12.
38. Meltzer, *Slavery*, pt. 2, 50–51.
39. Meltzer, *Slavery*, pt. 2, 75–76.
40. Meltzer, *Slavery*, pt. 2, 12.
41. De las Casas protested the enslavement of the Indians, and in the New Laws, issued in 1542 by the king of Spain, enslavement of Indians was officially abolished.
42. See "Encomienda," *Wikipedia, the Free Encyclopedia*, http://en.wikipedia.org/wiki/Encomienda.
43. After King Philip's War, a boatload of Pequot Indiana were shipped from Massachusetts to slavery in the West Indies on a ship ironically named *Seaflower*; see Nathaniel Philbrick, *Mayflower: A Story of Courage, Community and War* (New York: Penguin, 2006), xiv.
44. See Meltzer, *Slavery*, pt. 2, 51; see also Séamas Mac Annaidh, *Irish History* (Bath: Paragon Press, 2005), 114.
45. Meltzer, *Slavery*, pt. 2, 243–44.
46. On the development of European racism toward blacks, see Winthrop D. Jordan, *White over Black: American Attitudes toward the Negro, 1550–1812* (Chapel Hill: University of North Carolina Press, 1968).
47. Meltzer, *Slavery*, pt. 2, 139–49.
48. Meltzer, *Slavery*, pt. 2, 245.
49. Meltzer, *Slavery*, pt. 2, 250.
50. Meltzer, *Slavery*, pt. 2, 250.
51. Meltzer, *Slavery*, pt. 2, 255.
52. Meltzer, *Slavery*, pt. 2, 279–300; see also Kevin Bales, *Disposable People: New Slavery in the Global Economy* (Berkeley: University of California Press, 2004).

53. It is estimated by the U.S. Justice Department that at least 17,500 people are enslaved in fields, sweatshops, and brothels in the United States, a high percentage in California. In 1995, seventy-one Thai workers were founded imprisoned in a sweatshop in El Monte in the Los Angeles area; see "State Has Yet to Test Slavery Statute," *Los Angeles Times*, November 25, 2006, B1, B6.

• 5 •

Anti-Semitism, European Nationalism, and Zionism

This chapter traces the cultural and religious roots of anti-Semitism from antiquity and its transition into a racist ideology in the context of European nationalism in the nineteenth and twentieth centuries. Zionism as a Jewish nationalist response to European nationalist anti-Semitism is also discussed, as is its interaction with Palestinian nationalism in the context of the founding and development of the state of Israel.

The roots of anti-Semitism in European Christian societies go back to the ancient Greco-Roman world and especially to the founding and growth of the Christian churches. There was some hostility to the Jews in the ancient pagan world. One locus of this hostility was Egypt, where there were significant groups of Jews in major cities, such as Alexandria. Some Egyptian intellectuals realized that Egypt was the butt of the Jewish Exodus narrative, in which the Jews are depicted as miraculously escaping slavery in Egypt, during which time God rained down plagues on the Egyptians and drowned Pharaoh's army. Some Egyptians formulated a countermyth according to which the Jews were actually a leprous population whom the Egyptians had themselves driven out of Egypt. These sorts of stories were gathered together by the Egyptian priest Manetho in the third century B.C.E. and were repeated by some Hellenistic historians. They were countered by the first-century C.E. Jewish historian Josephus.[1]

There was also hostility to Jews in Greco-Roman culture that expressed a negative reaction to Jewish exclusivity. Greek culture saw itself as the highest civilization into which subject people should assimilate. Refusal to assimilate on the grounds that its gods were false and its manners unclean was an affront. Under the Greco-Egyptian rule of Antiochus Epiphanes (d. 163 B.C.E.), there were efforts at forced Hellenization of the Jewish temple in

59

Jerusalem. Imperial domination of Palestine by the Hellenistic and then the Roman empires led to Jewish struggles for independence under the Maccabees and then the Jewish wars of the first and early second centuries C.E. Jewish apocalyptic literature depicted the Greek and Roman empires as demonic, to be overthrown by God with the advent of a messianic reign in which the Jews would rule the world as God's people.[2]

Greco-Roman Gnosticism in the first and second centuries C.E. created a hostile view of the Jewish God as a demonic creator of a fallen world, over against a higher spiritual world from which human souls have been alienated and to which they must return. God is depicted as vaunting over the fallen world he had created with the cry, "I am the Lord thy God, I shall have no gods beside me." But this exclamation, instead of being a testimony to the true God of Jewish faith, is depicted as the epitome of the evil creator's arrogance and ignorance. Such negative views of the Jewish God were taken into Christian Gnosticism, as well as radical Paulinism by Christian theologians such as Marcion (d. 150 C.E.), who contrasts the evil Jewish God of law against the true God of love, who is the father of Jesus Christ.

But these negative views of Jews and Judaism were moderated by other tendencies in antiquity. Jewish intellectuals, such as the Egyptian Hellenistic Jew Philo (20 B.C.E.–50 C.E.), assimilated much of Platonism into Jewish philosophy. Counter to Greek traditions of contempt for the "Orient," there was also a Greek tradition of curiosity about the peoples of the Near East and India and a tendency to find ancient roots for its own traditions of wisdom in these Eastern peoples. Hellenistic Jews reciprocated by claiming that Plato had actually learned his teaching from Moses.[3] Roman rulers, as practical imperialists, sought to allow the conquered peoples of their empire their cultural and religious differences while supplanting their political leadership. While they warred against the Jews when they revolted again Roman rule and sought political independence, they accommodated to their religious particularities. The neopagan Roman emperor Julian (332–363 C.E.) claimed that each people had a guardian deity who gave them their particular religious practice, criticizing Christians for having abandoned their historic religion.[4]

Christianity took into its thought some of these pre-Christian cultural hostilities to Jews and Judaism. But it was the antagonism fueled by Christian rivalry with its parent faith that became the primary source and vehicle of hostility to the Jews inherited by Christian Europe. Christianity, from New Testament times, developed a diatribe against the Jewish people as a religious community. This diatribe was rooted in a rivalry between the Christian affirmation that Jesus was the "Christ," the Messiah expected by the Jewish tradition, and the rejection of this faith by the established Jewish religious leaders.

New Testament Christianity directed a bitter polemic particularly against the Pharisees, the leading rabbinic reformers at the time of Christian beginnings. The Pharisees are attacked in the Gospel of Matthew as "blind guides and hypocrites," as petty legalists strict in superficial matters but neglectful of "the weightier matters of the law, justice, mercy and faith" (Matt. 23:23). The Pharisees are described as "sons of those who murdered the prophets," "serpents, a brood of vipers, deserving of hell" (Matt. 23:31–33). In the Gospel of John, they are called children of the Devil. "You are from your father, the Devil, and you choose to do your father's desires. He was a murderer from the beginning and does not stand in the truth, because there is no truth in him. When he lies, he speaks according to his own nature, for he is a liar and the father of lies" (John 8:44–45).

These polemics developed originally in an intersectarian context within Judaism in which Christians positioned themselves as the true believers and interpreters of Jewish faith against its established leaders: the high priests, scribes, and Pharisees. They also blamed these leaders for having betrayed Jesus into Roman hands and thus being the ones primarily responsible for his death, even though he was executed as a political dissident by the Roman occupying power.[5]

As Christians were prevented from preaching their gospel within the synagogues and increasingly turned to Gentiles as their primary source of converts, these diatribes shifted from being intersectarian rhetoric to being a polemic against all Jews as a religious community. This was not a "racial" polemic but a religious one, one that called for Jewish believers to abandon their traditional religion for the Christian interpretation of Scripture. Many Christians, even in the second century C.E., came from Jewish backgrounds. Yet this religious polemic nevertheless created stereotypes of Judaism that were assumed to characterize all followers in the Jewish religion.

This polemic against "the Jews" hardened into fixed patterns in the *Adversus Judaeus* literature written by leading Greek and Latin church fathers in the second to fifth centuries C.E., patterns that informed Christian preaching and practices toward the Jewish community. In these writings, the Christian church is claimed to be the true heir to God's election of God's people, while the Jews have lost this election because they have rejected the Messiah. Following the language in the Gospels, the Jews are said to be the heirs of those who have always been apostate from God, those who killed the prophets, whose culminating perfidy is killing God's son and Messiah. Because of this apostasy, God is said to have cast them off, condemning them to be homeless wanderers subjugated to other people (the Roman Empire, with which the Christians now identify themselves).

Christian exegetes created a dichotomous interpretation of the prophets that split the left hand of judgment from the right hand of hope and promise. The prophets themselves understood judgment and promise to apply to the same people, God's people Israel. Israel is criticized for having failed to obey God and is threatened with punishment, some recent catastrophe being interpreted as such punishment for disobedience. But the prophet uses this polemic to call for repentance, for return to faithfulness, to be rewarded with victory over enemies, restoration to the land, and a flourishing society.

The Christians, in splitting these two sides of biblical prophecy, understood the judgmental side to apply exclusively to the Jews, while the side of hope and promise was taken to refer to the future Christian church. In this Christian view, the Jews are the ones who have always been apostate, their history a trail of crimes. They not only killed the prophets but have been idolaters and sinners of every description, having picked up their evil habits during enslavement in Egypt. Even in the time of the prophets, it was predicted that God would finally cast them off for their sins, turning instead to a new elect people from "among the Gentiles," namely, the Christian church.

Christian exegetes also employed the Platonic dualism between body and spirit to interpret the Jewish law and customs as being purely external, "carnal," understood only according to the "letter," while it is Christian teachings that are according to the "spirit," that transform the inner person. The Jewish law is interpreted as a provisional and punitive code, given to the Jews by God to restrain their extreme proclivity for vice. But it was intended by God from the beginning to transcend the Jewish law, both abrogating it and spiritually fulfilling it with the New Covenant, written on the heart, not simply in the flesh.[6]

In the first third of the fourth century, Christianity was transformed from a persecuted to the established religion of the Roman Empire. The emperor Constantine became a Christian in 312 C.E. and made Christianity the favored religion. Paganism was not disallowed. But by the reign of the emperor Theodosius (378–395 C.E.), only that form of Christianity declared "orthodox" through church councils was officially allowed. Both pagans and Christian heretics were denied official standing. In this new situation, the status of Judaism was unique. Under pagan Rome, Judaism had been given a special protected status. The Jews held full Roman citizenship, and their exemption from pagan worship was accepted, although they had to pay a special tax, the *fiscus Judaicus*. As a heritage of the Jewish wars of 113–116 C.E., they were forbidden to enter into Jerusalem. They were also forbidden to circumcise non-Jews. By the fourth century, Jewish communities were scattered throughout the Roman Empire and occupied a variety of economic positions, including agriculture.

As orthodox Christianity became the established religion of the empire, it sought to reshape Roman law to reflect its theological view of the Jews. Following the Christian belief that the redemption of the world would remain incomplete until the Jews converted and accepted Christ as their savior, the church allowed the Jews as a religious community to continue to exist within the now Christian empire. But at the same time, it insisted that they live in a miserable condition that would express their repudiation by God. Judaism was to exist to the end of time but as a pariah within history to testify to the election of the church and to witness its final triumph when Christ would return. At that time, it was believed that the Jews would acknowledge their error and be converted and that the redemption of the world would be completed. Meanwhile, the church would both continually pressure Jews to convert and enforce their pariah status as unconverted Jews. Jews were forced to listen to Christian conversion sermons.

The legislation that was developed by the church and Christian emperors, expressed in the Theodosian Code (439 C.E.), enforced this paradoxical status of the Jews. Among these laws was the prohibition of Jews proselytizing gentiles. Jews were forbidden to own Christian slaves. This had the effect of eliminating Jews from large-scale agriculture or manufacturing that was run by slave labor. This had nothing to do with the church forbidding Christians from owning slaves, which the church had never condemned. This also interfered with Jewish domestic and religious life since Jews commonly used non-Jewish servants to do tasks, such as lighting lamps, that Jews were forbidden to do on the Sabbath. Jews who had been forcibly baptized were forbidden to return to Judaism, and Christians were forbidden to marry Jews.

Other laws were developed that further reduced Jewish social standing. Jews were excluded from holding public office or acting as judges. The Jew was not to be in any position of power or authority over Christians, although they were forced to accept the role of *Decurion*, or local tax collector. This could be economically ruinous since *Decurions* had to make up from their own wealth the funds they were unable to collect. Jews were also forbidden to build new synagogues or repair old ones. Thus, the synagogue must become poor and squalid in comparison to the Christian church buildings. The church sought to prevent religious fraternizing between the two communities, such as Christians attending Jewish feasts and listening to sermons in synagogues. The repetition of some of these laws indicates that they were not always observed, and the two communities in fact continued to mingle for some time.[7]

These anti-Jewish laws and the vitriolic sermons of Christian preachers soon lent themselves to outbreaks of mob violence against Jewish communities. The leaders in such violence were fanatical monks who stirred up Christian mobs to pillage synagogues and cemeteries and forcibly baptize Jews. Roman emperors and local officials sometimes intervened against this violence, but they were often counteracted by bishops who objected to any compensation to the Jews for Christian violence. The most infamous example of this was the incident in 388 C.E. in which a Christian mob destroyed a synagogue in the town of Callinicum on the Euphrates River. The emperor Theodosius ordered the local bishop to provide funds to restore the synagogue, but Ambrose, the powerful bishop of Milan, intervened to insist that Christians must never contribute to the maintenance of "apostasy."[8]

In the Byzantine Empire, these laws were worsened in the Code of Justinian of 534 C.E. But in the West, these laws were no longer enforced after the fall of the Roman Empire in the West and the disappearance of centralized leadership during the period from 600 to 1000. Frankish kings gave Jews protected status as merchants. With the advent of Islam, Jews served as important trade links between the Christian West and the Islamic world. Muslim law made both Jews and Christians inferior to Muslims but also generally protected them from forced proselytizing as "people of the book." But Jews generally had broader opportunities for prospering in Muslim than in Christian lands.[9] In Muslim Spain particularly, Jews rose to a high level of both financial well-being and intellectual brilliance.

The major turning point of Jewish status in Christian Europe took place during the Crusades. Crusading armies on their way to destroy the "infidel" of the Muslim world frequently stopped along the way to pillage and massacre Jewish communities. Neither bishops nor Christian princes did much to protect Jews from these attacks despite their supposed protected status. Jews were forbidden to bear arms and so could do little to protect themselves. The massacres of Jewish communities by crusaders also fomented justifying myths in which Jews were depicted as stealing Christian children for ritual murders and profaning the Eucharistic host. With the fourth Lateran Council (1215 C.E.), the anti-Jewish laws of Roman times were revived and expanded. Jews were commanded to live in separate sections of town and to wear distinctive dress.

With the Crusades, Christians took over trade routes to the Islamic world, shutting out Jews. Jews were also excluded from owning land and from membership in guilds. Thus, Jews were economically marginalized, made to specialize in moneylending, a task forbidden to Christians since usury was defined as a sin. Thus was implanted the stereotype of the Jew as the rapacious moneylender.[10] In the later Middle Ages, major Jewish communities were expelled from Western Europe, from England in 1290, from France in 1390, and from most German cities in the mid-fourteenth to sixteenth centuries. Spain and Portugal, where Jews had flourished under Islamic rule, expelled the Jews in the late fifteenth century after the final expulsion of Muslims from Spain. Jews from northern Europe were pushed into Poland, while many Jews from Spain and Portugal were welcomed into the Islamic world.

In Spain, Jews were forced either to convert to Christianity or to leave. Many Jews converted, some maintaining their Judaism secretly, while others became believing Catholics. It is in this context that the Inquisition investigated and punished those Jews found to be secretly continuing their Jewish practices. Spain also decreed laws of "pure blood," which forbade a Catholic with Jewish ancestry from holding office in church or state. These laws reflected a transition from religious anti-Judaism to racial anti-Semitism. Since discriminatory laws against Jews were supposed to disappear once a Jew converted to Christianity, by defining Jewish ancestry as "impure blood," converted Jews were excluded on a purely "biological" (actually, historical) basis.[11]

There was some shift in this attitude toward the Jews with the Calvinist branch of the Reformation, particularly in England. There, Jews were seen as the people of the Old Testament in a way that was in more positive continuity with the Christian New Covenant. England particularly came to see itself as the "new Israel" as a nation, not simply as a part of a universal Christian church. Jews were seen more as ancestors than superseded Christ killers. During Cromwell's reign, the Jews were readmitted to England (1655). The laws of the ghetto were not revived. Jews were allowed to live anywhere and suffered under no restrictions other than those of other dissenters from the established Church of England. In the American colonies, the laws of the ghetto were never established. Jews received equal citizenship in the United States with the American Constitution in 1789.

Some Englishmen linked their national history with that of the Jews in another way. They came to believe that as part of the redemption of history, the Jews must go back to their historic homeland. This restoration of the Jews to Palestine would be a prelude to the return of Christ (and the final conversion of the Jews). Thus, the ancient Christian theme that the conversion of the Jews is necessary for the millennial culmination of history was linked with a new focus on the ingathering of the Jews to Palestine. The shift of emphasis laid the groundwork for Western Christian Zionism, a perspective that would play a significant role in English and American relations to the state of Israel in the twentieth century.[12]

The emancipation of the Jews from the ghetto and its restrictive laws took place in somewhat different ways in France, German cities, and Eastern Europe.[13] Jewish emancipation had been promoted by French rationalists in the eighteenth century, but it was the French Revolution that created the decisive break with the medieval past. For the French revolutionaries, all the separate "estates" of nobility, clergy, and commoners, with their distinct privileges or disabilities, were to be dissolved into the common identity of "citizen" of France. This meant that the corporate identity of the Jewish communities, with their distinct disabilities but also self-governance, needed to be dissolved in order for a Jewish resident in France to become simply a French citizen.

Religious identity could be maintained as private faith but no longer as a public status. As the French liberal Conte Clermont-Tonnerre declared in the French Constituent Assembly in 1789, "Everything must be denied to the Jews as a nation, and everything granted to them as individuals. They must not form either a political body or an order in the state; they must be individual citizens."[14]

Emancipation soon followed in the Netherlands. Napoleon freed the Jews in all the countries he occupied (1804–1815), but the Congress of Vienna sought to reestablish the pre-Napoleonic order. It was not until the Revolution of 1848 that Jewish emancipation was granted throughout German areas. However, the ghettos remained in Eastern Europe and Russia as well as in the Papal States[15] and in Spain. In Russia, Jews became scapegoats of revolutionary tensions against the oppressive rule of the czar. A series of government-organized pogroms (massacres) were directed against them in the late nineteenth and early twentieth centuries.[16] During this period, large numbers of Eastern European Jews migrated west, many to the United States.

The *Protocols of the Elders of Zion*, authored by the Russian secret police, justified these pogroms by claiming that a secret Jewish government, in existence since the time of Christ, was plotting the overthrow of Christendom and the establishment of the reign of the Antichrist over the world in the last age of world history.[17] This defamatory tract continues to be a carrier of anti-Semitism in the modern world, today also avidly read and believed in the Muslim world.[18]

The emancipatory promise of European nationalism proved contradictory. While Jews were told to dissolve any corporate identity as Jews to become simply citizens of the nation in which they resided, at the same time nationalists in France, Germany, and elsewhere began to think of their nation as possessing a particular spiritual essence or "nature" that Jews could not acquire. The old dualisms of carnality versus spirituality were repeated in secular nationalist terms. Jews were essentiality materialistic and lacked the spiritual essence of being French or German. They were rootless people, "internationalists," foreign to the French or German people, who were rooted in their particular soil. Jews were scapegoated for the new movements of secularism, industrialism, democracy, and/or socialism that threatened the traditional culture of Europe. Jews were depicted as an insidious "poison" threatening the vitality and spirit of European nations.[19] Thus, a racial nationalist anti-Semitism developed in Europe. Since these evil qualities were attributed to Jewish "nature," not to a faith or a culture that could be changed, the "final solution" to a racist anti-Semitism was expulsion (or extermination).

Faced with this renewed anti-Semitism, European Jews responded in one of three ways. Jewish liberals, heirs of the *Haskalah* (Jewish Enlightenment), pushed for a consistent secularization of their national society in which a plurality of private religious and ethnic identities could coexist with a national citizenship that all shared equally.[20] Such liberalism became characteristic of American Jews who sometimes became champions of other racially negated people, such as American blacks.

Another response was the various Hasidic movements in which groups of religious Jews sought to reinvent the corporate Jewish identity and distinctive traditional way of life of the ghetto but without its disabilities. This response developed particularly in Eastern Europe. Such groups were largely destroyed by the Nazi Holocaust. But before the war, some Hasidic groups migrated to the United States or to Palestine (now Israel), where they continue to exist as distinct communities in neighborhoods set apart from the rest of society.[21]

The third response was Zionism. This was by no means the majority response of Jews until after the Holocaust, when support for the state of Israel became de rigueur for Jewish identity throughout the Jewish Diaspora. Zionists argued that anti-Semitism was endemic to Christian societies. It could not be overcome by political and cultural reform. The only solution was to recreate Jews as a nation and to found a Jewish state where Jews would be the overwhelming majority and could deal with other nations of the world on a basis of equal power.[22] While a few Jews entertained the idea that some colonial power, such as Britain, might grant them land for a Jewish homeland in Africa,[23] for most Zionists, Palestine, the place of the ancient Jewish life, was the only possible place to reestablish such a Jewish nation. Here and here alone could Jews finally be "at home."

Most Zionists from 1880 to the founding of the state of Israel in 1948 were secular. The Hovevei Zion movement in Eastern Europe gathered groups of Jews to immigrate to Palestine to create agricultural socialist communities where Jewish national identity and the revived Hebrew language could be rooted in the traditional soil of the ancient homeland.[24] Political Zionism was founded by Theodor Herzl, an Austrian secular Jew horrified by the renewed anti-Semitism manifest in French society by the prolonged struggle over the Dreyfus case (a French-Alsatian Jew on the general staff of the French army who was used as a scapegoat by the French military for the sale of military secrets to the Germans during the Franco-Prussian War). Herzl's manifesto, *The Jewish State* (1896), became the basis for the World Zionist Movement (founded in 1897), which sought both

Jewish philanthropists and European colonial powers who would sponsor such a Jewish state in Palestine.[25]

Zionism drew on deep roots of Jewish messianism, which had long seen the return to Palestine, the rebuilding of the ancient temple, and the refounding of Jewish life there as an expression of the coming of the Messiah and the redemption of history. But most religious Jews in the late nineteenth and the first half of the twentieth centuries were hostile to Zionism. For religious Jews, only the Messiah could create this redemptive ingathering of Israel. It might be "hastened" by fervent piety, but it could not be accomplished by secular nonpracticing Jews.[26] But some religious Jews began to blend traditional Jewish messianism with Zionism, arguing that secular Zionist Jews could hasten the coming of the Messiah by effecting the return of the Jews to Palestine and "conquest" of the land, which could later flower into a revival of religious piety. Abraham Isaac Kook (1864–1935), Ashkenazi chief rabbi of Palestine under the British Mandate, led in this blending of Zionism and Jewish messianism.[27]

Although Theodor Herzl got little positive response to his proposal of a Jewish state from European political leaders between 1897 and World War I, a new opening was created by the war. Britain and France sought to divide up the tottering Ottoman control of the Middle East between themselves in the aftermath of the war. Britain particularly saw control of the area from Palestine to Mesopotamia, along with Egypt, as linked with its colonial control of India and much of East Africa.

At this time, the Zionist movement was lodged in London. Chaim Weizmann, leader of the Zionist movement, had established cordial relations with Lord Arthur Balfour, the British foreign secretary. This relation would bear fruit in 1917 when, on the eve of the British takeover of Jerusalem, Lord Balfour offered the Zionists a "Jewish homeland" under what was to become the British Mandate for Palestine. This offer of a "national home for the Jewish people" would facilitate Zionist immigration and settlement in Palestine, although Balfour also claimed that "nothing shall be done which may prejudice the civil and religious rights of existing non-Jewish communities in Palestine."[28]

The British patronizing of Zionism from 1917 until the eve of World War II was motivated by imperial strategic considerations, as would be the later close alliance of the United States with Israel from 1948 to today. Both have seen this relationship as buttressing the British or American global hegemony to control the region for the West over against the local Arab people's desires for self-determination. Both the British authors of this relationship in the 1920s, such as Lord Balfour and Herbert Samuel, high commissioner for Palestine under the British Mandate, as well as American leaders from Harry Truman to George W. Bush, have also been motivated by religious beliefs. They have seen themselves as part of a redemptive drama in which the return of the Jews to Palestine under the aegis of (their) Christian global power fulfills biblical prophecy for the final reign of peace on earth.[29]

From 1933 to 1945, the development of anti-Semitic nationalism in Germany bore terrible fruit in the control of Germany by the Nazi leaders. The new German leader, Adolf Hitler, shaped a pogrom to demote the well-assimilated German Jewish community from prosperity and social acceptance to pariahs, leading to final expulsion. During World War II, this goal of ethnic cleansing through expulsion was changed to one of physical extermination.[30] In the death camps of Nazism, some 6 million Jews, as well other despised groups, such as homosexuals and gypsies,[31] were exterminated. Neither the British nor the Americans offered any help to Jews seeking to escape from Nazism. Indeed, both powers prevented escape by forbidding Jewish settlement in the United States and British territories. The British, in order to placate Arab opinion, also forbade immigration to Palestine from 1939 to 1948.[32]

After the war, British and American public opinion was shocked by the revelation of the death camps. This sense of guilt and desire to compensate the Jews for their terrible losses helped motivate Western support for the partition of Palestine in 1947 and the granting of a Jewish state to the Zionists in 57 percent of historic Palestine, while the Arab Palestinians were to receive the remaining 43 percent for a Palestinian state. At that time, there were 590,000 Jews in Palestine who had acquired about 10 percent of the land, while Palestinian Arabs were 1,320,000 dwelling on 90 percent of the land.[33]

Neither Palestinian Arabs nor the Arab nations accepted this partition, which they saw as totally unjust. Several Arab nations sent armies to prevent the Jewish group from taking possession of the land granted by the United Nations. They were defeated by the well-organized Jewish army, which seized another 21 percent of the land and caused the flight and/or expulsion of about 800,000 Palestinians who became refugees in the West Bank, Gaza, Jordan, or Lebanon.[35] The land of these displaced Palestinians was mostly confiscated by the new Jewish state, which defined this land as the exclusive patrimony of the Jewish people.[35] This, then, is the root of the endemic Israel–Palestine conflict, which continues to smolder today.

It is beyond the limits of this brief chapter on European anti-Semitism to detail the ongoing Israel–Palestine and Middle Eastern conflict (some of it is dealt with in chapter 10). It remains to discuss two crucial matters that flow from the Zionist response to European anti-Semitism: 1) the Zionist concept of Jewish nationalism and the Jewish state and 2) the equation of anti-Zionism with anti-Semitism as a political response to criticism of the racial-ethnic policies of the state of Israel toward the Palestinian Arabs.

Zionism as an expression of Jewish nationalism, in the context of the founding of a Jewish state in what had been a majority Palestinian Arab society, contains a foundational demographic imperative. This imperative is that the state of Israel, wherever its national borders are drawn, contains an overwhelming majority of Jews, preferably at least 80 percent of the population. In order to create this Jewish majority in what had been an Arab-majority society, two things had to happen (and continue to happen). First, as many as possible of the Arab Palestinian community have to be expelled or persuaded to leave by all manner of means. Second, Jews from Europe and other regions of the world have to be persuaded to come and settle. These two demands, rapid or gradual expulsion of Palestinians, together with confiscation of their land and efforts to attract new Jewish settlers, have shaped and continue to shape the history of the state of Israel today.[36]

A second aspect of this demographic demand for a Jewish majority is the shaping of Israel's laws to give full citizen rights and privileges to only Jewish residents as well as the instant right to immigrate to Israel to Diaspora Jews. By contrast, Palestinians who remained in Israel after the 1948–1949 war were eventually given only a second-class citizenship, forbidden to serve in the army or to receive various benefits of army service, such as housing and college scholarship.[37] Palestinians, in what became (after 1967) the occupied territories of the West Bank and Gaza, are not given Israeli citizenship and are put under constant pressure, through continual land confiscation and military-legal repression, to leave the area.

Israel has not been satisfied to create a majority Jewish state in the 78 percent of the land occupied in 1949 but has sought to continually expand its control of the land and to remove Palestinians there. Thus, Zionism or Jewish nationalism must be defined as a religiously based ethnic nationalism (based on the rabbinic definition of who is a Jew) in which full citizenship is restricted to Jews. Palestinians can hold this citizenship only in a secondary way and in limited numbers.

The final issue for mention in this chapter is the effort to define any criticism of this Zionist view of Jewish nationalism and its resultant policies toward Palestinian Arabs as "anti-Semitism." This conflation of anti-Zionism with anti-Semitism draws on the horror toward anti-Semitism and the fear of being labeled an anti-Semite justifiably present in European and American cultures because of the terrible destruction of the Jews in the Holocaust, itself the culmination of a long history of European Christian anti-Semitism. By drawing on this Western desire to repudiate anti-Semitism root and branch, Zionist propagandists seek to silence any critique of Zionist policies toward the Palestinian Arabs. Since many Jews, in both Israel and the Diaspora, also make the same criticism of Israel's policies toward the Palestinians, this charge becomes more contradictory. Such Jews are silenced by calling them "self-hating Jews."[38]

This political use of the charge of anti-Semitism to repel and silence criticism of Israel's policies toward the Palestinians has been somewhat successful in maintaining control of Christian and Western political cultures and support for the state of Israel. But it also generates its own antagonism in which individuals angered by such policies in Israel take vengeance by attacks on Jewish symbols, synagogues, and cultural centers in the United States and Europe. Such use of anti-Semitism also degrades the meaning of anti-Semitism itself,[39] making it into a charge manipulated for political expediency rather than a serious and deep effort to overcome this cultural evil in non-Jewish societies and to create real coexistence and mutual friendship between different religious cultures—Jewish, Christian, and Muslim.

While some who are critical of Israel may be motivated by hostility to Jews, much of such criticism is based on a positive regard for Jews, Judaism, and the well-being of the state of Israel. Jewish ethicist Marc Ellis has severely critiqued the denial of injustice done to Palestinians by the Jewish establishment as undermining the heritage of Jewish prophetic tradition.[40] Many conscientious critics of Israel, such as the declarations of the American Friends Service Committee (which has been labeled anti-Semitic), do so both out of concern for the Palestinians and out of concern for Israel itself, whose policies of injustice to Palestinians threaten its own long-term viability as a state.[41] Christian–Jewish "dialogue" that demands silence about the Palestinians lacks integrity, based as it is on what Ellis has called the "ecumenical deal" between Christians and Jews in which each group collaborates in silencing each other's prophetic critics. Ecumenical relations between Christians and Jews are deeply undermined by the impasse over just treatment of the Palestinians and the efforts to silence the discussion by labeling it "anti-Semitic."

NOTES

1. Josephus, *Contra Apion*; see Rosemary Ruether, *Faith and Fratricide: The Theological Roots of Anti-Semitism* (Eugene, Ore.: Wipf and Stock Publishers, 1996), 24.

2. For example, the book of Daniel in Hebrew Scripture and the Intertestamental Apocalypses, R. H. Charles, *The Apocrypha and Pseudepigrapha of the Old Testament* (1913), vol. 2. The New Testament book of Revelations is the Christian version of this literature.

3. See Philo, *Vita Mosis* II, 17–24.

4. Julian, "Against the Galileans," in *Works*, vol. 3, ed. W. C. Wright (Cambridge, Mass.: Harvard University Press, 1961–1968), 321.

5. On the issue of the responsibility of the Jews for the death of Jesus, see Ruether, *Faith and Fratricide*, 72–73.

6. Ruether, *Faith and Fratricide*, 149–65.

7. Ruether, *Faith and Fratricide*, 184–91; see also James Parkes, *The Conflict of the Church and the Synagogue* (London: Socino, 1934).

8. Ruether, *Faith and Fratricide*, 192–94; for Ambrose's letters to the emperor Theodosius, see Ambrose, Letters 40 and 41.

9. On the relation of Islam to the Jews, see Rosemary Ruether and Herman Ruether, "The Community of Islam and the Peoples of the Book," in *The Wrath of Jonah: The Crisis of Religious Nationalism in the Israeli-Palestinian Conflict*, 2nd ed. (Minneapolis: Fortress, 2002), 27–35.

10. See James Parkes, *The Jew in the Medieval Community* (London: Socino, 1938), 273–306.

11. See Yitzhak Baer, *The History of the Jews in Christian Spain*, vol. 2, *From the Fourteenth Century to the Expulsion* (Philadelphia: Jewish Publication Society, 1966); see also Cecil Roth, *A History of the Marranos* (Philadelphia: Jewish Publication Society, 1947).

12. See Ruether and Ruether, *The Wrath of Jonah*, 69–84; see also Regina Sharif, *Non-Jewish Zionism: Its Roots in Western History* (London: Zed Books, 1983); Stephen Sizer, "The Historical Roots of Christian Zionism from Irving to Balfour: Christian Zionism in the United Kingdom (1820–1918)," in *Challenging Christian Zionism: Theology, Politics and the Israel-Palestine Conflict*, ed. Naim Ateek, Cedar Duaybis, and Maurine Tobin (London: Melisende, 2005), 20–31; and Donald Wagner, "From Blackstone to Bush: Christian Zionism in the United States," in Ateek et al., *Challenging Christian Zionism*, 32–44.

13. For an overview on the emancipation, see Jacob Katz, *Out of the Ghetto: The Social Background of Jewish Emancipation, 1770–1870* (Cambridge, Mass.: Harvard University Press, 1973).

14. See Leon Poliakov, *The History of Anti-Semitism: From Voltaire to Wagner* (New York: Vanguard Press, 1968), 217, 581 n. 10.

15. See Ferdinand Gregorovius, *The Ghetto and the Jews of Rome*, trans. Moses Hadas (New York: Schocken Books, 1966).

16. See Bernard D. Weinryb, "Eastern European Jewry since the Partition of Poland," in *The Jews: Their History, Culture and Religion*, vol. 1, ed. Louis Finkelstein (New York: Harper and Row, 1960), 321–71.

17. See Norman Cohn, *Warrant for Genocide: The Myth of the Jewish World Conspiracy and the Protocols of the Elders of Zion* (New York: Harper and Row, 1969).

18. See "Protocols of the Elders of Zion: Contemporary Usage and Popularity, the Middle East," *Wikipedia, the Free Encyclopedia*, http://en.wikipedia.org/wiki/Protocols_of_the_Elders_of_Zion.

19. See Ruether, *Faith and Fratricide*, 220; see also George Mosse, *The Crisis of German Ideology: Intellectual Origins of the Third Reich* (New York: Grosset and Dunlap, 1964), 88–107.

20. For U.S. Reform Judaism's rejection of Zionism in the late nineteenth century, see Ruether and Ruether, *The Wrath of Jonah*, 83.

21. For the Hasidic rejection of Zionism, see Michael Selzer, ed., *Zionism Reconsidered: The Rejection of Jewish Normalcy* (London: Macmillan, 1970).

22. See Ruether and Ruether, *The Wrath of Jonah*, 46–47. For an overview of the varieties of Zionism from the late nineteenth century to the founding of the state of Israel, see Arthur Hertzberg, *The Zionist Idea: A Historical Analysis and Reader* (New York: Meridian Books, 1960).

23. The British colonial office offered Herzl Uganda as a Jewish homeland in 1903, an offer that was indignantly rejected by a vocal minority at the Sixth Zionist Congress; see Ruether and Ruether, *The Wrath of Jonah*, 79.

24. Ruether and Ruether, *The Wrath of Jonah*, 47–49.

25. Ruether and Ruether, *The Wrath of Jonah*, 51–53; see also Hertzberg, *The Zionist Idea*, 199–230.

26. Ruether and Ruether, *The Wrath of Jonah*, 55.

27. Ruether and Ruether, *The Wrath of Jonah*, 56–58; Hertzberg, *The Zionist Idea*, 416–31.

28. Ruether and Ruether, *The Wrath of Jonah*, 79–80. Note that the Palestinian Arabs, at that time the overwhelming majority of Palestine, are referred to only as "existing non-Jewish communities," as though their presence there was accidental. Nothing is said about their having political or national rights. Arthur Koestler has referred to this document as "one nation solemnly promised to a second nation the country of a third." See "Balfour Declaration of 1917," *Wikipedia, the Free Encyclopedia*, http://en.wikipedia.org/wiki/Balfour_Declaration_of_1917.

29. Ruether and Ruether, *The Wrath of Jonah*, 78–79; on the Christian Zionism of the Christian right and the George W. Bush administration, see Donald Wagner, "From Blackstone to Bush," 37–44.

30. The literature on the Holocaust is large. For a basic account, see Doris Bergen, *War and Genocide: A Concise History of the Holocaust* (Lanham, Md.: Rowman & Littlefield, 2003); for the history of Nazi anti-Semitism, see Philippe Barrin, *Nazi Anti-Semitism: From Prejudice to Holocaust*, trans. Janet Lloyd (New York: New Press, 2005).

31. Bergen, *War and Genocide*, 190–93.

32. Ruether and Ruether, *The Wrath of Jonah*, 139–40. Several books have detailed the failure of the American Zionism movement to support rescue of European Jews during World War II; see Henry Feingold, *The Politics of Rescue* (New Brunswick, N.J.: Rutgers University Press, 1970); see also Leon W. Wells, *Who Speaks for the Vanquished? American Judaism and the Holocaust*, ed. Michael Ryan (New York: Peter Lang Press, 1987).

33. Ruether and Ruether, *The Wrath of Jonah*, 132.

34. Ruether and Ruether, *The Wrath of Jonah*, 134–35; see also Michael Palumbo, *The Palestinian Catastrophe: The 1948 Expulsion of a People from their Homeland* (London: Faber and Faber, 1987).

35. Ruether and Ruether, *The Wrath of Jonah*, 135; see also Uri Davis and Walter Lehn, "And the Fund Still Lives," *Journal of Palestine Studies* 7 (summer 1987): 3–33.

36. Ruether and Ruether, *The Wrath of Jonah*, 138–43.

37. Ruether and Ruether, *The Wrath of Jonah*, 143–59; see also Ian Lustick, *The Palestinians in Israel: Israel's Control of a National Minority* (Austin: University of Texas Press, 1980).

38. On the characterization of critical Jews as "self-hating Jews," see Bruce Jackson, "Jews Like Us," in *The Politics of Anti-Semitism*, ed. Alexander Cockburn and Jeffrey St. Clair (Oakland, Calif.: AK Press, 2003), 53–58.

39. For trenchant critiques of such charges of anti-Semitism by Jews, see the essays in Cockburn and St. Clair, *The Politics of Anti-Semitism*; see also Norman G. Finkelstein, *Beyond Chutzpah: On the Misuse of Anti-Semitism and the Abuse of History* (Berkeley: University of California Press, 2005).

40. See, for example, Marc Ellis, *Beyond Innocence and Redemption: Confronting the Holocaust and Jewish Power* (San Francisco: Harper and Row, 1990), and *O Jerusalem: The Contested Future the Jewish Covenant* (Minneapolis: Fortress, 1999).

41. See, for example, the collection of essays in American Friends Service Committee, *When the Rain Returns: Toward Justice and Reconciliation in Palestine and Israel* (Philadelphia: American Friends Service Committee, 2004).

· 6 ·

Racism in the United States: White, Black, Red, Brown, and Yellow

The term "race" is an inexact and highly contested term. In Western thought, the term "race" has often been conflated with such ways of grouping human beings as "tribe," "nation," and "lineage." Such categories do not differentiate between innate characteristics and those that are culturally constructed. The term is also used for all humans as one species, that is, "the human race." Greco-Roman thought believed that distinct "nations" with their religions and cultures had been established by different gods who stood under the one universal creator. All (men) could, however, become "Hellenes," members of civilized society, through (Greek) education.[1]

The Christian church played an ambivalent role in theories of human unity and diversity. It insisted that all humans were descended from a common ancestral pair, Adam and Eve, and thus are essentially one. But it also traced a division into three grouping as descendants of the three sons of Noah: Shem (Semites/Orientals), Ham (Africans), and Japheth (Europeans). It also saw the descendants of Ham as punished for the sin of their father (for uncovering his father's nakedness [Gen. 9:20–28]) by being made into the hewers of wood and drawers of water for the other peoples, thus justifying the enslavement of Africans.[2]

For the Christian church, the ultimate distinction was between believers and unbelievers. While unbelievers could be judged as evil through their worship of false gods (seen as demonic powers), this status was changeable through conversion. People of all nations could become one in Christ. Since Christ was also identified with the cosmic Logos of creation, conversion to Christ reestablished the original unity of mankind, disrupted by the building of the Tower of Babel (Gen. 11:1–9), which God punished by division of humans into different language groups.

The impetus for new speculation on differences among human groups came with European global expansion in the sixteenth century, colonization of other lands, and enslavement of African and "Indian" peoples. Western Europeans early developed an exaggerated response to skin color differences between themselves and Africans, adopting the dualistic symbolism of "white" and "black." Such polarized color symbolism easily was identified with other Christian moral and ontological dualisms, that is, spirit and matter, mind and body, good and evil, God and the Devil, being and nonbeing, qua "light" versus "darkness."[3]

Identifying Africans as "dark" inwardly as well as outwardly seemed justified as long as Africans were "pagans" but was challenged by the Christian demand that they should be converted and baptized. Thus, Europeans who wished to both evangelize Africans (and Indians) and enslave them had to find something "innate" in their inferiority that continued after conversion.

Some who sought to justify permanent slavery of Africans toyed with the idea of a plurality of ancestors, with Africans descended from a different, less human, more apelike ancestor,[4] but Christian teaching opposed this solution. Another way of establishing difference was through a theory of declension. Whites represent the original good humans, while other peoples of darker hue represent a corruption that affected their inner capacities as well as their color and physiognomy. Evangelization, together with slavery, could be seen as a way of rescuing such corrupted beings, teaching them obedience and discipline. New Testament texts, such as Ephesians 6:5, "Slaves be obedient to those who are your earthly masters," came to mind for such a viewpoint.

However, in the aftermath of the Civil War, the Thirteenth, Fourteenth, and Fifteenth Amendments to the Constitution, which freed the slaves and gave (male) freemen equal citizenship, ended the option of legal slavery. Whites, particularly in the South, soon began a process of taking equal citizenship from former slaves, first through the Black Codes in the 1870s that removed their right to hold political office and then through Jim Crow laws. From the 1890s into the 1960s, such laws both enforced disenfranchisement and created a system of separation of the races in public facilities.[5]

The need to justify legal separation and subordination lent new popularity to biological theories of race difference, with people of African descent always positioned as the bottom of the hierarchy of difference. Social Darwinism became the reigning pseudoscientific theory to justify such racial hierarchy. According to this popularization of Darwin's theories of evolution, humans had risen through a process of survival of the fittest from apelike animal ancestors to intelligent humans. People of northern Europe, variously called Nordic, Anglo-Saxon, Teutonic, or simply "white," were seen as the highest level of this evolution, while Asians, Indians, and Negroes were ranged below them in descending order of "primitive" brutality and stupidity. Since such evolution was seen as a very slow process over tens of thousands of years, the inferiority of the nonwhite races could be seen as quasi permanent, demanding either their exclusion or their subordination or even extermination.[6]

Such biological racism was particularly popular in the United States in the late nineteenth century where it justified a triumphant expansion of the superior American "Anglo-Saxon" into new colonial ventures in the Caribbean and the Pacific Islands as well as the disenfranchisement of blacks. As Thomas F. Gossett has shown in his 1963 volume *Race: The History of an Idea in America*, biological racism dominated American thought from the 1880s through the 1920s among historians, anthropologists, political scientists, linguistic and literary theorists, and popular novelists. Even the Social Gospel movement was not immune from racism. Josiah Strong particularly trumpeted the global triumph of God's elect people, the Anglo-Saxon Protestant, and the disappearance of lesser races.[7]

Although "nonwhites," Indians, Orientals, and blacks were always positioned in the lower levels of such racist theory, many American racists also differentiated among Europeans. One popular theory differentiated between Mediterranean, Alpine, and Nordic Europeans,[8] the ancestors, respectively, of southern Europeans, such as Spanish, Portuguese, and Italians; Eastern Europeans, such as Yugoslavians and Poles; and northern Europeans, which usually included Germans, Scandinavians, and English. The status of the Celts, Irish, and French was in doubt in this categorization. Much nineteenth-century American exaltation of Anglo-Saxons, as the quintessential ancestors of Americans, contrasted them to the "bestial" Irish. Only gradually did the Irish become "white" in the United States, accepted grudgingly into the family of Anglos.[9]

Race theorists generally assumed that intermarriage between racial groups always degraded the higher group to the level of the lower, producing debased offspring. In an analogy to dog breeding, the offspring were typically referred to as "mongrels." From 1900 to the 1920s, there was growing alarm in the United States about the increasing number of immigrants from Eastern and southern Europe, many of them Catholics or Jews. These inferior European "breeds" were seen as threatening the hegemony of the true "Nordic" or Anglo-Saxon "stock" that was supposedly the source of all the virtues of the American democratic political system and aggressive economic culture.

The climax of this racial fearmongering about the deleterious effect of immigrants from Eastern and southern Europe was the 1924 Immigration Act, which limited immigration to 150,000 annually with quotas for ethnic groups based on 2 or 3 percent of their proportion of the U.S. population according to the U.S. Census of 1890. Japanese were forbidden immigration altogether. The Chinese had already been excluded in 1888 and 1892 laws. This 1924 act gave the largest quotas to northern Europeans. Southern and Eastern Europeans, from which most Catholics or Jews came, were limited to small numbers.[10]

Racist thinking was built on an analogy to many cultural dualisms, as we have already seen in the polarized language of "white" and "black." Another dualism was the division of "animal" and "human" as an assumed contrast between the "dumb brute" and the "rational human." The idea of a "brute" typically combined intellectual and moral components. A "brute" is stupid, lacks creativity, and is physically repulsive, violent, and sexually rapacious.

Gender stereotypes also were used. The higher Anglo-Saxons or Nordics are often described as "manly," virile, aggressive, powerful, commanding, natural rulers, good looking, tall, blond, and muscular. Inferior races, by contrast, are often described as "effeminate," weak, passive, and sensuous. These contrasts are typically applied to males of both groups since women of the higher or lower races are mostly ignored. If women are mentioned as members of the inferior group, they may be seen as dirty sluts. Women of the superior group may be seen as tall, blond, and strong but primarily to produce virile male offspring since they themselves should not be seen as "manly."[11] Males of inferior races are always assumed to be lusting after white women, claims that were integral to episodes of white lynching of black men.[12]

The assimilation of immigrants into "American" identity came to be referred to as the "melting pot," but both the pot and the ability of some immigrants to "melt" were always subject to limitations. The pot itself assumed certain norms: light, pinkish skin with no noticeable characteristics of eye, nose, or hair texture suggestive of Orientals or blacks; the ability to speak American-accented English, preferably having lost any ability to speak any other language; and the adoption of American views of government and the economy. In the 1840s, this desire to assimilate meant that the Irish in America, widely imaged as brutish and apelike in New England cartoons, avoided joining abolitionists against slavery in order to identify with dominant white society.[13] Similarly, after the 1890s, many Germans, Italians, and Jews steered clear of public identification with socialism.

Some groups were allowed to "melt" into a reasonable facsimile of such an "American," while others could not. Most notoriously, those of African descent, no matter how intermarried with Europeans, so that their skin color and appearance became hard to distinguish from whites, were defined as black in American law if they had "one drop" of African blood.[14] American racism is notable for its refusal to create hierarchies of racial mixture, such as mulatto, octoroon, or mestizo, typical of French or Latin American society. In reality, of course, light-skinned and European-appearing mixed-race people, often enjoying better educational and social opportunities, were generally the first members of their "race" to succeed in America. But they still remained tagged as black, Oriental, Indian, or Mexican as long as any trace of their heritage in the "other" group was physically or culturally visible.

This dichotomy between "meltable" and "unmeltable" ethnics, those who can become "white" and those who cannot, highlights the peculiar character of the category of "white" in the United States. "Whiteness" is at once the norm of authentic Americanness and humanness and an empty, undefined center against which various racial "others" are defined as lesser Americans and nonnormative humans. To become "white" in America is to lose one ethnic historical particularity, as Irish or French or Finnish or Yugoslav. One's way of being Catholic or Jew (and today, Muslim) also should shed any marked appearance of difference. Such particularities may remain as residues in private identity but should be publicly invisible. Thus, "whiteness" may be described as a strategy of ethnic "erasure" that allows certain European-descended groups (today including some Europeanized Arabs) to be identified as one. In this fusion into "whiteness," the historical distinctiveness of each group is publicly repressed and ideally forgotten.

BLACKS IN THE UNITED STATES

Undoubtedly, the most vehement racism in U.S. ideology has been directed against descendants of Africans. Blacks were always classified as the bottom of any racial hierarchy. Blacks were the only group transported to North America as slaves. They were denied citizenship and the vote in the American Constitution, although listed as "three-fifths of a person" for purposes of reckoning state populations for the election of whites to the House of Representatives (U.S. Constitution, art. 1, sec. 2). Even those opposed to slavery as an institution, such as Thomas Jefferson, were convinced of the inferiority of the African and their unfitness for free citizenship. Those who sought to abolish slavery often coupled it with colonization proposals, that is, to send the free blacks back to Africa or to settle them in a distant land outside the United States. The American Colonization Society, founded in 1816, developed the plan to send free blacks to Liberia.[15]

Although slavery was gradually abolished in the northern states in the early nineteenth century, most whites refused to accept free blacks as equal citizens. Many northern states passed laws limiting the rights of free blacks, removing the right to vote, restricting free movement within and into the state, and barring them from certain types of employment and access to public schools. Whites burned black schools and gathering places where whites and blacks assembled together to discuss abolitionism or black civil rights. Since free blacks were often forced to take low-paying jobs, European immigrants, such as the Irish, often saw them as undercutting their jobs and wages. White working-class riots against blacks thus became common in northern cities.[16]

In the aftermath of the Civil War, the radical Republicans passed the three constitutional amendments to ensure equal citizenship to the freeman. They sought to enforce the laws of Reconstruction ensuring political participation by blacks in the legislatures of their respective states. Progressive state constitutions were written seeking to ensure political, social, and economic equality, guaranteeing blacks equal access to public services, abolishing property qualifications for voting, and creating an integrated school system. Southern whites fought back with terrorist violence through such groups as the Ku Klux Klan.

By 1877, the radical Republican leaders were no longer in power, and northern whites were increasingly disposed to let former Confederates and their descendants return to power and to repeal the egalitarian laws written during Reconstruction. New Black Codes disqualified blacks from voting through such strategies as property qualifications, literacy tests, and the grandfather clause (excluding anyone from voting not descended from someone who voted in 1865). Blacks were barred from equal access to employment and education. Many blacks were confined to sharecrop labor in agriculture where they were kept in permanent indebtedness to white landowners.

By the 1890s, these methods of disenfranchising and subordinating blacks were supplemented by elaborate Jim Crow laws that enforced separation in all public facilities. Separate parks, schools, libraries, and transportation became the rule. Blacks could not drink from the same water fountains, sit in the same seats, ride in the same elevators, walk on the same staircases, and even look out the same windows as whites. Efforts to challenge these laws were rejected when the Supreme Court ruled that the laws were legal as long as the separate facilities were "equal" (*Plessy v. Ferguson*, 1896), which, of course, was never the case.

For a hundred years, African Americans would struggle for full civil rights and social opportunities promised to them by the post–Civil War amendments and Reconstruction laws. Only with the Civil Rights Act of 1964 were the Jim Crow laws rejected and blacks guaranteed legal equality, but the struggle to overcome the deleterious cultural, social, and economic effects of more than 250 years of slavery and 100 years of discrimination still goes on today. Today a few blacks are making it into high political office at the state and national levels, with a black general and then a black woman scholar becoming secretary of state in the George W. Bush administration. In June 2008 Barack Obama, a black American with an African father, became the Democratic candidate for president of the United States. But at the same time, blacks are still almost two and a half times more likely to be poor than whites. The class hierarchy of U.S. society continues to be, in part, a race hierarchy, with blacks disproportionately in the lower rungs.

INDIANS IN U.S. HISTORY

Almost from the beginning of white settlement in the North American colonies, Indians were slated for removal from and expropriation of their lands. Puritan policy was expansionist, seeking to acquire more and more land and to remove the Indian presence from these lands, exterminating as many as possible in the process. It is not an exaggeration to say that the overwhelming consequence of the North America policy toward Indians has been genocidal.[17]

Indians were widely regarded as having no rights to the land since they failed to till it in the English manner. But even when Indians were or became farmers, whites soon found ways to uproot them from their land. Their cultures were seen as "savage" and their souls in the grip of the Devil. Successive wars between settlers and Indians during the colonial period had already pushed most of the Indians to the periphery of white settlement, with many Indians dying of diseases brought by the whites. The American Declaration of Independence treats the Indians not as potential American citizens but as hostile foreign nations to be kept at bay. There they are referred to as "merciless Indian savages whose known rule of warfare is undistinguished destruction of all ages, sexes and conditions."

During the period from 1776 to 1812, Indians east of the Mississippi were continually harassed and pressed to sign treaties ceding more land. Much Indian land in Indiana, Illinois, Ohio, Michigan, and Wisconsin was also taken over at this time.[18] From 1816 to 1850, the implementation of the policy of removal was carried out by the states and the federal government, often precipitated by private campaigns of frontiersmen. In 1830, Andrew Jackson persuaded Congress to pass the Indian Removal Act, which uprooted Indians east of the Mississippi and forced them to move west.

The Cherokees, who had accepted the demand that they become settled farmers, resisted the removal order. They appealed to the Supreme Court, where Chief Justice John Marshall upheld their rights. But President Andrew Jackson ignored the ruling and sent General Winfield Scott to forcibly remove them, herding them at bayonet point west. Thousands died on the way.[19]

Although the federal government promised that lands west of the Mississippi would be Indian territory permanently, the basic pattern of white expansion was to ignore such guarantees as soon as whites expanded into a region and began to settle the land. By 1885, remaining independent Indian tribes had been largely defeated and herded into dwindling reservations on land seen as useless by whites.[20]

Having crushed militant Indian resistance, U.S. policy from 1880 to 1934 was to forcibly assimilate the remaining Indians, thus extinguishing them as peoples with separate cultures, languages, and ways of life. Indigenous ceremonies were outlawed in 1894. Indian children were removed from their homes at a young age and sent to boarding schools, often run by church agencies funded by the federal government. There they were forbidden to speak their own languages or follow Indian customs. Discipline was harsh, and the death rates for children were high. Those who returned to their families as young adults were often permanently demoralized.[21]

In 1887, the Dawes-Severalty Act sought to break up communal landholding on reservations, allotting each family 160 acres and selling the rest on the open market. Fraud and taxes often deprived Indian families even of this allotment.[22] By the 1940s, the Indian population had dwindled to 300,000 and seemed on the way to extermination as a distinct people. Many leading American leaders frankly expressed the view that Indians were incapable of "civilization" and should "die off." Some stated this view sadly as an unfortunate but inevitable fact of "natural selection." Thus, Oliver Wendell Holmes opined in 1855,

> Theologians stand aghast at a whole race destined, according to their old formulae, to destruction, temporal and eternal. Philanthropists mourn over them, and from time to time catch a red man and turn him into their colleges as they would turn a partridge in among barn-door fowls. But instinct has its way sooner or later; the partridge makes but a trouble-some chicken and the Indian but a sorry Master of Arts, if he does not run for the woods, where all the *ferae naturae* impulses are urging him. These instincts lead to his extermination; too often the sad solution of the problem of his relation to the white race.... Then the white man hates him, and hunts him down like the wild beasts of the forest, and so the red-crayon sketch is rubbed down, and the canvas is ready for a picture of manhood a little more like God's own image.[23]

Other white leaders openly expressed the view that Indians were simply pestilent "varmints" and deserved to be killed off. Thus, Theodore Roosevelt, in his book, *The Winning of the West* (vol. 1, 1889), declared,

I supposed I should be ashamed to say that I take the Western view of the Indian. I don't go so far as to think that the only good Indian is a dead Indian, but I believe that nine out of every ten are, and I shouldn't inquire too closely into the case of the tenth. The most vicious cowboy has more moral principle than the average Indian.[24]

However, from the 1930s to the 1970s, the New Deal and the civil rights movement brought a modest revival of Indian life. Efforts to break up communal property were rescinded. Day schools replaced boarding schools, and native ceremonies, crafts, and languages were revived. But full religious freedom to Indians was granted only in the Religious Freedom Act of 1978. The Indian population made a rebound and was listed (together with Native Alaskans) at 2,475,956 in the U.S. Census of 2000.

But Indian problems in the United States are hardly over. The federal government prefers puppet chiefs to real self-government and uses tribal lands for weapons testing and dumping of toxic waste.[25] Although some Indians profit from new financial opportunities, such as casinos, the Indian population of the United States as a whole remains deeply demoralized, culturally conflicted, and educationally deprived. They rank among those with the highest poverty level in the U.S. population.

MEXICAN AMERICANS: THE BORDERS CROSS THEM

Mexicans were another expendable population that was "in the way" of white U.S. expansion across the continent. From the 1830s, the slogan of "manifest destiny" expressed the view that white Americans had a providential calling to expand from the Atlantic to the Pacific coasts.[26] Yet U.S. talks with Mexico in 1821 had accepted the northern borders of Mexico as including Texas, New Mexico, and California as well as parts of Utah, Colorado, Nevada, and Wyoming. In the 1830s, war broke out between Anglo settlers in Texas and the Mexican government, led by Antonio Lopez de Santa Ana. In 1836, these Anglo-Texans prevailed and declared themselves an independent state. In 1845, the U.S. Congress admitted Texas as a slave state into the Union, even though Mexico had abolished slavery in 1824.

In 1844, James Polk was elected president on a platform of western expansion to include both California and the Oregon territories, claimed by Britain. But the Mexican government refused to accept this annexation of Texas and turned down U.S. offers to buy the northwest Mexican territories. Polk engineered an "incident" on the Mexico–Texas border to declare war in April 1845. One group of U.S. troops marched south through Mexico and another west to California, with a third contingent landing at Veracruz and marching to Mexico City. By September 1845, the Mexican capital fell, and the Mexicans were forced to accept a peace treaty that ceded the Mexican northwest from Texas to California.[27]

During the war, there was debate in the United States about how much of Mexico to take over. Some wanted to annex all of Mexico, others only as far down as Veracruz. But the general consensus that emerged was that the territories north of the Rio Grande should suffice. This argument was based mostly on racial considerations. If the United States took more of Mexico, they would be forced to integrate much more of the Mexican population into their citizenry.[28]

The Mexican version of the Treaty of Guadalupe-Hidalgo signed by Mexico in February 1848 tried to ensure that Mexicans residing in the ceded territories, if they opted to remain, would receive full and equal U.S. citizenship and the rights to properties for which they held land grants from Mexico. But the version accepted by the U.S. Congress was vaguer on these points of civil, political, and property rights of Mexicans.[29] Moreover, the white settlers who soon crowded into California, with the gold rush of 1848, had no intention of leaving Mexican ranchers in California in possession of so much property or of accepting them as equal citizens. In the state constitution of 1849, both Indians and blacks were denied voting rights. This included many Mexicans of part Indian ancestry.[30]

Between 1850 and 1880, most of the vast territories claimed by Mexicans in California had been confiscated by whites by a variety of legal strategies and the Mexicans reduced to poverty and marginal legal status.[31] There were widespread massacres of Indians and lynchings of Mexicans. Despite a 100-year presence of Spanish/Mexican settlers that left its mark on the majority of place-names, California was on its way to becoming a white-dominated state. Similar patterns of confiscation of Mexican-claimed land also took place in New Mexico and Texas.

The war with Mexico and the U.S. takeover of the Mexican northwest was accompanied by virulent expressions of racism. The Spanish were regarded as an inferior "race" of Europeans lacking real "energy" and "manliness," corrupted by what was seen as an oppressive and false religion, Catholicism. The intermarriage of Spanish with Indians, creating a largely mestizo Mexican population, was viewed as a degrading "mongrelization" of what was already an inferior people. Whites commonly referred to them as "greasers." With its ranching elite stripped of its land, most Mexicans could be seen as people primarily capable of "stoop" agricultural work, to be allowed to enter the United States only when their cheap labor was needed. In the words of Pio de Jesús Pico, once a large landowner and the last governor of Mexican California, the Spanish Californians had become "strangers in their own land."[32]

THE CHINESE AND JAPANESE IN CALIFORNIA

Conflict between whites and Chinese in California first developed in the gold mines, where the Chinese were seen as undercutting white profits. Whites attacked Chinese laborers and sought to drive them out of the camps. As Chinese labor grew from the 1850s to the 1880s, so white antagonism against them also grew, led by white labor leaders who organized groups, such as the Anti-Coolie Union of San Francisco. The spokesmen for such groups claimed that the Chinese ran brothels and opium dens. Chinese women came only for the purpose of prostitution. Chinese were prevented from obtaining housing, and their children were segregated in schools.

The rhetoric of this anti-Chinese movement went far beyond the claimed threat to white wages; it expanded into a general racist indictment of Chinese humanity and culture. Their culture was portrayed as effete and degraded. It was claimed that they are by nature cunning, treacherous, sexually debased, vice ridden, and incapable of responsible citizenship. If not checked, they would flood the country, undercutting the very basis of American civilization. Thus, F. M. Pixley, speaking on behalf of white Californians before a joint congressional meeting on Chinese immigration in 1876, declared,

> The Chinese are inferior to any race God ever made. . . . I think that there are none so low. . . . Their people have got the perfection of crimes of 4000 years. . . . Divine Wisdom has said that He would divide this country and the world as a heritage of five great families. . . . The Yellow races are to be confined to what the Almighty already gave them, and as they are not a favored people, they are not to be permitted to steal from us what we have robbed the American savage of. . . . I believe that the Chinese have no souls to save, and if they have, they are not worth saving.[33]

In 1882, the federal government passed the Chinese Exclusion Act, suspending Chinese immigration for ten years. It was renewed for another decade in 1892 and made permanent in 1902.

Japanese immigration began to grow in the 1890s and soon attracted some of the same phobic hostility against the "yellow peril." However, Japan at this time was a rising Pacific empire and thus was seen as a danger to American expanding power in the Pacific, even as some American leaders were establishing diplomatic relations with it. In 1908, Theodore Roosevelt exchanged correspondence with the Japanese government in which it agreed to restrict Japanese immigration to the United States. In the Taft-Katsura agreement, Japan acquiesced to American control of the Philippines in exchange for American acceptance of the Japanese takeover of Korea.[34]

But the Japanese continued to prosper in California, bringing their wives and establishing families and businesses. They particularly specialized in intensive fruit and vegetable truck farming and by World War I owned or leased half a million acres of agricultural land in California. This prosperity sparked rising hostility from whites, and there were mass anti-Japanese demonstrations and petition campaigns. Valentine S. McClatchy, newspaper publisher and director of the Associated Press, enunciated this danger to white California supposedly posed by the Japanese:

> The Japanese are less assimilable and more dangerous as residents in this country than any of the other peoples ineligible according to our laws. . . . They come here specifically and professedly for the purpose of colonizing and establishing permanently [their] race. They never cease being Japanese. . . . California . . . has been making for 20 years the fight of the nation against incoming of alien races whose peaceful penetration must in time certainly drive the white race to the wall.[35]

This campaign soon led to direct violence. In Los Angeles, a "Swat the Jap" movement developed that vandalized Japanese property. In agricultural communities, vigilantes sought to drive Japanese out of town. In 1924, as noted before, the Immigration Act added the Japanese to the Chinese as totally excluded groups.

The shameful culmination of this anti-Japanese crusade occurred during World War II in which President Franklin Roosevelt accepted the argument that the Japanese, especially in West Coast states, represented a dangerous "fifth column" potentially allied with imperial Japan. In February 1942, he acquiesced to the demand to round up all Japanese in California, Oregon, and Washington into internment camps. Some 110,000 innocent people, 62 percent of them U.S. citizens, were forcibly uprooted and evacuated to ten "relocation centers" that consisted of poorly insulated barracks surrounded by barbed wire and armed guards in barren, inaccessible areas in the interior of the United States. Here these Japanese spent the years of the war, even as their sons were fighting for the United States in the armed services. When these interned Japanese were released in January 1945, many found their properties confiscated and had to begin again from nothing.[36]

In 1948, some compensation for property losses was paid to the former internees, but most were unable to fully recover their losses. In 1988, President Ronald Reagan signed legislation to apologize for the internment on behalf of the U.S. government, declaring that it was based on "race prejudice, war hysteria and a failure of political leadership." In 1992 in the Amendment to the Civil Liberties Act of 1988, $400 million was appropriated to ensure that all remaining internees received their $20,000 redress payments.[37]

But the danger remains that other targeted groups could suffer a similar internment under pressure from paranoid responses to apparent threats to U.S. security. In 1950, the U.S. Congress passed the Emergency Detention Act (as part of the McCarran Act) giving the attorney general the power to put American citizens in concentration camps without trial based on suspicion that such persons might "commit or conspire to commit espionage or sabotage."[38] This law is still on the books, so the danger remains that it could be used against some other group targeted by prejudice and war hysteria, such as Middle Eastern Muslims, in the context of the "war on terror" in the twenty-first century.

HAS AMERICAN RACISM BEEN OVERCOME?

In the 1930s, "scientific" support for race prejudice began to be undermined. A new school of anthropology led by Franz Boas disputed the concept of race differences and began to look at each culture in terms of its own distinctive worldview.[39] Recent developments in paleoanthropology have increasingly confirmed the unitary origins of all members of the human species. What had been the foci of claims of race differences, hair texture, skin color, and nose shape has been shown to be superficial, having no real connection with differences of intelligence and creative capacity. Culture, not differences of skin tone or slant of the brow, shape the way different human groups have formed their distinct social patterns and worldviews. But members of all humans groups have the capacity to excel in what is valued in their own culture as well as the ability to assimilate into other cultures, learning their languages and skills.

While racism has been largely dispelled on the level of anthropological science and is no longer respectable as political discourse in the United States, its shaping of social relations between "white" Americans and blacks, Indians, Mexicans, and Asians has hardly disappeared. In each of America's colonial wars since the 1898 Spanish-American War, the "others" slated for conquest and subordination have often been depicted in the rhetoric shaped by hostility to blacks, Indians, Mexicans, and Asians.

When the United States intervened in the Philippines in 1898 and carried on a destructive four-year war to suppress the Filipino independence movement, all the racist imagery shaped by contempt for "niggers," "savages," and "wily Orientals" was combined to stereotype the Filipino, even as other leaders paternalistically spoke of them as "our little brown brothers."[40] Whether fighting the Vietnamese nationalists in 1963–1975 or the Iraqi insurgency from 2003, still ongoing in 2008, the habits of racial hatred of "enemy" people of other colors, cultures, and religions and the genocidal methods shaped by Indian fighting keep reoccurring. Those we supposedly come to "liberate" soon come to hate Americans for their insulting mistreatment.

At home, those traditionally targeted as the "others" of American racism—blacks, Indians, and Mexican Americans—continue to suffer the legacy of unequal opportunity that shapes the likelihood of remaining disproportionately in poverty. Even Chinese, Japanese, and other Asians, such as Koreans, who today are often seen as "model minorities" highly successful in educational achievement and technological skills, have not completely escaped the scars of past exclusion or the shadow of anti-Oriental "paranoia" that could be awakened again.

Thus, the American "melting pot" continues to be formed by the mold of "whiteness," leaving those of other "colors" somewhat less able to "melt" into a common Americanness. What is needed and has yet to emerge is a different way of relating ethnic diversity to Americanness no longer based on the assumed norm of "whiteness."

NOTES

1. Julian, "Against the Galileans," in *Works*, vol. 5, trans. W. C. Wright (Cambridge, Mass.: Harvard University Press, 1961–1968), 321.
2. Thomas F. Gossett, *Race: The History of an Idea in America* (New York: Oxford University Press, 1997).
3. See Jordan D. Winthrop, *White over Black: American Attitudes toward the Negro, 1550–1812* (Chapel Hill: University of North Carolina Press, 1968).
4. Gossett, *Race*, 44–51.
5. Gossett, *Race*, 256–57; C. Vann Woodward, *The Strange Career of Jim Crow* (New York: Oxford University Press, 1986).
6. Gossett, *Race*, 144–75.
7. Gossett, *Race*, 176–97.
8. Gossett, *Race*, 354–55.
9. Noel Ignatiev, *How the Irish Became White* (New York: Routledge, 1995).
10. Gossett, *Race*, 406–8.
11. On such stereotypes of white manliness in American literature, see Gossett, *Race*, 123–43.
12. See Gossett, *Race*, 269–73.
13. Ignatiev, *How the Irish Became White*, 6–31.
14. See F. James Davis, *Who Is Black: One Nation's Definition* (University Park: Pennsylvania State University Press, 2001); see also Matthew Frye Jacobson, *Whiteness of a Different Color: European Immigrants and the Alchemy of Race* (Cambridge, Mass.: Harvard University Press, 1998).

15. Philip J. Staudenraus, *The African Colonization Movement, 1816–1865* (New York: Columbia University Press, 1961).

16. Ignatiev, *How the Irish Became White*, 150–59; see also Michael Feldberg, *The Philadelphia Riots of 1844: A Study of Ethnic Conflict* (Westport, Conn.: Greenwood Press, 1975).

17. See Ward Churchill, *A Little Matter of Genocide* (San Francisco: City Lights Books, 1997).

18. See Reginald Horsman, *Expansion and American Indian Policy, 1783–1812* (East Lansing: Michigan State University Press, 1967).

19. William T. Hagan, *American Indians* (Chicago: University of Chicago Press, 1993), 84–94.

20. See Dee Brown, *Bury My Heart at Wounded Knee: An Indian History of the West* (New York: Holt, Rinehart and Winston, 1970).

21. See David Wallace Adam, *Education for Extinction* (Lawrence: University Press of Kansas, 1995).

22. Janet A. McDonnell, *The Dispossession of the American Indian, 1883–1934* (Bloomington: Indiana University Press, 1991).

23. Oliver Wendell Holmes, *New England Society Orations*, from Gossett, *Race*, 243.

24. From Gossett, *Race*, 238 and note 20.

25. See Churchill, "Cold War Impacts on Native North America: The Political Economy of Radioactive Colonization," in *A Little Matter of Genocide*, 289–362.

26. See Albert K. Weinberg, *Manifest Destiny: A Study of Expansionism in American History* (Chicago: Quadrangle Books, 1935).

27. For a history of the Mexican-American War, see J. Jack Bauer, *The Mexican War, 1846–8* (New York: Macmillan, 1974).

28. See John D. P. Fuller, *The Movement for the Acquisition of all Mexico* (Baltimore: Johns Hopkins University Press, 1936).

29. See Richard Griswold del Castillo, *The Treaty of Guadalupe-Hidalgo: A Legacy of Conflict* (Norman: University of Oklahoma Press, 1990).

30. See Robert F. Heizer and Alan J. Almquist, *The Other Californians: Prejudice and Discrimination under Spain, Mexico and the United States to 1920* (Berkeley: University of California Press, 1971), 226–28.

31. See Leonard Pitt, *The Decline of the Californios: A Social History of the Spanish-Speaking Californians, 1846–1890* (Berkeley: University of California Press, 1998).

32. See www.socialhistory.org/biographies/pico. In an address at the time of the U.S. takeover, Pio Pico said, "Shall we remain supine while these daring strangers are overrunning our fertile plains and gradually outnumbering and displacing us? Shall these incursions go unchecked, until we shall become strangers in our own land?"

33. Quoted in Heizer and Almquist, *The Other Californians*, 167.

34. Bruce Cumings, *Korea's Place in the Sun: A Modern History* (New York: Norton, 1997), 141–42.

35. Roger Daniels and Harry H. I. Kitano, *American Racism: Exploration of the Nature of Prejudice* (Englewood Cliffs, N.J.: Prentice Hall, 1970), 52.

36. Morton Grodzins, *Americans Betrayed* (Chicago: University of Chicago Press, 1949).

37. See "Japanese American Internment," *Wikipedia, the Free Encyclopedia*, http://en.wikipedia.org/wiki/Japanese_American_Internment, 1, 9–10.

38. Daniels and Kitano, *American Racism*, 65.

39. Gossett, *Race*, 409–30.

40. See Leon Wolff, *Little Brown Brother: How the United States Purchased and Pacified the Philippine Islands at the Century's Turn* (New York: History Book Club, 2006).

· 7 ·

Social Ideologies: Sexism, Slavery, and Racism

This chapter delineates the major ideologies in the classical Western tradition that have justified sexism, slavery, and racism. It also mentions countervailing ideologies that have implicitly or explicitly opposed sexism, slavery, and racism and advocated equality between all humans and liberation from oppressive relations. The chapter discusses three major sources of such ideologies: religion, philosophy, and social sciences. By religious ideologies is meant primarily ideas derived from the Christian Bible: Old and New Testament and Christian tradition. By philosophy is meant primarily classical Greek thought from Plato and Aristotle. Social science ideologies refer to nineteenth- and twentieth-century Western systems of thought, particularly in psychology and anthropology.

It would, of course, be possible to widen the scope of this presentation to include other religions and philosophies. Hinduism in India undoubtedly provided religious and philosophical traditions that justified the caste system. Confucianism was used to justify class and gender hierarchy. But the focus here is on Western Europe and the United States and those ideologies that have shaped their traditional worldview, with its effects both on their own societies and on those they influenced around the world.

SEXISM: RELIGIOUS MANDATES

As we saw in chapter 3, patriarchy was already well established in the ancient Near East by the second millennium. Contrary to certain feminist claims, Judaism was neither its inventor nor an especially extreme example of it.[1] The patriarchal ordering of society was taken for granted in Hebrew Scripture, and there was no special effort to argue for it or justify it. Among key ideas and patterns of sexism in Hebrew society was the exclusion of women from leadership and public representation in religious and political assemblies and the belief that their female functions (menstruation and childbirth) rendered them "unclean," necessitating their further exclusion and untouchability in relation to the sacred (Lev. 12:2–5). Such a notion of woman's uncleanness is not peculiar to Judaism but is widely found in other cultures, such as in Africa and India.

In the New Testament, there is more explicit argument for the gender, generational, and slave hierarchies of patriarchy, an indication that this pattern was partly challenged in early Christianity, reflecting egalitarian movements in some contemporary forms of Judaism.[2] Hence, early Christian documents spend more time justifying patriarchal patterns as appropriate for the church. This is found most notably in what are called the "household codes" of the New Testament. These codes typically reiterate the threefold social hierarchy of the patriarchal family. Thus, we find in Ephesians 5–6,

> Wives be subject to your husbands as to the Lord. For the husband is the head of the wife as Christ is the head of the church, his body and is himself its savior. As the church is subject to Christ, so let wives also be subject in everything to their husbands (5:22–24). . . . Children obey your parents in the Lord, for this is right. . . . (6:1) Slaves be obedient to those who are your earthly masters with fear and trembling, in singleness of heart, as to Christ. (6:5)

Similar demands for subordination of women and slaves are repeated in 1 Timothy (2:11; 6:1–2) and 1 Peter (2:18–21; 3:1–2). 1 Peter also calls for submission to state authorities, the emperor, and governors (2:13–14). Submission to Christ is continually used as the pattern to reinforce social submission of women and slaves. In 1 Peter, submission to an unjust master who punishes unjustly and without reason is enjoined on the basis that this is like the redemptive suffering of Christ (2:20–24). This use of Christ to enforce subjugation is in contrast to Galatians 3:27–28, where baptism into Christ is said to overcome the divisions of Jew and Greek, slave and free, and male and female:

> For as many of you as were baptized into Christ have put on Christ. There is neither Jew nor Greek, there is neither slave nor free. There is neither male nor female, for you are all one in Christ Jesus.

Exactly what was meant by this seems to have been disputed both in New Testament times and in contemporary Christianity, some seeing it as a mandate for changed social relations and others as simply a "spiritual" oneness that does not change power relations.³

1 Timothy expresses what became the most important Christian justification for sexism, namely, the idea that women are both subordinate in the original "order of creation" and have become doubly subjugated because of their priority in causing sin to come into the world. Thus, 1 Timothy 2:11–14 declares,

> Let a woman learn in silence with all submissiveness. I permit no woman to teach or to have authority over men; she is to keep silent. For Adam was formed first, then Eve, and Adam was not deceived, but the woman was deceived and became a transgressor.

This passage read in its context shows that the author of 1 Timothy is actually contending against an alternative tradition with his own church where women did teach and had somewhat independent ministries. But in Christian tradition, this passage was read as an absolute reflection of early Christian practice, to be normative for all time.⁴

This idea that women are both naturally subordinate, because of their secondary status in the order of creation, and to be forcibly subjugated, as punishment for Eve's revolt against her subordination, causing sin to come into the world, is repeated in various forms in classical Christian teaching. Thus, St. Augustine, writing in the late fourth and early fifth centuries, taught that although women were created equally in the image of God and hence are redeemable, they were subordinate to the male in the original order of creation in their roles as wife and sexual partner. For Augustine, the relation of male and female mirrors the hierarchy of mind over body. In this relationship of male to female, it is the male who possesses the fullness of the image of God, while the female is included in the image of God only under the male, while in herself she represents the body. Thus, in his writing on the Trinity, Augustine says,

> How then did the apostle tell us that the man is the image of God and therefore he is forbidden to cover his head, but that the woman is not so, and therefore she is commanded to cover hers? Unless forsooth according to that which I have said already, when I was treating of the nature of the human mind, that the woman, together with her own husband, is the image of God, so that the whole substance may be one image, but when she is referred to separately in her quality as a helpmeet, which regards the woman alone, then she is not the image of God, but, as regards the man alone, he is the image of God as fully and completely as when the woman too is joined to him in one.⁵

For Augustine, although woman would have been subordinate in God's original intention for creation, she is also responsible for sin coming into the world because of her revolt against her subordination and disobedience to God's command. Her subordination has thus become punitive subjugation, and women must suffer this even if it means violence from her husband. Women are redeemed by patient acceptance of their forcible subjugation. In heaven, she will become man's spiritual equal according to the merits she has won through her meek and patient life on earth.

Thomas Aquinas, a leading Catholic theologian of the thirteenth century, also believed that woman is naturally man's subordinate. However, for Aquinas, this subordination is interpreted as biological inferiority. Influenced by Aristotle, Aquinas taught that woman was a defective human who lacked equal capacity for reason, moral will, and physical strength with the male. This means she must be under male domination and cannot represent any independent leadership either in the church or in society. Lacking full humanity, she cannot be ordained a priest. Christ had to be incarnated as a male because only males possess full humanity, and thus only males can represent Christ as priests.

Aquinas also thinks this original subjugation has been worsened because of woman's responsibility for sin. Woman is thereby punished both by forcible male domination and by the pains of childbirth. Woman does have a spiritual nature that allows her to be finally redeemed in heaven, but this redemption is predicated on her humble acceptance of her subordination on earth.[6]

Similar views are also found in the leading theologians of the Reformation: Luther and Calvin. For Luther, woman and man would have been perfect partners in Paradise, but this also meant that the man would have had preeminence and the woman would have accepted his leadership. However, because of her priority in sin, the woman now suffers both a forcible domination from her husband and the pains of childbirth.

For Calvin, woman was created equally in the image of God as far as spiritual capacity is concerned, but she was excluded in God's original order of creation from that part of the image of God that has to do with domination or government. With the Fall into sin, caused by woman's insubordination, woman's original subordination has been worsened to servitude. Although woman will be redeemed by humble submission to her wifely role, woman has to be strictly controlled since she still harbors the taint of subordination, which can be expressed not only by quarreling but also by such extreme evils as witchcraft.[7] While Dominicans were the leading witch persecutors in the fifteenth century, in the Reformation period it was Calvinists who were leading witch-hunters among Protestants.[8]

PHILOSOPHICAL MANDATES

Sexist ideologies in Western Europe also drew on philosophical mandates from Greek thought, especially Plato and Aristotle. Plato appears to be more egalitarian since he argues in the *Republic* that women are members of all three classes in his ideal society: philosopher-kings, warriors, and artisans. But it becomes evident that simply being members of each class does not mean that women actually exercise the leading roles of each class. Plato explicitly claims that women have inferior capacities in every arena, not only as philosophers and warriors but also as artisans. Thus, he argues that although "the gifts of nature are diffused in both; all the pursuits of men are the pursuits of women, but in all of them a woman is inferior to a man."[9]

This inferiority of women is defined ontologically in his creation story the *Timaeus*. Here humanity, as originally created by the gods, was male. Only when these males succumb to their passions are some reincarnated as females or even as animals:

> If they conquered these [the passions] they would live righteously, and if they were conquered by them, unrighteously. He who lived well during his appointed time was to return and dwell in his native star. And there he would have a blessed and congenial existence. But if he failed in attaining this, at the second birth he would pass into a woman, and if, when in that state of being, he did not desist from evil, he would continually be changed into some brute who resembled him in the evil nature he had acquired, and would not cease from his toils and transformations until he ... returned to the form of his first and better state.[10]

Aristotle goes further in justifying women's inferiority biologically and also insisting on their different roles in the family and society. For Aristotle, the male provides the soul or formative element in procreation, while the female provides the material that is formed by the soul. This difference determines "the specific characteristics of each of the sexes; that is, what it means to be male or to be female." Femaleness itself is seen as a defect. The female offspring is produced when the female material is incompletely formed by the male formative power. Thus, the "female is as it were a deformed male."[11]

This "deformed" nature makes women inferior in all her capacities of mind, moral will, and physical strength. Having a defective humanness, she is "naturally" servile:

> The rule of the soul over the body and of the mind and the rational element over the passionate is natural and expedient ... the male is by nature superior and the female inferior, and the one rules and the other is ruled;

this principle, of necessity, extends to all mankind. Where there is such a difference as that between soul and body, or between men and animals . . . the lower sort are by nature slaves, and it is better for them as for all inferiors that they should be under the rule of a master.[12]

These assumptions about male superiority and female inferiority as analogous to the relation of reason to the passions and mind to body not only shaped Christian theology, such as that of Thomas Aquinas, but also continued to be taken for granted in Western philosophy into the twentieth century. When women began to win the right to higher education and entrance into professions at the end of the nineteenth and early twentieth centuries, it was common for the social sciences to decry these developments, claiming that women's "weaker" nature would be impaired by "unnatural brainwork."

Some prominent educators and doctors argued that women have lesser physical energy than men and that what energy they have is needed for reproduction. If this limited energy is forced into their brain by education, they will become infirm, sterile, and even insane.[13] In the United States in the early twentieth century, this view was used to explain why middle-class white women who were beginning to go to college were having fewer children than blacks and working-class immigrants, thus fueling the racist and classist demographic fears of the white Anglo-Saxon Protestant ruling class of the time.

These fears of women's advancement into education and valued professions were reinforced by the popularity of Freudian psychology in the United States in the 1920s and again in the 1950s. Freud believed that women were biologically defective because of their lack of a penis and that this lack shaped their entire psychological development. The discovery of this lack is a deep psychological blow to the developing girl child. Some women refuse to accept their "castrated" nature and try to emulate men through attaining education and pursuing professions. Such pursuits Freud saw as pathological in women, a symptom of their "penis envy."

This pathology is resolved only when women give up such irrational desires for independence and accept their biological "destiny" to be inferior and dependent on the male. She can then be compensated for her lack of a penis by marriage and the bearing of a (male) child.[14] Thus, Freud provided a powerful stick with which to beat the "new woman" who was aspiring to higher education and professions and to dub her as "infantile" and "pathological" in comparison to those who accepted the traditional "feminine" roles.

SLAVERY

The traditional reinforcements of slavery in antiquity and early Christianity were generally part of the same patriarchal ideology as sexism, although with the additional dimension, in some cases, of racism toward ethnic groups seen as "naturally" slaves. However, slavery in antiquity was not confined to particular races and so did not usually draw on racial arguments.

This relation of ethnicity and slavery is complicated in the case of Judaism. For Jews, the central drama of national liberation was one of redemption of their people by God from slavery in Egypt. Since people of any ethnic group might find themselves enslaved in antiquity through such misfortunes as debt or kidnapping, Jewish extended families appointed a "redeemer" whose task was to liberate family members from slavery (generally through monetary payment).[15] Thus, the ideas of redemption and a "redeemer" were directly associated with liberation from slavery in Jewish thought, a connection also inherited by Christianity, which spiritualized the idea by speaking of redemption as liberation from the "bondage of sin."

In Leviticus, Jews are enjoined against making fellow Israelites into permanent slaves. If fellow Israelites become so impoverished that they must sell themselves and their families into slavery, they are to be treated as bonded laborers. They and their families are to be set free at the time of the Jubilee (in the fiftieth year): "For they are my servants, whom I brought out of the land of Egypt: they shall not be sold as slaves are sold. You shall not rule over them with harshness" (Lev. 25:39–43).

However, it is licit to acquire slaves from "among the nations" (i.e., the Gentiles): "it is from the nations around you that you may acquire slaves," Such Gentile slaves can be kept as property in perpetuity to be inherited by one's descendants. "These you may treat as slaves, but as for your fellow Israelites, no one shall rule over the other with harshness" (Lev. 25:44–46).

As we saw earlier in this chapter, the New Testament accepted slavery as part of the patriarchal social order and enjoined slaves to obey their masters, even those who are harsh and unjust (Col. 3:22–23; 1 Tim. 6:1–2; 1 Pet. 2:18–25; Titus 2:9–10). Slavery was accepted as a normal institution of society by Christianity, although some local churches helped ransom church members who had fallen into slavery. Augustine was responsible for the justification of slavery that became the basis of Church canon law.

For Augustine, there was no slavery in God's original order of creation in which God intended that humans have dominion over animals but not over each other. (Here Augustine differs from his view of sexism, which is a part of the original order of creation.) Slavery comes about through sin and thus represents a universal human fall from the original order of creation. For Augustine, this sin represents our universal bondage to sin, but it is also the particular sin of the ones who are enslaved. That is, an individual may sin by failing to obey constituted authority and be punished by being enslaved, or a group may revolt against their proper relation to ruling authorities and be enslaved, as in a just war. Thus, for Augustine, slavery is both a punishment the enslaved must accept for their sinfulness (or of their ancestors) and a duty imposed on those who must keep order in society and prevent rebellion.[16]

Greek philosophy reflected two major traditions about slavery in classical antiquity. The one represented by Aristotle, which we have already mentioned in connection with women, saw certain groups of people as "natural slaves" based on their insufficient reasoning capacities and lack of moral will. Those deemed "natural slaves" were seen mainly as "barbarians," that is, peoples from the fringes of the Hellenistic empires in the Middle East and Europe, although Aristotle does not consistently say that all barbarians are "natural slaves." But it is clear that it is the Greek-educated and property-owning elites who are assumed to be the "natural" slave masters, those in whom reasoning power dominates and thus who are suited to rule over others as the mind rules over the body.[17]

Aristotle's suggestion that "barbarians" were "natural slaves" because of their insufficient reasoning capacities was readily picked up during the sixteenth- and seventeenth-century European colonization and enslavement of indigenous people in Latin America to argue that indigenous peoples were "natural slaves."[18] That Africans were "natural slaves" was already a part of the Spanish tradition based on their identification as the descendants of Ham with Africans, as mentioned in chapter 6.

The second view of slavery in Greek philosophy is identified with the Stoic tradition. This tradition stresses the greater importance of moral slavery over actual physical slavery. For those of the Stoic tradition, all humans had equal moral capacity, but moral corruption was caused by falling into bondage to the passions. A person might be physically free but in bondage to the passions, while a person who is physically enslaved might be inwardly free and hence the moral equal of the greatest philosopher. This tradition was undoubtedly comforting to elites who found themselves unjustly enslaved or imprisoned by arbitrary power. But the tradition also tended to promote a passive acquiescence to the evils of actual slavery by making such physical enslavement appear unimportant compared to inner freedom.[19]

This Stoic view was taken over by Christianity, for which the important bondage was spiritual bondage to sin, not physical enslavement. Christ has freed us from the bondage of sin and made us servants of God. But this perspective was used to advocate the passive acceptance by slaves of even harsh treatment by slave masters. Augustine combines elements of both views. We are all sinners and hence in bondage to sin. Yet those in physical bondage deserve it by their actual sinfulness and should cultivate inner freedom while becoming completely compliant to the demands of even the harshest slave masters. Slavery is seen as part of the just ordering of a fallen society to repress sinful rebelliousness.

From the beginnings of slavery in human society until eighteenth-century Europe, there was no consistent antislavery tradition that argued that actual physical enslavement was wrong and should be opposed by moral people. Even in the mid- to late nineteenth century, there were philosophers and theologians who continued to justify slavery as part of the patriarchal order. Thus, in the United States on the eve of the Civil War, we find among leading theologians identified with the Reformed tradition in theological schools, such as Princeton University, arguments that linked slavery with the patriarchal order.

Both Frederick Ross, in *Slavery Ordained of God* (1857), and George Armstrong, in *The Christian Doctrine of Slavery* (1857), used the New Testament household codes to argue that slavery was parallel to the subjugation of women and children in the family. Blacks were like perpetual children who were incapable of independence and so must be cared for and made productive by being under the paternal authority of the slave masters.[20]

As we saw in chapter 6, the arguments for the enslavement of blacks in North America were joined to racism by the seventeenth century. Various arguments were used to define blacks as biological inferiors to whites, such as the belief that they were descended from a different set of ancestors than Adam and Eve, the parents of whites; that they represented a deterioration from the original status of humans; or that they represented a lower evolutionary stage of humans in the development of the human species from its ape ancestors. It was this social Darwinist view that came to dominate in the mid-nineteenth century and that continued to be used to argue for the denial of equality of whites and blacks, even with the abolition of slavery after the Civil War.

In the nineteenth century until the mid-twentieth, the sciences of anthropology and sociology were major vehicles that justified notions of racial division into distinctly superior and inferior races. It would not be until the 1970s that the notions that there are distinct races of humanity who possess distinctly different temperaments and intellectual and moral capacities became discredited among the social sciences.

In addition to social Darwinist theories of stages of evolution from ape to full humanity, American racism also drew on the biblical concept of an "elect" nation or chosen people of God. This concept of the chosen people or elect nation is central to Hebrew Scripture, but it was deprived of its nationalist exclusivism in classical Christianity by being identified with the Christian church in which "there is no more Jew nor Greek." In the Christian church, all nations are gathered into one universal chosen people of God.

This concept of the universal church as God's new elect people, however, also carried an anti-Jewish shadow side as well as hostility to peoples of other religions generally. But such prejudice based on religion or lack of adherence to the true faith was supposed to vanish when people of any race became converted to Christianity. In practice, however, the inferiority originally attributed to "others" because of wrong religion was often transferred to a concept of racial inferiority when a group previously despised became Christian, as we have seen in the case of converted Jews and also of converted blacks and Indians.

However, in the sixteenth century, the breakdown of the concept of a universal church into warring national churches in Western Europe helped to revive the identification of the "true" Christian church with an elect nation. Thus, the Spanish and the French in the sixteenth and seventeenth centuries each developed ideas of being both the true church and an elect nation chosen by God to defend the true church against rival Protestants and to extend that true church and national power over colonized peoples in North or Latin America. The English developed a rival view of being both God's elect nation and a true reformed church against "corrupt" Catholicism in wars of religion and national rivalry in Europe and also in competition for empire in North America.

It is this English view of being both an elect nation and a true reformed church that deeply shaped North American Protestant identity during the period of English settlement of the colonies of North America. When these English colonies broke from their "mother country" and became the United States of America, exclusivist national churches were rejected for separation of church and state. But North Americans continued to promote racist themes of a unique election of an "Anglo-Saxon" American people as God's elect, associated both with superior political institutions (democracy) and with superior moral-religious traditions.

From the 1840s to the 1920s, it continued to be common to define America's elect status in terms of other nations of the world with God's election of a uniquely superior "Anglo-Saxon race." Blacks, Indians, and later Mexicans, Filipinos, Chinese, and Japanese were shoved aside on the basis of the presumption that only "Anglo-Saxons" or at least Western Europeans (whites) were capable of this unique combination of superior morality and superior political institutions.

American global policy continues to be bedeviled by this assumption of a unique and superior entitlement of the United States to spread "democracy" qua the American political and economic system to the rest of the world, by force if necessary. Thus, the development of U.S. American empire has been deeply shaped by a U.S. American version of the idea of an "elect nation" chosen by God to rule the world.[21]

In summarizing these ideologies of sexist, proslavery, and racist thought, we note certain similarities between them not because the objects of prejudice are the "same" but rather because the dominating group projects similar patterns on the "others." The culture of the dominating group splits reality into binary dualisms, such as mind–body, good–evil, and innocent–corruption, projecting the negative side on the "other" while reserving the positive side for itself. These mythic projections tend to split into three perspectives. The other is seen as a natural "brute," closer to body than mind and hence suited primarily to physical labor rather than rational leadership. But the "other" can also be seen as rebellious against its own "natural" subservience and hence dangerous and demonic. Finally, the "other" may be romanticized or idealized as an auxiliary or helper of the dominant group. We will explore these three aspects of the ideology of the "other" in relation to five groups of sexual, religious, and racial "others": women, Jews, blacks, Indians, and (male) homosexuals.

Women are, first of all, Eve, the woman created to be subjugated to the male from the beginning, lacking full humanity and so incapable of autonomous existence, shaped to be the submissive wife and helpmeet in reproduction and housework. But Eve is also the rebellious wife who brought sin into the world. When she persists in her rebelliousness, she becomes the witch, the helpmeet of the Devil, the channel for the demonic. As witch, she should be destroyed by hanging or burning. Yet woman in her "ideal" nature is the mother of the male redemptive child who herself remains untouched by sexuality and sin. She is the Virgin Mary, the ideal embodiment of the spiritual "feminine" to be adored.

The Christian myth of the Jew also is compounded of a three-part "gaze." Jews are the people of the "Old Law," which cannot redeem, who have been superseded by the people of the New Testament, as grace over law, spirit over body. But Jews are also seen as crafty, demonic aliens; Christ killers who continually conspire against the Christian world; members of the "synagogue of Satan"; and the Elders of Zion, who plot to install the Devil, the Antichrist, as world ruler. Yet Jews can also be seen as the Chosen People, the ancestors of our faith, through whom Christ comes into the world. As in the current alliance of the United States and the state of Israel, the "original" and "new" chosen people can be seen as forming a "special relationship" to rule at least the Middle East if not the world.

African peoples brought to the Americas as slaves were also viewed through a three-part mythic gaze by whites. First, it was assumed that they were childlike beings that could never grow up into autonomous adults. Lacking adequate reason, they are suited primarily to servile labor. This view was extended to various other colonized peoples in U.S. history, such as Mexicans and Filipinos. But blacks, especially males, are also seen as dangerously rebellious, desiring to throw off white control and especially to desecrate the white man's most precious possession: the white woman. Thus, the dangerous black male is the rapist, the most heinous criminal whose crime must be punished by castration and lynching. But, on the other hand, when properly humble and submissive, the elderly black male becomes the Uncle Tom, who, with his wife, Mammy, loves and nurtures the white child in preference to their own children.

Native Americans likewise were viewed through a similar three-part gaze. First, they were seen as primitive, lacking adequate humanity and culture and incapable of being assimilated into white society. Then, in rebellion against white appropriation of their land, they became the "devil Indian," the incarnation of the demonic world that must be purged to redeem the land for God's true people. On the other hand, they could also be seen as the "noble savage," remnants of an innocent humanity in Paradise before the Fall into sin, from whom the white man might learn certain skills in hunting and tracking in the "wilderness" but who is sadly doomed to "vanish" before the triumphant expansion of a superior civilization.

Although they have always existed in societies, homosexuals have only recently come to be seen as a "minority group" in relation to dominant American society. Since the 1970s, Christian fundamentalists have come to define them as the major adversaries of a redeemed America. Gay males can be seen as "disordered" persons who have failed to mature or to develop a normative heterosexuality. As such, the Christian fundamentalist might look on them as people on whom to exercise compassion, extending to them the possibility of conversion from immature homosexuality to mature heterosexuality. But if they persist in their errors and even seek to legitimize them through legal rights, they become demonic aliens, "perverts" whose very existence threatens our children and society. Although American Christian fundamentalists have not recommended extermination for gays, this did happen in Nazi Germany. No romantic or idealized myth seems to have emerged among Christian fundamentalists toward gay (males), although others sometimes stereotype them as uniquely "feminine," sensitive, and artistic.

The corrective to these myths of the "other" cannot be an idealization or romanticization, which generally functions only to co-opt the other into subservience to the power of the dominant group, but rather a genuine friendship that accepts both difference and fellow humanity between men and women, people of different sexual orientations, and different religions and ethnicities. This means recognizing that as individuals and as members of groups, humans are complex, capable of the whole range of human gifts and weaknesses. There is no group qua group that is uniquely evil or capable only of somatic activities, nor is there any group that is totally innocent and good. We need to recognize that these binaries divide each of our hearts and cultures; they do not separate one group from another.

However, cultural maturation toward genuine acceptance of both difference and fellow humanness between ourselves and others continues to be very difficult not only for white Western males but indeed for all human groups as well. We often see what seems to be the defeat of one kind of prejudice, only to witness a backlash that revives this or some other prejudice in a new form. Thus, sexism continues to be revived in new forms, while anti-Semitic prejudice takes new forms in Europe and the United States as anti-Islamic and anti-Arab hostility.

NOTES

1. Some nineteenth- and twentieth-century feminist writings wrongly claimed that the ancient Near East and Egypt were egalitarian or matriarchal societies and that Judaism was responsible for the development of patriarchy. See Rosemary Ruether, *Goddesses and the Divine Feminine: A Western Religious History* (Berkeley: University of California Press, 2005), 267–71, 274–80.

2. An incorrect idea found in some Christian feminism is to contrast an egalitarian, prowoman view as distinctive of Christianity with what is presumed to be a monolithic patriarchy of Judaism. In fact, insofar as there was some challenge to patriarchy in early Christianity, it seems to have reflected some questioning of these patterns in some contemporary Jewish thinkers and movements. For example, the Therapuetae movement in Hellenistic Judaism featured a double monastery with men and women each having their own communities who studied during the week and worshipped together on the Sabbath. They also rejected slavery. See Philo, *On the Therapeutae*, in *The Essential Philo*, trans. and ed. Natum N. Glaser (New York: Schocken Books, 1971), 311–30.

3. See Ruether, *Goddesses and the Divine Feminine*, 23–24, 30–40.

4. Ruether, *Goddesses and the Divine Feminine*, 40; see also Dennis MacDonald, *The Legend and the Apostle: The Battle for Paul in Story and Canon* (Philadelphia: Westminster, 1983).

5. Augustine, *de Trinitate* 7.7.10

6. See Thomas Aquinas, *Summa Theologica* 1.92.1, ad. 1, and 1.99.2, ad. 2; for a full discussion of Aquinas's view of gender, see Kari Borresen, *Subordination and Equivalence:*

The Nature and Role of Woman in Augustine and Thomas Aquinas (Washington, D.C.: University Press of America, 1981), 141–334.

7. For views of gender in Luther and Calvin, see Rosemary Ruether, *Women and Redemption: A Theological History* (Minneapolis: Fortress, 1998), 117–26.

8. The leading witch-hunting manual by two Dominicans is the *Malleus Maleficarum* (1486). For a standard Puritan view, see William Perkins, *The Damned Art of Witchcraft* (1596). For primary documents on witch persecution in Europe, see Alan C. Kors and Edward Peters, eds., *Witchcraft in Europe, 1100–1700: A Documentary History* (Philadelphia: University of Pennsylvania Press, 1972).

9. Plato, *Republic* 5:455.

10. Plato, *Timaeus* 42.

11. Aristotle, *Generation of Animals* 738b, 737b.

12. Aristotle, *Politics* 1254a–b.

13. See especially G. J. Barker-Benfield, *The Horrors of the Half-Known Life: Male Attitudes toward Women and Sexuality in Nineteenth Century America* (New York: Harper, 1976), esp. 53–54.

14. See Sigmund Freud, "Some Psychological Consequences of the Anatomical Distinctions between the Sexes" (1925) and "Femininity" (1931) in *Standard Edition of the Complete Psychological Works of Sigmund Freud* (London: Hogath Press, 1961), vols. 19 and 22. For a summary of Freud's and also Jung's views of femaleness, see Rosemary Ruether, *New Woman, New Earth* (Boston: Beacon Press, 1995), 137–61.

15. Lev. 25:47–49; see also the word *ga-al* in "Redeem, Redeemer, Redemption," in *The Interpreter's Dictionary of the Bible*, vol. 4, ed. George Arthur Buttrick (Nashville: Abingdon Press, 1962), 21–22.

16. See especially Augustine, *The City of God* 19:14–16; see also Peter Garnsey, *Ideas of Slavery from Aristotle to Augustine* (Cambridge: Cambridge University Press, 1996), 206–19.

17. Garnsey, *Ideas of Slavery from Aristotle to Augustine*, 107–27.

18. Lewis Hanke, *Aristotle and the American Indians: A Study of Race Prejudice in the Modern World* (Chicago: H. Regnery Press, 1959).

19. Garnsey, *Ideas of Slavery from Aristotle to Augustine*, 128–52.

20. Frederick Ross, *Slavery Ordained of God* (1857), and George Armstrong, *The Christian Doctrine of Slavery* (1857).

21. See Rosemary Ruether, *America, Amerikkka: Elect Nation and Imperial Violence* (London: Equinox Press, 2007).

• 8 •

Political-Economic Ideologies: Liberalism, Socialism, and Fascism

The period from the Renaissance and Reformation in the fifteenth to sixteenth centuries through the Enlightenment in the eighteenth century was a time of gradual transformation of the economic, political, and social basis of European life and with it a transformation of worldview. The monopoly of established churches was in the process of being broken and with it the belief in the inferiority of the material and historical world in preference to the eternal world of life after death. The pessimistic belief that history was on a downward track leading to a more or less imminent apocalyptic end was changed to a more optimistic belief in ongoing progress toward an ever-improved society. Where apocalyptic habits of thought continued, they became revolutionary, aimed not at an end of this material world but at its radical transformation into a better world on earth.[1]

What counted as truth also changed. In the medieval and even Reformation worlds, trustworthy truth was disclosed through revelation from God that transcended the knowledge available through nature and human reason. These were seen as flawed by finitude and human sin. By contrast, the growth of science, based on empirical observation expressed through mathematical formulas, was now seen as providing universally reliable knowledge about the physical world. Revelation, by contrast, came to be discounted as superstitious—culturally and historically questionable. A new confidence in both the progressive improvement of knowledge through science and its application to technology to gradually overcome ignorance and misery and create a more prosperous world began to dawn in the Western consciousness.

At the same time, there was increasingly critical attack on the failures of established society and the widening gap between those profiting from new knowledge, trade, and technology and the impoverished masses. Tensions between hope and frustration spawned social movements and countermovements and, with these, ideological systems of critique of society and proposals for change. In this chapter, I summarize three basic ideological trends that have shaped nineteenth- and twentieth-century worldviews in the West: liberalism, socialism, and fascism.

LIBERALISM

The word "liberal" is rooted in the Latin word *liberalis*, meaning "pertaining to freedom." Thus, the word "liberal" points to liberty or freedom as a key value of the "modern" world. But these words, "liberty" and "freedom," raise the basic question: "free from what" and "free for what?" The variety of meanings of the word "liberalism" reflects the various answers to this question and also the contexts in which the question is asked. In this chapter, I summarize three different contexts in which the value of "freedom," or "liberty," is asserted: personal intellectual and cultural freedom, political freedom, and economic freedom or the "free market." I then discuss social welfare liberalism, which sanctions government interference to create equality of opportunity, and neoliberalism, which defends strict market freedom. What is meant by "freedom" takes on very different meanings depending on these different contexts.

Intellectual and cultural freedom has to do with freedom of thought and belief and freedom to communicate such beliefs to others. This includes freedom of the press, the right to assemble, and the right to petition the government for redress of grievances. These are the rights guaranteed by the First Amendment to the U.S. Constitution. A classic treatment of freedom of thought and individual lifestyle is John Stuart Mill's *On Liberty* (1859). In this treatise, Mill defends freedom of thought and communication of ideas as the best guarantee of increasing approximation of truth through the free marketplace of ideas. For Mill, any form of censorship assumes that the censor is in possession of infallible knowledge. But no human is in possession of infallible knowledge. Our knowledge, for Mill, is always fallible and partial. So the best guarantee of fuller truth is for all ideas to be open to discussion, without coercion in favor of any one viewpoint. This is the underlying assumption of what is called "academic freedom," or freedom to express differing opinions in an educational setting.

Mill, however, sees limits on who is capable of such intellectual freedom. It is reserved for adults, not for children, who are in a stage of dependency. It also is reserved for "advanced" societies, that is, Western Europeans. People in "backward states," that is, non-Europeans, he believes, are best ruled by benevolent despots. "Despotism is a legitimate mode of government in dealing with barbarians, provided the end be their improvement."[2] Mill does not develop this point. Presumably, such backwardness can be overcome through Western-style development, and then such "backward people" will become capable of freedom of the individual.

For Mill, freedom also includes freedom of action—freedom to choose different styles of life and not to be coerced into one way of living. For Mill, the only restraint on individual freedom to think and act should be that which harms others. "In the part which merely concerns himself, his independence is, of right, absolute. Over himself, over his own body and mind, the individual is sovereign."[3] It is here that critics have seen the Achilles' heel of Mill's concept of the sovereignty of the individual. Is there such a thing as an isolated individual whose thoughts and actions can have no harmful effect on others? If a man chooses to become a drunkard or to waste his money, has he no others with whom he is in relationship who are harmed by his actions? Clearly, the effort to translate into law the concept of the liberty of the individual as sovereign over his own thoughts and actions in a private sphere, protected against all interference from society, will run into continual debate about where this sovereignty ends and harm to others begins.[4]

Political liberalism seeks to guarantee basic civil liberties and the equality of all citizens before the law. It assumes the idea that governments are established through the "consent of the governed" and thus that all adult citizens have a right to vote and to participate in government. Who these adult citizens are has changed since the eighteenth century. The American Constitution assumed that these were white propertied males. Women, propertyless men, Indians, and slaves were excluded. In the subsequent two centuries, propertyless white men, blacks, and women came to be included in voting rights, although it took until 1965 to vindicate full voting rights for blacks.

The right to be protected from unjust government intrusion into one's property and person are major concerns of political liberalism. Some of these rights are enumerated in subsequent amendments in the Bill of Rights of the U.S. Constitution. These include the right of citizens to bear arms, to be protected against unreasonable search and seizures, not to be tried for the same crime twice (double jeopardy), not to be forced to witness against oneself, not to have one's property taken by the state without due compensation, the right to a speedy trial before an impartial jury in the area where the crime was committed, to be informed of the accusations and be able to confront the witnesses against oneself, to have access to a counsel for the defense, and to be protected against excessive bail and cruel and unusual punishment. Classical liberalism focuses on "negative liberty" or limited government; that is, government is restricted to certain public functions and prevented from interfering in private life.

Economic liberalism focuses on the free market, that is, the removal of any legal barriers to trade and the prevention of any government-imposed economic privileges for protected national industries, such as tariffs, subsidies, and monopolies. Economic liberalism believes that the market governs itself in the optimum way if it is left alone (laissez-faire) without government regulation of any kind. The classical theorist of this view is Adam Smith, found in his writings, such as the *Wealth of Nations* (1776). Smith expounded the theory of the "invisible hand" of the market, which regulates through its own mechanisms of supply and demand the appropriate levels of production, distribution of goods, employment of workers, wages, and prices. Government regulation of prices, wages, or protection of particular industries simply distorts these self-regulating processes of the free market.[5]

Smith was writing in the context of a primarily national market with small businesses and producers. It is questionable whether this same mechanism of self-regulation works in the context of large multinational corporations that are able to monopolize access to goods, markets, prices, and wages and drive small industries out of business. Today the defense of the "free market" functions mostly as an ideology that masks the global monopolizing powers of huge multinational corporations.[6]

There was rapid industrialization in the United States in the 1870s. Railroads, electricity, cars, and petroleum began to transform daily life. Huge fortunes were made by the few, while the vast majority labored under oppressive conditions for a pittance. A few hundred men had fortunes of over $1 million, while more than 80 percent of American workers made less than $500 a year. Farmers saw a sharp decline in commodity prices and were in chronic debt to railroads and food distributors.

The last decades of the nineteenth century saw a sharp bifurcation of social theories about what to do in this situation. Social progressives adopted the view that local, state, and federal government should adopt policies that ameliorated the injustice created by the raw pursuit of profits by the rich at the expense of workers. Such measures as minimum wages, protection of women workers, elimination of child labor, unemployment insurance, old-age pensions, government-sponsored health insurance, and the rights of workers to organize and bargain collectively would protect workers from the ravages of unfettered capitalism and satisfy for all citizens the needs of daily life. Human rights came to be defined not simply as negative rights (i.e., the protection of private freedoms from government interference) but as positive rights (i.e., the right to adequate food, housing, education, and health), with government as a major actor in ensuring these positive rights.

Over against these social progressives stood libertarian social Darwinists who argued for a radical version of free market economics and rejected any role of government in social amelioration. The leading theorist of social Darwinism was Herbert Spencer, who in the 1860s–1890s synthesized classical liberalism with the Lamarkian idea of the inheritance of acquired characteristics and Malthusian pessimism about the tendency of the poor to proliferate offspring. Spencer argued that the poor should not be helped by the state; rather, the unfettered workings of the free market would cause those who cannot make it to die off, thus ensuring the "survival of the fittest."

For social Darwinists, no social services or even charity should be given to people who have not earned these services by their own hard work. Such help only allows the unfit to survive and to pass down their feckless characteristics to their children. Thus, Spencerians opposed public schools, public libraries, public sanitation, public health, and even publicly financed postal systems. One should not be able to read books, go to school, have medical services, eat, be clothed, or have a roof over one's head if one cannot fully pay for these goods by one's own hard work. The role of the state is purely negative. It should do nothing that interfered with the laws of competition. Its job was to maintain unfettered market freedom to allow these laws of competition to play out freely and without interference.[7]

Such views were popular with American business leaders. Industrialist Andrew Carnegie was an enthusiastic follower of social Darwinism and a personal friend of Spencer. Through the first two decades of the twentieth century, these two views, progressivism and libertarianism, vied with each other for American allegiance. Although the United States had early adopted such public services as public schools and postal services, other ways of protecting workers or allowing them to organize against owners were violently resisted by American wealthy industrialists, backed by government troops. In the 1920s, American capitalism seemed to be permanently expanding, ensuring a comfortable life for all industrious citizens. The signs of vulnerability in this system—the huge gap between the few millionaires and the millions living on poverty wages or unemployed—were ignored. Much of the ostensible prosperity of the middle class was purchased through unsustainable loans and installment buying.

In 1929, this house of cards of American wealth came tumbling down. Fourteen million became unemployed, and the American national income contracted by more than 50 percent (from $87 billion in 1930 to $39 billion in 1933). Cycles of boom and bust, expansion, and depression were familiar in the previous half century of the American economy, but it was assumed that these cycles were self-correcting. But the Great Depression was the first time that such a "bust" seemed to have become "stuck," even getting worse, without a new stage of investment and expanded employment through market forces.[8]

Franklin Delano Roosevelt, the new president elected in 1932, called for emergency powers and began to make a large number of interventions in the U.S. economy. These included the use of public funds for public works, such as the building of dams and schools, as well as forest conservation and the promotion of the arts, providing new jobs for the unemployed. He expanded the federal government regulation of business by excess profit and progressive income taxes. Some of the protective legislation that social progressives had promoted for many years was passed, such as the Fair Labor Standards Act of 1938, which set minimum wages and maximum hours for workers and banned child labor under the age of sixteen. The Social Security Act of 1935 provided unemployment insurance, old-age pensions, and stipends for the handicapped and disabled and for impoverished dependent children.

These government interventions in the "free market" were fiercely resisted by social and economic conservatives, who continually accused the Roosevelt administration of "socialism."[9] But Roosevelt's New Deal found support in the revised theories of British economist John Maynard Keynes. According to Keynes the capitalist system is not fully self-correcting. If savings exceed new investment, leading to a fall in the economy and widespread unemployment, this will not automatically right itself if lack of money due to lack of jobs prevents people from buying expanded production. When this happens, a depression can become "stuck," with no incentive for businesses to invest to expand production. Thus, government investment in public works is necessary to put new investment and income into the economy to "prime the pump" for expanded business investment. Keynes developed a new economic theory that government regulation through public investment, manipulation of interest rates, and the selling of government bonds to create forced savings are necessary to manage the swings of the economy and prevent extremes of boom and bust. The Keynesian theory of government-managed capitalism became generally accepted in American public policy in the 1940s–1970s.[10]

But in the late 1970s and 1980s, there developed a widespread rejection of Keynesian economics and the welfare state under President Ronald Reagan in the United States and Prime Minister Margaret Thatcher in Britain. Several economic theorists, such as Friedrich Hayek,[11] argued that any government intervention in the economy was the high road to totalitarianism. Only a return to classical economic liberalism could restore the basis of a free society. A new generation of neoliberal economists came to power in the United States and Britain who argued for lessening government intervention in the market in favor of unfettered property rights of business.

In foreign policy, neoliberals use economic pressure (and, in some cases, military intervention) to dismantle welfare states, repealing legislation that supports wage and price controls and food, transportation, educational, or other subsidies for the poor. It seeks to undo any "restraints to trade" through tariff barriers or restrictions on investment to create a "level playing field" for international investors. Such neoliberal policies have come to dominate both American government policy and those of international banking under organizations such as the World Bank, the International Monetary Fund, and the World Trade Organization.[12]

These variations between types of liberalism set neoliberals (called neoconservatives in the United States) in deep conflict with traditions of welfare liberalism developed in the 1930s–1960s. It gives the term "liberalism" itself a contradictory profile in the United States. The term "liberalism" has come to define a whole spectrum of social and economic views from "left" to "right," including many variations in the "middle."

SOCIALISM

In contrast to liberalism, socialism believes that the free market and private property in a capitalist society favor the large owners of the means of production and impoverish workers. Capitalists make profits by lowering wages of workers as much as possible in order to create as large a profit margin as possible between the costs of production and the sale of products on the market. Low wages, extended hours of labor, poor working conditions, and failure to provide health care or pensions for workers are all ways of expanding profits, which is the "bottom line" in a capitalist economy.

This is why Marxist thought sees a built-in "class struggle" in capitalism.[13] The interests of the workers to make a living wage is in conflict with the interests of the owning class, which is to make as large a profit as possible by paying workers as little as possible and investing as little as possible in social services and environmental protection. Thus, to ameliorate the condition of workers through higher wages, protection in the workplace, and social benefits, it is necessary to intervene in the control of productive property. The property at issue here is not that of personal property (consumer goods, ownership of private cars and houses, and so on) but private ownership of the means of production (factories, mines, railroads, and oil and electrical companies).

The socialist tradition has been split on different ways of controlling economically productive property in order to ameliorate the condition of workers. Early socialism in the nineteenth century envisioned primarily some kind of collective ownership of property at the local level of communities of workers. Factories would be owned and managed by workers, thus eliminating the dichotomy between owners and workers. Communal ownership and management would mean that profits would be more fairly divided among all the workers.

The ideas of utopian socialism that prevailed in the first half of the nineteenth century, such as those of Robert Owen in England[14] and Charles Fourier in France,[15] envisioned complete self-sustaining communities where housing, land, productive enterprises, and social institutions, such as schools, would be owned collectively by the community, who would manage community life together to give equal benefits to all. Such utopian socialists often included a feminist dimension in their thought. Overcoming the dichotomy between private life, where women did the child care and housework, and productive paid labor, communal living would collectivize housework and child raising and allow women to participate equally in all aspects of community life.[16]

The kibbutz in early Israeli society is perhaps the most successful expression of this concept of a communal socialist society.[17] Another form of Israeli group production is the *Moshave*, which allows separate family ownership within a shared enterprise. A still more modest form of communal socialism is the producer collective in which individual producers exchange goods in a shared market. All these forms of communal socialism keep ownership and control on the local level with a high degree of direct participatory democracy.

In the mid-nineteenth century, the figures of Karl Marx and Friedrich Engels transformed socialism into an organized movement of workers engaged in revolutionary struggle to overthrow the capitalist control of private property and of the state. Marx and Engels scorned the earlier communal socialists whom they dubbed "utopian socialists" because they envisioned small socialist societies that reorganized ownership within the larger capitalist society, hoping that capitalism would "fade away" as such communal groups expanded. Marx and Engels favored a revolutionary process that would transform the entire economic system and state. Marxism envisioned a two-stage process of transforming society: a transitional stage in which the workers' party takes over the state (the state collectivizing productive property and reorganizing it to favor workers, abolishing the capitalist class), followed by communism, in which the state would "wither away."[18]

Unfortunately, Marx and Engels concentrated all their attention on the critique of the present capitalist system, with vague references to how socialism would be built by the worker-controlled state, leading to the final apex of human history, communism. In practice, this meant that when communist parties took over control of the state in societies, such as Russia in 1917, where there had been little development of industry, the stage of "building socialism" through state ownership of production came to be the actual meaning of "communism," with the "withering away" of the state indefinitely postponed to the future. Thus, the communist economic system became de facto the state-owned command economy managed by the Communist Party as a new ruling class[19] that brings together economic, political, educational, military, and police control of society, limiting the sphere of individual civil rights and political freedom.

However, prior to this development of state communism (or what some would call "state capitalism"), the socialist movement in Europe itself had evolved and split into different perspectives. In the late nineteenth century, socialism came to be organized primarily within each nation, focused on trade unions and political parties that mobilized working-class voters. By winning seats in parliaments, socialists gradually gave up a vision of a once-and-for-all revolutionary transformation of the whole economic system in favor of various kinds of reforms that protected workers' rights to unionize and to bargain collectively with owners. Taxation would provide health, education, and old-age pensions from the state.

Moderate socialists, such as Edward Bernstein,[20] rejected the goal of revolution for a gradual process of social reform through political democracy. In this process, social liberals, such as those found in the United States in the Progressive movement and the New Deal, and the social democrats within moderate socialism met and mingled. The welfare state, which began to be built in Europe and the United States in the 1930s and more fully in Europe after World War II, represents a synthesis of social liberalism and moderate democratic socialism, although this fact has been obscured by the phobia, particularly in the United States, of acknowledging the legitimacy of any element of socialism. In the welfare state, political and personal freedoms are preserved, but the free market and the unlimited control of productive property are attenuated to meet the social needs of all members of the society through such means as state-funded health care, child care, schools, unemployment insurance, and old-age pensions.

After the victory of communism in Russia in 1917, communists and socialists split, forming separate international organizations. Communists were identified with a revolutionary overthrow of the capitalist state, followed by total state ownership and management of the economy to control production, prices, and marketing. Socialists, by contrast, identify with democratic welfare states in which there is a preference for public ownership of basic utilities, but private ownership of the means of production is mostly preserved, subject to limitations to promote the common good, mainly through taxes and state regulation. Such democratic socialist welfare states were successful in much of Western Europe in the 1960s and 1970s but were challenged by rising neo-liberalism in the 1980s.

With the new independence of many countries in Asia and Africa, as well as rising criticism of injustice in Latin America, socialism became popular in many Third World countries. Some countries, such as China, followed the communist path of a revolutionary overthrow of the former social and political system, state takeover of both industrial and agricultural production, and total centralization of control in a Communist Party bureaucracy.[21] Vietnam, North Korea, and Cuba also followed the communist path. Other Third World countries, such as India, preferred to retain a democratic political system combined with socialist controls on the economy. Many socialists became highly critical of the communist system, which repressed political and individual liberties in favor of state control of all aspects of life. This was seen as a sellout of the original liberating vision of socialism for totalitarianism despite the supposed commitment to "workers' ownership" of the means of production and an economically egalitarian society.

Some Third World revolutionaries sought an alterative path to socialism. In Nicaragua, one such alternative was the Sandinista Revolution of 1979, which overthrew the oppressive dictatorship of the Somoza family that had monopolized much of the wealth of the country in the hands of the ruling family and governed by violent repression of dissent through the National Guard. This dictatorship had been both installed and supported by the United States for more than forty years.

The Sandinista vision was that of a "mixed economy": one-third state-owned production (particularly the railroads and public utilities), one-third private property, and one-third worker-owned and -managed cooperatives (particularly in agriculture).[22] The Sandinistas were committed to a democratic political process and wrote a new constitution safeguarding free and fair elections. The Sandinistas intentionally affiliated with the Western European Socialist International and not with the Communist International dominated by the Soviet Union.

But the United States made no distinction between communist states, such as China, Korea, Vietnam, and North Korea, and mixed economies, such as the one proposed by the Nicaraguan Sandinistas. It dubbed all of them "communists," enemies of freedom, and portrayed them as threats to an American democratic "way of life" identified with the free market. The United States waged major wars in Korea and Vietnam to "stop communism" in those countries. It exerted endless pressure through an embargo as well as an aborted invasion to undermine the communist regime in Cuba.

The United States failed to overthrow these governments, although it succeeded in distorting these regimes in favor of more repressive systems than might have been the case if they had been allowed to develop freely, with good relations with Western societies. It succeeded in causing the Sandinistas to lose the presidency in 1991, although the Sandinista Party remained powerful in the state legislature. In 2006, Daniel Ortega won the election to the presidency again, although it is a question whether the Sandinistas under his leadership continue to represent a progressive option for the Nicaraguan people.[23]

With the collapse of the Soviet Union in 1990 and the breakup of its constituent parts into separate nation-states, it appeared that any idea of a socialist alternative to capitalism had been thrown into the waste bin of history. The neoliberal concept of the free market, together with electoral "choice" between parties controlled by elites, had triumphed. This was declared to be the "end of history,"[24] free market capitalism having proved itself to be the only option for human society to which "there is no alternative." But many Latin American societies have become disillusioned with the effects of neoliberal global economics that have produced increasing gaps between the few very rich and the impoverished majority of the people, the eroding of any social services, and the neglect of the environment.

In the first eight years of the twenty-first century, a number of Latin American countries have elected new leaders from the "left" who seek to combine political democracy with economic protections from the ravages of the global "free market." Several of these, such as Venezuela's Hugo Chavez and Bolivia's Evo Morales, call themselves socialists, while Brazil's president, Lula da Silva, of the Workers' Party, identifies with a moderate social democracy. It remains to be seen whether some kind of social democratic mixed economy may yet emerge in Latin America as an alternative to the "free market" system championed by the United States.

FASCISM

It may seem strange to list fascism as a third major sociopolitical ideology of the twentieth century side by side with the two major competing ideologies of liberalism and socialism. But fascism should be mentioned and defined in order to make clear the ways in which it relates to and opposes both liberalism and socialism. The term "fascism" was first coined for the movement under Benito Mussolini that ruled Italy from 1922 to 1943. Here the term refers to a corporatist concept of the state as the organic expression of the nation as one. Here fascism opposed liberal individualism as well as Marxist class struggle. In the words of Mussolini's definition of fascism in his *Political and Social Doctrine of Fascism*, "The fascist concept of the state is all-embracing, outside of it no human or spiritual values can exist, much less have value. Thus understood fascism . . . interprets, develops, and potentiates the whole life of a people."[25] Thus, fascism exalts the idea of a unitary "national will," often identifying this with a charismatic leader as the embodiment of the national will.

Those with fascist views generally seek to dissolve the autonomy of any groups representing different sectors of the society, whether labor unions, student unions, different political parties, or peasant organizations. All differentiation must be dissolved under the corporate state embodying the whole nation. Fascism typically exalts war as revivifying the national will and so also prizes a militarist concept of masculinity against "softness," associated with femininity and homosexuality. Dissent against this corporate unity defined by the fascist nation-state is severely repressed by internal policy surveillance and imprisonment. Thus, fascism develops into the totalitarian police state.

Although only the Italian nationalist movement of the 1920s–1940s used the term "fascism" for itself, the term is often used more generically for various authoritarian and militarist movements of the period, particularly Nazism in Germany. "Fascism" was also used to describe the Phalange under Francisco Franco, who ruled Spain from 1939 to 1975, after a bloody civil war that defeated a leftist popular front government elected in 1936 and the *Estado Novo* of Antonio Salazar, who ruled Portugal from 1926 into the 1970s. In Nazism, the notion of organic nationalism became explicitly racist as it sought to expand its rule of Germany across Eastern and Western Europe on behalf of a supposedly Germanic or Aryan "race" and to either eliminate or subordinate as slave labor all "inferior races," Jews, Gypsies, Slavs, dissenting and "deviant" groups, communists, homosexuals, and the infirm.

The mass murders carried out by Nazism to engineer its dream of racial domination so horrified the world that no movement after 1945 has used the term "fascist" to identify itself. Thus, the term in more recent years has been used primarily as a slur against a regime that one opposes and accuses of seeking to establish a police state rather than a name that any movement uses for itself. This raises the question of the legitimacy of using the term for political opponents. In my view, it is possible to determine a number of characteristics of fascist types of political movements and to use the terms "fascist" or "tending toward fascism" for a regime that is characterized by most of these tendencies.

Central to this tendency is the idea of the corporate nation-state as a mystical unity to which must be subordinated any independent political organizations that represent divisions within the society. All such autonomous groups representing different social sectors are banned. Police repression is used against dissenting movements, labor and peasant unions, student unions, and human rights organizations, usually with the use of the police and army to arrest, torture, and kill dissenting leaders in a manner designed to terrorize other dissenters. Such regimes often come into power as a reaction against what is perceived to be a threat of a "takeover" by communist or socialist movements representing workers or peasants and so tend to represent the interest of large-business men and landowners who ally themselves with a military dictatorship to suppress what are seen as threats to their hegemony on wealth and power.

The national security states that came into power in Latin America, often with the covert or overt support of the United States, in Brazil (1964–1985), Argentina (1976–1983), Uruguay (1973–1985), Bolivia (1967–1982), Guatemala (1954–1996), and Chile (1973–1990) had these characteristics. Some U.S. critics of American policies during the Cold War and during the George W. Bush's administration's "war of terrorism" have claimed that the United States is becoming "fascist" not only because of its support of such national security states in other countries but also because of increasing reliance on police surveillance of those defined as "communists" or as "terrorists" within the United States. The curtailment of civil liberties found in the Patriot Act[26] in response to the terrorist attack on the World Trade buildings in New York and the Pentagon on September 11, 2001; domestic spying without warrants; the denial of habeas corpus to those defined as "enemy combatants; and the use of torture and "extraordinary rendition"[27] (the seizure of terrorist suspects to send them to foreign countries where they are tortured for information) are all seen as a slide within the U.S. government toward fascism.[28]

Clearly, the United States is far from taking on the full-blown characteristics of a corporate police state in which freedom of speech, assembly, and organization of dissenting movements is repressed. But critics are right to question these tendencies toward erosion of civil liberties, although the use of the term "fascist" probably throws more heat than light on what is going on.

Fascism is both antiliberal and antisocialist, yet it is important to see how both liberalism and socialism can, at times, make use of the totalitarian police state. When the free market and the rights of large corporate wealth by big business are exalted over all other values to demonize any aspect of socialism, free market liberals can come to prefer repression of civil and political liberties through a police state in order to defeat their leftist enemies. This is what happened with Latin American national security states.

However, when communism comes to power and identifies itself with the nationalization of all productive property and the regimentation of society around its goals, then communist states become totalitarian, as happened with Stalinism in the Soviet Union and the Maoist revolution in China. Thus, one can speak of a totalitarianism of the right (favoring big business) and a totalitarianism of the left (favoring control of the economy by the ruling Communist Party).

Although no one formula fits all societies, since each have their own cultures and histories, probably a mix of liberalism and socialism (or democratic socialism) represents the formula most likely to produce more equal sharing of social and economic benefits by all in the society, preserving political and civil freedoms while limiting the ability of big business to exploit workers and ravage the environment. The mistake of the Cold War was setting socialism and capitalism against each other as unalterably opposed, each demonizing the other, rather than seeking the optimal mixture of the two through forms of the welfare state and the mixed economy, which includes a lively sector of worker-owned and -managed cooperatives.

NOTES

1. See Rosemary Ruether, *The Radical Kingdom: The Western Experience of Messianic Hope* (New York: Paulist Press, 1970).
2. John Stuart Mill, *On Liberty* (New York: Bobbs-Merrill, 1956), 14.
3. Mill, *On Liberty*, 13.
4. See John Gray, *Liberalism*, 2nd ed. (Minneapolis: University of Minnesota Press, 1995), 51.
5. For an accessible account of Smith's thought, see Robert L. Heilbroner, *The Worldly Philosophers: The Lives, Times and Ideas of the Great Economic Thinkers*, 7th ed. (New York: Simon and Schuster, 1999), 42–74.
6. See David C. Korten, *When Corporations Rule the World* (San Francisco: Berrett-Koehler, 1995), 66–67.
7. Herbert Spencer's major writings are *First Principles* (1864; reprint, London: William and Norgate, 1884), *Man versus State* (London: William and Norgate, 1884), *Principles of Sociology*, 3 vols. (New York: D. Appleton and Co., 1899–1900), and *The Principles of Ethics*, 2 vols. (New York: D. Appleton and Co., 1892–1893). For an account of Spencer's influence in the United States, see Richard Hofstadter, *Social Darwinism in American Thought* (New York: George Braziller, 1959).
8. For a brief account of this period, see Heilbroner, *The Worldly Philosophers*, 248–52.
9. For the resistance to and red-baiting of the New Deal, see Blanche Wiesen Cook, *Eleanor Roosevelt, 1933–1938* (New York: Penguin, 1999), 497–99.
10. For Keynes's major works, see *The General Theory of Employment, Interest and Money* (New York: Harcourt Brace, 1936); see also Heilbroner, *The Worldly Philosophers*, 252–87.
11. See Friedrich Hayek, *The Road to Serfdom* (Chicago: University of Chicago Press, 1949).
12. Critiques of the World Bank and neoliberal economics abound. See, e.g., Kevin Danahern, *Fifty Years Is Enough: The Case against the World Bank and the International Monetary Fund* (Cambridge, Mass.: South End Press, 1994).

13. For a brief account of Marx's key ideas, see Rosemary Ruether, "Marx: The Secular Apocalypse," in *The Radical Kingdom*, 92–109.

14. See Donald E. Pitzer, "The New Moral World of Robert Owen and New Harmony," in *America's Communal Utopias* (Chapel Hill: University of North Carolina Press, 1997), 88–134.

15. On Fourier's utopian socialism and its expression in the United States, see Carl J. Guarneri, "Brook Farm and Fourierist Phalanxes," in Pitzer, *America's Communal Utopias*, 159–80.

16. On the role of feminism in English utopian socialism, see Barbara Taylor, *Eve and the New Jerusalem: Socialism and Feminism in the Nineteenth Century* (New York: Pantheon, 1983).

17. On the Zionist vision of utopian socialism, see Martin Buber, *Paths in Utopia* (Boston: Beacon Press, 1958).

18. This vision of the "withering away of the state" is described in Friedrich Engels, *Socialism: Utopian and Scientific* (1882; reprint, New York: International Publishers, 1935), 70, 72–73.

19. See Milovan Djilas, *The New Class: An Analysis of the Communist System* (New York: Praeger, 1957).

20. See Eduard Bernstein, *Evolutionary Socialism* (New York: Schocken Books, 1965); see also Henry Tutor and J. M. Tutor, eds., *Marxism and Social Democracy: The Revisionist Debate, 1896–8* (New York: Cambridge University Press, 1988).

21. See Adan Chan, *Chinese Marxism* (New York: Continuum, 2003).

22. See Geske Dijkstra, *Industrialization in Sandinista Nicaragua: Policy and Practice in a Mixed Economy* (Boulder, Colo.: Westview Press, 1992).

23. See Monica Baltidano, "Nicaragua from Sandinismo to Danielismo," *International Socialist Review*, November–December 2006, 31–35.

24. See Francis Fukuyama, *The End of History and the Last Man* (New York: Free Press, 1992).

25. Quoted in "Fascism," *Wikipedia, the Free Encyclopedia*, http://en.wikipedia.org/wiki/Fascism, 4.

26. For the text of the Patriot Act, See H.R. 3162, 107th Congress, October 24, 2001.

27. See Stephen Gray, *Ghost Plane: The True Story of the CIA Torture Program* (New York: St. Martin's Press, 2006).

28. See particularly the writings of Noam Chomsky, such as *Deterring Democracy* (New York: Verso Press, 1991) and *Hegemony or Survival: America's Quest for Global Dominance* (New York: Metropolitan Books, 2003). Richard Falk also uses the term "fascism" for the tendencies of the U.S. global empire in his *Declining World Order: America's Imperial Geopolitics* (New York: Routledge, 2004).

· 9 ·

Economic Class in the United States

The idea of economic or social class in the United States is generally seen as disturbing. The very term "class" used in public speech is regarded as "un-American," as the importation of an alien Marxist mind-set foreign to American culture. This hostility to the idea of class is a legacy of the American egalitarian tradition that claimed to have abolished class rule in the sense of a hereditary European aristocracy. In America, supposedly "all men are equal." When a politician points out that certain policies, such as George W. Bush's tax cuts, favor the rich, he or she is typically denounced as engaging in "class warfare," presumably something off limits in American political discourse. The use of such a term is usually sufficient to cause the politician to fall silent. What the politician does not do is to make the obvious retort: "No, it is you, President Bush, who are engaging in class warfare by promoting legislation that favors the superrich against the vast majority of Americans."

If Americans were asked to define "class," many would be hard put to do so. Most would reply that it is a question of income. Some people make much more money than others. High-paid sports personalities or entertainers may come to mind. But usually there is little sense that the wealthy form an organized group with dominating control over government, that is, a ruling class. Many Americans assume that anyone can become wealthy if he or she is "lucky" and "works hard."

In this chapter, I argue not only that there is a very wealthy group in the United States but also that it has organized control over the economy, that it dominates the federal government and the media of communication, and that at least a sector has hereditary characteristics. Moreover, income is secondary to the wealth of this group. For most Americans, income is money received from some institution that one does not own, that hires and pays you, but that also could fire you. Most Americans do not have millions or even hundreds of thousands of dollars in savings or other sources of income from stocks and bonds. Their income is their only source of money. If they are fired and lose their monthly income, unless they quickly find another job, they will shortly become poor. The definition of the truly rich, as distinct from a high-paid sector of the "working class," is that they will not become poor by losing their job. They could even afford to receive no income from a "job."

This means that what differentiates the truly rich from everyone else is ownership of wealth, not merely income. The truly rich as a ruling class own the means of production. They own land and housing from which they receive rent. They own the businesses and corporations or a controlling share of the stocks of such corporations. They have vast investments across the economy, increasingly internationally,[1] and a controlling share of bonds. Closely associated with this owning class are top chief executive officers who manage big businesses and corporate lawyers who defend the legal interests of the owning class. This second group not only is highly paid but also incorporates itself into the owning class through investments, often paid in lucrative stock options worth several times their stated income.

Moreover, this owning class forms an interlocking directorate of major corporations and policymaking institutions of the economy. They sit on one another's boards of directors. They use the same legal, accounting, advertising, and public relations firms. Thus, they form a corporate community.[2] The corporate community also interconnects through industry-wide organizations, such as the American Petroleum Institute, and nationwide business organizations, such as the National Association of Manufacturers, the U.S. Chamber of Commerce, and the Business Roundtable.[3] The largest and wealthiest corporations usually have the most interconnections with other corporations, banks, and other institutions of the corporate community. These corporations are the center of the network of the corporate community. Five giant corporations—General Electric, General Motors, Ford Motor, IBM, and Exxon—control 25 percent of industrial assets, and the top 100 control 75 percent.[4] The corporate community also bonds through a sense of having common enemies in the labor movement, liberal-leftist thinkers, environmentalists, and other anticorporate activists.

It is sometimes believed that other sectors of the economy could organize and provide a counterweight to the corporate elite. Half the stock issued by large corporations belongs to institutional investors: mutual funds, bank trust departments, and various kinds of pension funds. Representatives of union and public employee pension funds have had hopes to use their collective clout to influence corporate policy in ways beneficial to workers and the public. But the enforcement of leadership from the corporate sector over the Council of Institutional Investors reined in the power of activists. Likewise, farmers today no longer form an opposition sector. Most today are controlled by corporate agriculture or agribusiness. Small business (businesses with fewer than 500 employees), although they make 52 percent of the sales and employ 54 percent of the private workforce, lack the financial assets and cohesion to provide a counterweight to large corporations.[5]

The corporate community also extends their control over government and decision making through financing and control of the policy planning network. The corporate elite not only pays for these policy planning institutions but also provides them with crucial free services, such as legal and accounting help. They also serve as directors and trustees of these organizations and take part in their meetings. Some of these policy planning groups are long established, such as the Council on Foreign Relations, established in 1921; the Committee for Economic Development, established in the early 1940s; and the Business Council, created in the early 1930s as a quasi-government advisory group. These groups might be defined as moderate conservative. There are also more ultraconservative groups, such as the Hoover Institute and the American Enterprise Institute.[6]

Foundations set up by corporations and wealthy families of the corporate elite play a key role in financing these policy planning institutions. Foundations also set the direction of public policy by what they choose to finance. Thus, the Ford Foundation provided the financial basis for the War on Poverty in the 1960s by funding minority and community action organizations. In addition to the Ford Foundation, other leading foundations are the Packard Foundation, the Pew Charitable Trust, and the John D. and Catherine T. MacArthur Foundation. These last two have been important funders of environmental organizations, such as the National Resources Defense Council.[7]

The most concentrated work on policy planning is performed by key think tanks. Among the most influential of these are the Brooking Institution, the American Enterprise Institute, the RAND Corporation, and the Heritage Foundation, the last three on the ultraconservative side. Such think tanks are important not only in shaping policy ideas but also in recruiting and training the leaders for government service.[8] Thus, these policy planning organizations are a key part of the interface between business and government.

The corporate elite dominate the federal government in several ways. First, they largely finance the expensive campaigns for president and congressional offices. Generally only a person who is either independently wealthy or receives large funds from the wealthy can run for national office in the United States, although this has been modified recently by the success in using the Internet to generate millions of small contributions. This is also true on the state level, although here local elites play a larger role and national corporations a lesser role. Candidates for city office, depending on the size of the city, also depend on influential backers, although big money plays a lesser role, so such offices are more open to organizing from the grassroots.[9] But we concentrate here on the U.S. national government.

A second major way in which the corporate elite shape the federal government is through government appointees. They provide either from their own members or from those closely associated with them in ideas and relations to power and wealth, such as corporate lawyers, those who manage the executive branch of government (such as the departments of State, Treasury, Defense, and Justice), and Supreme Court nominees. There is little difference here between Democratic and Republican administrations. Both draw their appointees from the recommendations of the corporate elite, although there is some variation between selecting more ultraconservative representatives rather than more moderate conservative representatives between Republican and Democratic administrations. Through controlling who gets elected, who gets appointed to administrations, and who gets on the Supreme Court, the corporate elite gain the legislation and policies that favor their interests.

Three power blocs divide American politics: two directly represent the corporate elite and are insiders to government, and a third consists of outsiders. The insiders are divided between the ultraconservatives who are uniformly hostile to labor, environmental organizations, and other groups favoring limitations of their power and wealth, while a second, moderate conservative group favors some concessions to these groups to prevent polarization and even open warfare between the wealthy class and the vast majority of the society. The moderates are represented by the grants of big foundations to minority, community, and environmental organizations. These two inside blocks negotiate power between them, in some administrations leaning more to the ultraconservative side and in others to the more moderate side.

The third power bloc, consisting of outsiders, are represented particularly by organized labor, together with coalitions of liberal intellectuals, community organizations, and environmental groups. These groups gain some access to government when there is a split in the ruling elites, and they are able to ally with the moderate group and isolate the ultraconservative group.[10] These outsider groups also represent the danger of a voter revolt in which the vast majority of Americans might be mobilized to vote in ways that are critical of how the corporate elites favor the rich against them. Corporate control of elections depends not only on the control of financing by the wealthy but also on keeping the majority of the electorate confused, divided, and passive.

The corporate elite also control the mainline media of communication: newspapers of major cities, newsmagazines, radio, television news, films, and even book publishing. They do so through ownership of these media, which have become ever more concentrated in a few corporate hands, and by shaping the party line that is reflected in these media. This does not mean that there is no "freedom of the press" in the United States, but genuine dissenting opinion is confined mainly to alternative media, newspapers and magazines, and some radio programs and book publishers that command the attention of a small liberal-left intellectual elite but are not known to the majority of Americans. This control of the media has resulted in a remarkable level of control of political culture, eliminating dissenting thought from the mainstream. From the perspective of some European societies where dissenting thought is more mainstream in the print and television media, Americans seem remarkably ignorant about what is happening in the world.

The corporate elite also form a somewhat socially connected and cohesive group and are generally successful in reproducing themselves from generation to generation by getting their children into top schools and from there into high positions. Crucial to this social cohesion and reproduction of the corporate ruling class is a network of elite prep schools. These prep schools have high tuition, and although some may make some space for scholarship students, socially it is difficult for students to function in such schools unless they are socialized as members of the wealthy class. Such schools are essential for guaranteeing that the children of the corporate elite get into the most prestigious universities, such as Yale, Harvard, and Princeton, and from there are placed by family connections in business and political leadership positions.

The corporate ruling class also socializes through elite clubs, charitable activities, and parties, such as debutante balls. Networking instruments, such as the *Social Register*, have been important to identify them with each other, although these social activities may be less important than in the past. But in various ways, the corporate elite know one another and find social as well as economic and political ways to connect with each other.[11]

This means that the corporate elite as a moneyed ruling class also becomes at least partly hereditary. Major wealthy families who got their start particularly in the Gilded Age of the 1880s, such as the Rockefellers, Duponts, Mellons, and Phipps, and some, such as the Astors and Vanderbilts, going back even to the 1830s, have been able to carry on their commanding economic status from generation to generation. In the *Forbes* 400, representing the top fortunes in America, roughly a third inherited their status, although this does not mean that the family trusts do not continue to invest and engage in widespread wealth production today. Indeed, it is precisely because they inherit wealth that they have a running start in reproducing and expanding it.

But the wealthiest corporate owning class is also open to new talent. Each generation of new technology has created new millionaires and today billionaires, although one does not get on the bandwagon of new areas of wealth without some sources of "start-up" money; that is, few who become rich really start from "rags." In the 1910–1920 era, the new technology that brought new wealth was in automobiles, telephones, electricity, radio, and cameras. Since the 1980s, the new wealth has flowed from computer technology. Among the wealthiest today are those, such as Bill Gates, who made their fortune from computers.

A BRIEF HISTORY OF THE AMERICAN WEALTHY

Large divisions between the wealthy and the poor had long separated the settlers of the English colonies of North America. When John Winthrop, the first governor of the Massachusetts Bay Colony, wrote his plan for the "godly commonwealth" aboard the ship *Arbella* en route to New England, he made plain that this was not to be an egalitarian society:

> God Almighty in his most holy and wise providence hath so disposed of the Condition of mankinde, as in all times some must be rich, some poore, some highe and eminent in power and dignitie, others mean and in subjection.[12]

At the time of the American Revolution, the colonies had long been divided between rich merchants and landowners and humble servants, slaves who did not own their own bodies, and the range of middling classes.

For example, in 1776, Philadelphia was ruled by a wealthy merchant class that constituted about 10 percent of the population of the city but controlled more than 50 percent of its wealth. They controlled the trade between Britain, the port of Philadelphia, and the Caribbean. While owning the great trading houses in the city, they lived in elegant rural country estates where they copied the manners of the British aristocracy. Another 50 percent of the city consisted of artisans, from elite craftsmen to humble tradesmen. Together they controlled about 46 percent of the wealth but lacked political power. The remaining 40 percent of the city's population were day laborers, apprentices, indentured servants, and slaves who both were powerless and owned little or nothing.[13] In 1776, a radical group in the city representing the artisan class seized power in Philadelphia and wrote a new state constitution giving the vote to all males over the age of twenty-one who paid taxes. Thus, the middle group was enfranchised but not the poorest 40 percent.

The leaders of the American Revolution who shaped its Constitution consisted of this wealthy elite of planters (such as George Washington and Thomas Jefferson), elite merchants who controlled international trade (such as John Adams), and leading bankers (such as Alexander Hamilton). Many, like Adams, had reservations even about the expansion of democracy represented by the new Pennsylvania state constitution and had no intention of enfranchising white men without property much less women or slaves. They looked askance at the equalitarianism of Tom Paine's *Common Sense*. They preferred a bicameral legislature with a nonelected upper house or senate of the wealthy elite modeled after the House of Lords in England.[14]

The Revolution also saw new fortunes made from the spoils of war. One source of this was the lands of the more than 100,000 loyalists who left the country, much of whose property was confiscated. This eliminated about a third of the 1,000 largest prerevolutionary wealth holders, such as the Penns of Philadelphia and the Calverts of Maryland.[15] Many licensed privateers also operated from American ports, sending some 2,000 ships to capture 3,000 British ships and tow them with their cargo back to American ports, especially the ports of New England. The spoils from this piracy have been valued at $18 million, a huge sum at that time.[16]

The period from 1790 to 1860 saw contradictory trends in American wealth and poverty. On the one hand, this was the greatest period of expansion westward across the continent to California, buying up French lands under the Louisiana Purchase and seizing Indian lands and those of the Mexicans after the independence of Texas (1836) and the Mexican-American War (1846–1848). White men willing to move west had great opportunities to homestead cheap on free land and found new farms and businesses. Thus, this period has been called the era of "the common man," a time of great expansion of equality. On the other hand, new waves of immigrants, especially Germans and Irish, flooded the eastern seaboard. Industrialization began especially in New England, with the development of textile factories that employed women and children for long hours at low wages. Great inequality existed in eastern cities. In New York, the top 1 percent held 40 percent of the wealth in 1845; in Philadelphia, the top 1 percent held 50 percent of the wealth; and in Boston, the top 1 percent held 37 percent of the wealth.[17]

The Civil War again saw vast fortunes to be made from war profiteering. Large bankers financed the northern side of the war and gained vast profits sometimes for shoddy goods, guns that misfired, and uniforms that fell apart in the rain. But the largest economic shift took place at the end of the war when much of the wealth of the South was transferred to the North through debt transfers. Southern land was devastated. Planters lost their slaves, estimated as 30 percent of southern wealth. From 1860 to 1870, the southern share of national wealth declined from 30 to 12 percent.[18]

But the greatest expansion and concentration of wealth in the hands of the elite took place in the Gilded Age from 1875 to 1900. One of the major sources of wealth came from the building of the national railroad system across the continent. Much of this building was heavily subsidized by the U.S. government by confiscation of land through eminent domain for the railroad's routes and for materials and labor, but the great railroad barons profited. Contrary to laissez-faire ideology prevalent in the period, the U.S. corporate elite have never objected to government subsidies and protections for the rich, only for the poor.

The biggest fortunes rested on a combination of railroads, coal, steel, and oil. John D. Rockefeller and Andrew Carnegie led with fortunes of $200 million to $300 million. William Vanderbilt and William Astor were next with fortunes of $100 million to $200 million. Other high-wealth holders were Frederick Weyerhaeuser, Marshall Field, J. P. Morgan, Collis Huntington, Cyrus McCormick (International Harvester), and Philip Armour (meatpacking). Although much of this wealth was still concentrated in New York, wealth had become national. The top 1 percent of owners of great corporations held some 50 percent of the national wealth, while immigrants in sweatshops labored for a pittance.[19]

The first decade and a half of the twentieth century saw some victories for the Progressive movement and a reaction against this concentration of wealth in the hands of the few. "Trust-busting" sought to break up large monopolies. The passage of the income tax law placed most of the burden of taxation on the superrich. Direct election of the Senate ended the dichotomy between an elected "commons" and a Senate of wealthy appointees. But vast new profits arose from financing and providing the equipment for World War I. After the war, a new generation of technology—automobiles, electricity, telephones, radios, cameras, and refrigerators—seemed to put modern lifestyle in the hands of the middle classes. Buying on credit became the rage, with many in the middle classes going heavily into debt. Investing in the stock market gave even those of modest income the hope of making an easy fortune. Wealth was highly concentrated, with the top 1 percent holding about 45 percent of the wealth, but wages had not risen for most people.

This financial bubble of 1925–1929 burst on the dreadful day of the stock market crash of October 29, 1929. In the four years from 1929 to 1933, U.S. gross national product fell from $103 billion to $56 billion. Five thousand banks closed, wiping out the savings of 9 million Americans. Many new millionaires were also wiped out, but the fortunes of the very wealthy, such as the Rockefellers, Duponts, Fords, and Mellons, survived. Some made new fortunes, such as Joseph Kennedy of Boston, Massachusetts (liquor and movies). At the lower end, unemployment reached 25 percent of the workforce (counting mainly white males).

The New Deal brought a new coalition of the elite into power with more input from the West, from Jews, and from labor unions. But many of the laws proposed by the reformers were blocked by the power of southern Democrats. This was particularly the case with any reforms that would dismantle Jim Crow laws and bring greater equality for blacks, changes favored by the president's wife, Eleanor Roosevelt, but less so by her husband. A federal law to outlaw lynching was repeatedly blocked in Congress in the 1930s[20] and was never passed. There were some gains for the working-class majority, especially white males.

The Fair Standards Labor Act of 1938 set minimum wages and maximum hours for work, although women's minimum wages still fell below those of men. The poorest-paid agricultural and domestic work was not covered. Employment of children under the age of sixteen was banned. The Social Security Act of 1935 set up the "safety net" for the poorest: unemployment insurance, old-age pensions (Social Security), and stipends for the handicapped and disabled. Stipends were also provided for impoverished dependent children and would expand into Aid to Families with Dependent Children (welfare) in the 1950s to 1990s until it was dismantled by the 1996 Welfare Reform Act under President Bill Clinton.

World War II saw another wealth explosion, again much of it from government contracts for war construction. This included companies that built ships, airplanes, and military installations, such as Bechtel and Boeing. "Pearl Harbor turned on the lights in factories, warehouses and dockyards from Maine to California."[21] Workers, including women, who were able to shift to war production found their wages climbing by 50 percent or more. While wages rose, price controls kept down the cost of living, and wartime rationing prevented luxury buying. During the war years, many saved as much as a quarter of their take-home pay. At war's end, Americans were rolling in cash.

After the war, the G.I. Bill allowed many white males to go to college and make a down payment on a house for the first time. In 1951, the gap between rich and poor had narrowed with the top 1 percent now commanding only 29 percent of the wealth. By 1971, this had fallen to 20 percent. Thus, the years from 1945 to 1975 saw the most egalitarian period in American wealth distribution. While there were huge fortunes at the top, with the Mellon family and the Rockefellers expanding into the billions,[22] wealth was more evenly shared in the middle classes.

But the 1980s to the present saw a new explosion of wealth for those at the top, while the income of the middle classes and the poor slipped. A new generation of wealth from computer technology and global trade sparked the largest fortunes ever, with Bill Gates topping $46.6 billion and the five members of the Walton family (Wal-Mart) owning $18 billion each, for a collective $90 billion. In 1976, the top 10 percent of Americans owned 49 percent of all wealth, and the lower 90 percent owned 51 percent. In 1999, this had shifted, with the share of the top 10 percent rising to 73 percent and lower 90 percent falling to 27 percent of the wealth.[23]

The economic policies of President Ronald Reagan in the 1980s were key to this shift of wealth, combining tight monetary policy to curb inflation, tax cuts that favored the rich, and greatly increased defense spending. A neomercantilist policy prevented collapse of failing U.S. corporations and financial institutions with bailouts from the federal government, ultimately paid for by American taxpayers. In 1989–1992, at the ultimate cost of more than $250 billion, Washington set up the Resolution Trust Corporation to sell off the assets of hundreds of savings and loan institutions after reckless lending and financial mismanagement made them insolvent.[24] The tax burden shifted dramatically from the rich to the middle classes. In 1948, the middle class paid 5.3 percent of income taxes, and the top 1 percent paid 76.9 percent. By 1989, this had shifted to the middle classes paying 24.37 percent of the taxes and the top 1 percent only 26.7 percent.[25]

Middle- and lower-class Americans became increasingly overstressed in their struggle to keep up, often needing a second income from a spouse to stay in the middle-range income. When a spouse becomes a second earner, households also take on new expenses for child care, health care, and transportation. Americans were working longer hours than any group in the industrialized world. In 2005, U.S. workers worked an average of 46.2 hours a week, compared to 40.6 hours among Germans. They took an average of 3.9 weeks of vacation, compared to 7.8 weeks for Germans. Unlike Germany, where a four-week minimum vacation is required by law, America law has no requirement for mandatory vacations.

Fewer and fewer Americans had pension plans or health insurance through their work. While Americans pay more for health care than other industrialized countries, private business in 1995 provided only 27 percent of insurance policies, with many Americans depending on Medicare and Medicaid to meet their needs.[26] Corporation mergers often resulted in downsizing, with tens of thousands of workers laid off while chief executive officers got millions of dollars in bonuses. Between 1981 and 1996, 20 percent of Americans were laid off or had their jobs eliminated. Most of those laid off found other jobs, but 62 percent did so at lower pay. Many also lost health insurance benefits in the process.[27]

At the same time, the numbers of severely impoverished Americans has grown. From 2000 to 2006, those with incomes under $9,903 for a family of four ($5,080 for individuals) grew by 26 percent. It is estimated that

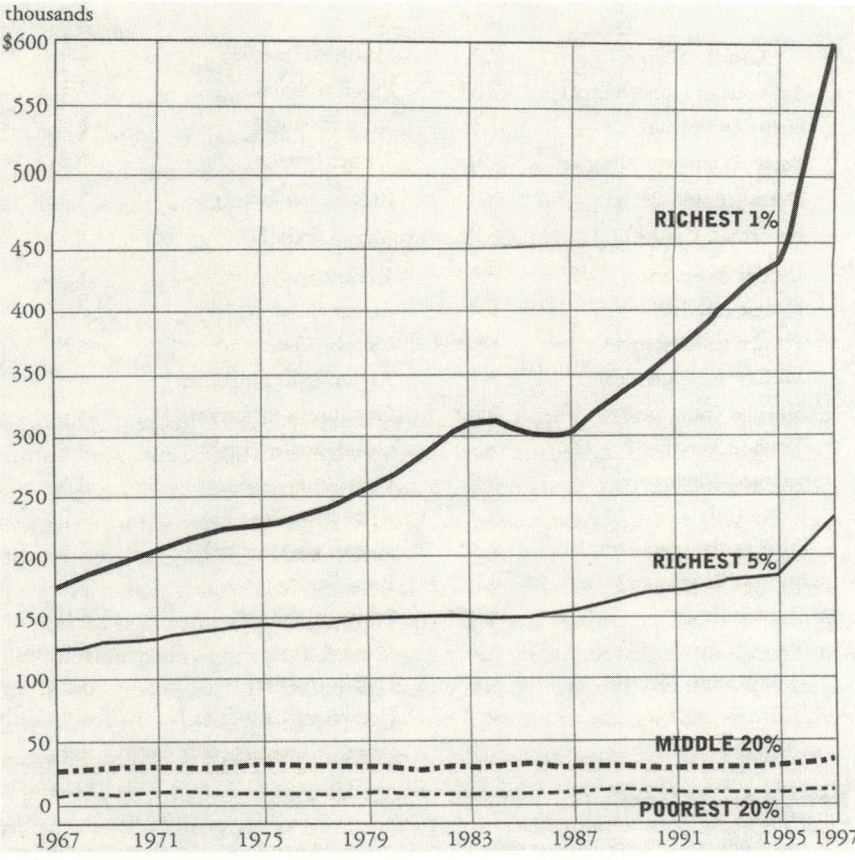

Household Groups	Share of All Income		Average After-Tax Income (Estimated)		Change
	1977	1999	1977	1999	
One-fifth with lowest income	5.7%	5.2%	$10,000	$8,800	12.0%
Next lowest one-fifth	11.5%	9.7%	$22,100	$20,000	9.5%
Middle one-fifth	16.4%	14.7%	$32,400	$31,400	3.1%
Next highest one-fifth	22.8%	21.3%	$42,600	$45,100	5.9%
One-fifth with highest income	44.2%	50.4%	$74,000	$102,300	38.3%
1 Percent with highest income	7.3%	12.9%	$234,700	$515,600	119.7%

Figures do not add to 100 due to rounding.

The Economic Polarization of America, 1967–1997

the numbers of severely poor people in the United States number 16 million, the largest number (1.9 million) in California and the second largest (1.6 million) in Texas.[28] From 1977 to 1999, the share of income of the richest 20 percent has grown, and that of the lower 80 percent has shrunk. In 1977, the lowest 20 percent had 5.7 percent of the income, the second 20 percent had 11.5 percent, the third 20 percent had 16.4 percent, the fourth 20 percent had 22.8 percent, and the top 20 percent had 44.2 percent. In 1999, this had shifted to the lowest 20 percent earning only 5.2 percent, the second 9.7 percent, the third 14.7 percent, the fourth 21.3 percent, and the top 50.4 percent. Thus, the top 20 percent gained 6.2 percent of the income at the expense of the other 80 percent.[29]

A *Time* magazine report of October 30, 2006, celebrating the expansion of the American population to 300 million outlined the reported income of 132 million Americans who filed tax returns in 2004. Since income taxes are filed by household, these figures include both single-person and multiperson households. According the federal figures for 2004 income tax returns, 90 percent of Americans make less than $100,000, 70 percent make less than $50,000, and 50 percent make less than $30,000. This means that half of American households report an income between extreme poverty and low income. Since the federal poverty line of $19,500 is recognized as unrealistically low and $35,000 would be a more realistic figure for a family of four to pull out of poverty, this means that half of Americans are in or near poverty. On the other side of the income spectrum, the top half of 1 percent report income from $500,000 to billions of dollars, with the top 9,677 reporting over $10 million (average $26.5 million).[30] The *Forbes* 400 richest people in America top $1 trillion.

But, as noted at the beginning of this chapter, the stratification of wealth is much greater by ownership than by income. It is estimated that in 1999, the top 1 percent of Americans own 49 percent of the wealth in terms of productive wealth and controlling interest in stocks and bonds. The top 20 percent own about 92 percent of the productive wealth, while the bottom 80 percent own only 8 percent of the wealth, mostly in consumer durables, such as houses and cars. For most middle-class Americans, ownership of a house is their chief asset. Since the value of houses has escalated over the past forty years, those who bought houses in the 1950s or 1960s have been able to use their home ownership as the main asset for their retirement. But this also means that many young people have been priced out of ever buying a home.

The debt level for individual Americans is very high. Almost everyone who buys a house, unless they are selling another house, does so with at least a twenty-year mortgage. Most people who buy cars also do so on time. Credit cards are used for daily purchases from groceries to gas. Thus, most people have high credit card debt as well. This means that as many as a third of Americans actually owe more than they own.

The United States of America, from its founding in 1776, has favored the rich for both economic benefits and political power. This has been partly balanced at certain periods when middle-class Americans experienced expanding prosperity and poorer Americans were provided with a "safety net." But these efforts to create a more justly shared economy have been counteracted by major economic booms that have favored the rich. The past twenty-five years have seen another such boom in which the economic wealth of the rich and superrich has escalated at the expense of the 80 percent of other Americans.

This also means that politically, especially at the federal level, the United States is more of a plutocracy than a democracy. The superrich and their corporate networks hold commanding power over who gets elected and who gets appointed to the federal government and judicial benches. Those who favor greater equality have an extremely difficult time getting elected and governing if elected. Proposals for reform of this system of commanding power in the hands of the wealthy abound in projects such as the group United for a Fair Economy.[31] But the enactment of such reforms is impeded by the same preponderance of power in the hands of the wealthy that is the cause of the problem.

NOTES

1. This chapter focused on the U.S. context, but it is important to remember that the ruling class is increasingly international; see Jeff Faux, *The Global Class War: How America's Bipartisan Elite Lost Our Future and What It Will Take to Win It Back* (Hoboken, N.J.: John Wiley and Sons, 2006).
2. See G. William Domhoff, *Who Rules America? Power and Politics*, 4th ed. (New York: McGraw-Hill, 2002), 15–16.
3. Domhoff, *Who Rules America?* 16.
4. Domhoff, *Who Rules America?* 20–21.
5. Domhoff, *Who Rules America?* 32–39.
6. Domhoff, *Who Rules America?* 69, 85–94.
7. Domhoff, *Who Rules America?* 74–77.
8. Domhoff, *Who Rules America?* 78–82.
9. See G. William Domhoff, *Who Rules America Now? A View for the '80s* (Englewood Cliffs, N.J.: Prentice Hall, 1983), 157–202.
10. Domhoff, *Who Rules America Now?* 143–49.
11. Domhoff, *Who Rules America Now?* 17–55.

12. From the *Winthrop Papers*, vol. 2 (Massachusetts Historical Society, 1931), 282, taken from Conrad Cherry, ed., *God's New Israel: Religious Interpretations of American Destiny* (Chapel Hill: University of North Carolina Press, 1998), 37.

13. See Eric Foner, *Tom Paine and Revolutionary America* (New York: Oxford University Press, 1976), 23–56.

14. In 1776, John Adams wrote a treatise, *Thoughts on Government*, in which he decried Paine's excessively "democratical" ideas. He argued for a bicameral legislature in which the desires of the common people would be balanced by wisdom of the wealthy elites; see Foner, *Tom Paine and Revolutionary America*, 122.

15. Kevin Phillips, *Wealth and Democracy: A Political History of the American Rich* (New York: Broadway Books, 2002), 12.

16. Phillips, *Wealth and Democracy*, 12–13.

17. Phillips, *Wealth and Democracy*, 13–31.

18. Phillips, *Wealth and Democracy*, 31–40.

19. Phillips, *Wealth and Democracy*, 41–46.

20. See Blanche W. Cook, *Eleanor Roosevelt: Volume II, 1933–38* (New York: Viking, 1999), 177–81, 243–47, 310–11.

21. Phillips, *Wealth and Democracy*, 74.

22. Phillips, *Wealth and Democracy*, 80. In 1957, the Mellons had a fortune of $1.6 billion to $2.8 billion and the Rockefellers $1.0 billion to $1.9 billion. J. Paul Getty's and the Dupont family's fortunes approached $1 billion.

23. Church Collins and Felice Yeskel, *Economic Apartheid in America: A Primer on Economic Inequality and Insecurity* (New York: New Press, 2000), 55.

24. Phillips, *Wealth and Democracy*, 105–6; compare with Collins and Yeskel, *Economic Apartheid in America*, 41.

25. Phillips, *Wealth and Democracy*, 96.

26. See James Heintz, Nancy Folbre, and the Center for Popular Economics, *Field Guide to the U.S. Economy* (New York: New Press, 2000), 124.

27. Heintz et al., *Field Guide to the U.S. Economy*, 45.

28. Tony Pugh, "U.S. Economy Leaving Record Numbers in Severe Poverty," *McClatchy Newspapers*, February 22, 2007.

29. Phillips, *Wealth and Democracy*, 129.

30. "What We Earn," *Time*, October 30, 2006.

31. Collins and Yeskel, *Economic Apartheid in America*, 127–219.

• *10* •

European Colonialism, 1492–1965

Colonization by European powers has at one time or another covered much of the globe. In the sixteenth century, Spain was the greatest world colonial empire, covering most of the Caribbean and Latin and Central America to Florida, while Portugal held the huge area of Brazil. In the nineteenth century, Spain lost its colonies in America to national independence movements, with its last Caribbean colonies, Puerto Rico and Cuba, as well as the Philippines, being taken over by the United States in the Spanish-American War of 1898. By the end of World War II, Spain had only a few remnants of empire in Africa, a sliver on the coast of Morocco, Equatorial Guinea, and the Rio de Oro region in Western Sahara.[1]

In the nineteenth century, England became the empire "on which the sun never set." In the seventeenth century, England planted colonies on the East Coast of North America and took over the French colonies in Canada in 1763. But it lost the American colonies in the American Revolution of 1776. Canada became a self-governing dominion within the British Empire in 1931. But in the nineteenth century, the British Empire spread over much of Asia and Africa. In 1945, the British Commonwealth and empire covered one-fifth of the land surface of the globe and about one-quarter of the world's population.[2]

In 1945, France had the next largest European empire. Although it had lost its Canadian territories to the British in the eighteenth century, it built a huge empire in Africa, including Algeria and Morocco and large areas in equatorial and western Africa, and in Indochina (Vietnam, Cambodia, and Laos) from the mid-nineteenth to the mid-twentieth centuries.[3] The Dutch colonies in 1945 consisted mostly of the Dutch East Indies, today Indonesia. The Portuguese lost its largest colony in Latin America, Brazil, in 1822 but in 1945 was still clinging to large territories in Africa (Angola, Mozambique, and Portuguese Guinea) as well as trading areas in Asia (Goa, Macao, and a part of Timor).[4] Belgium had one large colony, Congo, as well as the mandated territories of Ruanda-Urundi in Africa.

The Italians and Germans were late into the empire-building business, having been unified as nations only in 1870 and 1871, respectively. Germany participated in the European scramble for Africa in the late nineteenth century, taking over large territories in southwestern and eastern Africa. But it lost its African territories as a result of its loss of World War I to the Allied powers, with South-West Africa (Namibia) being mandated to South Africa and German East Africa (Tanzania) going to the British. The Italians ruled the North African area of Libya from 1912 and grabbed areas in northeastern Africa (Eritrea and central and southern Somaliland) in the 1880s but lost these when Italy was defeated in World War II.

The Middle East constitutes a distinct case in this history of empire. Historically, the lands surrounding the eastern Mediterranean from North Africa around the Near East to Greece and the Balkans had been controlled by the Ottoman Empire, reaching its greatest extent in 1683 (see map 1). It did not control Hungary for long, Hungary being taken under Austrian domination. The Ottomans lost Greece in 1829 and Bulgaria and Romania by 1878 after nationalist revolts. Other areas in the Balkans, such as Bosnia and Herzegovina, were absorbed into the Austro-Hungarian Empire. The Euro-

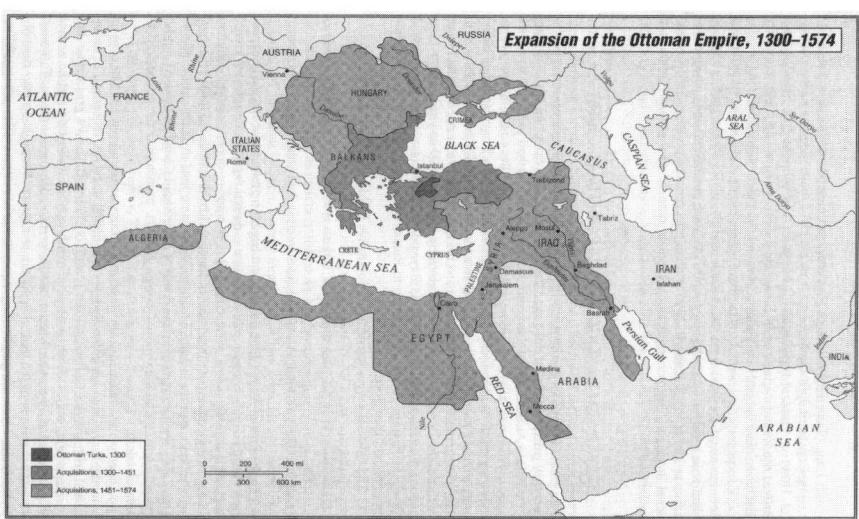

Map 1.   The Expansion of the Ottoman Empire, 1300–1574

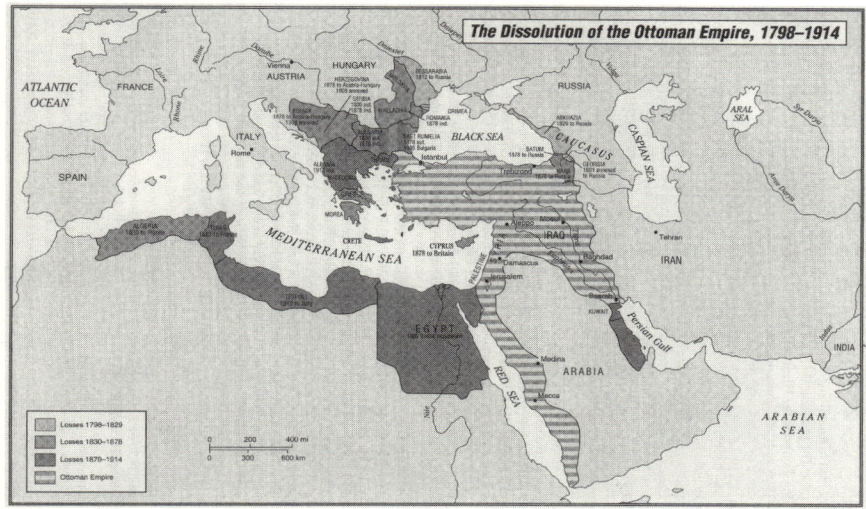

Map 2. The Dissolution of the Ottoman Empire, 1798–1914

pean empires, French, Italian, and British, divided North Africa from Morocco to Egypt between them. By 1914, the Ottoman Empire was seen as the "sick man of Europe," on the brink of dissolution, although it still ruled the area from Turkey to the end of the Arabian Peninsula (see map 2).

In World War I, Turkey sided with Germany. During this war, the French and British planned the division of the Ottoman territories between themselves. Turkey emerged as a self-governing nation in 1923. Iraq, Palestine, and Transjordan were given as mandate territories to Britain, while Syria/Lebanon was given to France. The bulk of the Arabian Peninsula became Saudi Arabia, but major territories around the southern coast and up the Gulf of Oman—Yemen, Oman, the United Arab Emirates, Qatar, and Kuwait—became independent states, mostly under British control until the 1960s.

After World War II, Palestine was divided by the United Nations into two states. The Jewish state of Israel received 55 percent of the land of Palestine, and a Palestinian Arab state received 45 percent. In the Arab-Israeli War of 1948–1949, Israel seized another 23 percent of historic Palestine, and the rest of the Palestinian state fell under Jordan (the West Bank) and Egypt (the Gaza Strip). In the 1967 Arab-Israeli War, Israel took over the West Bank and Gaza as well as the Golan Heights (from Syria) and the Sinai Peninsula (from Egypt). The Sinai was given back to Egypt in 1982, but Gaza, the West Bank, and the Golan Heights remain areas occupied by Israel.

Between 1947 and 1965, much of the land of these vast European empires in Asia, Africa, and the Middle East emerged as independent, self-governing nations. The European empires negotiated various relations of control over major resources and foreign policy with the former colonies. A new relation of the European powers and the United States with the former colonies emerged from the 1960s to the present, often called "neocolonialism." In this neocolonial system of relations, the United States has gradually emerged as the dominant world power, although Britain and France still wield considerable influence.

Neocolonialism means that European powers and the United States no longer rule dependent territories directly through their occupying troops and imperial bureaucracy. Rather, they control the area's resources indirectly through business corporations and the financial lending institutions they dominate, such as the World Bank and the International Monetary Fund. They intervene militarily, sometimes directly with their own troops (as in the wars in Korea and Vietnam) or indirectly with local surrogate armies that they fund and manipulate through such agencies as the Central Intelligence Agency to remove leaders (democratically elected or not) that they see as contrary to their global economic and political interests.

The United States seeks to exert hegemonic control over the globe through its vast network of military bases. This "empire of bases," as Chalmers Johnson calls it,[5] has been built over 100 years of military-economic expansion of the United States. Since the completion of the spread of the United States "from sea to sea" within the continental United States, every subsequent expansion of U.S. power has left a legacy of permanent military enclaves, except in those areas where the American military was defeated and their presence ousted, as in Vietnam. From Guantánamo in Cuba and military bases in Puerto Rico and the Philippines, the legacy of the 1898 Spanish-American War; to Germany, Italy, England, and Japan in the aftermath of World War II; and to Korea after 1945 and the Middle East after the 1991 Persian Gulf War, each expansion of U.S. power has added to the "empire of bases."

Today, with the wars in Iraq and Afghanistan, more bases are being added. Before this current round of wars, Johnson counted some 725 bases of various sizes in thirty-eight countries.[6] The Iraq War has added many more, some 109 in Iraq alone, four of them very large and apparently permanent. These bases operate as a network of neocolonial control of the United States over the globe, "projecting force" militarily, spying on other countries, and ensuring access to key resources, especially oil.

A detailed history of the successive waves of colonization and decolonization obviously goes far beyond the limits of this brief chapter. The economic and military aspects of neocolonialism are discussed in chapters 11 and 12, while its regional manifestations are explored in the three country studies of chapters 13 to 15 (Nicaragua, North and South Korea, and South Africa). In this chapter, I summarize briefly the two stages of European colonialism in the sixteenth to eighteenth centuries and in the mid-nineteenth to mid-twentieth centuries along with their subsequent waves of decolonization.

THE FIRST WAVES OF EUROPEAN COLONIALISM, 1492–1830

Columbus's "discovery" of America saw Spain plant its control through settlements in the islands of the Caribbean, such as Santo Domingo (1496), and then expand into Mexico with the conquest of the Aztec kingdom by Hernán Cortés in 1519–1521. Francisco Pizarro led the Spanish expansion down the west coast of Latin America and the conquest of the Inca Empire in 1532. Spanish explorers also went into northern Mexico, planting colonies as far as Florida and across the North American continent from Texas to California.

This period of exploration was followed after 1556 with a consolidation of Spanish control in the Americas. Spanish government was divided into four large regencies: the viceroyalty of New Spain (Mexico, including Florida and a region from Texas to California, Central America, and the Caribbean), the viceroyalty of New Granada (Venezuela, Colombia, and Ecuador), the viceroyalty of Peru (present-day Peru), and the viceroyalty of Rio de La Plata (Bolivia, Paraguay, Uruguay, and Argentina), governed by viceroys directly responsible to the king of Spain (see map 3).

All top positions in the state and church were reserved for *peninsulares* (Spaniards born in Spain). Creoles (Spaniards born in America) took the second rank of local leadership and came to dominate socioeconomic development. The most fertile tracts of land were divided into large *encomiendas*, or plantations divided among the leading Spanish conquistadores, to be used primarily for export production of crops such as sugar, with the indigenous people handed over to these landowners as serf labor on the pretext that their masters would make them "Christian." When many indigenous people either fled or died through harsh treatment, Africans began to be imported as slave labor. Spain ruled these vast regions (with the exception of Brazil, which was similarly settled and exploited by Portugal) for more than three centuries.

In the seventeenth century, the Dutch, British, and French were seeking to divide the North American continent among them, with the British pushing out the Dutch in New York and the French in Canada. French explorations and claims in the Midwest from Canada to New Orleans were bought out by the United States with the Louisiana Purchase of 1803, thus clearing the way for U.S. expansion westward.

140 Chapter 10

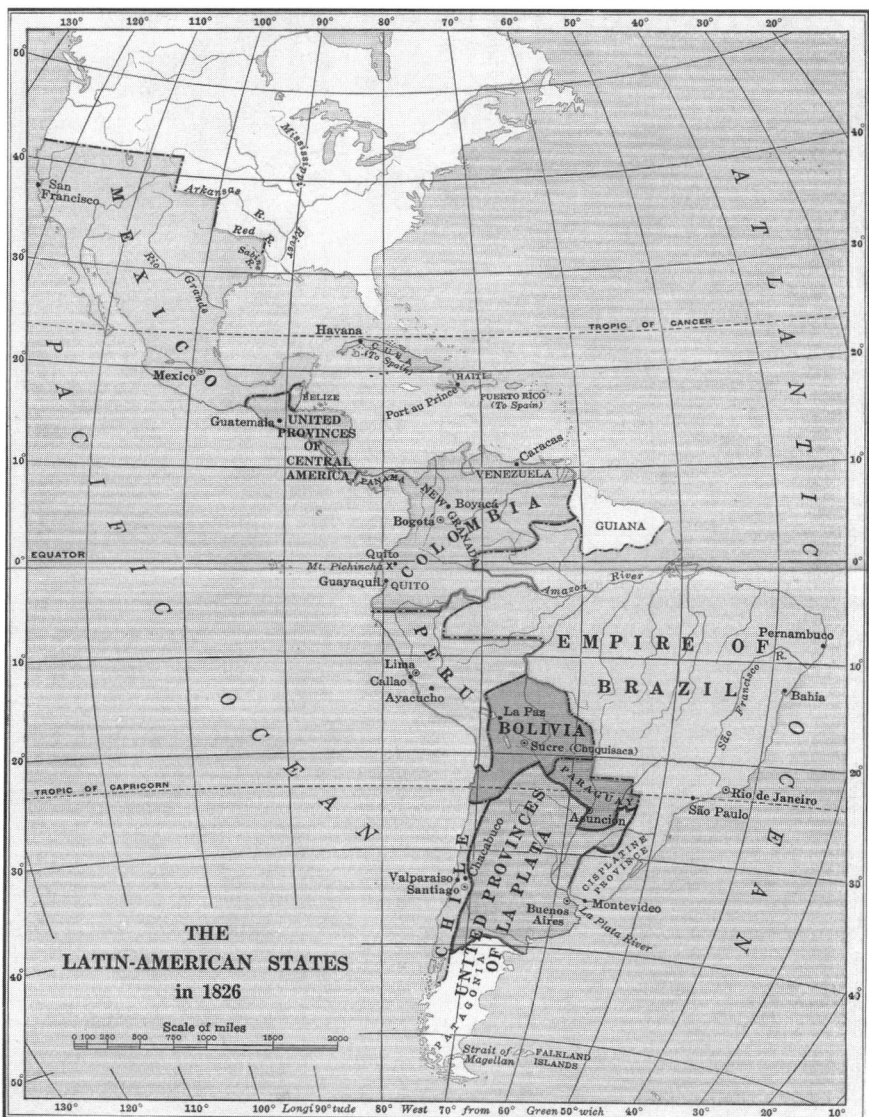

Map 3. Latin American Political Organizations in 1798

The center and staging ground of this control of Central and South America remained the Caribbean. This was the first area to be settled by the Spanish. It was to key ports in these islands that slaves were brought from Africa to be dispersed to plantations and where sugar was processed for export to Europe. Thus, the Caribbean was a center of exchange in the global market between Europe, Africa, and the Americas in the sixteenth to nineteenth centuries. The global trade created by these first three centuries of European colonization was a three-way traffic between Europe, Africa, and the Americas. The ships that brought the slaves from Africa also took from the Americas furs, tobacco, and silver and gold from the mines. They brought from Europe fashionable clothes, fine china, and ironware to be traded to the colonial elites. In North America, guns, trinkets, and liquor were traded to Indian tribes for furs. The profits from this three-way traffic flowed into the banks of London, Amsterdam, and Paris to fund European development and eventually the industrial revolution of the nineteenth century. The Spanish tended to use their gold and silver to decorate churches rather than as capital for economic expansion.

This huge flow of capital into Western Europe, especially to England, had major effects on Western European societies. The older artisan and peasant economy was disrupted. Much of the land tilled by small farmers was confiscated by large landholders and turned into large sheep-raising plantations for wool. The displaced peasants became the new working class of European cities. Rising health standards also created a population explosion. The surplus population was exported as the settlers of the colonies.

By contrast, the exploited areas of the Americas saw its indigenous population decimated by diseases, overwork, and war. From 90 million when the Spanish arrived, the indigenous population dropped to 3.5 million by the mid-seventeenth century. The dying Indians were replaced by black slaves as exploited labor in plantations and mines. The extractive practices of growing sugar and mining for precious metals stripped the land of its wealth, leaving it denuded and poisoned, even as those making a profit from the land moved on to other regions. Haiti, for example, was once densely forested and fertile. Today it is almost entirely deforested and its land stripped of its fertility.[7]

The Caribbean islands also were among the last regions to be liberated as independent nations. Puerto Rico and Cuba continued to be under Spain until seized as dependencies of the United States in 1898. The British allowed Jamaica independence in 1962 and the Bahamas in 1973. Guadeloupe and Martinique continue to be governed by France as part of the Overseas Department of France. The Dutch Antilles (Curaçao, Bonaire, St. Maartens, St. Eustatius, and Saba) remain Dutch dependencies. Dutch Guiana became independent of the Netherlands in 1975. The United States has long regarded control of the Caribbean, along with Central America, as central to its domination of the region, as its "backyard."

The last decades of the eighteenth century saw the stirrings of nationalist rebellion throughout the Americas. The successful American Revolution against the British in 1776 was an inspiration to peoples seeking to throw off the colonial yokes of Spain and France. The U.S. Americans themselves held out their revolution as a model to be followed by other people seeking democratic self-rule. But they were not prepared when the first area seeking independence from colonial power was the black slave state of Haiti, which succeeded in freeing itself from France by 1804 in bloody uprisings led by former slave Toussaint L'Ouverture. Americans in the United States had thought of their revolution as setting an example for other "white men," not for black slaves. Such a revolt was seen as setting a "bad" example for black slaves still groaning under the lash in the U.S. "land of the free."

Ideological influences also stirred revolt in the Spanish colonies, especially the views of Enlightenment thinkers such as Montesquieu, Voltaire, and Rousseau and the inspiration of the French Revolution with its Declaration of the Rights of Man and the Citizen. Wealthy Creole merchants and landowners chafed against limitations to their political power and economic expansion imposed by the Spanish mercantile system. The last straw was when the Napoleonic Wars in Europe reduced Spain and Portugal to dependencies of France. From 1810 to 1825, independence movements raged across the Spanish viceroyalties, led by Simon Bolivar in the north and San Martin in the south, while the priests Father Miguel Hidalgo and Father José María Morelos raised the flag of independence in Mexico.

These liberators imagined much larger independent states, corresponding to the old viceroyalties, but the emerging regions soon fell into factionalism. New Spain split into separate Caribbean states and Mexico, with Central America dividing into five small states. The New Granada region became three states, and the Rio de la Plata split into small states across the center of Latin America (Bolivia, Paraguay, and Uruguay) and the large state of Argentina. Such divisions allowed greater cohesion but also facilitated British neocolonial penetration of the Latin American region under the banner of "free trade." With the Texas revolt of 1835 and the Mexican-American War of 1846, the United States would carry off the northwest territories of Mexico into the United States.

Brazil followed a more leisurely course of independence from Portugal. When Portugal was occupied by France in 1807, the Portuguese king Joao IV sought to rule the Portuguese Empire from Rio de Janeiro. After his return to Portugal in 1822, Brazil became an independent monarchy under his son, Pedro I. Pedro II was deposed in 1889, and Brazil became a republic. Slavery was abolished at that time, and there began a process of separation of church and state and of industrialization.

THE SECOND WAVE OF COLONIZATION, 1850–1945

The second wave of colonization by European powers focused on Asia, Africa, and the Middle East. India is the prototype of the expansion of the

British Empire into Asia. The British East India Company had been engaged in gaining control of the area since the early seventeenth century. In 1858, with the Government of India Act, jurisdiction over "British India" (the presidencies of Bengal, Madras, and Bombay) passed from the dual control of the East India Company and the British Crown solely to the British Crown. All Indians in these areas became "subjects" of Queen Victoria. About half of India still remained under the rule of "native princes" but with considerable power in the hands of British "advisers."

Burma was seen as an outpost of the British Empire in India. It was conquered in three wars in 1824–1826, 1852, and 1885 and governed as a province of India until 1937. Britain acquired the Dutch bases in Ceylon during the Napoleonic Wars and extended British rule into the interior of the island between 1803 and 1818. The states that made up Malaysia were acquired piecemeal by Britain during the nineteenth century. It acquired the island of Singapore from the sultan of Johore in 1819. Singapore, Penang, and Malacca made up the Straits Settlements under the jurisdiction of the East India Company in 1826, to which the island of Labuan was added in 1846. The Federated Malay States, while still under their "native princes," came under British control by 1874–1896. North Borneo was acquired by the British North Borneo Company in 1881, and in 1901 the five states of Kedah, Kelantan, Trengganu, Johore, and Perlis passed under the jurisdiction of Britain.[8]

The French had established missionary and trading connections with Indochina in the eighteenth century but moved to conquer it only in the late nineteenth. They captured Saigon in 1861, extended their influence to Cambodia in 1863, and created the Indochinese Union of Cochinchina, Annam, Tonkin, and Cambodia in 1887.[9] The Dutch Empire in the East Indies dates from trading contacts from the seventeenth century. It secured territorial control over Java by 1750 and came to dominate the other islands in the nineteenth century although often governing indirectly through local rulers (see map 4).

The European colonization of Africa mainly took place during the "scramble for Africa" in the late nineteenth century, although several European countries had much earlier trading contacts with Africa, particularly on its coastal areas. The "scramble for Africa" refers to the period from the 1880s to 1910 when the European powers (Britain, France, Germany, Belgium, Portugal, and Italy) sought to divide up Africa between them.[10] Central to this process was the 1884–1885 Berlin Conference in which Otto von Bismarck, leader of recently unified Germany, invited diplomats of the other European countries to lay down the rules for division of the African continent. Among these rules were that no nation would stake a claim to a region of Africa without notifying the other powers and that no territory could be formally claimed before being effectively occupied by a European power.[11]

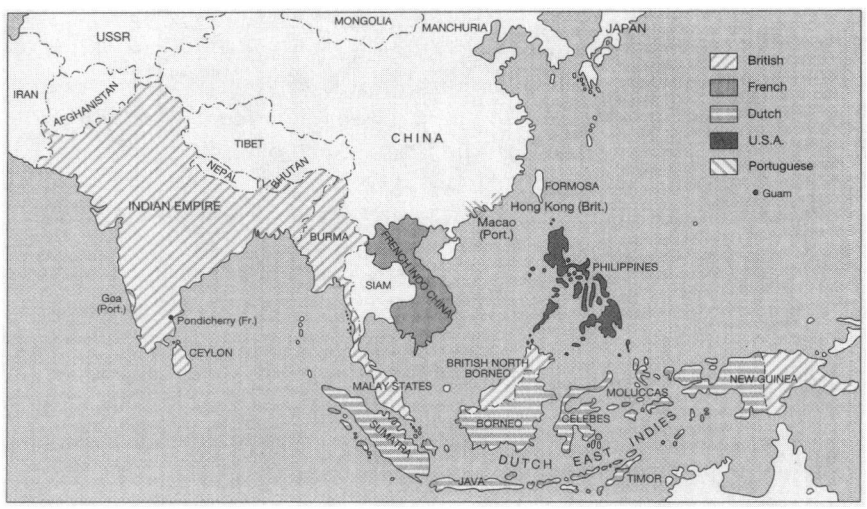

Map 4. Asia in 1939

The British had trading stations on the west coast of Africa from the seventeenth century and acquired the Cape Colony from the Dutch during the Napoleonic Wars. Ghana, or the Gold Coast, was established as a colony in 1874, but wars with the Ashanti Federation brought lands in the interior under British control. Nigeria was Britain's largest colony in tropical west Africa, acquired piecemeal. At the end of the Berlin Conference, Britain proclaimed a protectorate over the rivers of the Niger delta, and in 1886–1889, the Royal Niger Company acquired jurisdiction over a large area in the middle of Niger that was given over to the British government in 1899.[12] British colonization of Sierra Leone began as coastal station for freed slaves in 1788. The peninsula of Sierra Leone was acquired in 1807, but the hinterland became a protectorate only in 1896.[13] Gambia was the oldest British trading station dating from the time of Elizabeth I, but it was hemmed in by French colonial territories on all sides. In 1889, France and Britain agreed on its boundaries.[14]

The major African areas under British control consisted of territories running from southern and East Africa to Egypt, "from the Cape to Cairo." Starting with its possession of the Cape Colony, the British established control over South Africa with successive wars with the Boers (Dutch settlers), taking over the Transvaal and the Orange Free State by 1902. The intrepid Cecil Rhodes, who hoped to build a railroad from Cairo to the Cape, pushed north into what became Southern and Northern Rhodesia (Zimbabwe and Zambia, respectively) through his British South Africa Company, securing control in the 1890s.[15] Nyasaland (Malawi) had a different origin, being penetrated by Scottish Presbyterian missionaries who established an excellent educational system that allowed the graduates to establish themselves all over southern Africa as clerks. It became a British protectorate in 1891.[16]

The High Commission Territories—Basutoland (Lesotho), Buchuanaland (Botswana), and Swaziland—were remnants of conflicts in southern Africa in the nineteenth century. It was expected that they would be incorporated into South Africa, but their chiefs protested. The British promised that they would not be transferred against the wishes of their inhabitants, so they remained separate and eventually became independent countries.[17]

East Africa was also acquired in the 1880s. The Anglo-German agreement left both Kenya and Uganda in the British sphere of influence. The same agreement gave Tanganika to the Germans, but it became a British mandated territory after World War I.[18] North of these areas was the huge territory of the Anglo-Egyptian Sudan, technically a part of the Ottoman Empire, which became a British sphere of influence with its control of Egypt.

The French Empire in Africa, as in Asia, followed a different philosophy of colonization than the British. While the British in Africa preferred an indirect rule, governing through local chiefs, the French sought an assimilation of their colonies into the French culture and nation. Most of its territories were acquired in the "scramble for Africa" period. But they also extended French control south from their rule over the North African lands of Algeria, Tunisia, and Morocco. This included French West Africa, Senegal, French Guinea, Ivory Coast, Dahomey, Upper Volta, and part of Sudan and Mauritania as well as the equatorial areas of Chad, Gabon, Middle Congo (Congo Republic), and Ubanghi-Shari (Central African Republic). While the British sought to build continental dominance from north to south, the French sought control of Africa across the center from east to west. The two lines of colonial expansion met in Sudan, where the English and French avoided conflict by negotiating a separate sphere of influence (1899), demarcated by the Congo and Nile rivers.

The Dutch did not participate in the "scramble for Africa." The Portuguese expanded older trading stations on the west and east coasts of southern Africa into the large colonies of Angola and Mozambique. After World War II, they sought to assimilate these colonies into the "home" country by defining them as oversea provinces of Portugal. Leopold II of Belgium sought a large colony to be exploited as his personal possession, sending British explorer Henry Morton Stanley to acquire Congo for him in the 1880s. Leopold used it primarily to make huge profits from rubber and ivory. He treated the natives so harshly as slave labor, causing millions of deaths, that the Belgian government took it over and annexed it in 1908 as a colony of Belgium.

As mentioned earlier, Italy was late getting into colonialism because of its recent unification. It took territories in Eritrea and Somaliland in the scramble period and during Mussolini's rule in 1935–1936 conquered the one independent Africa country of Abyssinia (Ethiopia), which it lost to the British in 1941 (see map 5).

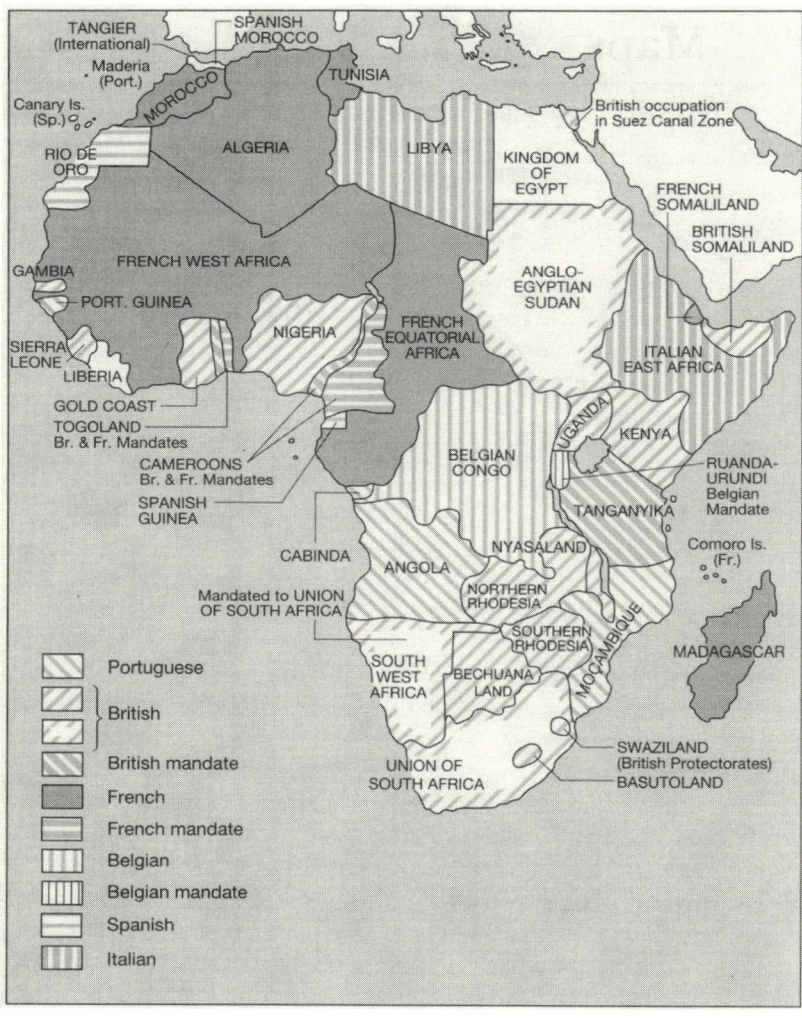

Map 5. Africa in 1939

DECOLONIZATION OF ASIA AND AFRICA, 1947–1990

The decolonization of Asia was complicated by World War II, during which the Japanese had occupied a large part of the European empires in Asia up to the borders of India. Korea had been a colony of Japan since 1905, and Manchuria fell under Japanese rule in 1932. Between 1941 and 1945, Japan sought to build an extensive empire, occupying Singapore, Hong Kong, Macao, French Indochina, Thailand, British Malaya and Borneo, and the Dutch East Indies, as well as the Philippines, controlled by the United States.

Japanese policy in these areas was to encourage local nationalists both to ally with Japan and to resist the European colonial powers. For example, in Burma, nationalist leaders, including Aung San, received military training from the Japanese. Aung San founded the Burma national army and fought with the Japanese. In 1943, the Japanese declared Burma an independent country. In Vietnam, the Japanese transferred power to the Vietminh under nationalist Ho Chi Minh when they left in August 1945.

This encouragement of anticolonial nationalists left a complicated legacy at the end of World War II. British Prime Minister Winston Churchill was determined to restore these Asian colonies to their former European rulers. Thus, he sought not only to take back the former British areas but also to restore Indochina to the French and Indonesia to the Dutch. Third World nationalists expected a rapid decolonization after the end of the war. Several areas of conflict between rising nationalists and colonial powers emerged at this time. One was when desires for independence conflicted with the determination of the colonial nation to cling to power. A second area of conflict arose when there was a large settler population in the colonized country that resisted turning over power to the indigenous majority.

A third area of conflict lay in the emerging Cold War divisions after World War II. Some Third World nationalists sought wider reforms, freeing their new nations from economic dependency on the colonizing country and allying with the Soviet Union or communist China, not necessarily because they were "anti-West" or "communist puppets" but as a way of claiming independence. Western powers were determined to keep the new nations within the Western sphere of economic and political power.

Thus, struggles over decolonization or North–South conflicts became intertwined with East–West or communist–capitalist conflicts. These conflicts are detailed more fully in chapters 11, 12, 13, and 15. This chapter briefly summarizes the processes of decolonization, some of which resulted in prolonged conflicts and others that appeared to take place fairly smoothly.

India led the way in a long struggle for national independence. The Indian National Congress was founded in 1885 and the Muslim League in 1906, but these at first did not press for independence. The struggle sharpened after 1919 with legal repression and military violence by the British. Mohandas K. (Mahatma) Gandhi emerged as a new leader who used a civil disobedience campaign (*Satyagraha*), first developed in South Africa, against these repressive measures. Gandhi transformed the Indian National Congress into a mass movement. The British government proposed reforms with broader Indian participation in government. Meanwhile, the leader of the Muslim League (Mohammed Ali Jinnah) began to demand autonomous regions or even an independent country. The "Untouchables" (outcastes) led by B. R. Ambedkar also complained that they were not represented and demanded the safeguarding of their rights.

In August 1942, the All-India Congress demanded that Britain "quit India" immediately and allow Indians to develop their own political arrangements. Gandhi and other leaders were jailed. After World War II, the British accepted Indian independence and sought to negotiate the conflicting demands of the Hindis and the Muslims. Partition into two countries, India and Pakistan, was finally seen as the only solution. At midnight on August 14–15, 1947, the two independent countries were inaugurated, with Jinnah as the governor-general of Pakistan and Jawaharlal Nehru as the first governor-general of India. But serious communal rioting broke out between the Hindu and Muslim communities in the autumn of 1947 in which up to 250,000 people died. About a million non-Muslims fled from Pakistan into India, while a comparable number of Muslims fled to Pakistan.[19]

A different history of decolonization took place in Indochina because of new entanglements with Cold War politics and the involvement of the United States as the emerging "policeman" of neocolonialism. The Japanese had turned over power to the nationalist Vietminh on August 18, 1945. Ho Chi Minh declared an independent Vietnam on September 2. But on September 13, British forces landed in Saigon and returned power to the French. The Vietnamese nationalists then began a struggle against French rule, with the French finally defeated at Dien Bien Phu on May 7, 1954.[20]

In July, the United Nations ruled that national elections were to be held within two years, but the United States rejected this solution (knowing the Ho Chi Minh would win).[21] They began to send "advisers" to support a separate noncommunist government in the south allied with the United States. Ho Chi Minh accepted aid from the Soviet Union, later allying with China (a communist regime since 1949). From 1965 to 1975, this became a full-fledged war that spread into Cambodia and Laos, causing enormous devastation and loss of life in all three regions. In April 1975, the United States conceded defeat and left. The communist forces then captured Saigon and created a unified nation.[22] Left-leaning regimes also emerged in Cambodia and Laos.

A prolonged struggle for independence also took place in the Dutch East Indies. Nationalist movements developed there from 1908, with Ahmed Sukarno founding the National Indonesian Party in 1927. The Japanese who occupied the area (1942–1945) encouraged Indonesian nationalism against the Dutch. At the end of World War II, Sukarno proclaimed the Indonesian Republic (August 17, 1945), but British and then Dutch troops arrived and reimposed Dutch control. But as resistance continued, the Dutch began to seek an arrangement similar to the British Commonwealth in which the Dutch would retain only titular power.

Fighting continued over the next three years, with Sukarno also suppressing indigenous communist movements. In January 1949, the Netherlands agreed to a complete transfer of sovereignty of the former Dutch East Indies (except Western New Guinea) to the Republic of the United States of Indonesia. This happened in December of that year, with Sukarno elected president. New Guinea was transferred into the republic in 1963. But struggles between separatist groups and the national government over disputed territories continue[23] (see map 6).

In Africa, the processes of decolonization progressed smoothly when indigenous leaders were willing to accept a large amount of control over the economy and foreign policy by the former colonial regime. But conflicts arose when leaders wanted more independence, especially when they sought more

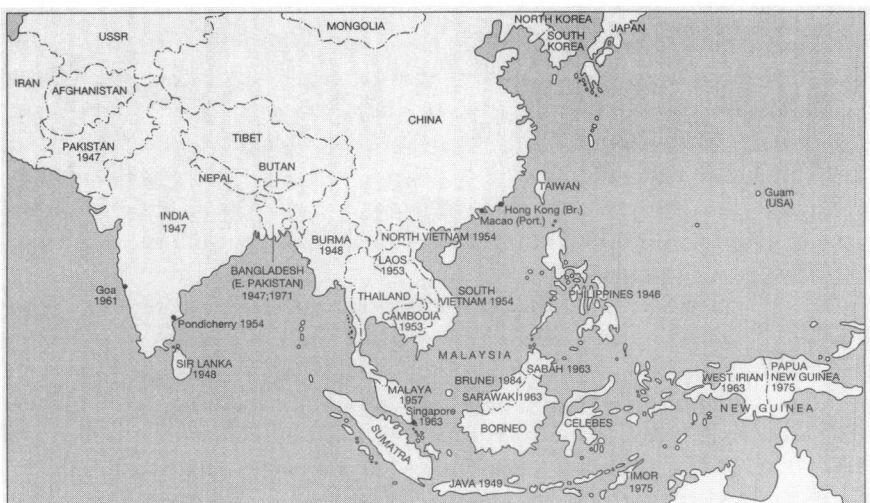

Map 6. The Chronology of Asian Independence

domestic economic reforms and reached out in alliances with the communist powers or when European settlers resisted giving power to indigenous Africans. Thus, in 1960 all the countries of French Equatorial and West Africa became independent but with arrangements in which they mostly remained members of the French community and accepted French control over their foreign policy.[24]

The British negotiated independence for Ghana, Kenya, Uganda, Zambia, Botswana, Burundi, Gambia, Lesotho, Malawi, Nigeria and Sierra Leone, Swaziland, and Tanzania between 1957 and 1968 after some initial struggles in which they sought to suppress more nationalist leaders, such as Kwame Nkrumah in Ghana, in favor of more moderate leaders representing the business classes. The major conflict that arose was in Southern Rhodesia (Zimbabwe), where a white settler population in control of the best land resisted giving power to indigenous Africans.

In 1965, white Rhodesians unilaterally declared their independence from Britain and attempted to impose a white settler regime on the African majority. From 1966 to 1979, there was protracted guerrilla warfare between Zimbabwe nationalists and this white settler regime (numbering only 250,000 compared to 7 million Africans). In 1979, a settlement was accepted in which twenty seats in the National Assembly would be reserved for whites and eighty for Africans. In April 1980, Rhodesia became the Republic of Zimbabwe.[25]

Portugal resisted decolonization after World War II and sought to integrate its two major colonies, Mozambique and Angola, more closely into Portugal, encouraging Portuguese to migrate there. In Angola, competing liberation groups were formed, creating a state of civil war in the 1960s. In 1974, a revolution in Portugal, overthrowing the fascist regime that had ruled there since 1928, facilitated a settlement. In 1975, the three warring liberation groups signed an agreement with Portugal, and Angola became independent.

In Mozambique, the liberation movement FRELIMO was founded in 1982, gaining control of much of the country by 1964. White settlers resisted African control. After the Portuguese Revolution in 1974, Mozambique became independent under the one-party rule of FRELIMO. But South Africa backed an opposition group, and civil war broke out, causing enormous death and destruction. A peace accord was signed in 1992, and UN troops withdrew by 1995.[26]

The independence of European colonies in North Africa and the Middle East has also been a source of major conflicts. One of the most prolonged struggles took place between France and independence movements in Algeria. There had been resistance to French colonization in Algeria since the 1870s. France responded by giving French citizenship to resident Europeans in Algeria, thus imposing a settler class on the indigenous population of Berbers and Arabs. Independence movements arose from 1900 but were divided between more secular groups and the much larger movements that identified with Islam as the national religion and culture.

After World War II, France negotiated a widened representation of indigenous Algerians but still under French control. A war of independence raged from 1954 to 1961, fought with great savagery on both sides. In 1982, an agreement was reached with the Algerian Provisional Government that gave full sovereignty to Algeria. Settlers had to choose between French and Algerian nationality. Most settlers returned to France, and Algeria became an independent country on July 3, 1982[27] (see map 7).

Thus, the process of decolonization, while appearing to go smoothly in some areas of Africa and Asia, in reality masked a resistance by the Western

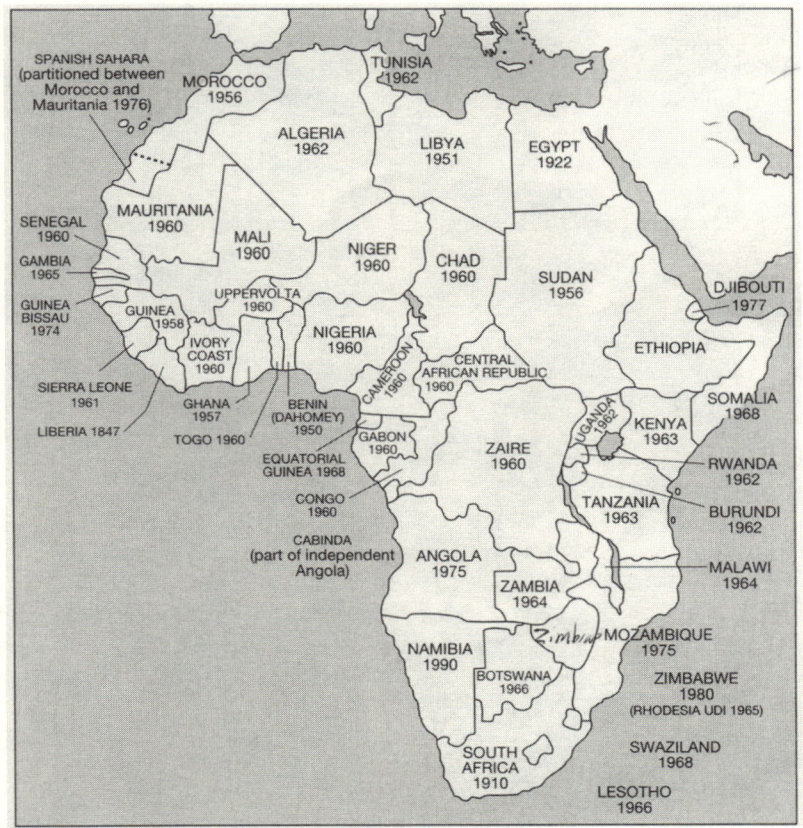

Map 7. The Chronology of African Independence

powers to real economic and political self-determination by former colonies that might pursue policies that differed from the European and, increasingly, American definitions of their global hegemony. This has resulted in a number of violent and prolonged wars and many lesser clashes that have come to define the world since World War II both during the Cold War (1950–1990) and after (1990 to the present). These conflicts would also affect Latin America countries, which, although independent since the 1820s, chafed under U.S. neocolonial control. It is to these conflicts that we turn in the following five chapters.

NOTES

1. Muriel E. Chamberlain, *European Decolonization in the Twentieth Century* (New York: Longman, 1998), 192–93.
2. Chamberlain, *European Decolonization in the Twentieth Century*, 3.
3. Chamberlain, *European Decolonization in the Twentieth Century*, 7–9.
4. Chamberlain, *European Decolonization in the Twentieth Century*, 10–11.
5. Chalmers Johnson, *The Sorrows of Empire: Militarism, Secrecy and the End of the Republic* (New York: Henry Holt, 2004), 151–85; see also Chalmers Johnson, *Nemesis: The Last Days of the American Republic* (New York: Henry Holt, 2006).
6. Johnson, *The Sorrows of Empire*, 154.
7. For an overview of this process, see Eduardo Galeano, *The Open Veins of Latin America: Five Centuries of the Pillage of a Continent* (New York: Monthly Review Press, 1973).
8. Galeano, *The Open Veins of Latin America*, 55–61.
9. Galeano, *The Open Veins of Latin America*, 174–75.
10. See Thomas Pakenham, *The Scramble for Africa, 1876–1912* (New York: Random House, 1991); see also Muriel E. Chamberlain, *The Scramble for Africa* (London: Longman, 1999).
11. "Scramble for Africa," *Wikipedia, the Free Encyclopedia*, http://en.wikipedia.org/wiki/Scramble_for_Africa, 8.
12. Chamberlain, *European Decolonization in the Twentieth Century*, 66, 71.
13. Chamberlain, *European Decolonization in the Twentieth Century*, 75–76.
14. Chamberlain, *European Decolonization in the Twentieth Century*, 77.
15. Chamberlain, *European Decolonization in the Twentieth Century*, 92–93, 99–100.
16. Chamberlain, *European Decolonization in the Twentieth Century*, 101–2.
17. Chamberlain, *European Decolonization in the Twentieth Century*, 103–5.
18. Chamberlain, *European Decolonization in the Twentieth Century*, 78–79, 84–85, 88–89.
19. Chamberlain, *European Decolonization in the Twentieth Century*, 45–57.
20. See Bernard Fall, *Hell in a Very Small Place: The Siege of Dien Bien Phu* (Philadelphia: Lippincott, 1967).

21. See William Blum, *Killing Hope: U.S. Military and CIA Interventions since World War II* (Monroe, Me.: Common Courage Press, 1995), 122–32.

22. Blum, *Killing Hope*, 174–78. See also Gareth Porter, *Perils of Dominance: Imbalance of Power and the Road to Vietnam* (Berkeley, CA: University of California Press, 2005).

23. Chamberlain, *European Decolonization in the Twentieth Century*, 183–86.

24. Chamberlain, *European Decolonization in the Twentieth Century*, 154–74.

25. Chamberlain, *European Decolonization in the Twentieth Century*, 97–99.

26. Chamberlain, *European Decolonization in the Twentieth Century*, 188–90.

27. Chamberlain, *European Decolonization in the Twentieth Century*, 158–62.

• *11* •

The Global Economy:
Neocolonialism and Neoliberalism

*N*eoliberal corporate globalization can be considered the third stage of European and U.S. colonialism, a colonialism based not on direct occupation of colonies but on control of each dependent nation's economy within the Western-controlled global corporate economy, backed up by the military power of the United States. This chapter delineates these patterns of Western control of the global economy, especially through the World Bank, the International Monetary Fund, and the World Trade Organization.[1] Chapter 12 details the system of U.S. militarism as the enforcer of this system of global neocolonialism, while chapter 16 discusses the acceleration of ecological impoverishment of the planet through military and economic exploitation.

As discussed in chapter 10, after World War II a process of political decolonization took place in which flag independence was conceded to most of the territories of European colonialism in Asia, Africa, and the Middle East. A few colonial powers, such as the Portuguese in Angola and Mozambique, refused to let go, and white settlers sought to block majority rule in Rhodesia and South Africa. This resistance necessitated long, bloody revolutionary struggles. But the general pattern that emerged from this process of decolonialism is neocolonialism, not full self-determination, in which the newly independent states control their own resources for their own people.

The United States emerged from World War II as the world's strongest military power and quickly assumed the role of the enforcer of the neocolonial system of control of the former colonies by the West. Third World liberation movements, seeking to throw off neocolonial hegemony over their nation's labor, wealth, and foreign policy, often adopted a socialist ideology and allied with the communist world against Western domination, although they sought nationalist forms of socialism, not dependency on the Soviet Union.

In response, the West, led by the United States, made anticommunism the ruling ideology of its foreign policy.

Although the United States thinks of "communism" and "socialism" only as code words for totalitarian dictatorship, for much of the Third World these terms carry the tradition of a quest for greater economic equality, while many Third World socialists would reject the stifling of civil liberties. But the U.S. ideological use of anticommunism did not allow a balanced discussion of these complexities. Rather, anticommunism functioned as a black-and-white rhetoric about good and evil, God and the Devil, qua capitalist "freedom" and socialist "dictatorship," presumably as a "puppet" of the Soviet Union.

This ideology was used to justify an attack on any social and political system proposed by Third World countries that aspired to a more just distribution of wealth and political power to the poor majority. By demonizing communism as atheistic totalitarianism and claiming to be the world champion of "democracy," the United States masked the fact that what this crusade was mostly all about was the maintenance of neocolonial Western-controlled corporate capitalism and the prevention of genuine locally controlled political and economic democracy.

With the collapse of the Soviet Union in 1990 and the emergence of the United States as the overwhelming leader of global economic and military power, the third era of colonialism, or neocolonialism, built during the Cold War, came into greater visibility. This has taken the form of a bid for U.S. imperial power rule over the rest of the world, not only over the former colonies of Asia, Africa, and the Middle East but also over Latin America, seeking also to divide and marginalize the European Economic Union lest it become an independent global power bloc. Great Britain, ambivalent about submerging itself as a small island nation within the European community, generally seeks to attach itself to the coattails of American empire and thus retain its global reach. This, perhaps, explains the desperate loyalty of former British Prime Minister Tony Blair to American military adventures in areas such as Iraq.

To understand this third phase of colonialism, manifest in corporate globalization, one has to examine the economic institutions that have been built over the sixty years since World War II to centralize control over planetary wealth. This effort to concentrate economic power in the hands of Western and especially U.S. elites also required the marginalization of the United Nations. For U.S. elites, the United Nations must be prevented from operating in any way as a representative world body of the world's nations that gives equal voice to Third World nations or indeed to any nation other than the United States.

The world system that has been built as the global extension of U.S. economic hegemony is what is called the Bretton Woods institutions: the World

Bank, the International Monetary Fund (IMF), and, since 1995, the World Trade Organization (WTO). The World Bank and the IMF were established between 1944 and 1947 to rebuild war-torn Europe. The IMF was created to administer the international monetary system. The World Bank was initially designed to provide loans for Europe's postwar reconstruction. The General Agreement on Tariffs and Trade (GATT), which became the WTO in 1995, is the global trade organization charged with fashioning and enforcing multilateral trade agreements. The World Bank and IMF are funded by the contributions of member nations, with the United States, providing 20 percent of the funds, as the largest donor. The G-8 nations—the United States, the United Kingdom, France, Germany, Italy, Canada, Japan, and (since 1990) Russia—monopolize the funding and control the decisions.

In the first two and a half decades, the Bretton Woods system was one of a controlled capitalism that promoted full employment and an expansion of the welfare state. As Manfred Stegner puts it, "Rising wages and increased social services secured in the wealthy countries of the global North a temporary class compromise."[2] This compromise collapsed in 1971 at the time when President Richard Nixon abandoned the gold-based fixed rate system. Several crises, including high inflation, low economic growth, and rising oil prices, led to the victories of conservative leaders, President Ronald Reagan in the United States and Prime Minister Margaret Thatcher in the United Kingdom, who championed a neoliberal dismantling of the welfare state. The rising neoliberal paradigm was further strengthened in 1989–1991 with the collapse of the command (state-controlled) economies of Eastern Europe. Shattering the postwar consensus of a controlled capitalism based on Keynesian principles of government regulation, free market theory became the new economic orthodoxy, advocating the downsizing of government and the deregulation of the economy.

Two other important developments also contributed to the new paradigm of a global free market without government regulation. One was the internationalization of financial transactions. As capital and security markets were deregulated, mobility among different segments of the financial system worldwide accelerated rapidly. There was an explosive growth of tradable financial value. By the late 1990s, nearly 2 trillion U.S. dollars were exchanged in global currency markets daily. These exchanges have nothing to do with actual investment in production; rather, they simply exploit profits through the rapid buying and selling of changing values of currency and stocks, taking advantage of weak banking regulations in developing countries.[3] With a flick of a computer button, billions of dollars can be moved around the world, buying stocks and bonds when the market goes up and selling when it goes down, creating vast profits for unaccountable financial traders but potentially throwing entire countries and regions of the world into financial crisis. The Asian financial crisis that hit Thailand, Japan, and South Korea in 1997–1998 was partly caused by such speculative trade in currency.[4]

A second key development was the emergence of transnational corporations that took advantage of a deregulated global labor market. Such transnational corporations exploited low wages for labor, cheap resources, and lack of environmental protections to locate their production throughout the world in a global system that integrated all stages of production and marketing. They created global commodity chains that produced, distributed, and marketed their products. Thus, Nike subcontracts 100 percent of its production to low-wage labor in Asia, China, South Korea, Malaysia, Taiwan, and Thailand. Such giant transnational corporations have come to dominate over 70 percent of world trade. Trade regulations under GATT and then the WTO increasingly were biased toward facilitating the global access of these giant transnationals at the expense of efforts of nations to regulate the conditions of labor and use of resources in their own countries.

Another key factor in the undermining of regulation of production in Third World countries was the emergence of their accelerating indebtedness. Since Europe quickly rebuilt itself without help from these financial institutions, already in the 1970s the World Bank and the IMF turned instead to lending for what came to be called the "development" of the "Third World," in actuality to consolidate control over the resources of the Third World by the West. In the 1970s, high U.S. military spending, the rise of multinational corporations, and the rapid increase of oil prices by the Organization of Petroleum Exporting Countries caused large funds to build up in international banks. Under Robert McNamara's leadership (1968–1981), the former secretary of defense who designed such murderous projects as the electronic battlefield in the Vietnam War, the policy of the World Bank became the promotion of high-volume, low-interest development loans to the Third World.[5]

McNamara favored large development projects, such as large dams and huge agricultural colonization and land-clearing schemes, often on poor soils in tropical forests in Latin America and Asia. Although claiming that the primary purpose of such development was overcoming poverty and that World Bank loans were carefully monitored for environmental impact, there was little evidence of either concern. Indeed, many large loans were made to military regimes that tortured and murdered their people, sometimes shortly after having overthrown a more democratic regime.[6] Many of these states in the hands of dictators, such as Ferdinand Marcos in the Philippines, used such funds for showy projects or stashed them into personal bank accounts. Many projects remained unfinished, with the benefits going to multinational corporations and national elites, not the local people. Masses of people were displaced by projects, such as large dams, without ever being appropriately resettled despite promises to do so.

The mounting debts accrued from such loans fed into an international debt crisis. This became evident in 1982 when Mexico announced that it could not pay its debts. International banks feared a general renunciation of debts by poorer nations that would cause a world monetary crisis and possible depression. The response to this debt crisis by the international banking system, led by the World Bank, was to devise structural adjustment programs aimed at forcing Third World countries to pay their debts at the expense of internal development.

The formula for structural adjustment entailed the following policies: 1) devaluation of local currency, thus making purchases more expensive for local people, as their money fell in value; 2) a sharp rise in interest rates on loans, thus increasing the costs of paying back the loans; 3) the removal of trade barriers that protected local industry and agriculture, with the effect that products from large multinationals could undersell and wipe out local production; 4) the privatization of public sector enterprises, such as transportation, water, telephones, and electricity, allowing the wealthy to buy up such enterprises and raise the prices, abolishing subsidies that made these services accessible to the poor; and 5) the deregulation of goods, services, and labor, that is, the removal of minimum-wage laws and state subsidies for basic foods, such as milk, bread, wheat, and rice, as well as subsidies for health and education. Prices rose for education, health, and food, making these inaccessible to the poorer classes.

Accepting this package of structural adjustment was mandatory if a country wanted to receive new loans to pay its debts. Each country was directed to focus on one or two traditional commodities, such as sugar or coffee, to earn money in international currency (dollars) to repay its debts at the expense of a diversified development of agricultural and industrial production for local consumption.[7]

The World Bank and the IMF have typically blamed governments of the Third World for their poor record in development and debt payment. Their claim was that local governments were inefficient and were wasting money in subsidized services to the people. Structural adjustment programs were billed as "austerity" measures that might cause temporary "pain" (to whom?) but would result in the whole economy eventually turning around and beginning to prosper. The proponents of these measures were confident that they would cause the economies of each country to rise. But the reality was mostly the opposite of these rosy predictions. By focusing on stepped-up production of a few export products, such as coffee, the international market for such products was glutted and prices fell so that even though the countries were producing and exporting more, they were earning less on their exports.

Local wages also fell, while prices rose. This was caused both by the devaluation of the currency and by the cutting of state subsidies on food, basic commodities, health, education, and transportation or the privatization of companies providing such services. For example in post-Sandinista Nicaragua in the 1990s, free local health clinics and centers for popular education were closed. Local hospitals no longer had funds to provide medicines, to repair old equipment, or to purchase new equipment. A person admitted to a hospital often found that friends or relatives had to go out and buy the medicines in a pharmacy that a patient needed.

Schools were privatized and became more expensive, and even state schools raised tuition beyond the reach of an increasingly impoverished majority. The gains in literacy and access to health under the revolutionary regime were rapidly lost. While the literacy campaign of 1980 had reduced illiteracy to less than 10 percent, ten years later it was back to 35 percent. Thus, the results of these structural adjustment measures were rising poverty, malnutrition, unemployment, homelessness (especially of children), and the turn to drugs and crime for relief and for money.[8]

These negative effects of structural adjustment were not confined to a few local cases, such as Nicaragua, but were general throughout the global community of nations. In 2001, the Center for Economic and Policy Research in Washington, D.C., used data from the United Nations and the World Bank itself to examine the progress in economic growth rates, education, and health in 170 countries for the periods from 1960 to 1980 and 1980 to 2000. These countries were divided into five groups, from the poorest to the most affluent. During the first twenty years from 1960 to 1980, it was typical of most of these countries to follow policies that protected local development. During the second twenty years, the World Bank's strictures against trade barriers and subsidies of local production prevailed, and such practices were discontinued.

The researchers found that for all the indices of economic growth, health (including increased life expectancy, both male and female, and lessening infant and childhood mortality), and education (both public spending on education and enrollment, male and female), these countries made more progress in the decades of 1960–1980, when welfare states were in force, than in the decades of 1980–2000, in the era of neoliberal economic policies, with the exception, in some cases, of the most affluent set of countries. Those hardest hit were the poorest two groups of countries.

In terms of economic growth, there was a fall across the board for all groups of countries. The poorest group went from a per capita growth rate of 1.9 percent annually in 1960–1980 to a decline of 0.5 percent a year during 1980–2000. For the second-poorest group of nations, there was a decline from an annual per capita growth rate of 3.6 percent in 1960–1980 to less than 1 percent in 1980–2000. Other groups also showed substantial declines in growth rates.

In health, progress in life expectancy was reduced for four out of the five groups, the biggest slowdown taking place in the second of the poorest group of nations. Since this fall occurred both in nations with a high level of acquired immunodeficiency syndrome (AIDS) and in those without large numbers of AIDS sufferers, it cannot be explained by the AIDS pandemic. Progress in reducing infant mortality was also considerably slower during the period of globalization (1980–2000) than in the previous two decades. The biggest decline took place in the three poorest groups of nations. Progress in education also slowed during the period of globalization. The rates of growth of primary, secondary, and tertiary (postsecondary) school enrollment was slower for most groups of countries, except for the richest group. This decrease was true both for the level of public spending on education and for enrollment and literacy rates.

Although it cannot be proved from these data that these declines in economic growth, education, and health were directly caused by the policies of the World Bank, the researchers declare that there is a prima facie case that these policies played a major role in causing these declines during the period when structural adjustment rules were imposed in contrast to the earlier period when they were absent and most countries were following policies protective of local development.[9] It is also well known that those developing countries that made rapid economic progress in the 1980s, such as the Asian "Five Tigers" (Japan, South Korea, Singapore, Taiwan, and Hong Kong), continued to follow patterns of state protection of local industries into the 1980s and resisted the World Bank strictures against such protective policies.[10]

The World Bank, IMF, and WTO sought to dismantle such protective practices, eventually for the Asian "Tigers" also but beginning with the weaker indebted countries. Interest rates escalated. Pushing high-interest loans to repay debts under the conditions of structural adjustment created a spiraling upward of a debt trap, even as the poverty of the countries supposed to repay these debts was spiraling downward. Poor countries were often able to pay only 30 to 40 percent of the interest in the loans, while the rest of the interest payment was added to the principal owed. Thus, even though the countries continued to squeeze their resources to repay their loans, their debts mounted year by year through compounding interest and the need for new loans. Hence, structural adjustment had the effect of creating a net extraction of wealth from the poor countries to the rich countries or, rather, to international banks. Instead of "trickling down" from the rich to the poor, as promised by neoliberal economists, such policies created a "gushing upward" of wealth from the masses of the poor of the world to an elite group of the superrich. As far back as 1988, $50 billion more was paid by poor countries to banks than was loaned to them by these banks, and this figure has continued to rise.

Structural adjustment had other major effects. By dismantling trade barriers, local production was devastated. Flooded by cheap products from transnational corporations, local industries and agriculture were forced out of business. Thus, in Nicaragua, peanut farmers and the local peanut butter industry could not compete with Skippy's peanut butter from the United States and went out of business. In Korea, rice farmers were put out of business by cheap rice from the United States and lost their land. Such destruction of local production was defended by neoliberal theorists as simply the inevitable working of "market laws." What was unacknowledged by such theorists is that large multinationals enjoy subsidies and tax breaks from their governments, while local industries in the Third World are not similarly allowed to protect their industries and agriculture. American rice is cheap not because American farmers are more efficient than Korean farmers, especially given the costs of transportation of such rice from the United States to South Korea, but because American farmers and food multinationals are subsidized by the U.S. government.[11]

Why did Third World governments accept such loans in the first place? Even more, why did they accept such destructive conditions for the continued repayment of these loans? It seems that there have been three reasons for such compliance. First, although the majority of people were suffering as a result of these policies, the wealthy elites who controlled the governments favored by the United States were prospering. Development loans were a major way for them to cash in on enormous profits by using these loans for their own projects. Second, the economists who were advising these governments were trained in the same schools of market neoliberalism as those of the World Bank and accepted its theories of the free market as unquestioned dogma. Finally, any government that resisted the structural adjustment package was made into a pariah, isolated, and denied further loans and markets. This was the strategy toward Nicaragua in the 1980s that brought down the Sandinista government and that has been applied for more than forty years against Cuba. These strictures are enough to bring most Third World governments into line.[12]

The system of global control of markets by international financial institutions and transnational corporations is being greatly extended since the 1995 emergence of the WTO. The WTO sets the market rules that not only prevent any trade barriers from being erected that protect local industries and agriculture but also enforce new rules that extend the ability of such transnational corporations to exploit wealth. Two such sets of rules are particularly notable: TRIMS, or trade-related investment measures, and TRIPS, or trade-related intellectual property laws.

TRIMS are designed to prevent local governments from protecting their own national financial institutions and property ownership from takeovers by foreign corporations. They forbid such laws as those that limit the percentage of an industry that can be owned by foreigners and that demand that a corporation use a certain percentage of local resources or labor or set minimum-wage levels or working and environmental conditions.

TRIPS prevent local industries from cloning their own versions of Western technology, such as computers. They also have been expanded to allow corporations to patent the genetic properties of seeds and plants and even human DNA, preventing local farmers from saving and using their own seeds and growing plants that have been a part of local agriculture and medicine for thousands of years because such seeds have been modified by Western technology and now are claimed as "owned" by Western patents. Corporations are also buying up aquifers and watersheds and forcing people to pay for water that they formerly used free from their own wells and streams.[13]

These market rules function on behalf of the unaccountable economic power of transnational corporations. David Korten, in his acclaimed book *When Corporations Rule the World*, has traced the process by which such corporations have shaken off any accountability to local or national governments. In the 1880s, corporations in the United States won the legal status of persons and were able to exploit the laws protecting the rights of persons under the Fourteenth Amendment to the Constitution (written to defend the rights of the freed slave, even as these freemen were themselves being deprived of these rights by Jim Crow laws). In the 1950s and 1960s, corporations uprooted themselves from accountability to local communities and in the 1980s became increasingly transnational, dismantling any national or international laws that might limit their freedom of movement and investment.[14]

One major effort to prevent any regulation that would limit the investment freedom of transnational companies was the Multilateral Agreement on Investment, which was negotiated in secret between 1995 and 1998 by the Organization for Economic Cooperation and Development, an organization representing the transnational corporations. The agreement sought to limit the legal ability of governments at all levels—local, provincial, and national—to regulate foreign investment and activities of foreign-based corporations. National borders could then become totally permeable to large corporations that could enter any country and buy up businesses, banks, and other assets. Governments would not be permitted to pass laws to protect their national assets, businesses, and banks; to regulate labor conditions; or to prevent human rights abuses or environmental damage. Although international outcry prevented this agreement from being accepted, investment liberalization is still the operating agenda of the WTO, which continues to seek to incorporate its rules into its trade regulations.[15]

The global system of transnational corporations and the Bretton Woods institutions means that Third World governments have lost much of their national sovereignty—their right or ability to protect their own national industries or shape their own development and foreign policies. These developments sparked a debate about the obsolescence of the nation-state. Some globalization thinkers argued that the nation-state was disappearing for a borderless world, governed by global corporations and financial institutions.[16] But this argument seems premature. There has also been backlash movements in many countries, including the United States, Europe, and the Third World, threatened by this loss of national sovereignty, that seek to restore the power of the nation-state.[17] It is more accurate to say that many small nations have become powerless in the face of international forces, while large wealthy nations, such as the United States, have become imperial powers.

What has become increasingly evident in the 1990s to the present is the growing gap between rich and poor worldwide, with some 85 percent of the wealth of the world in the hands of some 20 percent of the world's population, much of it concentrated in the top 1 percent, a global elite, while the remaining 80 percent share the remaining 15 percent and the poorest 20 percent, more than a billion people, live in deep misery.[18] In 1960, the richest 20 percent of the world's population had thirty times the wealth of the poorest 20 percent. By 1995, this gap had grown to eighty-two times. The richest 225 people in the world have a combined wealth of over $1 trillion, equal to the annual income of the poorest 50 percent of humanity, 3 billion people, while the richest three people have assets that exceed those of forty-eight of the poorest nations. In 1999, almost half the world's population was living on less than $2 a day and more than 20 percent, 1.2 billion people, on less than $1 a day, according to World Bank figures.[19]

As it became increasingly evident that the policies of the World Bank, IMF, and WTO were accelerating the poverty and de-development of the world's poorest people while enriching a small, mostly Western-based elite, a backlash against globalization has developed around the world. This took the form of both right-wing and left-wing antiglobalism movements. The right-wing backlash in the United States, Europe, and some Third World countries has taken the form of nationalist-protectionist movements, often championing national sovereignty and the rights of the racially dominant peoples of the country against immigrants in a way reminiscent of fascism of the 1930s, such as the German People's Union founded in 1971 by Dr. Gerard Frey in Bavaria.[20]

Alternatively, there have emerged movements on the left that might be called internationalist and egalitarian. These movements and their leading thinkers are not against globalization as a process of intercommunication of people around the world, but they champion what might be called globalization from below rather than globalization from above. They are concerned with creating a new global system that restores the self-government, cultures, and economic integrity of local people while linking them together in networks of global communication and mutual help.

Among major expressions of such internationalist and egalitarian movements of global mutual help from below are the Third World Network, based in Malaysia; the International Forum on Globalization, representing over sixty organizations in twenty-five countries; Global Exchange, based in San Francisco, California; and Focus on the Global South, led by Filipino economist Walden Bello and based in Bangkok.[21] The World Social Forum, which has met annually in Porto Alegre since 2001, has become the international gathering place for groups concerned with exchanging ideas and strategies on alternative forms of global relationship.[22]

A package of policy recommendations has emerged from these left egalitarian movements that are broadly shared. These include blanket forgiveness of all Third World debt, imposing a tax on international financial investments, the so-called Tobin tax, the abolition of offshore financial centers that give tax havens to wealthy individuals and corporations, implementation of stringent environmental protection agreements, the implementation of a more equitable global development agenda (together with a new world development institution to be financed by such measures as the Tobin tax on financial transactions but managed mostly by the global South), the establishment of global labor protection standards to be followed by all nations, greater transparency and accountability of national governments and international institutions to the public of every nation, and greater sensitivity to the issues of women in development.[23]

While such a consensus on what needs to happen is important, these networks that seek an alternative way of development are still far from being able to match the global wealth and power of the dominant economic system and its main military backer, the United States.

NOTES

1. This chapter reproduces much of the analysis on globalization and the Bretton Woods institutions found in Rosemary Ruether, *Integrating Ecofeminism, Globalization and World Religions* (Lanham, Md.: Rowman & Littlefield, 2004), 3–8, in a rewritten and expanded form.

2. Manfred B. Steger, *Globalism: The New Market Ideology* (Lanham, Md.: Rowman & Littlefield, 2002), 26.

3. Steger, *Globalism*, 26–27.

4. See Walden Bello, *The Future in Balance: Essays on Globalization and Resistance* (Oakland, Calif.: Food First and Focus in the Global South, 2001), 93–94.

5. See Bruce Rich, "World Bank/IMF: 50 Years Is Enough," in *50 Years Is Enough: The Case against the World Bank and the International Monetary Fund*, ed. Kevin Danaher (Boston: South End Press, 1994), 9–11.

6. Rich, "World Bank/IMF," 10.

7. See Bruce Rich, *Mortgaging the Earth: The World Bank, Environmental Impoverishment and the Crisis of Development* (Boston: Beacon Press, 1994), 186–289; Susan George and Fabrizio Sabelli, *Faith and Credit: The World Bank's Secular Empire* (Boulder, Colo.: Westview Press, 1994), 58–72; and John Cobb, *The Earthist Challenge to Economism: The Theological Critique of the World Bank* (New York: St. Martin's Press, 1999), 90–107.

8. On Nicaragua, see Sharon Hostetler et al., *A High Price to Pay: Structural Adjustment and Women in Nicaragua* (Washington, D.C.: Witness for Peace, 1995).

9. Mark Weisbrot, Dean Baker, Egor Kraev, and July Chen, "The Scorecard on Globalization, 1980–2000: Twenty Years of Diminished Development," www.cepr.net/publications/globalization_2001_07_11.htm (accessed March 27, 2007).

10. Walden Bello and Stephanie Rosenfeld, *Dragons in Distress: Asia's Miracle Economies in Crisis* (San Francisco: Institute for Food and Development Policy, 1992).

11. See particularly Walden Bello, *The United States, Structural Adjustment and Global Poverty* (London: Pluto Press, 1994).

12. See George and Sabelli, *Faith and Credit*, 112–34, 190–296.

13. See Vandana Shiva, *Biopiracy: The Plunder of Nature and Knowledge* (Boston: South End Press, 1997); Vandana Shiva, *Stolen Harvest: The Hijacking of the Global Food Supply* (Boston: South End Press, 1999); and Maude Barlow and Tony Clarke, *Blue Gold: The Battle against Corporate Theft of the World's Water* (New York: New Press, 2002).

14. David Korten, *When Corporations Rule the World* (San Francisco: Berrett-Koehler, 1995).

15. See Council of Canadians, *The MAI Inquiry: Confronting Globalization and Reclaiming Democracy*" (Toronto: Council of Canadians, 1999).

16. Steger, *Globalism*, 28–34.

17. Steger, *Globalism*, 86–104.

18. A useful primer on global inequality in its many dimensions is Bob Sutcliffe, *100 Ways of Seeing an Unequal World* (London: Zed Books, 2002).

19. See www.worldbank.org/poverty.

20. Steger, *Globalism*, 95–99.

21. Steger, *Globalism*, 111–13.

22. See Ruether, *Integrating Ecofeminism, Globalization and World Religions*, 139–41.

23. See Steger, *Globalism*, 146.

· 12 ·

U.S. and Global Militarism

*A*rmies have functioned through history and still today as the main way of enforcing imperial power. Military force ensures domination over populations and access to and continued control of economic resources by an imperial power. The United States has relied on its military in much of its process of expansion of power across the continent to clear the land of Indians and suppress their resistance and to seize the Mexican northwest in the Mexican-American War of 1846–1848. The rush of white settlers across the North American continent to California was a major tool in this expansion, settlers who often used their own firearms and other forms of violence to drive out Indians and Mexicans.[1]

The United States did not then think of itself as an imperial, militaristic nation. The founding fathers were suspicious of the military power of kings and elites, and many cautioned that the new nation should not keep any standing army. Thomas Jefferson was responsible for inserting into the Declaration of Independence the complaint against the English king that "he has kept among us, in times of peace, Standing Armies without the Consent of our legislatures." In his letters, Jefferson expressed reservations that the new federal Constitution did not provide "clearly and without the aid of sophisms for . . . protection against standing armies."[2] Jefferson's concern was reiterated in his first annual message as president in 1801: "Nor is it conceived needful or safe that a standing army should be kept up in time of peace."[3] James Madison, the primary author of the Constitution, wrote, "Of all enemies to public liberty, war is, perhaps, the most to be dreaded, because it comprises and develops the germ of every other. War is the parent of armies; from these proceed debts and taxes; and armies and debts and taxes are the known instruments for bringing the many under the dominion of the few."[4]

American policy from the Revolutionary War to World War II was not to maintain a large standing army but rather to recruit armies at a time of war and disband them when the war was over, retaining a small professional army between wars. When the Spanish-American War broke out in 1898, the United States had not fought a war since the Civil War thirty years earlier (other than Indian fighting), and its army had dwindled. Most of the 306,760 troops who eventually served in these wars had to be quickly recruited, trained, and equipped to be sent to the Caribbean and the Pacific to fight. This process was highly confused, without a clear central authority. As a result, many soldiers were sent to Cuba with wool uniforms in a tropical summer without adequate guns and horses or tents to keep off the rain.

However, Theodore Roosevelt already envisioned the United States as becoming a major imperial nation to rival the British. As assistant secretary of the navy under President William McKinley in 1897, he had begun to expand the navy for that purpose.[5] The Spanish-American War was the first time that the United States began to maintain an occupying army in lands beyond the North American continent.[6] In 1903, Congress set up for the first time a general staff to plan and coordinate future wars. The Army War College was also founded that year as a permanent institution to prepare for war, and independent state militias were coordinated into the National Guard.[7] The Marine Corps, developed as an adjunct of the U.S. Navy, was repeatedly sent from 1900 to the mid-1930s to occupy countries such as Haiti, the Dominican Republic, and Nicaragua, which were seen as threatening U.S. interests. Still, a large army was not maintained between wars. The army that was sent to Europe in 1916 was mostly recruited for that war and disbanded thereafter.

World War II represented the largest military mobilization that the United States had ever undertaken. Total servicemen mobilized were over 16 million. Yet after the war, it was assumed that most of this army would be disbanded and its war industries converted to civilian use. The U.S. military was almost totally demobilized in the years immediately after 1945. But this began to be reversed by 1947 when the United States redefined its foreign policy as one of active intervention to prevent "communist takeover" of emerging nations. The concept of the "cold war" was developed to rationalize the maintenance of a war footing in times where there was no declared war.

The distinction between times of war as times of exceptional mobilization of an army and times of peace became blurred. A "cold" war meant that the army must remain ever on the ready for whenever the war might turn from "cold" to "hot." On March 12, 1947, President Harry Truman set the foundation for the idea of a cold war by describing the world as split between two alternative ways of life: freedom versus totalitarian slavery. The American people must be ready to oppose totalitarian slavery and commit themselves to military interventions to preserve "freedom" at any time and in any place in the world.

From this 1947 declaration of the existence of a permanent state of war until today, there has been a continuous expansion of military spending in the United States. Total U.S. servicemen during the Korean War were 5.7 million, of whom 33,741 died in battle. The Vietnam War saw the total U.S. servicemen expanded to 8.7 million, of whom 47,410 died in battle. A permanent network of U.S. military bases began to develop around the world. Some of these, such as those in Italy, Britain, Germany, Japan, and Korea, date from the end of World War II.

Between 1950 and 2003, the United States experienced four periods of intense military mobilization with huge spurts of purchases of weapons. The first of these was the Korean War from 1950 to 1953, although only a small part of these armaments were used to fight that war. Most of the military budget went into the development of nuclear weapons and the stocking of the huge Cold War military garrisons being built in Britain, Germany, Italy, Japan, and South Korea. Defense spending rose from about $150 billion in 1950 to over $500 billion in 1953 (measured in 2002 dollars).

The second buildup was during the Vietnam War. Defense spending was over $400 billion in 1968 (in 2002 dollars). The third boom was during Ronald Reagan's presidency when there was a renewed Cold War and outcry that the United States was "falling behind" in the arms race with the Soviet Union. Under Reagan, there were huge investments in new weapon systems and high-tech research for the Strategic Defense Initiative (so-called Star Wars). Spending hit about $450 billion in 1989.[8]

To the surprise and consternation of U.S. cold warriors, the Soviet Union unraveled rapidly after 1989, and it appeared that the rationale for the Cold War was disappearing. For many in the United States, the end of the Cold War was seen as mandating a major reduction of the military buildup of the previous forty years. Many called on the U.S. government to cut the military budget by half and to use the savings for a major renewal of infrastructure and social services of American society, which had been defunded in the Reagan years. Speaking hopefully of a "peace dividend," such people looked forward to the chance to rebuild roads, bridges, schools, and libraries; to alleviate poverty; and to invest in health, education, and environmental protection.

The American military-industrial establishment saw this call for a major conversion from military to peacetime spending as highly threatening and quickly began to search for new enemies to justify the maintenance and even expansion of military expenditures. They insisted on the necessity of being able to fight "two wars at once" and held up as still dangerous enemies states such as Cuba, Iran, Iraq, North Korea, and Libya, though the global danger of these states appeared unconvincing at the time.

In the early 1990s, some in the George H. W. Bush administration began to search for a new rationale for U.S. military expansion beyond the Cold War. Early in 1992, Paul Wolfowitz, then undersecretary of defense for policy, circulated a draft of a new defense planning guide that openly acknowledged that the United States was now the sole superpower and thus that its military purpose should be seen as the maintenance of a permanent preeminence of the United States over the entire globe. The United States should go beyond the capacity to defeat existing competitors for world power to project such overwhelming capacity for force that any potential competitors would be convinced that "they need not aspire to a greater role or pursue a more aggressive posture to protect their legitimate interests." This stance of preeminent power should be directed not only against potential adversaries, such as China, but also in relation to advanced industrial nations, such as Europe and Japan. In short, America's purpose in maintaining a huge army was no longer defense but imperial rule.[9]

This proposal, leaked to the press in March 1992, aroused an outcry of opposition. The Bush administration claimed that Wolfowitz's draft was mere speculation and not official policy. But Dick Cheney, then secretary of defense, issued a sanitized version of it later in the year.[10] During the presidency of Bill Clinton (1993–2001), there were some rhetorical gestures in the direction of a "peace dividend" but no real cuts in military spending. But Republican conservatives out of power began to plan for a new stage of military expansion. They argued that the United States was in danger of losing its global dominance and also that U.S. dominance now had a new purpose, namely, imperial preeminence in all regions of the globe.

In 1997, these thinkers established the Project for the New American Century, headed by leading neoconservative Irving Kristol, to promote this view. In their 2000 report *Rebuilding American Defenses*, they argued for both a renewal and an expansion of American military power and a transformation of its purpose. No longer confined to defending the "West" against communism, the American military now existed to maintain a Pax Americana around the world. They projected four core missions for this military: 1) to defend the American homeland, 2) to develop the capacity to fight and win multiple simultaneous wars, 3) to carry out constabulary duties worldwide wherever there were threats to American interests, and 4) to engage in a major upgrading of American forces through new technology, including the militarization of space and cyberspace. Active-duty strength should be expanded to 1.6 million and defense spending extended to reach 3.5 to 3.8 percent of the U.S. gross national product, about $500 billion a year.[11]

The authors of the report expressed some concern whether the American people were ready for such a revolutionary development of the role of the United States and its military in the world, "absent some catastrophic and catalyzing event—such as a New Pearl Harbor."[12] On September 11, 2001, this new Pearl Harbor occurred. Four American airplanes were seized, two of them crashing into the World Trade Center, one purportedly into the Pentagon, and a fourth into a field in Pennsylvania. The official version of what actually happened on that day and who was responsible for it continues to be contested, although the major American media have steadfastly refused to take such questioning seriously, labeling it mere "conspiracy theory."[13]

What is not in doubt is that these events were immediately seized on by the new President, George W. Bush, and his cabinet, made up of many of the neoconservatives, such as Dick Cheney and Paul Wolfowitz, who had already been arguing for an imperial expansion of the American military to both effect such an expansion and carry out major invasions. They called for invasions not only of Afghanistan, arguably partially responsible for the attack because of its harboring of the al-Qaeda terrorists, but also of Iraq, which bore no such responsibility. With 9/11, "terrorism" became the new rationale, replacing the "communist" threat, for open-ended, never-ending war.

Few Americans questioned the appropriateness of responding to such a terrorist attack with full-scale war designed to battle other countries with high-tech armies and airpower. Since the terrorists were said to have been armed only with box cutters and were mostly Saudi Arabians operating outside any relation to their national state of origin, why war was the appropriate response to such terrorism needs to be questioned. International police work conducted cooperatively between nations would actually be the more appropriate response to stateless terrorists. This has been the European response to terrorist acts, such as the bombing of the London transportation system by mainly "homegrown" terrorists on July 7, 2005.

Yet for Bush and his cabinet, there was no question that full-scale war and a great expansion of the U.S. military were the only imaginable responses to this attack. Thus, in 2001–2002, the Bush administration launched a new expansion of military weapon purchases supposedly to meet this threat of terrorism. On March 14, 2002, the House of Representatives passed a military budget of $393.8 billion, the largest increase in defense outlays in almost twenty years.[14] By 2008, this military budget has expanded to $585 billion. When the military portion of other government agencies is added to this figure, it actually reaches $727 billion for current military spending. If one adds to this past military expenses (i.e., veterans' benefits and interest on the national debt created by military spending), the total figure comes to $1.188 trillion, or 51 percent of the total federal budget.[15]

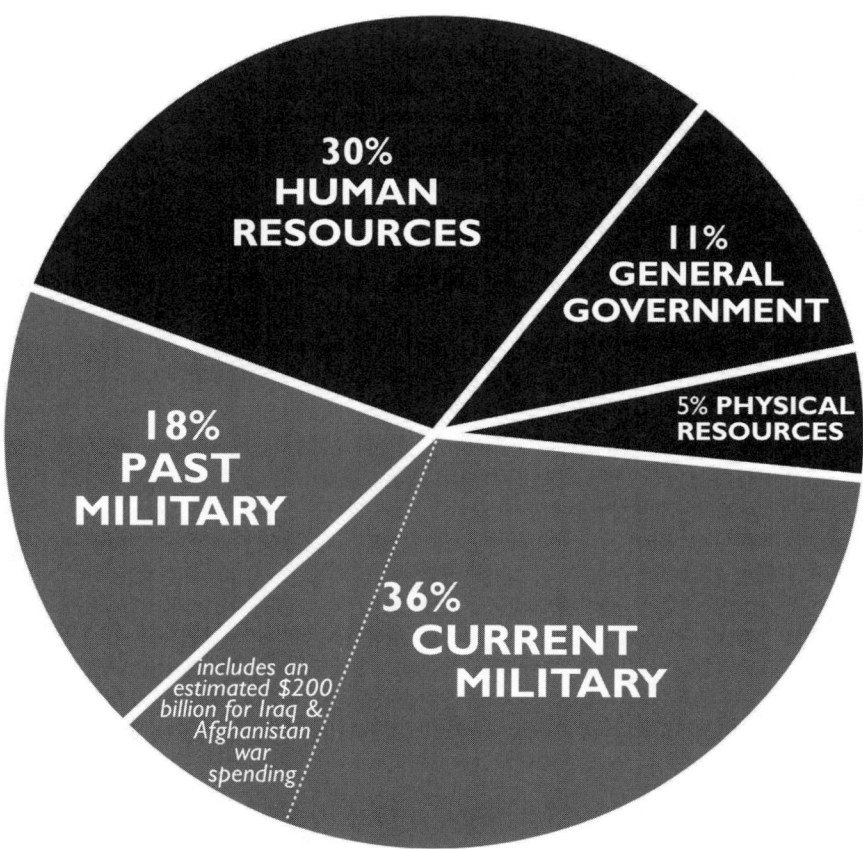

The Federal Budget Pie Chart, 2008

This level of military spending by the United States far outpaces that of any other country. In 2001, the next highest spender, Russia, had a military budget of $65 billion, a sharp drop from the end of the Cold War in 1990 when that country's military budget was $300 billion. China in 2001 had a military budget of $47 billion, and Japan in 2002 was $42.6 billion. Among Europeans, in 2002 the United Kingdom spent $38.4 billion, France $29.5 billion, and Germany $24.9 billion. Those whom the United States defined as members of the "axis of evil" spent a relative pittance compared to the United States or even the Europeans. Iraq's budget in 2001, before the U.S. invasion, was $1.4 billion, North Korea $1.4 billion, Libya $1.2 billion, and Cuba $0.8 billion. The forty-five highest-spending countries other than the United States together spent $442.5 billion. Thus, the United States far outspends the next forty-five countries combined.[16]

In addition to outspending the other nations of the world put together, the United States is also the world's major arms dealer. Since 2001, U.S. military sales have totaled $10 billion to $13 billion a year. In fiscal 2006, arms sales agreements of $21 billion were signed by the Pentagon. From 2001 to 2005, the United States delivered 2,099 surface-to-air missiles to nations in the developing world, 20 percent more than Russia, the next largest supplier. The United States is also first in military training of armies around the world. In 2008, the Pentagon has commitments to train militaries of 138 nations at a cost of nearly $90 million. No other nation comes close to this record.[17]

Global military spending in 2004 was $1.3 trillion, or about 5.5 percent of world gross national product. This amounts to about $2.5 million a minute. Such vast outlays of money for the military deplete global wealth worldwide for social welfare. Much of the world's social needs for education, health, eradication of poverty and malnutrition, and ecological repair could be funded with even half of what the world is spending on the military. Militarism also does vast damage to human society and the environment. It is estimated that 50 million to 51 million people have died in wars or war-related injuries from 1945 to 2000.[18] In addition to the many millions killed in the wars that have ravaged the world since World War II, many millions more are left permanently injured, both physically and psychologically. The families of the injured are also deeply stressed by having the ongoing care of these wounded family members.

The violence from war does not stop when the war is officially over. Not only is there the task of rebuilding the destroyed homes, schools, hospitals, businesses, factories, electrical plants, bridges, and the entire infrastructure of society, but the land remains littered with antipersonnel weapons and land mines. Many fields needed for farming are made inaccessible by the presence of such land mines. Farmers seeking to till such fields and children playing in them are injured and killed by such exploding mines. Sometimes the land has been poisoned by being sprayed with herbicides to reduce forest cover for guerrillas. It takes many years to heal such long-term effects of war, even if the country is lucky not to have another outbreak of violence.

PENTAGON CAPITALISM AND THE EMPIRE OF BASES

As the U.S. military spread its network of power around the world, it has exhibited forms of "crony capitalism" and "state capitalism" that are shocking expressions of rampant exploitation and waste. This has been the case at least since the 1960s. Already in 1970, Seymour Melman published a volume titled *Pentagon Capitalism: The Political Economy of War*,[19] in which he documented this pattern of military waste. Melman showed how the government-funded system of military production and the companies that produce its hardware tend to maximize costs (gold plating), systematic inefficiency, and waste.

The effects of this primacy of military production also erode the civilian economy, causing deindustrialization. There has been a loss of technological competitiveness to Germany and Japan and a decline of heavy industries in areas such as steel and production of railway cars. Defunding public services in favor of war funding also erodes the public service economy. The infrastructure of cities, roads, bridges, and transportation services is neglected. Education, health services, social welfare, libraries, and environmental protection suffer as the federal budget continually favors military over civilian interests.

Military spending is also a key factor in the shift of the United States from being a creditor to being a debtor nation. The national debt has grown since World War II, but it particularly accelerated during the Reagan years of the 1980s into the twenty-first century.[20] On August 4, 2007, the national debt stood at $8.948 trillion. This works out to be a debt of $29,569.10 for every man, woman, and child in the United States.[21] This enormous national debt is increasingly owned by foreign companies and nations. For example, of the $4.9 trillion in treasury bonds and bills, $2.2 trillion is held by other countries, including China and Saudi Arabia.[22] Many observers see this pattern of deficit spending as a house of cards that is bound to crash, leaving the U.S. economy in ruins.[23]

A pattern of exploitation and waste by companies under government contract has also grown rampant under the George W. Bush administration. Government contracts for "rebuilding Iraq" and support services in military bases around the world are farmed out to a list of favorite companies without competitive bidding, such as Bechtel and Halliburton and the latter's subsidiary Kellogg Brown and Root. Vice President Dick Cheney served as the chief executive officer of Halliburton and still retains large economic interests in it. According to Pratap Chatterjee in his book *Iraq, Inc: A Profitable Occupation*, "This company practically designed the modern system of outsourcing the American military with the help of one man: Dick Cheney."[24]

In 2003, Halliburton earned $3.9 billion from contracts with the U.S. military. Halliburton consistently charged high prices for materials that could have been obtained much more cheaply from local sources. It often charged for services that were not delivered. In February 2004, the *Wall Street Journal* reported that in July 2003, Halliburton billed the U.S. government for 42,042 meals a day but served only 14,053. In the first several months of 2002, Halliburton overcharged as much as $16 million for meals for U.S. troops, according to military auditors.[25]

Halliburton avoided giving jobs to Iraqis, who were 70 percent unemployed after the U.S. conquest, preferring to bring in more expensive labor from India and the United States. While Iraqis were paid $100 a month for rote labor, Indians received $300 a month and Texans $8,000 a month. In Chatterjee's words,

> Ultimately the company doesn't care how much it spends, because under its contracts the government pays Halliburton for costs plus a small margin of profit of one percent. In addition to its direct costs, Halliburton can bill as cost a percentage of its overhead, all the way up to its Huston office. ...Thus the more money the company spends the more profit it can make, making a mockery of the private sector's highly touted efficiency.[26]

Since the Spanish-American War over 100 years ago the American military has built a continually expanding "empire of bases." Each time the American military has been present in a country, except in those cases where it was defeated and its presence ousted, as in Vietnam, an ongoing legacy of military bases has been established, from Guantánamo in Cuba in 1900 to Iraq after 2003. Before the U.S. invasion of Iraq in 2003, there were no U.S. military bases in that country. Now there are 109 bases, four of them very large and apparently intended to be permanent.

Chalmers Johnson, the major authority on this "empire of bases," sees this as a new form of empire building not by establishing colonies but rather through establishing military bases through all parts of the world. From these bases, the United States "projects force" in the region, using military pressure to back up American neocolonial penetration of the surrounding countries. In 2003, Johnson counted 725 such bases of various sizes in thirty-eight countries, seventeen very large, eighteen middle sized, and 690 small. In 2005, this had expanded to 737 bases, sixteen very large, twenty-two medium sized, and 699 small.[27]

These are only the bases that are officially acknowledged since others are secret, disguised, or not reported in the official *Base Structure Report*, as in Kosovo, Afghanistan, Iraq, Israel, Kyrgyzstan, Qatar, and Uzbekistan, as well as military and espionage stations in Britain, disguised as Royal Air Force bases.[28] Johnson sees five post–Cold War "missions" served by these bases: 1) maintaining absolute military predominance over the rest of the world; 2) spying on military and civilian communications of friends and enemies alike; 3) controlling as much of the sources of petroleum as possible; 4) providing work and income for the military-industrial complex, including companies such as Halliburton and Bechtel; and 5) providing members of the military and their families with a comfortable life.[29]

All these bases enjoy extraterritorial status, so crimes committed by their personnel are handled by American courts. The United States negotiates a "status of forces agreement" with the "host" country to ensure that its personnel are not tried by local laws. Thus, the American "empire of bases" is like microcolonies beyond the jurisdiction of the occupied country. These bases are typically surrounded by bars and brothels to provide entertainment for the base personnel, so they are seen as both corrupting the local culture and being the spark for endless incidents, such as rapes and drunken driving, that cause injuries and deaths to local people. Thus, the bases become the occasion of outrages that focus anger on their presence.[30]

The building of such bases and their servicing and security are outsourced to corporations, such as Halliburton and Bechtel, and security firms, such as Dyncorp, so the same patterns of cost overruns, exploitation, and waste that Chatterjee documented in Iraq applies to this whole "empire of bases." In addition to these many bases, the Central Intelligence Agency maintains a network of secret prisons where suspects in the war on terrorism can be clandestinely tortured.[31] Robert Higgs, senior fellow in political economy at the Independent Institute, characterizes the American military-industrial complex as

> a vast cesspool of mismanagement, waste and transgressions not only bordering on but often entering deeply into criminal conduct. . . . The great arms firms have managed to slough off much of the normal risks of doing business in a genuine market, passing on many of their excessive costs to the tax-payers, while still realizing extraordinary rates of return on investment.[32]

THE PROLIFERATION OF NUCLEAR WEAPONS AND U.S. RESPONSIBILITY

In 1945, the United States, having developed atomic weapons in its secret laboratory in Los Alamos, New Mexico, dropped two of them on the Japanese cities of Hiroshima and Nagasaki, incinerating hundreds of thousands and leaving thousands more with radiation sickness that was passed down to their children and grandchildren. Whether this use of atomic weapons to "end the war" with Japan was really necessary to "save American lives," as the United States claimed, or whether it was impelled more by a desire to test these weapons continues to be debated.[33] In any case, this creation of atomic weapons led to an immediate effort by the United States to maintain an absolute monopoly over their possession, as a powerful tool of control over the rest of the world.

In 1950, President Truman authorized the development of a still more potent weapon, the hydrogen bomb. But the U.S. monopoly on such weapons was broken in 1950 when the Soviet Union produced its own atomic bomb. Between 1960 and 1970, the United Kingdom, France, and China became nuclear powers, and after 2000, India and Pakistan also developed such weapons. Israel is estimated to have between sixty and eighty nuclear warheads, but these remain unacknowledged.[34] North Korea tested seven ballistic missiles on July 5, 2006, and has announced its willingness to conduct its first nuclear test.[35]

The creation of an atomic weapon by the Soviet Union in 1950 helped precipitate the domestic anticommunist witch-hunt of the McCarthy era in search of those guilty of "leaking" military secrets to the Soviet Union. As other European powers and China developed such weapons, the United States changed its policy to an effort to restrict their possession to its allies, preventing those it saw as its enemies and Third World nations from developing them. As the terrible danger to all humanity of a nuclear exchange between the United States and the Soviet Union became evident, there was a worldwide outcry against their development. In 1970, the Nuclear Non-Proliferation Treaty was signed by the United States. By December 1998, it had been signed by 185 nations, including Iran and Iraq (both signed it in July 1968).

The Nuclear Non-Proliferation Treaty not only seeks to prevent other nations from acquiring such weapons but also pledges to "achieve at the earliest possible date the cessation of the nuclear arms race and to undertake effective measures in the direction of nuclear disarmament." For thirty-seven years, the United States has violated the intention of this treaty, developing new nuclear weapons designed to be used in conventional warfare against those who do not themselves possess these weapons. On nineteen occasions, since the U.S. bombing of Japan, the United States has contemplated the use of nuclear weapons (not counting the current threat to Iran).[36]

Some of the most notable occasions were during the Korean War (see chapter 14). In December 1950, General Douglas MacArthur submitted a list of "retaliation targets" across the border of North Korea and China for which he desired thirty-four atomic weapons. In an interview, MacArthur declared, "I would have dropped between thirty and fifty as atomic bombs . . . strung along the neck of Manchuria." This would have created "a belt of radioactive cobalt" from the Sea of Japan to the Yellow Sea. "For at least 60 years there would have been no land invasion from the North."[37]

The use of nuclear weapons was also contemplated in Vietnam. In April 1954, as the French were on the verge of defeat at Dien Bien Phu, American aircraft carriers carrying atomic weapons were ordered into the Gulf of Tonkin. Secretary of State John Foster Dulles is reported to have offered his French counterpart Georges Bidault the option of dropping two atomic bombs on Dien Bien Phu. Bidault pointed out that the use of atomic bombs in such a context of close armed conflict would kill the French as well.[38] When the United States renewed the war in Vietnam, it again contemplated the use of nuclear weapons several times in 1968 and 1969.

The world stood aghast in 1962 when there appeared to be the possibility of an exchange of nuclear weapons between the U.S. and Soviet missiles installed in Cuba. The crisis ended when Soviet leader Nikita Khrushchev agreed to dismantle the missiles. But the United States continues to develop nuclear weapons with the intention of using them or threatening to use them to control enemies, particularly those who seek to develop their own nuclear weapons. In an April 17, 2006, *New Yorker* article, investigative journalist Seymour Hersh revealed that the Bush administration was contemplating using nuclear weapons, so-called bunker busters, against underground facilities in Iran, where it claimed the Iranians were developing the capacity to create nuclear weapons.

Such bunker busters do not just explode underground. Physicians for Social Responsibility, using software developed by the Pentagon and leased to Harvard University, have estimated that the use of such nuclear weapons on underground Iranian research facilities would generate a blast in which 2.6 million people would die within forty-eight hours and a million more would suffer immediate injuries. Radioactive dust would be carried eastward, exposing 10 million more to fallout.[39]

The Nuclear Non-Proliferation Treaty forbids such use of nuclear weapons to threaten a nonnuclear power. Such aggressive development of nuclear weapons by the United States fatally undermines the intention of this treaty by creating a double standard that has the opposite effect from the intended diminishment of the proliferation of such weapons. By seeking to maintain a monopoly on such weapons for its allies while threatening its political and ideological enemies with them, the United States divides the world into elite nations that possess such weapons and second-class nations that do not. Possession of nuclear weapons thus becomes a status symbol. Every nation that wishes to establish itself as a first-rank power and to protect itself against other nuclear powers believes that it must have such weapons. To demand that a nation desist from developing such weapons while holding them to its head as a threat fuels the urgent need to have them.

The curbing of nuclear proliferation as well as the proliferation of other weapons of mass destruction, such as chemical and biological weapons, is a losing game under these rules. There is only one way that the expansion of such weapons can be curbed, and that is to recognize that the curbing and reduction of such weapons must apply equally to all nations. In the Middle East, Iran can agree to disarm only if Israel agrees to disarm and the Middle East as a whole is declared a nuclear-free zone. North Korea might cancel its nuclear weapons program if the United States and South Korea would cease pointing such weapons at North Korea. Those who have not yet produced such weapons can be persuaded not to acquire them only if those who have them begin the process of giving them up.

This call for universal disarmament must also apply to the United States and to Russia, both of which still possess the largest arsenals of such weapons. In 2006, the United States possessed 10,104 nuclear weapons, about 5,735 operational, while Russia possessed 16,000, 5,830 considered operational. The next largest holders of nuclear weapons are France with 470 and China with 400.[40]

This point is so obvious that it is hard to understand why it is so continually avoided. The first step must be to insist that universal disarmament must be the context for the discussion of nonproliferation. Only if this is the goal will it become possible to curb and eventually abolish such weapons. If genuinely universal disarmament of nuclear armaments could begin, it would be possible to initiate a discussion of the need to move away altogether from war as the way to solve international conflicts. War needs to be superseded by negotiation of conflicts between nations within the world forum of nations. It is this discussion of the ultimate renunciation of war altogether that should be put back on the table if we are to end the violence that threatens all humanity and the planet itself in the twenty-first century.

NOTES

1. On the violence of white settlers against Indians, Mexicans, and Chinese in the first decades of the U.S. takeover of California, see particularly Robert F. Heizer and Alan J. Almquist, *The Other Californians: Prejudice and Discrimination under Spain, Mexico and the United States to 1920* (Berkeley: University of California Press, 1971).

2. Thomas Jefferson to James Madison, 1787; see "Thomas Jefferson on the Military," http://etext.virginia.edu/jefferson/quotations/jeff1480.htm, 2.

3. "Thomas Jefferson on the Military," 2.

4. Quoted in Chalmers Johnson, *The Sorrows of Empire: Militarism, Secrecy and the End of the Republic* (New York: Henry Holt, 2004), 44–45.

5. See Edward J. Marolda, ed., *Theodore Roosevelt, the U.S. Navy and the Spanish-American War* (New York: Palgrave, 2001).

6. See Thomas Schoonover, *Uncle Sam's War of 1898 and the Origins of Globalization* (Lexington: University Press of Kentucky, 2003).

7. Johnson, *The Sorrows of Empire*, 45–46.

8. Johnson, *The Sorrows of Empire*, 55–56.

9. See Andrew J. Bacevich on what he calls the "Wolfowitz indiscretion" in *American Empire: The Reality and Consequences of U.S. Diplomacy* (Cambridge, Mass.: Harvard University Press, 2002), 43–44.

10. See Patrick E. Tyler, "U.S. Strategy Calls for Insuring That No Rivals Develop," *New York Times*, March 8, 1992, 11; see also James Mann, *Rise of the Vulcans: The History of the Bush War Cabinet* (New York: Viking, 2004), 211–13.

11. Project for the New American Century, *Rebuilding America's Defenses*, September, 2000, available at www.newamericancentury.org/RebuildingAmericasDefenses.pdf. On the new militarism promoted by the neoconservatives, see Andrew J. Bacevich, *The New American Militarism: How Americans Are Seduced by War* (New York: Oxford University Press, 2005), esp. 147–74.

12. Bacevich, *The New American Militarism*, 51.

13. Reputable authors have argued that the official story that Islamic terrorists were responsible for these events contains many contradictions and that the Bush administration either knew about these plots months ahead of time and allowed them to happen in order to facilitate military expansion or even planned the attack themselves; see David Ray Griffin, *The New Pearl Harbor: Disturbing Questions about the Bush Administration and 9/11* (Northampton, Mass.: Olive Branch Press, 2004).

14. Johnson, *The Sorrows of Empire*, 56.

15. See the pie chart of the War Resister's League for fiscal year 2009 at www.warresisters.org/piechart.htm.

16. "Military Spending: U.S. vs. the World," www.cdi.org/issues/wme/spendersfyo4.html.

17. See Frida Berrigan, "A Nation of Firsts Arms the World," www.todispatch.com/index.mhtml?pid=196017.

18. When deliberate genocides by governments are added to the toll, it is estimated that 214 million to 225 million have died from 1900 to 2000; see Milton Leitenberg, "Deaths in Wars and Conflicts, 1945 and 2000," www.pcr.uu.se/conferences/Euroconference/Leitenberg_paper_pdf.

19. Seymour Melman, *Pentagon Capitalism: The Political Economy of War* (New York: McGraw-Hill, 1970).

20. See http://mwhodges.home.att.net/federal-debt-dollars.gif.

21. From the U.S. National Debt Clock, http://brillig.com/debt_clock/8/4/2007.

22. U.S. National Debt Clock, "Debt: To Whom Is It Owed?" http://brillig.com/debt_clock/8/4/2007.

23. See Jeff Faux, *The Global Class War: How America's Bipartisan Elite Lost Our Future and What It Will Take to Win It Back* (Hoboken, N.J.: John Wiley and Sons, 2006), esp. 179–200.

24. Pratap Chatterjee, *Iraq, Inc: A Profitable Occupation* (New York: Seven Stories Press, 2004), 39. For mercenary armies in Iraq and elsewhere, see Jeremy Scahill, *Blackwater: The Rise of the World's Most Powerful Mercenary Army* (New York: Nation Books, 2007).

25. Chatterjee, *Iraq, Inc*, 23.

26. Chatterjee, *Iraq, Inc*, 28, 29.

27. Johnson, *The Sorrows of Empire*, 151–52, 154; compare with Chalmers Johnson, *Nemesis: The Last Days of the American Republic* (New York: Henry Holt, 2006), 139.

28. Johnson, *Nemesis*, 140.

29. Johnson, *The Sorrows of Empire*, 151–52.

30. Johnson has detailed how this pattern of conflict has worked in the major U.S. base in Okinawa, Japan; see Johnson, *Nemesis*, 171–207.

31. See Stephen Grey, *Ghost Plane: The True Story of the CIA Torture Program* (New York: St. Martin's Press, 2006).

32. Robert Higgs, "Free Enterprise and War, a Dangerous Liaison," *Independent Institute*, January 22, 2003, www.independent.org/tii/news/030122Higgs.html, quoted in Johnson, *The Sorrows of Empire*, 308–9.

33. See Gar Alperovitz, *The Decision to Use the Atomic Bomb and the Architecture of an American Myth* (New York: Knopf, 1995).

34. Seymour M. Hersh, *The Samson Option: Israel's Nuclear Weapons and American Foreign Policy* (New York: Random House, 1991).

35. See "Nuclear Powers of the World," in *The World Almanac and Book of Facts, 2007* (New York: World Almanac Books, 2007), 853.

36. See the Peaceweb, www.himahima.cojp/PeaceWeb/Peace/E/pNuclear2_1.html.

37. See Bruce Cumings, *Korea's Place in the Sun: A Modern History* (New York: Norton, 1997), 291.

38. See Bernard B. Fall, *Hell in a Very Small Place: The Siege of Dien Bien Phu* (New York: Lippincott, 1966), 307.

39. See Physicians for Social Responsibility, "Medical Consequences of a Nuclear Attack On Iran: Fact Sheet," May 2006, www.psr.org/site/PageServer?pagename=security_main_iranfactsheet.

40. *The World Almanac and Book of Facts*, 2007.

· 13 ·

Nicaragua in the Caribbean and Central American Context

The Caribbean was the first area colonized by the Spanish with the arrival of Columbus in 1492. In the following centuries, this area was divided between the many colonizing nations—Spain, France, England, and Holland—each imposing its language on the colonized islands and seeking footholds in the region that was the staging area for the intercontinental interchange of slaves, precious metals, raw materials, and manufactured goods. Early on, the United States began to see the Caribbean and Central America as its "backyard" and to seek control over the region as well as the rest of Latin America.

Although the Monroe Doctrine, excluding other European powers from intervention or settlement in the Western Hemisphere, was enunciated by President James Monroe in 1823, it was only at the end of the nineteenth century, after the United States had expanded to California and seized northwestern Mexico in the Mexican-American War of 1846–1848, that the United States was in a position to actively intervene in the Caribbean and Central America. This intervention began with the Spanish-American War of 1898 when the United States intervened in a Cuban struggle for independence from Spain to make Cuba an American dependency while also seizing Puerto Rico as a colony.

THE CARIBBEAN

For the next thirty years, the United States continually intervened in conflicts seen as threatening U.S. interests in the Caribbean, at times sending its marines for extended periods of occupation. The island Columbus called La Española was ceded by Spain to France in 1795. In 1801, the Haitians declared their independence of France. The eastern end of the island continued to be disputed into the mid-nineteenth century, with local people declaring an independent Dominican Republic in 1844 and Spain briefly occupying the region (1861–1865). The United States intervened in 1904 and took charge of the Dominican Republic's finances. As conflicts continued, the United States sent a contingent of marines who occupied the country from 1914 to 1934. When they departed, they left in place a dictator supported by the United States, Raphael Trujillo, who reigned with an iron fist until he was assassinated in 1961. American troops were sent again in 1965 to prevent the victory of leftist rebels.[1]

Haiti, the eastern third of the island, was also the scene of continual U.S. intervention. In 1905, the United States took over a custom receivership of Haitian finances. Then the marines occupied the country from 1915 to 1934. The marines disbanded the Haitian national army built during the revolution and substituted a U.S.-trained National Guard to suppress regional dissidents. Although it departed from direct occupation in 1934, the United States has continually used its economic power to prevent real reform, ruling through the Haitian elite.[2]

American interest in Central America in the nineteenth century had particularly to do with plans to build a canal from the Caribbean Sea to the Pacific Ocean to shorten the journey from the East Coast to the West Coast of the United States and to Asia. Whoever controlled this canal would have a major role in controlling world trade. Two routes were contemplated, one across the isthmus of Panama (then part of Colombia) and one across Nicaragua, sailing west on the San Juan River, across Lake Nicaragua, and then crossing the short costal area to the Pacific. The United States sought to control both regions to prevent any other European power from building a rival canal.

When the United States decided on the Panamanian route at the end of the nineteenth century, it first sought to negotiate a treaty with Colombia to pay for the rights. But the Colombian government objected to the amount offered by the United States, so President Theodore Roosevelt facilitated a revolution in which Panama seceded from Colombia and declared itself an independent country (1903).[3] The United States immediately recognized Panama and negotiated a treaty in which it paid Panama $10 million plus $250,000 a year for rights to the Canal Zone in perpetuity. American troops remained in Panama until 1914 and intervened periodically to quell "unrest" seen as threatening U.S. interests. A treaty giving Panama gradual control of the canal and phasing out U.S. military bases was signed under President Jimmy Carter in 1977.

NICARAGUA

The United States also intervened continually in Nicaragua, initially to control the region for a possible canal and then to prevent Nicaragua from negotiating with another country to build a rival canal. The United States briefly supported and then opposed an American adventurer, William Walker, who in 1855 seized the country and declared it a slave state with English as its official language.[4] In the nineteenth and early twentieth centuries, Nicaragua was continually rent by rivalries between two factions of the ruling elite: liberals based in Leon and conservatives in Granada.

In 1893, the liberal José Santos Zelaya was elected president. Zelaya gradually became more dictatorial, but the United States objected to him as a strong nationalist who sought to shape an independent role for Nicaragua in Central American trade. He also tried to negotiate with Germany for an independent canal route across Nicaragua. In 1909, U.S. Marines landed and displaced Zelaya, putting the conservative Juan Estrada in power.[5] The United States intervened again from 1912 to 1925 to prop up the conservatives and to organize Nicaraguan economic assets, negotiating permanent naval bases in the Caribbean Corn Islands and the Pacific Gulf of Fonseca. The marine contingent returned in 1926 when a guerrilla war broke out led by nationalist leader Augusto César Sandino. American troops pursued Sandino for seven years, failing to apprehend him or to halt his movement, even carrying out the first example of heavy bombing from airplanes in 1927.[6]

Meanwhile, the United States was developing an alternative strategy to control Nicaragua, namely, the building of a National Guard independent of either party to act as the surrogate for the marines. The United States chose a "new man" fluent in English, Anastasio Somoza Garcia, to head it. As the U.S. forces withdrew, Somoza took over as ruling power. In 1934, Somoza claimed that he was arranging a truce with Sandino and invited him to a meeting. Sandino came with two of his generals, but as he left the presidential palace, he and his generals were seized on direct orders from Somoza and assassinated. For good measure his brother, Socrates Sandino, and one of Sandino's generals were arrested and also shot.[7]

For the next forty-three years, Anastasio Somoza and his two sons, Luis and Anastasio, would rule Nicaragua with a heavy hand and the full support of the United States. The Somoza family would monopolize control of large areas of agricultural land for major export products, such as sugar, cattle, and coffee. Somoza acquired numerous factories, such as cement and textiles, and took charge of major national utilities, such as the railroads, electricity, and water. He owned the national banks and the National Insurance Company. He controlled all public regulations, contracts, and licenses and used these to eliminate any competition. He ruled particularly through his control of the National Guard, which he converted into a tool to repress any competition or dissent, torturing and murdering any opponents.[8]

The struggle against the Somoza dictatorship began among university students in 1944–1948 and again in 1959–1966. In 1961, one such student leader, Carlos Fonseca Amador, founded the Sandinista Liberation Movement (Frente Sandinista de Liberación National [FSLN]). After several disastrous military encounters with the National Guard in the early 1960s, the FSLN began to organize as a more clandestine guerrilla movement, even learning from some aged members of Sandino's guerrilla movement from the 1930s how to survive in the jungles with support of local peasants as well as how to build an urban support network among students and workers.[9]

A major turning point in the growing national opposition was the 1972 earthquake, which demolished much of central Managua. Aid flowed into Nicaragua from many countries that Anastasio Somoza Debayle proceeded to loot with a free hand, doing little reconstruction of the damage.[10] This blatant show of corruption turned more middle-class and church leaders against the dictatorship. Groups in the Catholic Church, as well as sectors within Protestantism, also began to change their politics in the 1970s. Influenced by liberation theology, radical priests shaped Christian base communities (comunidades eclesiales de base) that brought together biblical study and socioeconomic transformation on behalf of the poor. Such base communities became a recruiting ground for supporters of the FSLN.[11]

In 1977, the FSLN began to build its strategy for a final military offensive to overthrow the Somoza rule. Several popular opposition groups were formed that ranged from favoring removing the Somozas and moderate reform without revolution to revolution in alliance with the FSLN. Many supporters of the regime began to fade away, some departing with their assets to Costa Rica or the United States. Somoza fought back viciously, refusing to quit. Meanwhile, the FSLN and its allies began to shape a government of national reconstruction in exile. President Carter sought to negotiate a more moderate reform alternative that would keep the national elites in power but without Somoza. On July 15, 1979, Carter gave up his effort to retain the National Guard and leading members of the Somocista Liberal Party in power and informed Anastasio Somoza Debayle that he should resign. Somoza submitted his resignation the next day. On July 17, he and members of his family, the National Guard general staff, and Liberal Nationalist Party leadership hurried to the Las Mercedes airport and flew to Miami, with others departing over the next two days. The new revolutionary leadership took over, with the victorious FSLN columns marching into the city on July 19, 1979.[12]

The new rulers of Nicaragua encountered enormous destruction. Between 40,000 and 50,000 Nicaraguans had died in the final two years of the struggle, and another 300,000 were wounded. Hundreds of thousands had been displaced or left homeless. Huge areas of residential, commercial, and industrial property in every important population center had been bombed, and the social and economic fabric had been shattered. Starvation and disease were rampant. The departing elites had emptied the national treasury, leaving the Sandinistas with a $1.6 billion national debt.[13] The Sandinistas faced a daunting task of rebuilding a shattered country and economy while seeking to make a social revolution at the same time.

The Sandinistas defined their revolutionary system as a mixed economy, a third remaining in private hands, a third state owned, and a third to be allocated for peasant cooperatives. The huge Somoza estates, many largely unused, were confiscated to carry out land distribution to the peasants. State utilities, railroads, electricity, and water, which also had been owned by the Somozas, were to be state owned but run in a way that favored popular access to these services. A plurality of political parties were each given equal access and funding to participate in the political process, to be guaranteed through an electoral board and reformed constitution to ensure free elections. A literacy campaign involving thousands of university students and coordinated by Jesuit Fernando Cardenal, the new minister of education, brought popular education to the poorest areas of the country and reduced illiteracy dramatically in a year's time.[14] A parallel health campaign built popular health centers to bring free medical services to the poor. Labor, peasant, and women's unions were developed to expand the popular base of the revolution. Two other priests also served in the new cabinet under President Daniel Ortega: diocesan priest Ernesto Cardenal, minister of culture, and Maryknoll priest Miguel D'Escoto, minister of foreign affairs. The presence of these priests in the Sandinista government displeased the Vatican, which suspended their priestly functions while they were in office.

The Roman Catholic Church in Nicaragua at this time, as in much of Latin America, was deeply polarized. A sector of the Catholic Church in Nicaragua identified with liberation theology and supported the Sandinistas. But the hierarchy, especially the archbishop Obando y Bravo, became hostile to the Sandinistas and supported the traditional propertied classes. The Vatican became increasingly condemnatory of liberation theology and persecuted liberation theologians. A sector of the Protestant churches also adopted liberation theology and supported the Sandinistas. As progressive Catholic priests found it difficult to work in official Roman Catholic institutions, they sometimes found a base for their work in ecumenical, Protestant-funded institutions, such as the Centro Ecuménico Antonio Valdivieso in Managua.[15]

The Sandinistas defined themselves as democratic socialists and intentionally allied with the European Socialist International (to which the British Labor Party and other Western European socialist parties belong), not to the Communist International, seeking to avoid what some saw as the Cuban mistake of too close a dependency on and identification with the Soviet Union. But opposition from the United States quickly developed. After the victory of the Sandinistas, Carter cut funding to Nicaragua and began to funnel aid to non-Sandinista groups, including remnants of the notorious National Guard. But it was when Ronald Reagan became president in 1981 that U.S. efforts to overthrow the Sandinistas shifted into high gear.

Reagan became obsessed with trying to destroy the Sandinista regime, insisting on seeing it as a "communist" beachhead of Soviet control that would soon spread across Central America and even invade Texas if not stopped. The Sandinistas were accused of exporting revolution by sending arms to the guerrillas of El Salvador, although most of the evidence for these charges was fabrications that were hardly believed by the Central Intelligence Agency (CIA) itself. By 1982, Reagan was providing major funding to the "contras" (counterrevolutionaries, at first made up mostly of National Guardsmen who had fled into Honduras and were engaging in petty sabotage across the northern border of Nicaragua).

In 1981, Reagan authorized $19 million to support the contras. An additional $43 million was authorized in 1983 and $27 million more in 1985. By the spring of 1986, the contras had received $130 million and in June 1986 received $100 million more. By 1988, the contras had been given over a billion dollars in support from the United States.[16] This vast funding, plus arms and air support from the United States, allowed the contras to greatly expand their numbers and carry out extensive sabotage of Sandinista efforts to develop the impoverished country. Schools, health clinics, and agricultural cooperatives were attacked and roads mined to blow up trucks bringing produce to market. Nicaraguan ports were mined, and the fishing industry was decimated. Cutting off aid and embargoing trade and loans from international banks, the United States sought to strangle the Nicaraguan economy, preventing oil for fuel or spare parts for machinery from being imported.

As a result, the Sandinista government had to divert most of the resources of the country from social and economic development to national self-defense. In 1980, more than half the government budget went for health and education and only 18 percent to the military. By 1987, this had been reversed, with the military consuming more than half the budget and health and education less than 20 percent.

Nicaragua's Central and Latin American neighbors sought to negotiate a peace process that would end this U.S. intervention. This took the form of the Contadora group (Panama, Mexico, Colombia, and Venezuela) and then President Oscar Arias of Costa Rica's Central American Peace Accord. But the United States blocked all these efforts. The Nicaraguans also took their case against the United States to the World Court, accusing the United States of systematic sabotage and mining of its ports. The World Court ruled in their favor by twelve to three and awarded Nicaragua $17 billion in damages, requiring that the United States repair the damage that had been done, a ruling that the United States ignored, refusing to pay.

When the U.S. Congress began to turn against Reagan's contra funding in the latter 1980s, forbidding further aid, Reagan arranged for such funds to be sent through covert channels under the notorious Colonel Oliver North.[17] Reagan and his supporters insisted that Nicaragua was a totalitarian communist state that prevented free elections and repressed the free press, even though the Sandinistas had been elected by a two-to-one vote in 1984 that had been certified by international observers as allowing multiparty candidates and being both free and fair.

In February 1990, a second national election was scheduled to be held. The United States confected a coalition party, the United Nicaraguan Opposition (UNO), made up of various opposition parties, led by Violeta Chamorro, the widow of popular Conservative Party journalist Pedro Joaquin Chamorro, who had been assassinated by Somoza in 1971. Unlimited funding and propaganda materials were channeled to this opposition party, while President George H. W. Bush pointedly made clear that the contra war and the embargo would continue unless the Nicaraguans voted the Sandinistas out of power. Exhausted by the war, the strangling of the economy, and the carnage of young people in the fighting (another 30,000 Nicaraguans had died in the fighting against the contras in the 1980s), Nicaraguans, especially women, voted for the UNO. The UNO, to the surprise of many Nicaraguans, including many who had voted for it, won 60 percent of the vote, although the Sandinistas remained the largest party in the National Assembly.

Contrary to the U.S. myths of Sandinista totalitarianism, the FSLN bowed to the decision of the people and to their own democratic constitution and electoral process and allowed Violeta Chamorro to assume the presidency and the representatives of opposition parties to take their seats in the National Assembly. But since the Sandinistas remained the largest party, led by Daniel Ortega, with his brother, Humberto Ortega, still in charge of the Sandinista national army (which replaced the National Guard of the Somoza era), and since much of the land redistribution to peasant cooperatives remained in place, the United States was unsatisfied with its victory. Nicaragua received little of the promised aid from the United States, which sought to undo the various reforms of the revolution. Funds continued to be channeled to opposition parties. There were efforts to intimidate voters by threatening to cut off remittances of Nicaraguans working in the United States to their relatives in Nicaragua if they voted for the FSLN in order to prevent Daniel Ortega from winning subsequent elections.

The World Bank and the International Monetary Fund swung into action to force Nicaragua to repay its loans by accepting the structural adjustment package of reforms. Confiscated land was to be given back to its former owners, many of whom had fled to Miami. State utilities, such as the national telephone service and the railroad, were to be privatized, being bought up by wealthy businessmen who removed the subsidies that allowed the poor access to services. The health and literacy centers were closed, hospitals and schools were privatized or raised their fees, and education and medical service became inaccessible to most Nicaraguans. Many of the former contra fighters, as well as elements of the Sandinista army, had not been integrated into the society and became roaming bandits. Urban poor youth turned to drugs and thievery, many living in homeless bands in the streets.[18] Thus, the gains of the revolution quickly evaporated, and rising poverty soon ranked Nicaragua with Haiti as the poorest countries in the Caribbean–Central American region.

Daniel Ortega, who remained the head of FSLN, however, by no means had given up his desire to be returned to power as Nicaragua's president. He moved continually to the right, seeking a coalition with the right-wing Liberal Party and the president, Arnaldo Alemán, to share power. Alemán was in the process of looting $100 million from the treasury, and he and Ortega agreed to grant each other immunity from criminal prosecution. The two leaders also agreed to lower the percentage needed to win the presidency from 45 to 35 percent. Ortega also sought to form an alliance with the Catholic Church, represented by Archbishop Obando y Bravo, his previous archenemy, agreeing to support a draconian change in the abortion law to forbid women from obtaining a therapeutic abortion even if their lives were in danger.

In November 2006, Ortega won the presidency with a lesser percentage of the national vote than he received in the two previous elections when he had lost. In his inauguration on January 10, 2007, Ortega appeared flanked by Venezuelan President Hugo Chavez and Bolivian President Evo Morales, thus staking his claim to be a part of the coalition of leaders of a new Latin American left.[19] But little remains of the Sandinista agenda of the 1980s in Ortega's actual practice. A fervent desire to maintain his own power seems to have replaced any revolutionary zeal to better the lot of the poor majority of Nicaraguans. The business classes of Nicaragua no longer see him as a danger. The Sandinista Party has split, with a Sandinista Renewal Movement

Party opposing Ortega, denouncing him as representing "Danielismo" (i.e., his personal power) rather than authentic Sandinista principles of social and economic betterment of the Nicaraguan people.[20]

GUATEMALA

Nicaragua was not the only Central American country where the United States invested heavily in the Cold War era to prevent reformers from coming to power. Guatemala and El Salvador also represent major expressions of such intervention. From 1898, Guatemala was ruled by oppressive dictators Manuel Estrada Cabreza and Jorge Ubico, representing the big landowners. The U.S.-owned United Fruit Company was virtually a state within a state. It owned vast plantations linked to its own railroads, ports, and power companies; gave starvation wages to its workers; and paid little taxes. In 1944, a reform movement developed, modeled on the U.S. New Deal. Ubico was overthrown, and a new democratic constitution affirmed the right of workers to unionize, votes for women, social security, and expanded education.

Under the new constitution, reformers Juan José Arévalo (1945–1951) and Jacobo Arbenz (1951–1954) were elected. Arbenz initiated a land reform program, much needed in a country where 2.2 percent of the landowners owned 70 percent of the arable land and where peasants labored in slave conditions on plantations and were kept in continual debt peonage. Arbenz expropriated large tracts of unused land and distributed it to 100,000 landless peasants. He offered to pay United Fruit $525,000 for this land, which was United Fruit's own declared valuation of it for tax purposes.[21] United Fruit demanded $16 million. Arbenz also supported the unionization of factory and farmworkers. A few seats in the congress were held by communist representatives of the Guatemala Labor Party. But these leftists neither dominated Arbenz's government nor in any way were linked to the Soviet Union, which ignored Guatemala.

Nevertheless, in Washington, at the urging of United Fruit, a propaganda war was unleashed, labeling the Arbenz government as "communist" and a tool of the Soviet Union. A plan to topple the Arbenz regime, hatched under President Truman, was revived under the Eisenhower administration in 1953 by John Foster Dulles, who was secretary of state, and his brother, Allan Dulles, head of the CIA, both with ties to United Fruit. The Latin American press was flooded with stories of the "communist danger" in Guatemala, and plans were developed for an invasion, led by army Colonel Carlos Castillo Armas. Arms presumably from the Soviet Union were planted, foreign credit to Guatemala was cut off, and there was a campaign of bombing of ports, the international airport, military barracks, radio stations, schools, and the national palace. Nicaraguan dictator Anastasio Somoza happily agreed to be the base for this military attack. By late June 1953, the Guatemalan army was convinced that they had no choice but to capitulate and to force Arbenz to resign.[22]

Armas was flown in as the new national leader and quickly initiated a purge of reform leaders. Thousands were rounded up, tortured, and killed. A law was passed allowing the government to declare anyone a communist with no right of appeal. The agrarian reform law was canceled and the land returned to United Fruit. Three-fourths of Guatemalan voters were disenfranchised on grounds of illiteracy. A reign of terror was unleashed against union leaders and dissidents of any kind. The Guatemalan army became a state within a state, with its own schools and banks, making and breaking presidents.[23] In the civil war that raged until 1996, some 200,000 Guatemalans were killed (mostly by the army), more than 450 villages were destroyed, and 1.5 million indigenous people were driven from the countryside into army-controlled labor camps, refugee camps in Mexico, or squatter areas on the edges of cities.

In 1996, peace accords were negotiated between the Guatemala government and the guerrillas with the mediation of the Catholic Church. The accords contained promises to reduce of the power of the army, end forced conscript recruitment, protect the human rights of the indigenous people, carry out land reform, and restructure taxes and public finances to address social needs. Although there is no longer an armed conflict, there has been little progress in the past twelve years (1996–2007) in reducing the impunity with which the army acts against peasant peoples and their leaders or in increased spending for the social needs of the people.

Moreover, the peace accords opened the way for the imposition of the neoliberal model of development under the World Bank and the business elite. Large areas of free trade zones allow for the exploitation of cheap Guatemalan labor. Public assets are transferred to private companies, including foreign owners. Social spending for health and education is reduced, and poverty has grown. There has been no reform in taxes that allow the rich to pay little and thus deny state resources for social needs. Loans from the World Bank have been spent mostly on roads and other infrastructure projects that benefit the *maquila* factories of the free trade zones and the second homes of the rich, while poor *campesinos* pick lettuce, tomatoes, and flowers for export on land once owned by their grandfathers. Thus, the promises of the peace accords have borne little fruit for most Guatemalans yearning for a better life.[24]

EL SALVADOR

A parallel story of struggle for reform, guerrilla war, state repression, and unfilled promises of peace accords unfolded in El Salvador in the past seventy-five years. In the early 1930s, labor leader Farabundo Martí sought to organize peasants and workers, declaring a general strike in 1932. Striking workers and peasants were rounded up; 30,000 were massacred. Martí himself was executed. General Maximiliano Hernández Martínez ruled as dictator from 1932 to 1944 on behalf of the "fourteen families," or the big landowners, and institutionalized military rule.[25] In the 1960s, there were efforts at reform that were resisted by the oligarchy. American aid began to flow to the El Salvadorean military already in the 1950s, but it opened to a gush in the 1980s under the presidency of Ronald Reagan, when more than $6 billion is estimated to have come from the United States to prop up the military and the reigning oligarchy.[26]

After repeated frustration of reform and the stealing of elections, sectors of reformers fled into armed struggle in the late 1970s, naming themselves the Faribundo Martí Front for National Liberation (FMLN) after the executed labor leader of the 1930s. Again, as in Nicaragua, a progressive sector of the church sided with social justice and began to organize base communities and peasant cooperatives. The oligarchy responded by stepped up attacks on church leaders, including priests. "Be a patriot—kill a priest" was the slogan of one death squad, printed on leaflets dropped from the air.[27] Rutilio Grande, a popular parish priest dedicated to the poor, was gunned down with his driver and a young boy on March 12, 1977, as he took sacraments to a sick person.

The assassination of Rutilio Grande radicalized the new bishop of San Salvador, Oscar Arnulfo Romero, who began to speak out against the repression in sermons broadcast by radio. He called on President Carter, "Christian to Christian," to stop the U.S. military aid. In his last sermon, he addressed the El Salvador army with the words, "I beseech you, I beg you, I order you, in the name of God, stop the repression."[28] The next day, an assassin, sent by Roberto d'Aubussion, founder of the ruling Nationalist Republican Alliance Party (ARENA), stepped into the center aisle of the church where Romero was saying mass and put a bullet into his heart. In December of the same year (1980), four North American church women supporting social justice were seized as they traveled from the airport, raped, and massacred.

As in Nicaragua, President Ronald Reagan insisted on seeing the struggle in El Salvador not as a civil war between an oligarchy and those seeking democratic and social reform but as another beachhead for communist "infiltration" from Nicaragua, Cuba, and ultimately the Soviet Union that, if not stopped, would take over all Central American and threaten the United States itself.[29] With the latest high-tech military weapons and airpower, the military was able to continually bomb the countryside. The residents of entire villages were rounded up and massacred, and survivors fled to refugee camps in Honduras. An estimated 75,000, mostly civilians, died in the twelve-year civil war.

Despite the carnage, the FMLN grew stronger. In November 1989, they planned a major offensive that they hoped would wrest power from the oligarchy and bring them to power. Although they failed, the strength of the offensive made clear to the U.S. military advisers that all the money and stepped-up repression were not ending the civil war. Moreover, in the midst of the FMLN push, on November 16, 1989, the shocking massacre of six Jesuits and their housekeeper and her daughter occurred at the Jesuit residence at the Central American University. These six Jesuits represented the elite intellectuals of progressive Catholicism. One of the Jesuits, distinguished theologian Ignacio Ellacuría, had just returned from Spain on the invitation of the junta, claiming that he was needed to help negotiate peace with the FMLN. Instead, they were plotting his assassination. These murders horrified the world and led to an insistence on peace negotiations that even the United States had to heed.

It took until early 1992 for the war to come to an official end, when a UN commission negotiated a cease-fire between the two sides. The FMLN were to lay down their arms and become a legal political party that could participate in the democratic process. A UN truth commission issued its report on the civil war in March 1993, confirming that the main perpetrators of the many massacres during the war were the government, not the FMLN, although they were charged with some crimes, including killing several mayors. The commission called for the dismissal of forty high-ranking military leaders and a number of government officials who were charged with approving the violence.[30]

Although "peace" has come to El Salvador in the sense of the end of the civil war, the poverty has changed little. ARENA continues to be elected and to stay in power, funded by the United States as its chosen instrument to deliver the resources of El Salvador to the United States, including seeing to the passage of the Central American Free Trade Agreement, which would lock El Salvador and all of Central America into a subservient economic relation to the United States. While the FMLN has become a political party, the United States continues to apply funding and political pressure to prevent it from winning the presidency in a national election.[31] However, the FMLN has won office in many local municipalities in El Salvador, and these towns have been credited with being the most fairly and justly administered in El Salvador.³²

As can be seen from the narrative given in this chapter, U.S. interventions and manipulation of the countries and peoples of the Caribbean and Central America extend for more than a century. While claiming at times to defend "democracy," the intention of the United States has ever been to prevent real self-government on behalf of the majority of the people and to keep control of the resources and strategic location of the region either through direct military occupation or through surrogate local elites and military forces organized on their behalf. It is a shameful story, largely unknown or misrepresented to the American people themselves.

NOTES

1. See Howard J. Wiarda and Michael J. Kryanek, *The Dominican Republic: A Caribbean Crucible* (Boulder, Colo.: Westview Press, 1992).

2. For an excellent analysis of Haitian social history and U.S. intervention, see Michel-Rolph Trouillot, *Haiti: State against Nation: The Origins and Legacy of Duvalierism* (New York: Monthly Review Press, 1990).

3. For Roosevelt's description of his tactics in facilitating the Panamanian Revolution, see his *Autobiography* (New York: Charles Scribner's and Sons, 1925), 511–29. As he put it, "I did not lift a finger to incite the revolutionists . . . I simply ceased to stamp out the different revolutionary fuses that were already burning" (525).

4. For William Walker's intervention in Nicaragua, see John A. Booth, *The End and the Beginning: The Nicaraguan Revolution* (Boulder, Colo.: Westview Press, 1985), 18–20.

5. For Zelaya's policies, see Booth, *The End and the Beginning*, 22–25.

6. Booth, *The End and the Beginning*, 41–46.

7. Booth, *The End and the Beginning*, 51.

8. Booth, *The End and the Beginning*, 46–95.

9. On the student movement and the building of the FSLN, see Booth, *The End and the Beginning*, 109–13.

10. On Anastasio Somoza Dubayle's exploitation of the aid given for the 1972 earthquake, see Booth, *The End and the Beginning*, 81.

11. On the role of the churches in the revolution, see Booth, *The End and the Beginning*, 134–37. The most famous of the Catholic base communities that later became part of the revolution was that developed by Ernesto Cardenal on the island of Solentiname. See Ernesto Cardenal, *The Gospel in Solentiname* (Maryknoll, N.Y.: Orbis Books, 1976).

12. Booth, *The End and the Beginning*, 174–82.

13. Booth, *The End and the Beginning*, 183.
14. On the literacy campaign, see Booth, *The End and the Beginning*, 232–34; see also Leonor Blum, "The Literacy Campaign, Nicaraguan Style," *Caribbean Review* 10 (winter 1981): 18–21.
15. A good overview of the period 1975–1983 is Philip Berryman, *Religious Roots of Rebellion: Christians in the Central American Revolution* (Maryknoll, N.Y.: Orbis Books, 1984); see also Philip Berryman, *Liberation Theology* (Philadelphia: Temple University Press, 1987).
16. On these figures, see Magda Lanusa, "Nicaragua: Ecological Debt and the Model of Indebtedness, Impoverishment and Predatory Destruction," in *Jubilee South*, 7, www.Jubileesouth.org/journal/Nicaragua.htm (accessed March 31, 2007).
17. On the Iran-Contra scandal, see Lawrence Walsh, *Firewall: The Iran Contra Conspiracy and Cover-Up* (New York: Norton, 1997); see also Peter Dale Scott and Jane Hunter, *The Iran Contra Connection: Secret Teams and Covert Operations in the Reagan Era* (Boston: South End Press, 1987).
18. This description depends on my own visits to Nicaragua during the 1990s.
19. See Max Blumenthal, "The Kinder, Gentler Daniel Ortega," *The Nation* (February 5, 2007), www.thenation.com/doc/20070205/Blumenthal (accessed March 15, 2007).
20. See Mónica Baltodano, "From Sandinismo to 'Danielismo,'" *International Socialist Review*, November–December 2006, 31–35.
21. Thomas P. McCann, *An American Company: The Tragedy of United Fruit* (New York: Crown, 1976), 49.
22. For a good account of the coup, see Stephen Schlesinger and Stephen Kinzer, *Bitter Fruit: The Untold Story of the American Coup in Guatemala* (New York: Doubleday, 1982).
23. For the ongoing repression in Guatemala, see William Blum, *Killing Hope: U.S. Military and C.I.A. Interventions since World War II* (Monroe, Me.: Common Courage Press, 1995), 72–83, 147–48, 229–39; see also Susanne Jonas, *The Battle for Guatemala* (Boulder, Colo.: Westview Press, 1991), and Eduardo Galeano, *Guatemala: Occupied Country* (New York: Monthly Review Press, 1969).
24. See "Ten Years of Peace: A Critical Look at the Legacy of the Peace Accords," *Report on Guatemala* 27, no. 4 (winter 2006–2007): 2–8.
25. See Jenny Pearce, *Under the Eagle: U.S. Intervention in Central America and the Caribbean* (Boston: South End Press, 1982), 221; see also Raymond Bonner, *Weakness and Deceit: U.S. Policy and El Salvador* (New York: Times Books, 1984), and Clifford Kraus, *Inside Central America: Its People, Politics and History* (New York: Summit Books, 1991), 53–109.
26. See Blum, *Killing Hope*, 357.
27. Blum, *Killing Hope*, 354; see also Kraus, *Inside Central America*, 70.
28. Oscar Arnulfo Romero, *Voice of the Voiceless: Four Pastoral Letters and Other Statements* (Maryknoll, N.Y.: Orbis Books, 1985).
29. *New York Times*, March 7, 1981, cited in Blum, *Killing Hope*, 352.
30. Blum, *Killing Hope*, 365–66.

31. See Blum's account of the U.S. tactics to prevent the FMLN from winning the March 1994 election in *Killing Hope*, 267–69. In a January 2005 trip to El Salvador, I was told of the intense propaganda used by the United States to prevent an FMLN national victory, including threats to withdraw aid and a telephone campaign paid for by the United States through ARENA to get Salvadoreans in the United States to telephone relatives and tell them that their remittances from the United States would be blocked if they voted for the FMLN.

32. This is the result of a study of municipalities in El Salvador, which reported that all of the best-run towns were governed by the FMLN, as reported to me during a study trip to El Salvador in January 2005.

· 14 ·

The Two Koreas: Divergent Systems, Hope for Reunification?

The division of Korea into two states, North and South, communist and capitalist, today represent an extreme case of the perpetuation of a Cold War division into rival systems and ideologies. This division was shaped in the end of World War II as advancing Soviet troops met those of the United States in the Korean peninsula. Yet Korea has a much older history and memory of being a united people who have seen themselves as uniquely homogeneous. It is one of the few nations where ethnic and linguistic identity coincides with national boundaries. This heritage of unity underlies the continuing protest against the division into two states and the ongoing quest for unification. This chapter discusses this longer memory of shared history, followed by such a deep bifurcation into rival ways of life that unification today seems a distant dream.

Koreans trace their history back 5,000 years or more. According to legend, the first, or Old Choson, dynasty was founded in 2333 B.C.E. and included much of the peninsula and into Manchuria.[1] If such a unified dynasty existed, it had fallen into many small states by the third century B.C.E. In the early Common Era, three regional states emerged: in the north (Koguryo), the center (Silla), and the south (Paekche). These three kingdoms were briefly unified by Silla in 676 C.E., falling apart in the ninth century until the establishment of the Koryo dynasty, from which the name "Korea" derives. In 1392, the Yi, or new Choson, dynasty unified the peninsula, lasting until Korea was taken over by Japan in 1910.[2]

Although proud of its own independence and self-sufficiency, Korea of the Three Kingdoms and Choson eras looked to China as its cultural mentor. Both Buddhism and Confucianism were introduced into Korea in the Three Kingdoms era, with Buddhism seen as the predominant religion. With the founding of the Choson dynasty, Buddhism became marginalized, and some of the vast landed estates of the monasteries were confiscated. Women's status was sharply demoted.[3] Confucianism became the state ideology and Chinese the official language of education and state records. An aristocracy emerged that combined large landowners and a scholar-bureaucrat class who earned their positions through a civil service exam based on the Confucian classics.

This landowner-scholar-bureaucrat class (*yangban*) was sharply distinguished from the masses of the peasantry and outcast groups, such as butchers. Slaves also existed, making up about 30 percent of the population. This aristocracy set itself apart from those who worked with their hands. They despised merchants and traders, discouraging the emergence of a commercial middle class. A popular shamanistic culture remained strong among the poorer classes and women, rooted in a vibrant sense of the presence of spirits in nature as well as goblins and ghosts representing unhappy and malevolent spirits. Thus, Korean culture has been deeply shaped by the layering of three traditions, popular shamanism, Buddhist spirituality, and Confucian civic ethics, traditions that often mingle within the same family.

Christianity brought a fourth religious tradition, one that historically has sought to "convert" Koreans from the other three traditions and yet often mingles within the same household. Catholicism first came to Korea in the sixteenth century and Protestant Christianity in the late nineteenth. Today Christians make up about 26 percent of South Koreans. Since 1948, North Korea has been shaped by another imported tradition, militant atheistic Marxism, which seeks to discredit all three historical traditions and Christianity as well. Yet many see this North Korean Marxism as reflecting continuing elements of a Confucian heritage of paternalistic loyalty to the ruler, creating a distinctively Korean Confucian communism.[4] Even in division, common traditions shape both Koreas while taking significantly different forms.

During its long history, the Choson dynasty repelled several major invasions from outside: the Japanese during 1592–1598 and the Manchus in 1627 and again in 1636. From the seventeenth century, resistance to foreign power was expressed in a fierce culture of autarchy in Korea. Koreans saw themselves as self-sufficient, complete in their inherited culture and social system, and repelled foreigners who sought to bring new ideologies and subordinate Korea to outside powers. Particularly in the nineteenth century, as Western powers, Britain, Germany, and the United States, as well as older historic neighbors, Russia and Japan, vied for control of Korea, those who saw themselves as bringing the benefits of a superior culture and way of life of modernity were astonished and outraged by the persistent Korean refusal to "open up" to such outside influence. Korea sought to fend off any foreign presence by closing its borders to all nations except its historic mentor, China, which, at this time, was itself being picked apart by competing Western imperial powers. Korea became labeled the "hermit kingdom."[5]

But this period of resistance to foreign powers would end in humiliating defeat and colonization by its neighbor Japan, which it had traditionally seen as its equal, not its superior. Unlike Korea, Japan in the nineteenth century pursued an aggressive policy of westernization, copying Western technology and education, rapidly industrializing, and seeking to rival the Western powers at their own game of imperial dominance. The British and the Americans in particular came to see Japan as the one "enlightened" nation among otherwise retrograde Asians and sought to do business with it. In 1895, Japan defeated China, thus disempowering Korea's traditional mentor and protector.[6]

Russia was seeking to impose its power in the north of Korea, even proposing a division of the peninsula between Russian and Japanese spheres of influence, but in 1895 the Japanese drove the Russians out of Korea, murdering the Choson empress Myeongseong. Japanese victory over Russia was further confirmed in 1904–1905 when the Japanese defeated the Russians in the Russo-Japanese War. Korea was made into a protectorate of Japan in 1907 and then annexed it in 1910 with the acquiescence of both Britain and the United States.

The United States had just finished appropriating its first colonies outside the North American continent with the Spanish-American War of 1898, which brought the Philippines, Guam, Hawaii, Cuba, and Puerto Rico under its sway. President Roosevelt saw this growing Japanese power in Korea as an opportunity for the United States to confirm its own colonization of the Philippines by coming to a power-sharing agreement with Japan. Notes exchanged between Roosevelt and Japan (the Taft-Katsura Agreement) acknowledged that the United States would accept Japanese occupation of Korea if Japan accepted the U.S. occupation of the Philippines.[7]

JAPANESE COLONIZATION, 1910–1945

The era of Japanese colonization was deeply humiliating to Koreans and has left painful memories. Yet it also contributed to patterns that would shape both North and South Korea in the second half of the twentieth century. Japan sent hundreds of thousands of bureaucrats to Korea, replacing the old *yangban* Confucian-trained scholar–bureaucrats with Japanese administrators. It created a highly centralized system that supervised every aspect of

Korean life down to the village level and repressed dissent. It also built a modern system of roads, railroads, ports, and communication infrastructure throughout the land.

Japan left the old *yangban* in place as landowners but directed them to expand their holdings and to discipline the peasants to extract higher yields of rice for export. It also constructed heavy industry, steel mills, automobile plants, petrochemical complexes, and enormous hydroelectric facilities, all to serve the Japanese empire, not the colonized Koreans. Korean workers typically received much lower pay than a Japanese doing a comparable job, although some Koreans ready to collaborate became business managers, police, and officers in the Japanese army. But mainly, the Japanese wanted the Koreans as the foot soldiers and laborers for their empire.

Large numbers of Koreans were uprooted into other provinces of Korea, sent to other parts of the Japanese Empire, or brought to Japan as workers. By 1945, more than 11 percent of the Korean population was abroad. Ten thousand of these Korean forced laborers died when the United States bombed Hiroshima and Nagasaki. The survivors of the first atomic bombs scattered back to Korea with no attention to the consequences of the radiation they had suffered.[8] Between 100,000 and 200,000 Korean women were forcibly recruited as sex slaves or "comfort women" to serve as prostitutes for the Japanese army during World War II.[9]

Resistance to Japanese colonialism persisted through the thirty-five-year period. There were continual clashes between Korean guerrillas and Japanese troops in the early years of the occupation. The Japanese arrested 50,000 in 1912 and another 140,000 in 1918. In March 1919, there were nationwide independence demonstrations that were put down with fierce repression by the Japanese.[10] Some Koreans went into exile in China and the Soviet Union and founded early communist and nationalist resistance groups. When Japan annexed Manchuria in 1931, many Koreans joined with Manchurians to fight the Japanese. It was in the context of this Manchurian guerrilla resistance that Kim Il Sung and much of the later North Korean leadership emerged. North Korean leadership after 1945 to the present continues to base its legitimacy on this heritage of resistance to Japan.[11]

In the last years of World War II, Japan stepped up its efforts to mobilize the human capital of its empire. The Greater Asia Co-Prosperity Sphere was created after Pearl Harbor, recruiting labor for all parts of its empire. Two and a half million young people were organized into thousands of youth organizations. There was a concerted effort at thought control, with an ideology of Japanese national uniqueness drilled into every person in Japan and its colonies. Hundreds of Shinto shrines and prayer halls were built throughout Korea and Koreans made to worship at them. Koreans were forced to take

Japanese names and to speak Japanese. All this collapsed on August 15, 1945, when Japan surrendered, ending the war in Asia.

THE DIVISION AND THE KOREAN WAR: 1945–1953

At the end of World War II, the Soviet troops had reached the northern half of Korea, and the American troops had occupied southern part of Korea. President Franklin Delano Roosevelt had talked of a trusteeship between the United States, the Soviet Union, and Britain to share control of Korea and "prepare it" gradually for independence, but he died on April 12, 1945. At midnight on August 10, 1945, John J. McCloy of the U.S. State-War-Navy Coordinating Committee directed two young colonels, Dean Rusk and Charles Bonesteel, to withdraw to an adjoining room and, within thirty minutes, to find a place to divide Korea. They chose the thirty-eighth parallel because it would place the capital, Seoul, in the American zone. No Koreans or anyone else were consulted about this decision.[12] But it became the fateful decision for a Korea newly liberated from Japan and expecting to be a united, independent country. When General Douglas MacArthur issued General Order Number One for the Japanese surrender, he also announced the division of Korea into two zones: Soviet and American.

The Americans soon set about building the apparatus of a South Korean state, including its army. Kim Il Sung began to do so under the Soviets, although he was chosen as leader not by the Soviets but by the Korean guerrillas who returned with him from fighting in the anti-Japanese resistance in Manchuria.[13] During the war, popular committees of nationalists and leftists had emerged in the southern areas of Korea, determined to shape a new democratic socialist Korea. But the American occupiers soon set about repressing these popular committees and favoring the military, police, and business leaders who had served under the Japanese. Calls for land reform were rejected. In August 1948, the United States ended the occupation period, setting up the Republic of Korea and bringing the seventy-year-old Syngman Rhee, an anticommunist nationalist who had been in exile in Washington, D.C., since 1911, back to be the new president. The United States retained its own military troops in Korea, and these remain today.

From 1945 to 1947, there were vehement protests by Koreans of this policy, which maintained the leadership structure of Japanese colonialism. When these protests were violently repressed, the protestors fled to the hills and organized guerrilla bands that fought the new Korean government. These guerrilla bands were not sent from North Korea but rather represented local dissenting forces in the south.¹⁴ In 1949–1950, the South Korean army, supported by U.S. troops, engaged in a systematic campaign to eradicate this guerrilla resistance.

Neither Syngman Rhee nor Kim Il Sung accepted the division of Korea into two states, and both hoped to end it by invading and defeating the other side. In 1949, there were continual border skirmishes between the two sides. Early in 1950, about 100,000 battle-trained Korean guerrillas who had fought with Chinese returned to North Korea. This infusion of new troops gave Kim Il Sung the basis for what he hoped would be a winning army to conquer the south. Although Stalin initially supported Kim Il Sung's plan and sent military supplies, he did little to continue this support during the war.¹⁵ Thus, the conflict must be seen primarily as a civil war reflecting deep divisions within Korea, south as much as north, rather than one orchestrated by the Soviet Union or China. Without the U.S. Army, Kim Il Sung would have quickly overwhelmed the army of the Republic of Korea and occupied all of Korea.

On June 23, 1950, the North Korean army invaded and quickly took Seoul. They pressed farther on south, aided by South Korean guerrillas. The people's committees were reconstituted. Leftists were released from prison, and a redistribution of land in every province was begun.¹⁶ The Americans quickly mobilized for a counterattack. In mid-September, General MacArthur landed at Inch'on. Seoul was recaptured by the end of the month, but MacArthur soon revealed an intention that went beyond merely restoring the borders at the thirty-eighth parallel. Rather, he rolled on deep into North Korean territory, marching toward the Yalu River dividing Korea from China, thereby showing that his plan was to conquer it and reunify Korea under the Republic of Korea. The army of the Democratic People's Republic of Korea withdrew before this advance and positioned itself for guerrilla war against the American onslaught.¹⁷

This invasion, which threatened to go beyond Korea into China, brought the entry of China into the war. Hundreds of thousands of Chinese would come to the aid of the North Koreans. This combined Chinese–Korean offensive cleared the north of invading troops in little more than two weeks. By the end of December, Seoul was about to fall again. By the spring of 1951, the line between the two areas was reestablished at the demilitarized zone, but the United States was determined to dismantle the North Korean power and so continued the air war for another two years. At one point, MacArthur contemplated bringing thirty to fifty nuclear bombs and creating a radioactive belt of destruction across the border of Korea with Manchuria.¹⁸ MacArthur was removed as commander of the war on April 11, 1951, not because Truman was against using nuclear weapons but because he saw MacArthur as insubordinate. The use of nuclear weapons was again contemplated by Eisenhower at the end of the war when there were conflicts over the armistice.

In the 1951–1953 air war, the United States dropped vast numbers of heavy bombs as well as massive chemical weapons, including napalm, on North Korea. Almost all modern buildings were destroyed, as were government buildings and industry, transportation, and much of the housing. Dams were wiped out, flooding the spring rice planting.[19] The population survived by digging tunnels to live underground. This underground world continues to exist today as the last-ditch defense of North Korea in a future war.

A million and a half North Koreans died in the 1950–1953 war, one in eight of the total population, while a million South Koreans died, one in twenty of the population. Most of these casualties were civilians. One hundred and twenty-five thousand Chinese died. The United States lost 54,589. The war solved nothing but simply froze the conflict in place for the next half century and more.[20]

SOUTH KOREA: POLITICS AND THE ECONOMY, 1953–2008

The Rhee regime in South Korea became increasingly authoritarian after the war. There were many political executions, and thousands were jailed as political prisoners. The economy remained stagnant. There was some land reform in 1951, ironically based on the land reform the North Koreans had undertaken during their three-month occupation of the south. Landlord dominance was ended in the countryside, but also radical peasant and labor organizations had been destroyed by the war.[21] In the spring of 1960, large student protests against the Rhee regime broke out, and the eighty-five-year-old Rhee was forced to retire.

For less than a year, Korea experienced a lively experiment with democracy and a free press. Some radicals even suggested that the time had come for unification talks with the north. But this period of freedom was ended by a military coup in May 1961. Colonel Park Chung Hee, a product of the Japanese military, active in military intelligence during the Korean War, took over and ruled with a heavy hand until he was assassinated by his own director of the Korean Central Intelligence Agency (KCIA), Kim Jae Kyu, in 1979.

Park ruled through a new political party, the Democratic Republican Party, with a centralized authoritarian structure and huge funding base provided by his private supporters, including foreign friends in Japan and the United States. The KCIA was also organized with help from the American CIA, coming to dominate public life, censoring newspapers, and muzzling dissent in universities. Dissidents were subjected to torture. The KCIA also operated abroad, especially in the United States, spying on Koreans in other countries and bribing congressmen. Park declared himself president for life and made the National Assembly a rubber stamp for his decrees. In another page taken from the Japanese era, Park imposed the *Yushin* (revitalizing) ideology designed to indoctrinate all Koreans to be a "big happy family" docilely accepting his centralized control.

Park initiated a phase of heavy industry building, with new steel, petrochemical, automobile, shipping, and nuclear energy industries. The economy prospered even as the society became more authoritarian. Park and subsequent South Korean presidents followed a state-led development program and state protection of national industry that reflected the pattern learned from the Japanese but violated the neoliberal orthodoxy of free trade favored by the World Bank.[22] American and Japanese firms were encouraged to relocate in Korea where productivity was high and labor costs were low, with an educated and "disciplined" (no unions allowed) workforce. Textiles and light electronic manufactures were among the first major industries. A small number of large corporations came to control most of the wealth, while urban workers were paid less than $110 a month for a sixty-hour workweek.

After Park's assassination in October 26, 1979, a new group of generals organized another coup within the military, with General Chun Doo Hwan, head of the military committee for national security, assuming power. Students and workers again organized massive protests. Martial law was declared. When new protests broke out in the provincial capital of Kwangiu, Chun put down the rebellion brutally, killing over 2,000. Chun assumed the presidency in February 1981, purging 800 politicians and 8,000 government officials and jailing 37,000 journalists, students, teachers, and labor organizers in remote "purification" camps. In 1987, Chun handpicked his own successor, Roh Tae Woo, again with massive demonstrations of public protest.

Roh relaxed some of the restrictions on political activity and labor organizing, and labor unions quickly increased their membership. Strikes and lockouts over wages and working conditions broke out. The 1993 election of Kim Young Sam reduced the power of the military in politics for the first time. The press became freer. But it was only in 1997 that a member of an opposition party, Kim Dae Jung, was elected. Thus, through a fifty-year popular struggle, often led by students, the authoritarian patterns of South Korean politics was gradually relaxed, and something closer to a democratic society emerged.

Kim Dae Jung, elected in 1997, had been a longtime opposition leader since the Rhee regime. He was elected to the National Assembly in 1961, but this assembly was dissolved by Park after his military coup. Elected again in

1963, he became the spokesman for the New Democratic Party. Park attempted to assassinate him by ordering his car rammed by a heavily loaded truck, but he survived with injuries. When Kim Dae Jung objected to Park's imposition of martial law banning all political activity, Park had him arrested by the KCIA, which planned to execute him, but protests brought his release. He was then placed under house arrest. After leading more protests, he was arrested in 1976 and sentenced to five years in prison, commuted to house arrest in 1978. When Chun seized power in 1980, Kim Dae Jung was again arrested and sentenced to death. This sentence was then commuted, and he was allowed to go into exile in the United States.

When Kim Dae Jung returned from exile in 1985, he was again put under house arrest but was cleared of all charges in 1987. He ran for president several times and was finally elected in 1997, signaling in his own person the long struggle of South Korea for democracy. He took office during a time of financial crisis and was able to pull the economy back from bankruptcy. He also declared a new "sunshine" policy of constructive engagement with North Korea, visiting Pyongyang and signing a joint declaration of peace with North Korean leader Kim Jong-Il on June 15, 2000. His policies of openness to North Korea have been continued by his successor, Roo Moo Hyun, contrary to the hostile views of North Korea cultivated by President George W. Bush. Kim Dae Jung received the Nobel Peace Prize in 2000.[23]

The churches in South Korea, both Protestant and Catholic, have played an ambivalent role in this long struggle for democratization against military dictators. In the early 1970s, a small sector of the churches involved in industrial mission began to develop a Korean version of liberation theology, called *Minjung* theology, and to work in solidarity with the struggles of workers to unionize and with student protests.[24] But much of Korean Protestantism is conservative, politically and theologically. Megachurches cultivate a charismatic type of Christianity and identify with a "prosperity gospel" that hopes for economic success through divine favor.

NORTH KOREA: SOCIETY AND ECONOMY

Superficially, North and South Korea appear to be radically different systems, the south prosperous, successful, capitalist, and democratic on the American model and the north a repressive command economy and totalitarian state on the Stalinist model, impoverished and stagnant. But more careful observation reveals some deeper similarities. North Korea was devastated by the Korean War, as we have seen, and spent its first few years after the war in intensive reconstruction. North Korea inherited a heavy industry base from the Japanese era that was taken over by the North Korean state after World War II (previously, it had not been privately owned but owned by the Japanese state). After rebuilding following the war, industrial growth rates became among the highest in the world, with a focus on steel, railroads, coal, and hydroelectric energy. But this growth slowed in the late 1960s as expansion ended and plant depreciation and technological obsolescence took their toll.[25]

For several decades, the Democratic People's Republic of Korea had a successful agricultural system, becoming self-sufficient in food by the mid-1970s. It relied on cooperative farms based on the traditional villages, not huge state farms, and peasants were allowed to sell produce individually from small private plots. However, by the 1990s, North Korean agriculture fell into difficulties, with the loss of markets from the former Soviet Union, several floods and bad harvests, and the confiscation of the rice harvest to feed the North Korean army as well as for export to earn cash. The result was food shortages and malnutrition and even starvation in the poorest rural areas.

The North Korean political system is a centralized authoritarian state ruled by one family, Kim Il Sung, and then his son Kim Jong-Il. This family rules through a highly organized mass party and centralized top-down administration with weighty bureaucracies, the top leaders of which enjoy special privileges, while there is a socioeconomic leveling of the rest of the population. The press is tightly controlled, and there is little freedom of expression. This system represents a kind of marriage of Stalinism and a distinctly Korean Confucian paternalism, with every North Korean constantly exhorted to see the supreme leaders as "beloved fathers," the "head and heart" of the body politic and the "supreme brain" of the nation.

This authoritarian paternalism is combined with a fierce insistence on self-reliance and freedom from a dependency on foreign governments, or *juche*. This commitment to autarchy makes North Korea a new version of the traditional Korean "hermit kingdom" closed to the outside world.[26]

While the North Korean economy was successful in expanding heavy industry in the 1960s and 1970s, it has mostly failed (or refused) to enter into the new industrial revolution of the 1980s of communication technology. Television, cell phones, and computers, ubiquitous in the south, are mostly absent in the north. However, health care is well developed, with a life expectancy on a par with second-rank industrial countries, and literacy is nearly universal. The cities are clean, with few cars on the streets and only the elite driving state-owned Mercedes and Volvos. The North Korean countryside has a bucolic antiquarian feel, with deep green, well-tended fields and peasant villages with few television sets or consumer durables. But at the same time, there is little abject poverty or the social pathology of many urban, industrial countries.[27]

In the 1990s, with the loss of the Soviet bloc nations as trading partners, North Korea has sought new outside markets for its goods, particularly weapons, trading with Third World countries such as Zimbabwe. It has a program of nuclear energy as a part of its quest for energy self-sufficiency. It has also aspired to possess nuclear weapons, a program that has caused it to be listed as a "rogue" nation by the West and named as one of the "axis of evil" by President George W. Bush. Although North Korea continually has sought to end tensions with the United States and to achieve a permanent peace treaty, its nuclear ambitions have stood in the way of further diplomatic reconciliation with the United States.[28]

However, the U.S. press and government seldom help Americans understand what lies behind this North Korean drive for nuclear weapons. As we noted earlier in this chapter, North Korea was seriously threatened by U.S. plans to drop nuclear weapons during the Korean War. Since that war, the U.S. and the South Korean armies have periodically conducted "team spirit" exercises in which they practice war scenarios against North Korea, including the use of nuclear weapons. Both armies have stockpiled nuclear weapons in the South for possible use against the north since the Korean War.

North Korean memory is deeply shaped by the vast destruction it suffered in 1950–1953, and it keeps its underground bunkers in place in case of another such attack. North Korea maintains a large army of some 1 million soldiers with another million in reserve, more than a tenth of the population. By contrast, South Korea's army is 686,000 but much more technologically advanced and backed by 35,000 American troops. Thus, North Korea lives as a barrack state in constant fear of renewed attack and sees the possession of nuclear weapons as a major deterrent against such an attack by the United States.

North Korea might be willing to give up these weapons if it were assured that the United States would make peace and normalize relations with North Korea. Improved relations with North Korea demands a willingness of the United States and the West to see the world from the North Korean point of view rather than constantly reiterating the view that it is both a failed state that should disappear and a rogue state that should be nuked.[29]

PROSPECTS FOR PEACE AND REUNIFICATION?

There are many obstacles to improved relations between North and South Korea and eventual reunification. The biggest obstacle is the United States, which has still not negotiated a peace treaty with North Korea and continues to harbor the hope that it can be made to disappear as a separate state by some combination of military violence and economic collapse. The United States has been less than friendly to efforts of recent South Korean presidents, Kim Dae Jung and Roh Moo Hyun, to relax tensions. At the same time, each side of this divide fears being taken over by the other side. South Koreans would not want to live in the North Korean system, and North Korea fears being absorbed into the South Korean system. Some South Koreans also fear a collapse of the north that would make them responsible for impoverished North Korean peasants.

Yet both sides have great strengths. If the best of both systems were put together and the enormous wealth and effort that have been used for more than fifty years to fight each other put to constructive use, a united Korea would be a prosperous and powerful state. Some Asian neighbors, such as Japan, might not want to see such a strong state on their doorstep. The best approach is a gradual relaxation of tensions and the negotiation of peaceful economic cooperation. Freedom of travel, tourism, and academic and technical exchange would build new relations, modifying differences on both sides. Perhaps only after a considerable period of such exchange might it be possible to create a reunified Korea.[30]

NOTES

1. Bruce Cumings, *Korea's Place in the Sun: A Modern History* (New York: Norton, 1997), 23–24.
2. Cumings, *Korea's Place in the Sun*, 26–46.
3. Cumings, *Korea's Place in the Sun*, 48–50.
4. See Bruce Cumings, *Divided Korea: United Future?* Headline Series no. 306 (New York: Foreign Policy Association, 1995), 53–58.
5. Cumings, *Divided Korea*, 87–94.
6. For this era of Korean foreign relations, see Key-Hink Kim, *The Last Phase of the East Asian World Order: Korea, Japan and the Chinese Empire, 1860–1882* (Berkeley: University of California Press, 1980).
7. Cumings, *Korea's Place in the Sun*, 142.
8. Cumings, *Korea's Place in the Sun*, 183–84.
9. See George Hicks, *The Comfort Women: Japan's Brutal Regime of Enforced Prostitution in the Second World War* (New York: Norton, 1995).
10. Cumings, *Korea's Place in the Sun*, 147.
11. Cumings, *Divided Korea*, 21.
12. Cumings, *Divided Korea*, 25.
13. Cumings, *Divided Korea*, 29.
14. Cumings, *Korea's Place in the Sun*, 245.
15. Cumings, *Divided Korea*, 30–31.
16. Cumings, *Korea's Place in the Sun*, 270.

17. Cumings, *Korea's Place in the Sun*, 275–81.
18. Cumings, *Korea's Place in the Sun*, 291.
19. Cumings, *Korea's Place in the Sun*, 293–94.
20. For a more detailed study of the war, see Rosemary Foot, *The Wrong War: American Policy and the Dimensions of the Korean Conflict, 1950–1953* (New York: Cornell University Press, 1985). Bruce Cumings has written a two-volume study of the origins the war, *The Origins of the Korean War* (Princeton, N.J.: Princeton University Press, 1981, 1990).
21. Cumings, *Divided Korea*, 38.
22. For a good overview of the South Korean political economy, see Woo Jung-en, *Race to the Swift: State and Finance in Korean Industrialization* (New York: Columbia University Press, 1991).
23. http://nobelprize.org/nobel_prizes/peace/laureates/2000/dae-jung-bio.html.
24. See the Commission on Theological Concerns of the Christian Conference of Asia, *Minjung Theology: People as the Subjects of History* (Maryknoll, N.Y.: Orbis Books, 1983),
25. Cumings, *Divided Korea*, 74
26. Cumings, *Korea's Place in the Sun*, 403–14.
27. This description come from Cumings, *Divided Korea*, 74.
28. Cumings, *Korea's Place in the Sun*, 464–84.
29. For an expanded development of Bruce Cumings's view of the North Korean system and viewpoint, see Bruce Cumings, *North Korea: A Different Country* (New York: New Press, 2004).
30. See Cumings, *Korea's Place in the Sun*, 287–94.

• 15 •

South Africa: Constructing and Deconstructing Apartheid

South Africa lies at the southern end of the African continent. It is a largely arid land with only 10 percent that is arable. It is rich in minerals and metals, such as diamonds, gold, coal, iron, and uranium. According to 2006 figures, the population is 44.2 million, 75 percent African, 14 percent white, and 11 percent Colored and Asian.[1] These figures represent a diminishment of the white percentage of 17 percent in 1990, with many whites migrating in the 1980s and 1990s to escape the struggle against apartheid.

South African history represents an extreme example of a European colonialism of an African land that assumed the form of a concerted effort to separate the white and black populations and to create a legal, economic, and political system of white domination. The struggle to dismantle apartheid is also remarkable for its uniting of national and international forces for reform of this system, but it also reveals the limits of such reforms in terms of achieving real justice for the African majority. This chapter seeks to provide a concise history of the several aspects of this conflict, the construction of apartheid, the struggle to dismantle it, and the successes and the limits of this effort.

EUROPEAN COLONIALISM AND SETTLEMENT, 1500–1910

Bushmen hunter-gatherers and Khoi San pastoralists settled in South Africa as early as 25,000 years ago, while different Bantu people began to migrate into the area from 2,500 to 1,500 years ago.[2] Europeans, such as the Portuguese, seeking a route to Asia in late fifteenth century, sailed around the

Cape but did not settle. The Dutch were the first to establish a colony in the Cape, in 1652, but at first as a station to provide passing ships with food and water.[3] The British also saw the usefulness of the Cape as a fueling station and seized it in 1795, relinquishing it in 1803 and retaking it in 1806. It was ceded to the British by Holland in 1814.[4]

The Dutch settlers were antagonized by this British takeover, and many packed their ox-drawn wagons and migrated north to occupy what they believed was open land in the central High Veld, which eventually became the two Boer (Dutch South African) republics of the Orange Free State and the South African Republic of the Transvaal. In their efforts to expand into the Natal region, they conflicted with an expanding Zulu kingdom. On December 16, 1836, they defeated the Zulus in the battle of Blood River, killing several thousand. These events convinced the Calvinist Boers that they were especially blessed as God's New Israel with the lands they were settling as their promised land. Thus, the trek north and its battles with the Zulu became a part of their national lore.[5]

However, it would be the British who would eventually subdue the Zulus of Natal and establish their control over the region. Lacking willing local labor, the British imported over 150,000 indentured servants from India to work in sugar plantations, thus establishing the Asian population of South Africa.

Diamonds were discovered near Kimberley in 1869, and gold was discovered in Witwatersrand in 1886. These discoveries brought floods of new European immigrants as well as black laborers to the mines.[6] It also brought conflicts with the British in the Cape and Natal who sought to control this wealth. A brief war was fought in 1880, with the Boers victorious, followed by a second more protracted war from 1899 to 1902. When the British seized the major cities, such as Pretoria, Boer farmers took to guerrilla warfare. The British responded with scorched-earth tactics and rounded up tens of thousands of Boer women and children into concentration camps, where some 26,000 died of disease and neglect.[7] These deaths brought cries of concern from some humanitarian sectors of British society.

On May 31, 1902, a peace treaty was signed in which the two Boer republics acknowledged British sovereignty. In 1910, the two British colonies of the Cape and Natal and the two Boer republics were united in the Union of South Africa, which was given British dominion status, similar to Canada. The British High Commission territories—Basutoland (Lesotho), Bechuanaland (Botswana), Swaziland, and Rhodesia (Zimbabwe and Zambia)—continued under direct British rule. Only whites could be elected to parliament.

PROTOAPARTHEID, 1910–1948

Certain patterns of separation of the races and the subordination of blacks and Colored (mixed-race people) were already in place before the Union or developed during the period from 1910 to 1948. The British had already introduced pass laws in the nineteenth century in the Cape Colony and Natal regulating the movement of blacks from tribal areas into that occupied by whites. Color bars separated whites and blacks in the workplace, reserving skilled jobs for whites and barring black workers from striking.[8] But the most important piece of legislation was the 1913 Land Act, which allotted 6 percent (later expanded to 13 percent) of the land for blacks, 75 percent of the population, in separate parcels, strung along the east coast and northern border, designated for different tribal groups. This left 87 percent of South Africa, including all the prime agricultural land, in the hands of whites. Blacks could not buy or rent land or even work as sharecroppers outside their designated areas. Thousands of blacks living on land outside these areas were uprooted and forced into black reserves.[9]

A black middle-class opposition began to organize, forming the South African Native National Congress in 1912, renamed the African National Congress (ANC) in 1923. The ANC sought respectability and used only legal appeals to oppose the growing segregation.[10] Even prior to the formation of the ANC and partly as a model for it was the work of Mahatma Gandhi, who pioneered both nonviolent direct action and legal opposition to defend the rights of the Indian populations in Natal and the Transvaal.[11] White Afrikaner nationalism began to organize against the "black threat," forming the secret *Broederbond* (Brotherhood) to promote Afrikaner culture and language, standing behind the newly formed Nationalist Party. During World War I, South Africa, fighting on the British side, invaded the German colony of South West Africa (Namibia), occupying it until it was granted independence in 1990. This independence was achieved after more than twenty years of guerrilla warfare against South African occupation led by the Southwest Africa People's Organization (SWAPO).

CONSTRUCTING APARTHEID, 1948–1990

In 1948, the Nationalist Party, some of whom, such as John Vorster, had been pro-Nazi during World War II, won the national election on a platform of apartheid or separation of the races. Having won the election, the new government immediately began implementing apartheid legislation to separate whites not only from blacks but also from Coloreds and Asians. Those Cape Coloreds who were property owners had voted in the previous South African union but were now stripped of their voting rights.

A series of laws fixed the new system of apartheid in place.[12] These included the Prohibition of Mixed Marriages Act and the Immorality Act (1949, 1950), which forbade interracial marriage or sexual relations between whites and those of a different race; the Population Registration Act (1950), which required all citizens to be registered as white, black, or Colored; the Suppression of Communism Act (1950), which banned the South African Communist Party or any other party that the government labeled "communist"; the Group Areas Act, the Bantu Authorities Act, and the Prevention of Illegal Squatting Act (1950, 1951), which partitioned the country into different areas for the different races, created separate government structures for blacks, and mandated the demolition of black housing deemed illegal "squatting"; the Reservation of Separate Amenities Act (1953), which forbade those of different races from using the same drinking fountains, restrooms, and so on; the Bantu Education Act (1953) and the Extension of University Education Act (1959), which created a separate system of inferior education for blacks and abolished alternative mission schools for blacks, later setting up separate universities for whites, blacks, and Coloreds, while the Afrikaans Medium Decree (1974) forced all schools to use the Afrikaans language as the medium of instruction in mathematics, the social sciences, geography, and history at the high school level, a language spoken nowhere except in South Africa; the Industrial Conciliation Act (1959), which separated workers by color, preventing interracial unionizing; and the Promotion of Black Self-Government Act (1958) and the Black Homeland Citizenship Act (1970), which attempted to create the legal fiction that blacks were "citizens" of their own racial reserves and not citizens of South Africa. Blacks were defined as working in South Africa with specific permits as "immigrant" labor.

The apartheid system did not allow blacks to run businesses or have professional practices in white areas without a special permit. It segregated all facilities: transportation (buses and trains), hospitals, and even ambulances. Blacks had to carry passes at all times and could be arrested and deported to their "homeland" if found without one. All facilities for blacks, such as schools and hospitals, were markedly inferior to those for whites, if they existed at all. Black areas rarely had plumbing or electricity. Even beaches were segregated, with the best beaches reserved for whites. Most important, blacks were declared citizens of their homelands, not of South Africa, and so could no longer obtain a South African passport for travel. No other country recognized the "native reserves" as independent countries except South Africa.

The homeland system broke up black families. Men of working age might spend most of the year working in the mines, living in a hostel that gave each man only a shelf as a bed and a place to keep belongings. Adult women might work most of the year as a domestic in a white family, living in a small room or in a shack behind the main house.[13] Both had holidays to see their families only a few days a year. Meanwhile, nonworking women, children, the handicapped, and the elderly were crowded into the reserves, where they scratched out a living from arid ground and gathered water from polluted streams. The government also implemented a policy to destroy long-established black and Colored areas, such as Sophiatown near Johannesburg and District Six in the center of Cape Town, forcing their removal to distant, separate areas, bulldozing the buildings and constructing new communities for whites in their place.[14]

THE ANTIAPARTHEID STRUGGLE, 1952–1990

The ANC had already been formed in the earlier period but in 1952 began to move from legal appeals through the courts to more direct actions to resist the apartheid laws through strikes, protest marches, and boycotts in what was called the Defiance Campaign. In 1960, more radical members of the ANC split from it to form the Pan-Africanist Congress (PAC). They led nationwide demonstrations against the pass laws. One group of about 5,000 converged nonviolently on the local police station in Sharpsville on March 21, 1960, singing and offering themselves for arrest for not carrying their passbooks. A group of about 300 police fired on them, killing sixty-nine and injuring 186. All these were black, and most were shot in the back as they were fleeing.[15] After the massacre, both the ANC and the PAC were banned by the South African government.

These events impelled the resistance to apartheid to go underground and to begin to use new methods of sabotage and armed struggle, although the ANC continued to use nonviolent methods of protest as well. Prime Minister Hendrik Verwoerd declared a state of emergency, arresting tens of thousands of demonstrators, including many of the ANC and PAC leaders. In June 1964, Nelson Mandela and seven others were put on trial for treason and sentenced to life imprisonment, while other leaders, such as Oliver Tambo, escaped from South Africa to lead the struggle in exile.

Resistance spread to all sectors of black society. Unions went on strike. The South African Students' Organization developed the Black Consciousness Movement under the leadership of medical student Steve Biko. This movement stressed the need for political freedom to be accompanied by cultural freedom, by pride in black identity.[16] High school and even grade school students went on strike, refusing to attend schools where the medium of instruction was Afrikaans, a language that limited the ability of black students to go on to universities within or outside South Africa that required fluency in English. A generation of South African youth committed themselves to revolutionary struggle with the motto "liberation before education." In 1977, Biko was arrested and beaten to death in prison, while hundreds of young people were killed or injured by police firing on their protest marches.

The churches played an important role in the antiapartheid struggle in South Africa. South Africa is more than 80 percent Christian, divided between the white Dutch Reform churches and their subsidiary "Colored" and black "daughter" churches; the English churches, including Anglican, Methodist, and Roman Catholic; and African Independent churches. In the 1960s, a progressive sector of the English churches and black and Colored Dutch reform churches began to develop a protest against apartheid. A black South African liberation theology developed in the 1970s.[17]

In 1985, the antiapartheid sector of the churches published the *Kairos* document, which divided the theology and practice of the churches into three groups: a state theology that justifies apartheid as a biblical doctrine of the separation of the races, a church theology that counsels reconciliation of the races but without structural change, and a prophetic liberation theology that denounces apartheid as injustice and demands its dismantling.[18] In the 1980s, churches often sheltered protest meetings that were officially banned by the government. Desmond Tutu, bishop of the Anglican Church of Cape Town, emerged as the leader of the South African Council of Churches, which called for the end of apartheid.

The South African military stepped up its attacks on what they saw as "terrorist bases" in border countries, allying with antigovernment guerrilla groups, such as the National Union for the Total Independence of Angola and the Mozambican National Resistance. They also struck at SWAPO groups based in Namibia. Assassinations of exiled ANC leaders abroad were carried out not only in bordering African countries but in Brussels, Paris, Stockholm, and London as well. Ruth First, leading antiapartheid speaker and wife of ANC leader Joe Slovo, was killed by a parcel bomb in Maputo. Vast damage to land, buildings, and people, mostly civilians, in bordering countries resulted from these cross-border attacks.

Protest against South African policies became international. In November 1962, the UN General Assembly condemned apartheid. In 1976, an arms embargo against South Africa was made mandatory by the United Nations. A movement to divest from South Africa spread to many countries. South

African sports teams were barred from participating in international sports events, and tourism was boycotted. A university boycott restricted foreign lecturers from teaching at white South African universities unless they also spoke at black and Colored universities. The churches also joined in the protest. In 1982, the World Alliance of Reformed Churches declared apartheid a heresy and excommunicated Reformed churches that defended it as a biblical teaching. The World Council of Churches and denominational bodies encouraged divestment.

South Africa found itself increasingly isolated in the world, even though cooperation with the divestment campaign was by no means universal. Both President Reagan in the United States and Prime Minister Margaret Thatcher of Britain resisted it as contrary to free trade principles. Thatcher condemned the ANC as a Marxist "terrorist" organization.[19] African countries were all antiapartheid, with the frontline states forming the Southern African Development Coordination Conference in 1980 to promote regional development independent of South Africa. Nigeria led the thirty-two-nation boycott of the 1986 Commonwealth Games because of Thatcher's lack of support for the sports boycott of South Africa.

During the last decade of apartheid, the white South African government stepped up its repression of dissent. Stricter censorship was imposed on the media. A new state of emergency was declared in 1986. Tens of thousands were detained without trial and many tortured under the Internal Security Act. The president could rule by decree without reference to the constitution or the Parliament. Certain areas were declared "unrest areas" where extraordinary measures could be employed to crush protest. Police and soldiers patrolled towns in armed cars, destroying black squatter camps and detaining thousands of blacks and Coloreds. At the same time, black-on-black violence broke out: militants killed those who collaborated with the police and army by putting burning tires around their necks. Those who bought from white-owned shops were forced to drink soap powder and kerosene.

At the same time, the South African government sought to make some reforms to mollify the protest. Pass laws were modified. There was an attempt to separate Asians and Coloreds from blacks by creating a tricameral legislature where Colored and Asians had a vote and token representation, but real power still remained with the white Parliament. In 1989, Prime Minister P. W. Botha suffered a stroke and resigned, and F. W. de Klerk took his place. De Klerk realized that much more extensive reforms were necessary. In February 1990, he announced that he would repeal discriminatory laws and lift the ban on the ANC, the PAC, the Communist Party, and the United Democratic Front (formed in the 1980s and led by churchmen Desmond Tutu and Allan Boesak). Political prisoners not guilty of common-law crimes were released.

On February 11, 1990, Nelson Mandela was released after twenty-seven years of imprisonment.[20] South Africa relinquished its control of Namibia, which became an independent state on March 21, 1990.

DISMANTLING APARTHEID AND BEYOND

From 1990 to 1991, the legal apparatus of apartheid was dismantled.[21] All the apartheid laws cited previously were repealed. A whites-only referendum in March 1992 gave the government authority to negotiate a new constitution with the ANC and other parties. In December 1991, the Convention for a Democratic South Africa began negotiations to form a multiracial transitional government and new constitution. In 1993, the draft of the new constitution was published. The final draft of the constitution was approved in December 1996 and took effect on February 4, 1997.

The new constitution is the most liberal in the world. It has an extensive bill of rights that explicitly forbids discrimination on the grounds of "race, gender, sex, pregnancy, marital status, ethnic or social origin, colour, sexual orientation, age, disability, religion, conscience, belief, culture, language and birth" (2.9.3).[22] It is unique in forbidding discrimination based on sexual orientation. It guarantees the freedom and security of the person, including the right not to be detained without trial or to be tortured or treated in a cruel, inhuman, and degrading way. The guarantee of bodily and psychological integrity includes the right to make decisions concerning reproduction, to control of one's body, and not to be subjected to medical or scientific experiments without informed consent. (2.12. 1 and 2). All slavery, servitude, or forced labor is forbidden (2.13).

Freedom of expression, according to the bill of rights of the South African constitution, includes freedom of the press and other media, freedom to receive or impart information or ideas, freedom of artistic creativity, academic freedom, and freedom of scientific research. Such freedom, however, does not include propaganda for war, incitement of imminent violence, or advocacy of hatred based on race, ethnicity, gender, or religion (2.16). Freedom of assembly and association and freedom to demonstrate, picket, or present petitions is guaranteed (2.17 and 18). Every citizen has the right to vote and stand for elected office as well as to form a political party and campaign for that party or cause (2.19). Section 21 of the bill of rights guarantees freedom of movement and freedom to leave or enter the republic, to reside anywhere in the republic, and to have a passport. Section 22 guarantees the right to choose a trade, occupation, or profession freely. Section 23 on labor relations guarantees the rights of workers to form a union, participate in its activities, strike, and engage in collective bargaining.

Section 24 on the environment states that everyone has a right to an environment that is not harmful to their health and well-being. The environment should be protected for present and future generations through legislation and other measures "to prevent pollution and ecological degradation, promote conservation and ensure ecologically sustainable development while promoting justifiable economic and social development."

Section 25 forbids arbitrary deprivation of property except for public purpose and with just compensation. Section 26 guarantees everyone access to adequate housing and forbids eviction from a home or demolition of a home without a court order. Section 27 guarantees everyone health-care services, including reproductive health care, sufficient food and water, and social security, including social assistance for themselves and their dependents if they are unable to support themselves. Section 29 guarantees everyone the right to a basic education in the language of their choice. Sections 30 and 31 guarantee the right to use the language and participate in the cultural life of their choice. With these and other provisions, the bill of rights of the South African constitution seeks not only to dismantle apartheid legislation but also to guarantee that such laws should never be passed again.

On April 27, 1994, a new national election was held with universal adult suffrage.[23] The ANC won 62.7 percent of the vote, while the National Party captured most of the white and Colored vote. At midnight on April 26–27, 1994, the old flag of South Africa was lowered, the old national anthem was sung, and the new rainbow flag of South Africa was raised, and the former anthem of the ANC, *Nkosi Sikelel'i Afrika* (God Bless Africa) was sung as the new national anthem (co-official with the old one, *Die Stem*). On May 10, 1994, Nelson Mandela was inaugurated as the new president of South Africa. The old Bantustans, or "African homelands," were abolished. South Africa was divided into nine provinces where people of any race could live: Western Cape, Northern Cape, Eastern Cape, Northwest, Free State, Kwa Zulu Natal, Gauteng, Northwestern Province, and Mpumalanga.[24]

Despite these stunning transformations of South African law and its political system, many of the economic patterns of apartheid continue, having been deeply hewn into the structure of the society even before the formal apartheid period. In the first years of the 1990s, when it became evident that a new multiracial democratic state would take over with the ANC as its majority party, the wealthy white South African business class dug in for continued economic dominance. Key utilities that had been state owned but run primarily for the benefit of whites were privatized and sold to wealthy white businessmen. Thus, the white elite assured themselves that the key companies that provided water, electricity, energy, fuel, and public transportation would continue to be controlled by whites, even though the new government might seek to extend these amenities to black townships and former homelands.

All the economic assets of South Africa continue to be overwhelmingly owned and controlled by whites. Since part of the negotiation for a multiracial democratic state ensured that there would be no forced land reform, all the best land, 80 percent of arable land, continues to be in the hands of white farmers. The mines and major industries are also owned almost entirely by whites. Five large corporations control 75 percent of the business of South Africa. The country continues to have one of the most unequal income distributions of the world. Five percent of the population, almost entirely white, own 88 percent of the wealth, while 60 percent of the population, almost entirely black, make less than R42,000 per year (about U.S.$7,000). Poverty is mostly defined by skin color, with blacks making up 90 percent of the poor.

A small black educated and politically empowered black elite has developed that has power in government and represents teachers and intellectuals, small businessmen, and professionals. They have adopted a lifestyle similar to whites with gated homes and black domestics in shacks in their backyard. The ANC adopted the Black Economic Empowerment policy, which sought to ensure that government contracts employ blacks, Colored, and Asians in proportional numbers to whites, which ironically had the effect of continuing these racial classifications from apartheid times but now for the purpose of "affirmative action." Better and more permanent housing with electricity and water has been developed in former townships where a few years before blacks and Colored were driven out by police for squatting. But these reforms have yet to make a deep effect on the economic hierarchy of the society.

Moreover, the ANC government has accepted the World Bank and International Monetary Fund guidelines for "development" according to neoliberal principles.[25] This means that 25 percent of the government budget is devoted to repayment of the national debt inherited from the apartheid regime. The privatization of utilities and the cutting of social services by the government have meant the raising of prices for basic utilities, such as water and electricity, and the cutting off of these amenities from those who are unable to pay.[26] Government and businesses have been downsized, cutting 100,000 jobs a year and causing an unemployment rate of 35 percent. These measures have actually increased the gap between rich and poor since 1994.[27]

In addition, postapartheid South Africa is plagued by a heightened level of violent crime. Former military personnel were not integrated back into the society.[28] In addition, the antiapartheid struggle left a legacy of millions of youth who have failed to get an adequate education to participate in the new society, as they engaged for years in protest marches rather than attending classes. These uprooted and uneducated black youth become the social base of gangs engaged in robberies and rapes within their own communities although occasionally invading white areas as well. From 1994 to 2001, violent crime increased by 33 percent. In 2002, South Africa experienced 114.8 murders per 100,000 inhabitants, the highest murder rate in the world, five times greater than the second highest, Brazil. There have also been attacks on white farmers, with roughly 313 white farmers being killed annually since 1994.[29] Although these attacks reflect black resentment against the continuing monopoly of the arable land by whites, it does nothing to effect a real land redistribution where blacks could effectively take their place as productive farmers.

In addition, since the late 1980s, South Africa had suffered from a rising epidemic of AIDS, which now affects 5.5 million South Africans, or 20 percent of adults. This was not helped by President Thabo Mbeki, who succeeded Nelson Mandela as president of South Africa in 1999. Mbeki insisted that the HIV infection did not cause AIDS and that a focus on the epidemic reflected racist views of blacks. He has softened these views in recent years after much protest, but his stance helped prevent a concerted effort to curb HIV/AIDS through effective means of prevention and cure. Thus, South Africa stands to lose millions of working-age men and women, leaving many children homeless or to be raised by grandparents.

The dismantling of apartheid as a system of legalized racial discrimination has been one of the stellar human accomplishments in the past two decades, carried out finally not by arms but by political negotiation between white and black leaders. But the victory also reveals its limitations. Racial discrimination has been abolished, but its economic effects continue to shape South Africa as a society in which the hierarchy of rich and poor is extreme and still runs largely along racial lines.

NOTES

1. *World Almanac and Book of Facts* (New York: Simon and Schuster, 2007), 828.
2. On the African settlement of the area, see Robert Ross, *A Concise History of South Africa* (Cambridge: Cambridge University Press, 1999), 6–20.
3. Ross, *A Concise History of South Africa*, 21–25.
4. Ross, *A Concise History of South Africa*, 35.
5. Ross, *A Concise History of South Africa*, 39–42; see also "History of South Africa," *Wikipedia, the Free Encyclopedia*, http://en.wikipedia.org/wiki/Special:Search?search=History+of+South+Africa&fulltext=Search, 10–11.

6. See William H. Worger, *South Africa's City of Diamonds: Mine Workers and Monopoly Capitalism in Kimberley, 1867–1895* (New Haven, Conn.: Yale University Press, 1987).

7. Ross, *A Concise History of South Africa*, 72–75; see also "History of South Africa," 12–13.

8. "History of South Africa in the Apartheid Era," *Wikipedia, the Free Encyclopedia*, http://en.wikipedia.org/wiki/History_of_South_Africa_in_the_Apartheid_Era, 4.

9. Ross, *A Concise History of South Africa*, 88–90.

10. Ross, *A Concise History of South Africa*, 85–86.

11. See Robert A. Huttenbach, *Gandhi in South Africa: British Imperialism and the Indian Question, 1860–1914* (Ithaca, N.Y.: Cornell University Press, 1971).

12. For this list of apartheid laws, see "History of South Africa in the Apartheid Era," 5–6.

13. See Jacklyn Cock, *Maids and Madams: Domestic Workers under Apartheid* (Johannesburg: Ravan Press, 1980).

14. On the story of Sophiatown, see Don Mattera, *Gone with the Twilight: The Story of Sophiatown* (London: Zed Books, 1987); on District Six, see Hettie Adams and Hermione Sutter, *William Street, District Six* (Diep River, South Africa: Chameleon Press, 1988).

15. Ross, *A Concise History of South Africa*,129.

16. Ross, *A Concise History of South Africa*, 141–43; see also Steve Biko, *I Write What I Like* (Harmondsworth: Penguin, 1988).

17. See Allan Boezak, *Farewell to Innocence: A Socio-Ethical Study of Black Theology and Black Power* (Maryknoll, N.Y.: Orbis Books, 1977); see also Itumeleng Mosala and Buti Tihagale, *The Unquestionable Right to Be Free: Black Theology from South Africa* (Maryknoll, N.Y.: Orbis Books, 1986).

18. Kairos Theologians, *Challenge to the Church: A Theological Comment on the Political Crisis in South Africa: The Kairos Document and Commentaries* (Geneva: World Council of Churches, 1985).

19. See "History of South Africa in the Apartheid Era," 14.

20. See Nelson Mandela, *Long Walk to Freedom: The Autobiography of Nelson Mandela* (London: Little, Brown, 1994).

21. See Patti Waldmeir, *Anatomy of a Miracle: The End of Apartheid and the Birth of a New South Africa* (New York: Norton, 1997).

22. For this and subsequent references to chapter 2 of the bill of rights of the South African constitution, see www.info.gov.za/documents/constitution/1996/96cons2.htm.

23. See R. W. Johnson and Lawrence Schlemmer, *Launching Democracy in South Africa: The First Open Election, April, 1994* (New Haven, Conn.: Yale University Press, 1996).

24. See Ross, *A Concise History of South Africa*, 191.

25. See Ishmail Lesufi, "Six Years of Neoliberal Economic Policies in South Africa," in *Globalization and Post-Apartheid South Africa*, ed. Abebe Zegeye, Richard L. Harris, and Pat Lauderdale (Toronto: de Sitter Publications, 2005), 22–34.

26. On militant resistance in Soweto to this rise of electricity prices in South Africa and the formation of the Soweto Electricity Crisis Committee and the Anti-Privatization Forum, see the interview with the leading organizer, Trevor Ngwane, in Tom Mertes, ed., *A Movement of Movements: Is Another World Really Possible?* (London: Verso Press, 2003), 111–34.

27. See Vicki Short, "A Revealing British Documentary on Post-Apartheid South Africa," www.wsws.org/news/1998/may1998/pilg-m20.shtml; see also P. Eric Louw, "Globalization and the New South Africa," in *The Rise, Fall and Legacy of Apartheid* (Westport, Conn.: Praeger, 2004), 193–203.

28. See Ian Liebenberg, Rialize Ferreira, and Marlene Roefs, "Loyal Service and Yet Demobilized—What Now? Demobilization and Economic Reintegration of South Africa's Demobilized Military Personnel," in Zegeye et al., *Globalization and Post-Apartheid South Africa*, 35–53.

29. "History of South Africa," 20.

· 16 ·

Ecology: The Context for All Social Systems

The biosphere of planet earth is the context in which humans exist. We are latecomers to the planet. Our species, *Homo sapiens*, emerged a mere 300,000 to 400,000 years ago and has become a dominant species on the planet only in the past 5,000 to 8,000 years, since the development of plow agriculture, cities, class hierarchy, and systems of dominating power of some over others. This is a tiny moment within the 4.6-billion-year history of the earth, the first billion years of which were expended simply stabilizing the earth's atmosphere.

Life in the form of prokaryote cells (bacteria reproducing by binary fusion) emerged only 3.8 billion years ago and eukaryotes with nucleated cells, chromosomes, proteins, and sexual reproduction a billion years later. Five hundred million years ago, vertebrates were established, and life forms rapidly colonized the earth's surface from the seas where life first developed. During the Mesozoic era, the age of the reptiles, dinosaurs dominated the earth for 170 million years, far longer than humans have existed. Their sudden demise was probably caused by a meteorite hitting the earth and the ensuing climate change.

DIMENSIONS OF THE ECOLOGICAL CRISIS

Our own era, the Cenozoic era, emerged over the past 65 million years after the demise of the dinosaurs. This is the age of fish, birds, flowers, and mammals, from which the first hominids developed from chimpanzee-like animals about 23 million years ago, with *Homo sapiens* emerging from *Homo erectus* less than half a million years ago.[1] It is this earth of the Cenozoic era that humans know as "our earth," a planetary paradise with its variety of plants and animals. It is this earth that is threatened by the rapid expansion of the human species as the dominant species, particularly over the past 200 years, with humans rapidly multiplying from 500 million in 1650 C.E. to 1 billion in 1850 C.E. to 2 billion in 1930 and 4 billion in 1975. In 2006, humans numbered 6.528 billion. Despite extensive efforts at population control, human population will probably not be stabilized until the second half of the twenty-first century at 11 billion to 12 billion.

This enormous expansion of one species, humans, is colonizing every area of habitable land, destroying forest, marsh, and plain habitats that supported the vast variety of planet and animal species that developed over the past 50 million years. Thus, the earth is experiencing vast die-offs of tens of thousands of flora and fauna. By 2000, as many as a million different species of plants and animals had disappeared since 1650, representing as much as 20 percent of the species of the earth.[2] This rapid destruction continues despite intentional efforts around the world over the past thirty years to protect endangered species.

This formidable destruction compares to the vast die-off of life at the end of the Cretaceous (last period of the Mesozoic era) period, when it is estimated that some 47 percent of marine life and 18 percent of land vertebrate families died. But this is the first time such widespread destruction of the diversity of evolutionary development has been caused by the expansion of one species, humans, at the expense of the whole. This vast destruction of other plants and animals threatens our own survival. It is caused not only by the continual encroachment of humans on the habitats of most other earth creatures but also by the poisoning of air, water, and soil, which form the basis for our own existence. For example, in many areas, the rivers, lakes, and oceans have grown so toxic that the fish population has been greatly diminished, and people dare not eat the fish that remain because of fears of being sickened. Thus, a major source of food on which human have relied for tens of thousands of years is disappearing.

The ecological crisis that presently threatens the survival of many of the plants and animals of the Cenozoic era, as well as humans themselves, can been seen as the interconnection and mutual enhancement of five major trajectories: population expansion; energy use, especially reliance on fossil fuels; methods of food production; deforestation and destruction of habitat for nonhuman species; and, in and through these four, increasing pollution of air, water, and soil.

We have just mentioned the exponential growth of human population in the past 350 years in which human numbers doubled in shorter and shorter periods of time. The most notable period of expansion was from 1930 to 1975, when humans expanded from 2 billion to 4 billion in a mere forty-five years. The next thirty-two years (1975–2007) added another 2.5 billion, a considerable slowing of the pace of expansion but still adding a huge number of humans. The issue of population expansion is a controversial one since it touches on issues of gender (the status of women as the reproducers) and sexuality in areas where the world's religions and the moral cultures, developed over the past 2,500 years, are often hostile to proposals for birth control and female reproductive and sexual agency.

Some have argued that the issue of curbing population expansion is implicitly genocidal, seeking to reduce the numbers of less wanted groups—that it is poverty and the lack of just distribution of wealth, not population, that is the issue. This, however, is a false dichotomy. Ecologists have shown that the ecological footprint created by humans should be seen as a multiplication of three factors: population × consumption × technology.[3] In other words, one must look at all three factors in their interconnection: human numbers, how much groups of humans consume, and what kind of resources are used to produce, process, transport, and deliver such goods that are consumed as well as disposal of the wastes of this whole process.

Thus, the same-size population that uses primarily the human body for labor and transportation and that has a subsistence economy, producing and gathering its own food, using local materials for clothes, building material and fuel, and reusing or recycling its wastes, makes a much smaller environmental impact than a similar number of people who consume a great variety of foods and goods transported from distant regions, using fossil fuels and electricity for energy to produce, transport, and process its goods and to heat buildings, which discards wastes in a polluting way at each stage of production and consumption. If we imagine the first group as having an environmental impact of one and the second group as consuming ten times more than the first and using technology that uses ten times the energy, then the environmental impact of the second group is 100 times that of the first group.

This is in fact approximately the difference between the environmental impact of the average American compared with that of a Third World person living in a subsistence lifestyle. This does not mean, however, that poor populations are irrelevant to the problem of ecological crisis; rather, all populations should be seen in their interrelationship with the other two factors of consumption and technology. Moreover, most of the poor populations of the world are not living sustainably; rather, their very poverty means they are marginalized by the modern productive systems of the world. They may be stripping available forests for wood and discarding wastes without adequate sewage facilities. They may be living in the more polluted areas without access to clean water. Thus, the proliferation of the numbers of the poor also causes environmental degradation, even as they are also victims of such degradation.

It is, however, the high-consuming and high-technology rich populations that cause the most environmental damage, and this damage multiplies as their numbers and their way of life spreads. For example, U.S. Americans own about 940 automobiles for every 1,000 persons, almost one for every man, woman, and child. By contrast, the Chinese own about eight automobiles for every 1,000 persons, or about 15 million autos, but this is up from only 1 million automobiles in 1990. With a population of 1.2 billion, the increase of automobile ownership by fifteen times greatly increases the ecological impact of this enormous population whose cities now suffer from some of the most toxic air pollution of any urban areas of the world.

The ecological impact of populations is greatly multiplied by the kinds of energy they use. Since the dawn of modern industrialization, this has been mostly fossil fuels: coal, natural gas, and petroleum. Fossil fuels today account for 78 percent of energy use, 33 percent petroleum, 27 percent coal, and 18 percent natural gas. The burning of fossil fuels releases many gaseous by-products into the air. Carbon dioxide in the earth's atmosphere is now 25 percent higher than in preindustrial times. Such gases cause air pollution and acid rain that destroy forests and soil fertility. It is also the major cause of global warming, which is creating more violent weather patterns, such as stronger hurricanes, and melting ice caps that threaten to inundate low-lying islands and coastal areas where many of the world's cities are located. The ocean current that brings temperate weather to northern Europe could also be affected, causing it to become much colder, while increased heat in tropical areas would be devastating for farming in these regions.[4]

Not only is the burning of fossil fuels a major source of environmental damage, but fossil fuels are also scarce resources that are rapidly being used up. Although new sources of petroleum may still be discovered or exploited, these tend to be less accessible and cause greater environmental damage in extraction, such as tar sands that lie under the muskeg of northern Alberta, Canada. Although these tar sands are estimated to contain as much as 175 billion barrels of proven oil reserves, almost as much as Saudi Arabia, they are very costly to extract. To extract just one barrel of oil from these tar sands, it is necessary to mine two to four tons of tar sands, burn 250 cubic feet of natural gas, or use 1,000 cubic feet of gas to inject steam underground, then burn another 500 cubic feet of gas to upgrade the bitumen into synthetic oil, using five barrels of water. The whole process would release 2.5 times as much carbon dioxide as conventional oil production. The use of water for such extraction could use up as much as 25 percent of Alberta's groundwater.[5]

The extraction of readily accessible petroleum has already peaked worldwide and will become increasingly scarce by 2020.[6] The result of the growing scarcity and expense of extracting oil is a major cause of the oil wars around the world. This is a major reason for the U.S. desire for global domination through military bases in so many parts of the world (see chapter 12).

Soil erosion, the pollution of soil and water from industrial and domestic wastes, and acid rain are major causes of decreasing fertility of the soil. This affects the ability to increase the food supply for the growing population. The production of basic grains, the foundation of the human diet, increased 2.6 times between 1950 and 1984, during which time the human population almost doubled. But the ability to increase the production of basic grains has been disappointing since that time.[7] Much of the confidence in the possibility of expanding the world's food production was based on the Green Revolution, which provided new high-yield grains to farmers in Asia, Africa, and the Middle East. But these new grains demanded high inputs of water, petroleum-based pesticides and fertilizers, and mechanized farming equipment. The Green Revolution promoted an agribusiness model, biasing agriculture to large mechanized farms and away from the small farmer. As oil prices escalated in the 1970s–1990s, the costs of fuel, fertilizer, and pesticides became out of reach of smaller farmers. Water tables were depleted by unsustainable use of water for irrigation, and petroleum-based pesticides and fertilizers polluted the soil and waters. Thus, the initial hope of the Green Revolution turned into a disaster for many Third World farmers.[8]

Humanity faces a future where food production may not be able to keep up with population expansion. But the primary cause of famine at present is not lack of enough food but rather lack of access to food. An elite few feast on a food procurement system that markets a great variety of foods worldwide, while the rural poor who produce the crops often lack adequate basic food for daily life, and the urban poor are malnourished by innutritious "fast food." Chronic undernourishment affects some 20 percent of humanity worldwide (over 1 billion).[9]

Deforestation is also a major effect of expanding human populations, converting trees into lumber and the land into farms and grazing areas for cattle. Deforestation is a major cause of extinction of animal and plant species, contributing to the rapid destruction of the diversity of life. The soil of rain forests, in the tropics particularly, is often fragile and becomes quickly barren when stripped of its forest cover. Lack of forests also promotes drought. Abundant green plants respire water vapor through the pores in their leaves, creating clouds that moderate the climate by blocking and reflecting the sun's rays, while the water vapor stored in the clouds returns to the earth as rain. So the loss of forests disrupts the hydrologic cycle of evaporation and precipitation.

All these factors—how we produce our food, run our machinery, transport our goods and ourselves, and dispose of our wastes—are interlinked elements in a global ecological crisis. Humanity stands on the brink of huge disasters worldwide in the next few decades. How we respond to these crises in the first quarter of the twenty-first century is critical for human survival and that of many species of flora and fauna of the earth, especially the larger mammals. These crises had already been clearly recognized in the 1980s, summarized in the *World Watch Report* of 1990. Unfortunately, many of the world's leaders, particularly those of the United States during the George W. Bush administration, have frittered away precious time denying the problem and even undermining environmental legislation that had been passed in earlier administrations.[10]

STEPS TOWARD EARTH HEALING

In the following pages, I summarize a few of the major steps that need to be taken to modify, if not reverse, these destructive trends.[11]

Population

The main issue here is to promote a culture of reproductive choice. A major obstacle to this is the culture of several of the world's patriarchal religions that condemn contraceptives and fear women and youth becoming independent of family patriarchal controls if they are able to control their own fertility. Those concerned to slow human population have often not done this persuasively, whether it be the coercive "one-child" policy of the Chinese government or Western efforts to force contraceptives on suspicious populations. The major challenge is thus to approach these issues holistically with an emphasis on community health and the well-being of the whole family.

The education and empowerment of women and the improved economic well-being of the family have proved to be crucial to a willingness to reduce unchosen pregnancies, but it takes a major cultural change to accept this as a gain for the family and the whole community. Within the context of improved health of family members, better education for women, and the economic well-being of the whole family, a variety of contraceptives need to be made available inexpensively. Everyone should be taught how to use them correctly and encouraged to use them as the normal way of life. The creation of children needs to be valued as a planned decision to be undertaken when there is adequate means and social support to raise each child well.

Energy

The first step to addressing the problem of disappearing fossil fuels, as well as the dangerous pollutants that their use emits into the air, is to find ways of using such fuels much more efficiently through energy-conserving machinery, emission controls, and environmental design of buildings. But these steps must be seen as part of a transition toward rapid conversion from reliance on fossil fuels to more and more use of renewable and less polluting sources of energy, such as solar, wind, water, and thermal. Government subsidies must shift from supporting the petroleum industry toward subsidizing renewable energy. As fossil fuels become more expensive and renewable sources of energy more economical, researchers, manufacturers, and consumers will move toward these alternatives.

A third component in reducing energy use is to drastically reduce the amount of transportation required to move people and products. This will require some major changes in the modern lifestyle. Humans must reconstruct more organic decentralized communities where living, working, production, trade, and cultural amenities are within reach of walking, biking, and nonpolluting public transportation, such as the electric tram. The private gas-guzzling car needs to be phased out, not expanded as the status symbol of modernity. Long-distance traveling and shipping need to be greatly lessened by producing food and goods more regionally. Electronic communication should replace most of the air travel that forces business people and communicators to fly long distances on a regular basis.

Food

Local food production should be greatly diversified, replacing monocrops grown for national and worldwide marketing with a variety of foods grown close to where they will be marketed. A model for this is community-supported agriculture, which successfully grows a great many fruits and vegetables seasonally for local marketing, partly supporting themselves by subscriptions by community members who pay the farm yearly and receive boxes of fresh foods weekly within days of its actual harvesting. Restaurants that prize fresh vegetables and fruits also choose to patronize nearby community-supported farms.[12]

There needs to be a great reduction of the national and global food transportation chains that fly and ship food around the world. This would mean a return to eating in season and canning, freezing, and drying foods for winter. The human diet needs to be converted to eating lower on the food chain, using meat occasionally for special occasions or in small amounts as in traditional Asian cooking but focusing mostly on grains, fruits, and vegetables. Factory farming for mass meat production should be phased out. This would greatly expand the grain food available for human consumption that is presently being fed to animals to produce meat.

Since it takes approximately ten pounds of grain to produce one pound of meat, greatly reducing meat eating would release a great amount of grain for humans. It would also lessen the destruction of land presently trampled by grazing animals and the pollution of waters caused by putting their excrement into streams and lakes rather than recycling it as fertilizer. Food also needs to be grown organically, using organic fertilizer and pest control and recycling all agricultural wastes to rebuild soils, to feed animals, and to make fuels and other products. Methods of drip irrigation also should be adopted that use water much more efficiently by dropping it directly onto plants roots rather than spraying water on entire fields, much of which simply runs off into streams and eventually into oceans.

Pollution

Eliminating the burning of fossil fuels for housing, transportation, and factories; eliminating petroleum-based fertilizers and pesticides for organic methods; and recycling all industrial and domestic wastes would greatly reduce the threat to human and planetary life from air, water, and soil pollution and would help stabilize global warming. Some wastes, such as the by-products of nuclear energy production and fluorocarbons from spray cans, that cannot be recycled and that cause great harm to the atmosphere should be eliminated from production altogether. Human societies should function like healthy forests or meadows in which the death or waste side of the life cycle of production and consumption is fully integrated into the creation of new products, the renewal of soils, and the feeding of animals. Recycle everything and don't produce what cannot be recycled should be the maxim for healthy human societies.

Protecting Forests and Biodiversity

Putting endangered species of plants and animals on a "list" to be protected is ineffective if it is taken out of the context of the habitat where such species live. Thus, what needs to be protected are much greater areas of forests and "wildlands" where the diversity of species can maintain themselves within natural balances of predators and prey. Protecting "favorite" animals, such as deer, while killing off predators, such as wolves, simply creates a population explosion of deer, which then starve to death. Finding accurate ways of mimicking "natural" ways of forest management is a major challenge.

Preserving wildlands should not necessarily mean sweeping away all human inhabitants and turning such areas over to tourism. Societies should consider allowing the indigenous people who traditionally lived in such forests and used its products in moderation to manage the forests rather than eliminating all the indigenous people in favor of state park services, as was done in the U.S. program of setting aside national forest preserves. Forests and wildland should not simply be juxtaposed to human habitat as though these formed mutually exclusive realms. Rather, wetlands, forests, and green areas need to be redeveloped in ways that are interspersed with human habitation. Thereby, habitat would be renewed for a variety of plants and animals and human settlements protected from storms and floods that are aggravated by the loss of forests and wetlands.

BUILDING ECOLOGICAL SOCIETIES: LOCAL, REGIONAL, STATE, AND GLOBAL ORGANIZING

Building ecological societies will take tremendous effort on every level of human organization—local, regional, state, and global. The problem is not that we do not know what to do. The problem is the will to do it. Presently, those elites with the preponderance of wealth and power are for the most part clinging to a system that is doomed but from which they profit. Most ordinary people feel confused and powerless. Even if they have some ideas of what should be done, they feel unable to do much because living "ecologically" is presented to them as something that will cost more than their present lifestyle and that they have to do as an isolated individual against the dominant system that controls their daily options.

Just as the destructive and wasteful ways of producing goods and disposing of wastes are a system, so ecological ways of living must become a system—one that becomes normal for everyday life. When recycling means making a special effort to carry your trash to a distant "recycling center," only a few highly motivated individuals are likely to do it. Once recycling becomes built into the municipal system of trash collection, then everyone can—and most will—collaborate with it. Thus, ecological living requires both converting systems and converting cultures that support those systems. I discuss some examples of efforts to do this on local, regional, state, and global levels.

The local level of transformation is crucial for such change, although it needs to be supported by many forms of networking and communication across local, national, and international groups. Religious communities, churches, mosques, synagogues, and temples can play key roles in such transformation, both generating the new ecological culture that is needed, spiritually and ethically, and modeling such changes in their own buildings and lands. Most Christian denominations have issued statements calling for concern for the environment, but only a few have really mandated study and action on a practical level.

There are a few Christian denominations that have published adult study curricula for such work in churches. One of these curricula is Sharon Delgado's *Hope for the Earth*.[13] This ten-week study guide is based on the Methodist "quadrilateral" of the four sources for theology: Scripture, tradition, reason, and experience. Each week, passages from Scripture, church tradition, and science are studied to provide the basis for understanding why changes are required. Each week, some area of action is decided on and put into practice, such as examining the lighting use in the church and changing all the lightbulbs from inefficient incandescent bulbs to long-lasting fluorescent bulbs.

The ten lessons of the curriculum move on an ascending scale from smaller actions within the church to larger efforts in the community that relate to national and global concerns. The goal is not only to make some changes in practice but also to build an ongoing "green group" within the congregation to continue to educate the church toward becoming a green community and to inspire its members to carry their learning into other institutions of their daily life: their homes, schools, and businesses. It is crucial to spread examples of "green communities" that are implementing ecological practices on a level larger than the individual.

Another effort of organizing is the regional levels. An interesting effort to work on this level is the Interreligious Sustainability Project of Greater Chicago. This project was put together by a partnership between the Center for Neighborhood Technology, a well-established ecological and social justice organizing center in downtown Chicago, and several faculty of the theological schools of Chicago, especially the Lutheran School of Theology and the Meadville-Lombard school in the Unitarian-Universalist tradition. This combination of theologians and environmental activists spent many months charting the environmental issues of greater Chicago and producing a study guide, "One Creation, One People, One Place."

This study guide mapped the concentrations of population, poverty, race, health, employment, environmental pollution, and other factors on to the map of greater Chicago (the City of Chicago together with its suburbs and exurbs). These maps showed the relationship between these issues in different neighborhoods of the region. This study guide became a tool for community organizing. Organizers went neighborhood by neighborhood seeking to establish a groups of religious congregations of all traditions—Christian, Jewish, Buddhist, Muslim, and others—that would be willing to come together to study the guide, find how the place where they lived fit into its data, and come up with projects for environmental care for their neighborhood. These projects might be anything from improving waste disposal to restoring a green space in their area and would be carried out with an awareness of being part of a network of local projects within the greater Chicago bioregion.[14]

Constructing a new ecological society means changing laws and seeing that ways of implementing these laws are developed. Changes of law need to happen on the municipal, state, and federal levels. Cities have the power to make significant changes in areas such as waste disposal, water conservation, encouraging alternative energy use, and setting aside green spaces. The states within the U.S. system can pass major laws having to do with matters such as regulating car and factory emissions, waste management, forests, water use, and the like. Finally, the federal government bears responsibility for setting environmental standards for the whole country.

Unfortunately, during the George W. Bush administration, the federal government began to undermine environmental laws that had already been passed, so some states have begun challenging the laggard attitudes of the federal government on questions such as alternative energy and climate change.[15] Environmental nongovernmental organizations are vital in doing the research and lobbying for better laws on all these levels of government, sometimes suing offending corporations.[16]

Finally, there is a vital role that must be played in creating a new global ecological world society by international bodies. Since 1959, there have been hundreds of treaties between nations and under the United Nations to protect the environment and regulate use of common resources such as oceans. One of the most successful treaties was the 1987 Montreal Protocol on the Protection of the Ozone Layer.[17] This treaty involved a limited type of air pollutant, chlorofluorocarbons, emitted by refrigerators and aerosol cans, that played a role in depleting the ozone layer of the stratosphere. Since these chemicals could easily be replaced by other nonpolluting ones, it was fairly easy to get global agreement and compliance for this treaty.

Global climate change is a far more difficult issue for the world's nations to agree on. There is now widespread agreement among scientists that emissions from burning fossil fuel are a major factor in causing global temperatures to rise, with potentially disastrous effects of rising sea levels and changing weather patterns.[18] But since it is the wealthiest, most developed nations, such as the United States, that cause most of these emissions, while it is some of the poorest nations, especially small island nations, that may suffer the most, the global politics of gaining an agreement of what to do is controversial. The UN Climate Change Conference in Kyoto, Japan, in December 1997 revealed this conflict between industrialized and developing nations and between environmentalists and large economic interests.[19]

The 1997 Kyoto Protocol committed industrialized and former Eastern bloc nations to reduce their greenhouse emissions to 5.2 percent below 1990 levels by 2008–2012, a very inadequate level of reductions given the urgency of the problem. But the United States continually acted as the spoiler at these meetings, arguing for the inconclusiveness of the data and the unfairness of the cuts demanded of high-polluting nations, such as the United States. In March 2001, the new president, George W. Bush, withdrew the United States altogether from the negotiations. But most of the world's nations have continued with the negotiations, with 140 nations, but not the United States signing the protocol, which went into effect in 2005. But it is evident that even this protocol is only a bare beginning in tackling this problem.[20]

It is evident that creating ecological societies is a global issue that demands widespread changes in culture, technology, and practices of economic organization and daily life. Global agencies, such as the United Nations, the World Bank, and global nongovernmental organizations, play vital roles in seeking consensus of the kinds of changes that are needed. Environmental crises are fairly recent issues for global consideration. It is only with the 1972 Stockholm Conference on the Human Environment that this issue appeared on the global agenda. The world's nations have adopted over seventy declarations, charters, and treaties on the environment since that time.

One effort to create a global framework for the environmental issue was the World Charter for Nature adopted by the UN General Assembly in 1982. This was the first intergovernmental declaration to affirm respect for nature as the foundation of human and planetary well-being.[21] However, this declaration did not explore the links between environmental degradation and poverty and equitable human development and was drafted before the UN World Commission on Environment and Development articulated the concept of sustainable development in its 1987 report "Our Common Future." Thus, there began an effort to formulate a fuller statement that would bring together the issues of poverty, economic justice (including gender and race relations), and the environment. This became the Earth Charter.[22]

The Earth Charter Initiative was launched in 1994 by Maurice Strong, former secretary-general of the Stockholm Conference and of the UN Conference on Environment and Development, and Mikhail Gorbachev, president of Green Cross International. During 1995–1996, extensive research was conducted on international law, science, world religions, ethics, and environmental issues to draft the Earth Charter. Consultations were conducted in many different areas around the world to promote a global dialogue and reach a consensus on the key principles that should be a part of this charter. Representatives from thirty countries and seventy organizations participated in an international consultation in the Peace Palace in The Hague in May 1995. The drafters of the Earth Charter were very concerned that the declaration be as universal as possible, reflecting the many cultures, religions, and ethical traditions of the world, not a statement that seemed purely "Western."

Early in 1997, the Earth Charter Commission was formed with five cochairs representing Asia and the Pacific, Europe, Latin America and the Caribbean, North America, and Africa and the Middle East. Drafts of the charter were tested and revised in meetings in all parts of the world in 1997–1999, including online discussions. During January and February 2000, further revisions were made in the draft in a meeting at the headquarters of the UN Educational, Scientific and Cultural Organization in Paris. A completed version of the charter was issued in March 24, 2000, but with the possibility of still further revisions.[23] The Earth Charter hopes for an eventual endorsement by the United Nations, but in the meanwhile it seeks to function as a "people's charter," gaining endorsements on the level of local and national meetings and commitments to implement its principles. Thus, it seeks to work in a bottom-up fashion, gaining widespread acceptance before seeking formal UN endorsement.

The full text of the Earth Charter appears in an appendix of this book. The Earth Charter seeks to bring together in one comprehensive global vision the issues of respect for nature, universal human rights, economic justice, and a culture of peace as the basis of a sustainable global society. It organizes these issues under four major headings: "Respect and Care for the Community of Life," "Ecological Integrity," "Social and Economic Justice," and "Democracy, Nonviolence and Peace." It concludes the closing section on "The Way Forward" with the words, "Let ours be a time remembered for the awakening of a new reverence for life, the firm resolve to achieve sustainability, the quickening of the struggle for justice and peace and the joyful celebration of life." With this charter, spokespeople of the world community seek a global vision and way of life that bring together the values traditionally assigned to religion, ethics, and spirituality and those usually assigned to government and business: peace, political democracy, and economic justice. The charter thus seeks to be the basis for a global covenant between the earth's peoples with each other and with their common earth home.

NOTES

1. Some of the details of this account of planetary evolution and especially its approach to ecological crisis by situating it in evolutionary history is drawn from Heather Eaton, "The Revolution of Evolution," *Worldviews: Environment, Culture, Religion* 11, no. 1 (2007): 6–11.

2. See Edward C. Wolf, *On the Brink of Extinction: Conserving the Diversity of Life*, Worldwatch Paper no. 78 (Washington, D.C.: Worldwatch Institute, 1987); see also Paul and Anne Ehrlich, *Extinction: The Causes and Consequences of the Disappearance of Species* (New York: Random House, 1981).

3. This is called the ecological equation; see Paul R. Ehrlich, Anne H. Ehrlich, and John P. Holdren, *Human Ecology: Problems and Solutions* (San Francisco: Freeman, 1973), 12–13, 206–7.

4. See the issue on global warming, *Time*, April 3, 2006.

5. See "Security and Prosperity Partnership and Petroleum," www.commonfrontiers.ca.

6. In 1983, Lester Brown of the World Watch Report estimated that at the 1983 level of use, easily available supplies of petroleum would be consumed in thirty-five years; see *Population Policies for a New Economic Era*, Worldwatch Paper no. 53 (Washington, D.C.: Worldwatch Institute, 1983).

7. Lester Brown, *Changing the World's Food Prospect: The Nineties and Beyond*, Worldwatch Paper no. 85 (Washington, D.C.: Worldwatch Institute, 1986).

8. See Vandana Shiva, *The Violence of the Green Revolution: Third World Agriculture, Ecology and Politics* (London: Zed Books, 1991).

9. See Rosemary R. Ruether, *Gaia and God: An Ecofeminist Theology of Earth Healing* (San Francisco: HarperSanFrancisco, 1992), 92–96.

10. See Robert Kennedy Jr., *Crimes against Nature: How George W. Bush and His Corporate Pals Are Plundering the Country and Hijacking Our Democracy* (New York: HarperCollins, 2004).

11. Somewhat different versions of these steps to ecological change are found in previous publications; see Ruether, *Gaia and God*, 258–65; see also Rosemary Ruether, *America, Amerikkka: Elect Nation and Imperial Violence* (London: Equinox Press, 2007), 269–72.

12. See Rosemary Ruether, *Integrating Ecofeminism, Globalization and World Religions* (Lanham, Md.: Rowman & Littlefield, 2005), 152–53 and notes 50, 51, p. 171.

13. Sharon Delgado, *Hope for the Earth: A Handbook for Christian Environmental Groups* (Washington, D.C.: Geneva Board of Church and Society, 1995).

14. The website for the Center for Neighborhood Technology of Chicago is www.cnt.org.

15. For example, in 2003, states, led by New York, sued the federal government over the protection of the Clean Air Act; see www.oag.state.NY/US/press/2004/Oct/Oct27b_03.html.

16. The Grinning Planet website lists twenty-one major environmental groups, organizations or nongovernmental organizations: Audubon, Bluewater Network, Center for the American Dream, Earth Action Network, EarthJustice, Earth Rights International, Environmental Defense, Environmental Working Group, Friends of the Earth, GRACE: Global Resource Action Center for the Environment, Greenpeace, National Environmental Trust, Natural Resources Defense Council, National Wildlife Federation, Resources for the Future, Sierra Club, Union of Concerned Scientists, Wilderness Society, World Resources Institute, Worldwatch Institute, and Wildlife Fund International; see http://grinningplanet.com/5005/environmental-groups-ngos.htm.

17. For the Montreal Protocol on Substances That Deplete the Ozone Layer, see www.ciesin.columbia.edu/TG/PI/Policy/montpro.htm.

18. For the UN Framework Convention on Climate Change, see http://unfccc.int/essential_background/convention/item/2627.php.

19. On the World Council of Church's work on climate change and the Kyoto treaty, see David G. Hallman, "Climate Change, Ethics and Sustainable Community," in *Christianity and Ecology: Seeking the Well-Being of Earth and Humans*, ed. Rosemary R. Ruether and Dieter T. Hessel (Cambridge, Mass.: Harvard University Press, 2000), 453–71.

20. See Loren R. Cass, *The Failure of American and European Climate Policy: International Norms, Domestic Politics and Unachievable Commitments* (Albany: State University of New York Press, 2006).

21. For the text of the 1982 World Charter for Nature, see http://sedac.ciesin.org/entri/texts/world.charter.for.nature.1982.html.

22. For the history of the development of the Earth Charter, see www.earthcharterusa.org/ec_history.htm.

23. For the Earth Charter, see www.earthcharter.org.

· 17 ·

Social Systems and the Church's Mission

Chapter 1 examined the theological status of social systems. Are they expressions of the "orders of creation" rooted in divine decree and therefore sacrosanct and unchangeable? Or are they demonic powers contrary to God's will for creation against which the church is called to struggle? In response to Walter Wink's work on this issue, I suggested that some kinds of social systems are necessary to organize our relation to one another and to the other earth creatures, politically, economically, and culturally. Humans always live in relationships of some kind. But the actual historical expressions of social systems as states, economies, and cultures have become deeply distorted, creating injustice and oppression. They have indeed become a "dominator system," as Wink claims (see chapter 1).

In my view, the redemption of creation means the overcoming of this dominator system not beyond but within creation itself. The mission of the church is to be an expression (not the only or exclusive expression) of a struggle to overcome this dominator system and to transform the ways humans connect with each other and with the earth into more loving, life-giving, peacemaking relations. In the words of the Lord's Prayer, "God's Kingdom come," that is, "God's will be done on earth, as it is in heaven." "Heaven" is the paradigm of where God's will is fully manifest. Our mission is not to flee earth for some transcendent realm called "heaven" but to put ourselves in harmony with this divine will for just, peaceful, and loving relationships, to bring them to earth, to make them present on earth.

Historically, the Christian churches have been deeply ambivalent toward social systems, such as patriarchy, with its subjugation of women and acceptance of slavery, class hierarchy, racism, colonialism, militarism, and ecological destruction. The Christian churches are themselves hierarchical social systems that have been modeled largely after and reflect the social systems of society. Typically, they have counseled passive support for the existing social hierarchies, either suggesting that the bodily form of society is irrelevant to the salvation of the soul or else that these social systems themselves are unchangeable reflections of God's divinely created "order of creation" and thus must be honored and obeyed.

However, there has always been a sector of the churches that has denounced some aspects of the social systems, whether it be the Roman Empire in the early centuries of the church's history, the landholding aristocracy of the Middle Ages, slavery in nineteenth-century colonialism, women's subjugation by modern feminism, and global economic colonialism and imperialism in twentieth-century anticolonial movements. In the 1960s–1990s, liberation theologies appeared throughout the Christian churches in Latin America, Africa, and Asia. Feminist and black theologies arose in North America. These movements denounced patterns of injustice and called for transformation toward egalitarian societies.

Such liberation theologies have always been minority movements in the churches. Some have made significant impact both on the churches and on the social realities of their nations, especially when the liberation theologies have been expressions of larger struggles in the society. Thus, feminism in the churches has been successful within liberal Protestantism in bringing about women's ordination and the integration of women's leadership in the churches. Likewise, racial segregation was dismantled in the churches, and black men and women took their place as leaders at all levels. In our chapters on Central America, South Korea, and South Africa, we have noted the importance of the church component of the liberation struggle in those societies.

But the churches have typically stopped short of advocating a deep transformation of the class hierarchy of wealth and poverty and the global colonial and economic patterns of domination or imperial power, especially of their own nation. In response to challenges, reactionary movements have arisen in the churches, which seek to repress more critical voices and to realign the churches with the ruling classes and the racial and gender hierarchies. In this chapter, I sketch the complexity and ambivalence of the Christian, particularly Protestant, churches in the United States in relation to the messianic claims of the United States itself as a nation that sees itself as chosen by God with a unique mission to dominate the continent and even the whole world.

This notion of "America" as an elect nation was not a totally unique development in the United States. In its origins, it emerged from the expansionist nationalisms of the Reformation and Counter-Reformation era in Europe in the sixteenth and seventeenth centuries. Each of the European nations, especially the major ones (Spain, France, and England), competed with each other both for dominance in Europe and for overseas colonies. Each imagined themselves as God's new elect people to defeat heresy, defend true Christianity, and rule the world in God's name.[1]

The American colonies—and then the United States—inherited their own version of this mixture. The Massachusetts Bay Colony carried from its English forebears the dream of a godly commonwealth governed by a reformed ministry and magistracy (political leaders). But it clashed with Puritan Separatists, Baptists, and Quakers, who entertained hopes for a purified church separated from an apostate church and state. Weak versions of the Anglican established church reigned in Maryland (despite its Catholic beginnings), Virginia, and the Carolinas. The American Revolution, with its new Constitution and Bill of Rights, sought to settle these disputes over church and state by firmly separating the two, making religious choice a private option while decreeing that the state should favor no particular religion: "Congress shall make no law respecting an establishment of religion or prohibiting the free exercise thereof" (Amendment 1, Bill of Rights).

But the colonists also inherited from their English ancestors the vision of being an elect nation, chosen by God to rule the world in God's name.[2] For their Puritan forebears, this meant creating the true reformed church, the ministry of which would shape a godly people and, together with a reformed magistracy, a godly commonwealth. For the American revolutionists in the new nation, this notion of being an elect people morphed into a political version of the true faith. Americans were seen as shaping a reformed state that had thrown off the monarchies and aristocracies of a debased European world and creating a democratic republic. This reformed political order was the "light to the nations" that the rest of the world should follow.

The idea that the United States was the bearer of the reformed political religion, democracy, was mingled with racist notions of being a superior people. White Anglo-Saxons were seen as having unique capacities for democracy not possessed by inferior races: Indians, blacks, and Orientals, and debased mixtures of the three, such as Mexicans and Filipinos. Thus, the elect white Anglo-Saxon Protestant (WASP) nation is said to have a unique mandate from God to fulfill its Manifest Destiny, to press across its North American continent "from sea to shining sea," pushing lesser races out of the way and then to leap its boundaries to begin a global domination in the Caribbean and the Pacific, at each stage bringing its redemptive political gifts for "democracy" that would lift lesser peoples from their benighted forms of government, economics, and culture.[3]

This combination of disestablishment of all religion, together with the messianic claims of the United States as a nation-state, poses special challenges to what it means to be a church in the United States. The disestablishment of all religious bodies blurs the distinctions between state church and free church from the European context. In the United States, all churches are "free churches," that is, private religious options with no special status in relation to the state. At the same time, there is an expectation that religion in general should shape good public citizens who follow the dominant moral values and obey the law. In other words, Christianity in the United States is both disestablished as particular legal church entities and culturally established as religious and ethical mandates for being "true Americans."

In theory, all religious bodies in America are "equal" in their common status of being politically disestablished yet culturally established. Yet some have been more equal than others. For the first 150 years of American history, the "mainstream" Protestant churches, especially the Anglicans, Presbyterians, Congregationalists, and Methodists, were assumed to be the normative exemplars of American religious-civic culture. Jews, Catholics, and more marginal forms of Protestantism, such as Pentecostal and black, were allowed but with reservations as to whether they were fully "American" until they had proven themselves able and willing to assimilate into the WASP public culture. Today a similar reservation is extended to Buddhists and particularly to Muslims.

Mainstream Protestantism in the nineteenth century and the first half of the twentieth often tacitly identified with the American messianic mission to save the world for its superior democratic and capitalist way of life. This was only partly challenged at the turn of the century by a significant movement of Christian socialism among Protestants who sought to reform the American economic system to create better pay and working conditions for the working class, including democraticizing the workplace to bring in elements of worker ownership and management. This movement was led by theologians and pastors such as Walter Rauschenbusch, whose books *Christianity and the Social Crisis* (1907), *Christianizing of the Social Order* (1912), *The Social Principles of Jesus* (1916), and *Theology for the Social Gospel* (1917) expressed its principles.

For Rauschenbusch, Christianity must recover the heart of the gospel of Jesus, which is faith in the coming kingdom of God. This kingdom is not otherworldly but rather the progressive establishment of justice on earth. "the redemption of social life . . . from all forms of slavery in which human beings are treated as mere means to serve the ends of others."[4] Freedom and the democratic ordering of life are central to such establishment of a redeemed society. For Rauschenbusch, the United States is already well along in this establishment of democratic freedom, but it needs to take another step by making the workplace democratic through worker participation in management.

Rauschenbusch largely ignored antiblack racism in American life at a time when Jim Crow reigned, disenfranchising blacks and separating them from any equal access to American life. He also had little interest in equality for women at a time when the women's suffrage movement was at its height. His advocacy of a living wage for the working man assumed that women could then become full-time housewives.

One leader of the Social Gospel, Josiah Strong, was a full throttle enthusiast for the centrality of the United States in the redemption of the world. Strong was a clergyman who represented the American Home Missionary Society for Ohio. In 1885, he laid out his vision of the unity of American imperial expansion with the triumph of Christ's kingdom on earth in his *Our Country: Its Possible Future and Present Crisis*.[5] Strong believed that the millennial redemption of the earth was no longer in the distant future but the crucial turning point "in the world's salvation may depend on the next twenty years of United States' history,"[6] propelled by the expansion of American power. This American expansion he sees as going hand in hand with the Christianizing of the world. Christianizing also multiplies the desires of the people of the earth for worldly goods, for which American industrial productivity is particularly capable of supplying. Thus, Christianizing, the expansion of American power, and the expansion of American markets are all of one piece.

For Strong, the Anglo-Saxon Protestant is uniquely God's elect people for this economic, political, and religious mission. The Anglo-Saxon Protestant American uniquely blends moneymaking capacity and an aggressive energy to push into and settle new lands and colonize lesser peoples:

> It seems to me that God, with infinite wisdom and skill, is training the Anglo-Saxon for a hour that is sure to come in the world's future . . . then will the world enter upon a new stage of its history—*the final competition of the races, for which the Anglo-Saxon is being schooled*. . . . Then this race of unequaled energy, with all the majesty of numbers and the might of wealth behind it—the representative, let us hope, of the largest liberty, the purest Christianity, the highest civilization—having developed particularly aggressive traits to impress its institutions upon mankind, will spread itself over the earth.[7]

Strong admits that the United States is not perfect. There are some impediments to the fulfillment of America's millennial role, represented by the threats of Mormonism, of the expanding Roman Catholic immigrant population, and of liquor and socialism. But he hopes that these threats can be eliminated by the Home Missionary Movement. Protestants, especially the wealthy, need to be converted to seeing their own wealth as belonging wholly to Jesus to be used to uplift and convert their fellow citizens to true Christianity and American civil values:

> Thus America must be converted to become God's instrument to save the world:
> Ours is the elect nation for the age to come. We are the chosen people. We cannot afford to wait. The plans of God will not wait. Those plans seem to have brought us to one of the closing stages of the world's career, in which we can not longer *drift* safely to our destiny. We are shut up in a perilous alternative. Immeasurable opportunities surround and overshadow us. Such, as I read it, is the central fact in the philosophy of American Home Missions.[8]

Not all American Protestant leaders were willing express such enthusiasm for American messianic identity. Reinhold Niebuhr, who became the leading critic of the naive optimism of the Social Gospel and the theologian of the Cold War, expressed reservations about it. However, he was convinced that the greatest threat from messianic zealotry came from communism with its belief in the worldwide triumph of a socialist utopia. Human sinfulness must ever impede fully realized redeemed conditions on earth, and those who purport to create heaven on earth inevitably repress dissent and assert absolute control in order to deny the ambiguity of their achievements. Thus, for Niebuhr, utopians end by becoming totalitarians.

Niebuhr recognized that American national ideology also made strong messianic claims, but he believed that it was finally pragmatic, with checks and balances that prevented absolute power from emerging. Thus, he took a forgiving "ironic" view of American beliefs in their own messianic destiny and saw the United States as the main force that was essential to curb the dangers of communism.[9] In this way, Niebuhr conceded a redemptive role to the United States, primarily as the savior of the world from communism.

In the 1960s, the United States was rocked by another wave of self-criticism and calls for reform. This was the civil rights movement, which struggled to end the long legacy of racism in American life with its Jim Crow system of racial apartheid. Some of the major leaders were black clergymen, especially the charismatic Martin Luther King Jr. But the white Protestant liberal establishment, as well as Catholics and Jews, also joined in this struggle, marching arm in arm with King in the civil rights protests.

King enunciated what might be called a liberation theology version of American civil religion. He endorsed the vision of the United States as called to be a place of "liberty and justice for all," but he also decried the United States as having betrayed that vision, especially to its black citizens. Drawing on the powerful rhetoric of the biblical prophets, such as Amos 5:24, "Let justice roll down like waters and righteousness like an every-flowing stream," King called the United States to deep personal and institutional repentance of its long practice of racism.

In his later years, King began to question the Vietnam War and American imperialist adventures generally. In a speech at Riverside Church in New York City on April 4, 1967, King declared that the United States had long been on the "wrong side of a world revolution."[10] King also proposed a new stage of struggle against injustice in America, the Poor People's Campaign, which would bring together the economically disadvantaged of all races to struggle for a more just economic order. In these two initiatives, King went beyond the critique of racism and the dismantling of Jim Crow laws to question American imperialist militarism and economic injustice. While the "liberal" establishment in American society was willing to endorse the first goal of ending Jim Crow laws, they were mostly not ready for these new questions. King had gone "too far."

The civil rights movement was followed by a series of other movements that also sought to redress historical injustices in American society. The women's movement sought full equality for women; the Chicano movement and the American Indian movement questioned the historical patterns of injustice toward these communities. The gay rights movement challenged "compulsory heterosexuality" and sought legal and social acceptance of gay Americans. In 1973, the Supreme Court struck down the laws prohibiting abortion, making it legal in the first two trimesters.

These movements, with their deep questioning of the established white patriarchal social and economic system at home and U.S. power abroad, sparked a vehement reaction from right-wing religious and secular forces in American society. In the late 1970s, a new union of religious fundamentalists and neoconservative political leaders was formed that swept Ronald Reagan into power with the 1980 presidential election. This coalition continued to expand its power in society and politics and also in the churches into the twenty-first century with the reelection of George W. Bush in 2004.

This coalition of political-economic conservatives and religious fundamentalists created a new division within American Christian churches. In the first half of the twentieth century into the 1960s white male liberals were in charge of the mainstream Protestant churches. They were open to a moderate reform of American society to include women and blacks in leadership and the ending of outright discrimination against any group. But in the last quarter of the twentieth century, they were told that their brand of liberal Christianity was losing and that the future lay with evangelical conservatives, indeed that liberal causes were not authentically "Christian" at all but godless secularism. For a while, the liberal Protestant establishment seemed confused, demoralized, and unable to find its voice in the face of a triumphant, politicized, antiliberal evangelicalism.[11]

Conservative evangelicalism had long been a part of American Christianity and society, but in the first half of the twentieth century, it was apolitical, following a free church tradition that separated religion from politics, and defensive against a confident liberalism that controlled the church bureaucracies and seminaries.[12] Thus, the new fact of late twentieth-century America is the politicization of conservative evangelicalism, its alliance with neoconservative forces that were previously secular and often non-Christian, and the virtual takeover of the Republican Party by this new coalition.[13]

This coalition of religious and sociopolitical conservatisms has created new schisms in the American Christian churches, schisms that often run within rather than between Christian denominations, dividing social justice from "good news" Methodists, progressive from conservative Presbyterians, and liberal from traditionalist Episcopalians. Even Roman Catholics have become deeply divided, as in Opus Dei versus liberation and feminist theology Catholics, with the retrenchment of the papacy of John Paul II and Benedict XVI against Vatican II reforms.[14]

Right-wing versus progressive forms of Christianity seem particularly divided on sexual and gender issues. Conservative Christians reassert patriarchy as the divinely established "order of creation," with male headship in the family and society. Women ideally should stay home as "full-time housewives." Liberals have more or less accepted that women have equal human capacities, that there are many different forms of the family in society, and that men and women should be partners both in the home and in society.

Likewise, conservatives see homosexuality as sinful and perverse, against God's created order of nature and society. Liberals are inclined to accept homosexuality as a "natural" expression of human sexual "orientation" along with heterosexuality. They are generally ready to accept homosexuals as equally capable of being good and competent leaders or ordained ministers in the church and teachers, politicians, or managers in social institutions. Most would allow gays to marry and raise children.

For conservatives, abortion is murder from the moment of conception. For liberals, abortion is unfortunate but at times a lesser evil to forced, unchosen childbirth. The best alternative would be to avoid abortion by maximizing the choice of a woman whether to get pregnant through effective sexual education and birth control.

Abortion and gay marriage have become the "hot-button" issues in American life both in the church and in politics, with feminism versus antifeminism being the unstated subtext behind these conflicts.[15] But the liberal–conservative split in American Christianity extends to other issues.

Conservative evangelicals often combine an individualized view of salvation that rejects social reform as a part of the church's mission, with a politics of American messianic imperialism that believes that America is God's chosen nation to "rule the world."[16] They are generally hostile to any understanding of the work of the church as including the overcoming of racism, sexism, and economic injustice.

In the 1990s, this fundamentalist hostility to social reform had extended to ecological issues. Fundamentalists generally endorse a view that the earth has been given to humans to dominate and use as we will, while our true goal in life is beyond the earth, in a heaven transcendent to creation. However, the appearance of a united evangelical front on the environmental crisis has begun to change. A wing of evangelicals has begun to emerge who argue that concern for peace, overcoming poverty, and care for creation is truly biblical and that Bible-believing Christians must be concerned with these issues.[17] This is provoking a deep split within the evangelical churches, with leaders of the Christian right establishment seeking to refute and discredit the "creation care" evangelicals.[18]

While liberal Christians in the United State were struggling to find a voice against the charge that they lacked deep and compelling faith, the radical political agenda of the neoconservative–fundamentalist alliance has begun to be thrown into question. The fusion of Christian fundamentalism and American messianic imperialism has become evident in the crusading language of President George W. Bush. This had led some Christian liberals to believe that they should play down support for women's rights, legal abortion, and gay rights, issues that have little explicit basis in the Scriptures. Rather, they should take their stand on a critique of American imperial identity, global economic injustice, and militarism, all issues for which there is a great deal of biblical precedent in the prophetic and apocalyptic traditions of both testaments.

In the first decade of the twenty-first century, a "progressive Christianity" movement has begun to emerge that seeks an alliance with liberal and liberationist Christians and creation care and anti-imperial evangelicals around a common focus on ecological sustainability, economic justice, and a critique of militarism. However, it remains to be seen whether this alliance will entail hiding the issues of women's rights, reproductive rights, and gay rights under the carpet. Will women, gays, and young people again be sold out so that white Christian males can forge a new power alliance for a "progressive" politics? Significantly, the American Episcopal Church has been under insistent pressure from African churches and the World Anglican Communion to renounce its acceptance of gay bishops and play down women's leadership as priests and bishops. They have stood firm in refusing to do so.

The denunciation of American imperial messianism has never before been central to any theology of American Christianity, left, right, or center. But a critique of this ideology is emerging in the twenty-first century as a major theme of public opinion worldwide thanks to the exploitation of such language by the Bush administration. A focus on anti-imperial theology is also upheld by a new wave of biblical studies, especially of the New Testament, which argues that antiempire was central to the self-understanding of the early church.[19]

One of the most forthright expressions of this anti-imperial Christianity is the July 15, 2006, document issued by the World Alliance of Reformed Churches (WARC), the global body for Presbyterian and Reformed churches, titled "An Ecumenical Faith Stance against Global Empire for a Liberated Earth Community."[20] This study document was written by a group of theologians, primarily from the Third World, at a consultation called by WARC to articulate further the critique of global injustice made at the WARC world meeting in Accra, Ghana, in August 2004.

This 2006 document declares the U.S. world empire to be the primary global evil against which Christians must take a stance today. This empire, which combines military and economic domination, victimizes and impoverishes the whole earth and its people and is threatening a new stage of nuclear war. It is dismantling the basic safeguards of human rights, with the practice of torture and denial of habeas corpus to those imprisoned without charges. Moreover, it buttresses itself with an appeal to a religious ideology, based on a false messianism that is the opposite of authentic faith in Jesus Christ, himself crucified by the power of empire.

Resistance to such an empire is seen as crucial to authentic Christian faith, along with the defense of peace, social justice, and ecological integrity. Jesus' ministry, crucifixion, and resurrection stand in the context of rejection of empire and a hope for a redemptive alternative to such systems of oppression. Central to Christian faith is a rejection of the quest for absolute power, imperial justifications for war, and messianic pretensions that usurp the saving role of Christ, which is founded on good news to the poor and liberation of the captives. All Christian churches, not just WARC churches, are called to examine the challenge of the gospel to global empire and to engage in a process of shaping their understanding of faith, worship, and the mission of the church in the light of this resistance to empire.

The document concludes with these words: "the global empire with its unprecedented reach, represents a massive threat to life. In the face of this pervasive and death-dealing reality of world-wide hegemony, we are inspired by Jesus of Galilee to resist empire and to renew communities of life. This reality has economic, political, social, cultural and spiritual dimensions. It presents life and death challenges to Christians, as empire uses religion to justify its domination and violence and makes claims that belong to God alone."

Has a progressive Christianity that unites liberal and liberationist stances found its voice in this document? The proliferation of books since 2003 by American thinkers, many of them originally conservative, against American empire makes it clear that a new anti-imperial political rhetoric is beginning to emerge[21] with which a Christian reappropriation of New Testament anti-imperialism can make a powerful alliance. However, the tendency to forge this alliance at the expense of women and gays should not be accepted. Yet it will not be easy to hold these issues together within a new version of "progressive Christianity."[22] Yet a progressive Christianity that would really bring together personal human rights, including the rights of women and gays, economic justice, and ecological integrity, within the context of critique of global American empire might offer a coherent alternative to fundamentalist neoconservatism.

Progressive Christians will find that they must struggle in at least three arenas simultaneously. They must contest the efforts of fundamentalists to take over their church, whether congregation or denomination, and its seminaries and other institutions, affirming an anti-imperialist and prosocial justice vision of Christian faith. They must seek a broad-based alliance for all justice issues, without selling out some vulnerable groups. This also means that they must unite ecumenically with the progressive wing of Christians across all denominations who share a similar theological and ethical vision. Finally, they must reach out to other religions and the nonreligious for allies in a common struggle for justice, peace, and the integrity of creation. Here the authors of the Earth Charter and progressive Christians would find themselves on common ground.

Christians can no longer assume that redemption in Christ is the privileged trajectory to save the world. In this sense, the mission of the church must be decentered in world history. But at the same time, Christians can and should affirm that redemption in Christ should be one language among others for a vision of a planet that all peoples can inhabit in justice and peace. Christian hopes join the hopes of every religion and human tradition that seek more loving and just ways of living together on a renewed earth.

NOTES

1. Rosemary R. Ruether, *America. Amerikkka: Elect Nation and Imperial Violence* (London: Equinox Press, 2007), 8–30.

2. See William Haller, *The Elect Nation: The Meaning and Relevance of Foxe's Book of Martyrs* (New York: Harper and Row, 1963).

3. Haller, *The Elect Nation*, chaps. 2–6.

4. Walter Rauschenbusch, *Theology for the Social Gospel* (New York: Macmillan, 1918), 142–43.

5. Josiah Strong, *Our Country: Its Possible Future and Present Crisis* (New York: Baker and Taylor, 1885).

6. Strong, *Our Country*, 15.

7. Strong, *Our Country*, 222.

8. Strong, *Our Country*, 264.

9. Reinhold Niebuhr, *The Irony of American History* (New York: Charles Scribner and Sons, 1954).

10. This speech is found in James Melvin Washington, ed., *A Testament of Hope: The Essential Writings and Speeches of Martin Luther King* (San Francisco: HarperSanFrancisco, 1991), 231–44. King's arguments against the war are also found in his book *The Triumph of Conscience* (New York: Harper and Row, 1967).

11. I base these remarks primarily on my own experience teaching at several mainstream liberal Protestant seminaries, particularly Garrett-Evangelical Theological Seminary in Evanston, Illinois, from 1965 to 2002, where I observed efforts to respond to this challenge from conservative evangelicals by confused attempts to move to the "center."

12. See George Marsden, *Fundamentalism and American Culture: The Shaping of Twentieth-Century Evangelism, 1870–1925* (New York: Oxford University Press, 1980).

13. On the politicization of right-wing Christianity, see especially Sara Diamond, *Roads to Dominion: Right-Wing Movements and Political Power in the United States* (New York: Guilford Press, 1995).

14. See Mary Jo Weaver and R. Scott Appleby, eds., *Being Right: Conservative Catholics In America* (Bloomington: Indiana University Press, 1995).

15. See Rosemary Ruether, "The Family Agenda of the Christian Right," in *Christianity and the Making of the Modern Family: Ruling Ideologies, Diverse Realities* (Boston: Beacon Press, 2000), 156–80.

16. See Pat Robertson, *The New World Order* (Dallas: Word Press, 1991).

17. Jim Wallis has long been a leader of an evangelical social justice position; see his *God's Politics: Why the Right Gets It Wrong and the Left Doesn't Get It* (San Francisco: HarperSanFrancisco, 2005).

18. The statements of the Evangelical Creation Network can be seen at www.creationcare.org. A leading theologian of this network is Steven Bouma-Prediger; see his *For the Beauty of the Earth: A Christian Vision for Creation Care* (Grand Rapids, Mich.: Baker Academic, 2001).

19. The anti-imperial context of the New Testament has long been emphasized by New Testament scholars, such as Richard A. Horsley, but this has become more popular in the first decade of the twenty-first century, thanks to the Bush administration. See Richard A. Horsley, *Jesus and Empire: The Kingdom of God and the New World Disorder* (Minneapolis: Fortress Press, 2003), and Richard A. Horsley, ed., *Paul and Em-*

pire: Religion and Power in Roman Imperial Society (Harrisburg, Pa.: Trinity Press International, 1997).

20. This statement is available at http://warc.jalb.de/warcajsp/side.jsp?news_id =809&part_id=0&navi=6.

21. For example, Chalmers Johnson, *The Sorrows of Empire: Militarism, Secrecy and the End of the Republic* (New York: Henry Holt, 2004), and Gary J. Dorrien, *Imperial Design: Neoconservatives and the New Pax Americana* (New York: Routledge, 2004).

22. See the article by Frances Kissling, former president of Catholic for a Free Choice, criticizing the neglect of issues such as abortion by "progressive" evangelicals, such as Jim Wallis: "Looking for Salvation in All the Wrong Places," *The Nation*, April 24, 2006.

Appendix

The Earth Charter

PREAMBLE

We stand at a critical moment in Earth's history, a time when humanity must choose its future. As the world becomes increasingly interdependent and fragile, the future at once holds great peril and great promise. To move forward we must recognize that in the midst of a magnificent diversity of cultures and life forms we are one human family and one Earth community with a common destiny. We must join together to bring forth a sustainable global society founded on respect for nature, universal human rights, economic justice, and a culture of peace. Towards this end, it is imperative that we, the peoples of Earth, declare our responsibility to one another, to the greater community of life, and to future generations.

EARTH, OUR HOME

Humanity is part of a vast evolving universe. Earth, our home, is alive with a unique community of life. The forces of nature make existence a demanding and uncertain adventure, but Earth has provided the conditions essential to life's evolution. The resilience of the community of life and the well-being of humanity depend upon preserving a healthy biosphere with all its ecological systems, a rich variety of plants and animals, fertile soils, pure waters, and clean air. The global environment with its finite resources is a common concern of all peoples. The protection of Earth's vitality, diversity, and beauty is a sacred trust.

THE GLOBAL SITUATION

The dominant patterns of production and consumption are causing environmental devastation, the depletion of resources, and a massive extinction of species. Communities are being undermined. The benefits of development are not shared equitably and the gap between rich and poor is widening. Injustice, poverty, ignorance, and violent conflict are widespread and the cause of great suffering. An unprecedented rise in human population has overburdened ecological and social systems. The foundations of global security are threatened. These trends are perilous—but not inevitable.

THE CHALLENGES AHEAD

The choice is ours: form a global partnership to care for Earth and one another or risk the destruction of ourselves and the diversity of life. Fundamental changes are needed in our values, institutions, and ways of living. We must realize that when basic needs have been met, human development is primarily about being more, not having more. We have the knowledge and technology to provide for all and to reduce our impacts on the environment. The emergence of a global civil society is creating new opportunities to build a democratic and humane world. Our environmental, economic, political, social, and spiritual challenges are interconnected, and together we can forge inclusive solutions.

UNIVERSAL RESPONSIBILITY

To realize these aspirations, we must decide to live with a sense of universal responsibility, identifying ourselves with the whole Earth community as well as our local communities. We are at once citizens of different nations and of one world in which the local and global are linked. Everyone shares responsibility for the present and future well-being of the human family and the larger living world. The spirit of human solidarity and kinship with all life is strengthened when we live with reverence for the mystery of being, gratitude for the gift of life, and humility regarding the human place in nature.

We urgently need a shared vision of basic values to provide an ethical foundation for the emerging world community. Therefore, together in hope we affirm the following interdependent principles for a sustainable way of life as a common standard by which the conduct of all individuals, organizations, businesses, governments, and transnational institutions is to be guided and assessed.

PRINCIPLES

I. RESPECT AND CARE FOR THE COMMUNITY OF LIFE
1. **Respect Earth and life in all its diversity.**
   a. Recognize that all beings are interdependent and every form of life has value regardless of its worth to human beings.
   b. Affirm faith in the inherent dignity of all human beings and in the intellectual, artistic, ethical, and spiritual potential of humanity.
2. **Care for the community of life with understanding, compassion, and love.**
   a. Accept that with the right to own, manage, and use natural resources comes the duty to prevent environmental harm and to protect the rights of people.
   b. Affirm that with increased freedom, knowledge, and power comes increased responsibility to promote the common good.
3. **Build democratic societies that are just, participatory, sustainable, and peaceful.**
   a. Ensure that communities at all levels guarantee human rights and fundamental freedoms and provide everyone an opportunity to realize his or her full potential.
   b. Promote social and economic justice, enabling all to achieve a secure and meaningful livelihood that is ecologically responsible.
4. **Secure Earth's bounty and beauty for present and future generations.**
   a. Recognize that the freedom of action of each generation is qualified by the needs of future generations.
   b. Transmit to future generations values, traditions, and institutions that support the long-term flourishing of Earth's human and ecological communities.

In order to fulfill these four broad commitments, it is necessary to:

II. ECOLOGICAL INTEGRITY
5. **Protect and restore the integrity of Earth's ecological systems, with special concern for biological diversity and the natural processes that sustain life.**
   a. Adopt at all levels sustainable development plans and regulations that make environmental conservation and rehabilitation integral to all development initiatives.

b. Establish and safeguard viable nature and biosphere reserves, including wild lands and marine areas, to protect Earth's life support systems, maintain biodiversity, and preserve our natural heritage.
c. Promote the recovery of endangered species and ecosystems.
d. Control and eradicate nonnative or genetically modified organisms harmful to native species and the environment, and prevent introduction of such harmful organisms.
e. Manage the use of renewable resources such as water, soil, forest products, and marine life in ways that do not exceed rates of regeneration and that protect the health of ecosystems.
f. Manage the extraction and use of nonrenewable resources such as minerals and fossil fuels in ways that minimize depletion and cause no serious environmental damage.

6. **Prevent harm as the best method of environmental protection and, when knowledge is limited, apply a precautionary approach.**
   a. Take action to avoid the possibility of serious or irreversible environmental harm even when scientific knowledge is incomplete or inconclusive.
   b. Place the burden of proof on those who argue that a proposed activity will not cause significant harm, and make the responsible parties liable for environmental harm.
   c. Ensure that decision making addresses the cumulative, long-term, indirect, long distance, and global consequences of human activities.
   d. Prevent pollution of any part of the environment and allow no build-up of radioactive, toxic, or other hazardous substances.
   e. Avoid military activities damaging to the environment.

7. **Adopt patterns of production, consumption, and reproduction that safeguard Earth's regenerative capacities, human rights, and community well-being.**
   a. Reduce, reuse, and recycle the materials used in production and consumption systems, and ensure that residual waste can be assimilated by ecological systems.
   b. Act with restraint and efficiency when using energy, and rely increasingly on renewable energy sources such as solar and wind.
   c. Promote the development, adoption, and equitable transfer of environmentally sound technologies.
   d. Internalize the full environmental and social costs of goods and services in the selling price, and enable consumers to identify products that meet the highest social and environmental standards.

e. Ensure universal access to health care that fosters reproductive health and responsible reproduction.
f. Adopt lifestyles that emphasize the quality of life and material sufficiency in a finite world.

8. **Advance the study of ecological sustainability and promote the open exchange and wide application of the knowledge acquired.**
    a. Support international scientific and technical cooperation on sustainability, with special attention to the needs of developing nations.
    b. Recognize and preserve the traditional knowledge and spiritual wisdom in all cultures that contribute to environmental protection and human well-being.
    c. Ensure that information of vital importance to human health and environmental protection, including genetic information, remains available in the public domain.

III. SOCIAL AND ECONOMIC JUSTICE

9. **Eradicate poverty as an ethical, social, and environmental imperative.**
    a. Guarantee the right to potable water, clean air, food security, uncontaminated soil, shelter, and safe sanitation, allocating the national and international resources required.
    b. Empower every human being with the education and resources to secure a sustainable livelihood, and provide social security and safety nets for those who are unable to support themselves.
    c. Recognize the ignored, protect the vulnerable, serve those who suffer, and enable them to develop their capacities and to pursue their aspirations.

10. **Ensure that economic activities and institutions at all levels promote human development in an equitable and sustainable manner.**
    a. Promote the equitable distribution of wealth within nations and among nations.
    b. Enhance the intellectual, financial, technical, and social resources of developing nations, and relieve them of onerous international debt.
    c. Ensure that all trade supports sustainable resource use, environmental protection, and progressive labor standards.
    d. Require multinational corporations and international financial organizations to act transparently in the public good, and hold them accountable for the consequences of their activities.

11. **Affirm gender equality and equity as prerequisites to sustainable development and ensure universal access to education, health care, and economic opportunity.**
    a. Secure the human rights of women and girls and end all violence against them.
    b. Promote the active participation of women in all aspects of economic, political, civil, social, and cultural life as full and equal partners, decision makers, leaders, and beneficiaries.
    c. Strengthen families and ensure the safety and loving nurture of all family members.
12. **Uphold the right of all, without discrimination, to a natural and social environment supportive of human dignity, bodily health, and spiritual well-being, with special attention to the rights of indigenous peoples and minorities.**
    a. Eliminate discrimination in all its forms, such as that based on race, color, sex, sexual orientation, religion, language, and national, ethnic, or social origin.
    b. Affirm the right of indigenous peoples to their spirituality, knowledge, lands, and resources and to their related practice of sustainable livelihoods.
    c. Honor and support the young people of our communities, enabling them to fulfill their essential role in creating sustainable societies.
    d. Protect and restore outstanding places of cultural and spiritual significance.

IV. DEMOCRACY, NONVIOLENCE, AND PEACE

13. **Strengthen democratic institutions at all levels, and provide transparency and accountability in governance, inclusive participation in decision making, and access to justice.**
    a. Uphold the right of everyone to receive clear and timely information on environmental matters and all development plans and activities which are likely to affect them or in which they have an interest.
    b. Support local, regional, and global civil society, and promote the meaningful participation of all interested individuals and organizations in decision making.
    c. Protect the rights to freedom of opinion, expression, peaceful assembly, association, and dissent.

d. Institute effective and efficient access to administrative and independent judicial procedures, including remedies and redress for environmental harm and the threat of such harm.
   e. Eliminate corruption in all public and private institutions.
   f. Strengthen local communities, enabling them to care for their environments, and assign environmental responsibilities to the levels of government where they can be carried out most effectively.
14. **Integrate into formal education and life-long learning the knowledge, values, and skills needed for a sustainable way of life.**
   a. Provide all, especially children and youth, with educational opportunities that empower them to contribute actively to sustainable development.
   b. Promote the contribution of the arts and humanities as well as the sciences in sustainability education.
   c. Enhance the role of the mass media in raising awareness of ecological and social challenges.
   d. Recognize the importance of moral and spiritual education for sustainable living.
15. **Treat all living beings with respect and consideration.**
   a. Prevent cruelty to animals kept in human societies and protect them from suffering.
   b. Protect wild animals from methods of hunting, trapping, and fishing that cause extreme, prolonged, or avoidable suffering.
   c. Avoid or eliminate to the full extent possible the taking or destruction of nontargeted species.
16. **Promote a culture of tolerance, nonviolence, and peace.**
   a. Encourage and support mutual understanding, solidarity, and cooperation among all peoples and within and among nations.
   b. Implement comprehensive strategies to prevent violent conflict and use collaborative problem solving to manage and resolve environmental conflicts and other disputes.
   c. Demilitarize national security systems to the level of a nonprovocative defense posture, and convert military resources to peaceful purposes, including ecological restoration.
   d. Eliminate nuclear, biological, and toxic weapons and other weapons of mass destruction.
   e. Ensure that the use of orbital and outer space supports environmental protection and peace.

264 *Appendix*

    f. Recognize that peace is the wholeness created by right relationships with oneself, other persons, other cultures, other life, Earth, and the larger whole of which all are a part.

THE WAY FORWARD

As never before in history, common destiny beckons us to seek a new beginning. Such renewal is the promise of these Earth Charter principles. To fulfill this promise, we must commit ourselves to adopt and promote the values and objectives of the charter.

    This requires a change of mind and heart. It requires a new sense of global interdependence and universal responsibility. We must imaginatively develop and apply the vision of a sustainable way of life locally, nationally, regionally, and globally. Our cultural diversity is a precious heritage and different cultures will find their own distinctive ways to realize the vision. We must deepen and expand the global dialogue that generated the Earth Charter, for we have much to learn from the ongoing collaborative search for truth and wisdom.

    Life often involves tensions between important values. This can mean difficult choices. However, we must find ways to harmonize diversity with unity, the exercise of freedom with the common good, short-term objectives with long-term goals. Every individual, family, organization, and community has a vital role to play. The arts, sciences, religions, educational institutions, media, businesses, nongovernmental organizations, and governments are all called to offer creative leadership. The partnership of government, civil society, and business is essential for effective governance.

    In order to build a sustainable global community, the nations of the world must renew their commitment to the United Nations, fulfill their obligations under existing international agreements, and support the implementation of Earth Charter principles with an international legally binding instrument on environment and development.

    Let ours be a time remembered for the awakening of a new reverence for life, the firm resolve to achieve sustainability, the quickening of the struggle for justice and peace, and the joyful celebration of life.

ORIGIN OF THE EARTH CHARTER

The Earth Charter was created by the independent Earth Charter Commission, which was convened as a follow-up to the 1992 Earth Summit in order to produce a global consensus statement of values and principles for a sustainable future. The document was developed over nearly a decade through an extensive process of international consultation, to which over five thousand people contributed. The charter has been formally endorsed by thousands of organizations, including UNESCO and the IUCN (World Conservation Union). For more information, please visit www.EarthCharter.org.

Bibliography

CHAPTER 1: SOCIAL SYSTEMS

Grossman, Richard L., and Frank T. Adams. *Taking Care of Business: Citizenship and the Charter of Incorporation.* Cambridge, Mass.: Charter, Ink., 1993.
Korten, David C. *When Corporations Rule the World.* San Francisco: Berrett-Koehler, 1995.
Ruether, Rosemary. *America, Amerikkka: Elect Nation and Imperial Violence.* London: Equinox Press, 2007.
Wink, Walter. *Engaging the Powers: Discernment and Resistance in a World of Domination.* Minneapolis: Fortress Press, 1992.
———. *Naming the Powers: The Language of Power in the New Testament.* Philadelphia: Fortress Press, 1984.
———. *The Powers That Be: Theology for a New Millennium.* New York: Doubleday, 1998.
———. *Unmasking the Powers: The Invisible Forces That Determine Human Existence.* Minneapolis: Fortress Press, 1986.

CHAPTER 2: MODELS OF CHURCH AND STATE

Barron, Bruce. *Heaven on Earth: The Social and Political Agendas of Dominion Theology.* Grand Rapids, Mich.: Zondervan, 1992.
Beaume, Colette. *The Birth of an Ideology: Myths and Symbols of Nation in Late Medieval France.* Berkeley: University of California Press, 1991.
Bremer, Francis J. *The Puritan Experiment: New England Society from Bradford to Edwards.* Hanover, N.H.: University Press of New England, 1995.
Cherry, Conrad, ed. *God's New Israel: Religious Interpretations of American Destiny.* Chapel Hill: University of North Carolina Press, 1998.

268 *Bibliography*

Greenslade, S. L. *Church and State from Constantine to Theodosius*. London: SCM Press, 1954.
Haller, William. *The Elect Nation: The Meaning and Relevance of Foxe's Book of Martyrs*. New York: Harper and Row, 1963.
Kirk, John M. *God and the Party: Religion and Politics in Revolutionary Cuba*. Tampa: University Press of Florida, 1989.
Littell, Franklin H. *The Anabaptist View of the Church: An Introduction to Sectarian Protestantism*. Hartford, Conn.: American Society for Church History, 1952.
Maclear, J. F. *Church and State in the Modern Era*. New York: Oxford University Press, 1995.
Morgan, Edmund. *Roger Williams: Church and State*. New York: Harcourt, Brace and World, 1967.
Phelan, John Leddy. *The Millennial Kingdom of the Franciscans in the New World*. Berkeley: University of California Press, 1970.
Renna, Thomas J. *Church and State in Medieval Europe, 1050–1314*. Dubuque, Iowa: Kendall/Hunt, 1974.
Sanders, Thomas G. *Protestant Concepts of Church and State: Historical Backgrounds and Approaches for the Future*. New York: Holt, Rinehart and Winston, 1970.
Sider, Ronald. "An (Ana)baptist Theological Perspective on Church-State Cooperation." In *Welfare Reform and Faith-Based Operations*, edited by Derek Davies and Barry Hankins. Baylor, Tex.: J. M. Dawson Institute of Church-State Studies, 1999.
Strayer, Joseph P. "France: The Holy Land, the Chosen People and the Most Christian King." In *Action and Conviction in Early Modern Europe*, edited by Theodore K. Rabb and Jerrold E. Sergel. Princeton, N.J.: Princeton University Press, 1969, 6–10.
Sturzo, Luigi. *Church and State*. Notre Dame, Ind.: Notre Dame University Press, 1962.
Wilson, John F., and Donald L. Drakeman, eds. *Church and State in American History: Key Documents, Decisions and Commentary from the Past Three Centuries*. Boulder, Colo.: Westview Press, 2003.

CHAPTER 3: PATRIARCHY AS A SOCIAL SYSTEM

Amadiume, Ifi. *Male Daughters, Female Husbands: Gender and Sex in an African Society*. New York: Zed Books, 1987.
Bradley, Keith. *Slavery and Society at Rome*. Cambridge: Cambridge University Press, 1994.
———. *Slaves and Masters in the Roman Empire*. New York: Oxford University Press, 1987.
Dixon, Suzanne. *The Roman Family*. Baltimore: Johns Hopkins University Press, 1992.
Ehrenberg, Margaret. *Women in Prehistory*. London: British Museum Publications, 1989.

Gardener, Jane. *Family and "Familia" in Roman Law and Life*. New York: Clarendon Press, 1998.
Glancy, Jennifer A. *Slavery in Early Christianity*. Oxford: Oxford University Press, 2002.
Kadel, Andrew. *Matrology: A Bibliography of Writings by Christian Women from the First to the Fifteenth Century*. New York: Continuum, 1995.
Lacey, Walter Kirkpatrick. *The Family in Classical Greece*. Ithaca, N.Y.: Cornell University Press, 1986.
Leick, Gwendolyn. *Mesopotamia: The Invention of the City*. London: Penguin, 2001.
Lerner, Gerda. *The Creation of Patriarchy*. New York: Oxford University Press, 1986.
Martin, M. Kay, and Barbara Voorhies. *Female of the Species*. New York: Columbia University Press, 1975.
Pollock, Susan. *Ancient Mesopotamia: The Eden That Never Was*. Cambridge: Cambridge University Press, 1999.
Ruether, Rosemary. *Women and Redemption: A Theological History*. Minneapolis: Fortress Press, 1998.
Saller, Richard P. *Patriarchy, Property and Death in the Roman Family*. Cambridge: Cambridge University Press, 1994.
Sandy, Peggy. *Women at the Center: Life in a Modern Matriarchy*. Ithaca, N.Y.: Cornell University Press, 2002.
Schneider, David M., and Kathleen Gough, eds. *Matrilineal Kinship*. Berkeley: University of California Press, 1961.
Treggiari, Susan. *Roman Marriage, "Iusto Coniuges" from the Times of Cicero to Ulpian*. Oxford: Clarendon Press, 1991.

CHAPTER 4: MODERNIZING PATRIARCHY

Bales, Kevin. *Disposable People: New Slavery in the Global Economy*. Berkeley: University of California Press, 2004.
Cunningham, Hugh. *Children and Childhood in Western Society since 1500*. Harlow: Pearson, 2005.
Evans, Sara. *Personal Politics: The Roots of Women's Liberation in the Civil Rights Movement and the New Left*. New York: Vintage, 1970
Faux, Marion. *"Roe v. Wade": The Untold Story of the Landmark Supreme Court Decision That Made Abortion Legal*. New York: Macmillan, 1988.
Flexner, Eleanor. *Century of Struggle: The Women's Rights Movement in the U.S.* New York: Atheneum, 1972.
Gluck, Sherma Berger. *Rosie the Riveter Revisited: Women, the War and Social Change*. Boston: Twayne, 1987.
Heywood, Colin, *A History of Childhood*. Cambridge: Polity Press, 2001.
Hindman, Hugh D. *Child Labor: An American History*. New York: Sharpe, 2002.
Jones, Jacqueline. *Labor of Love: Labor of Sorrow: Black Women, Work and Family from Slavery to the Present*. New York: Basic Books, 1985.

Kennedy, David M. *Birth Control in America: The Career of Margaret Sanger.* New Haven, Conn.: Yale University Press, 1970.

Kraditor, Eileen S. *The Ideas of the Women's Suffrage Movement, 1890–1920.* Garden City, N.Y.: Anchor Books, 1971.

Kuehn, Thomas. *Law, Family and Women: Toward a Legal Anthropology of Renaissance Italy.* Chicago: University of Chicago Press, 1991.

Meltzer, Milton. *Slavery: A World History.* New York: Da Capo Press, 1993.

Ruether, Rosemary. *Christianity and the Making of the Modern Family: Ruling Ideologies, Diverse Realities.* Boston: Beacon Press, 2000.

Ruether, Rosemary, and Eleanor McLaughlin, eds. *Women of Spirit: Female Leadership in the Jewish and Christian Traditions.* New York: Simon and Schuster, 1979.

Ryan, Mary P. *The Cradle of the Middle Class: The Family in Oneida Country, New York, 1790–1865.* Cambridge: Cambridge University Press, 1981.

Scharf, Lois. *To Work and to Wed: Female Employment, Feminism and the Great Depression.* Westport, Conn.: Greenwood Press, 1980.

Smith, Hildah L. *Reason's Disciples: Seventeenth Century English Feminists.* Chicago: University of Illinois Press, 1982.

Tilly, Louise A., and Joan W. Scott. *Women, Work and Family* New York: Holt, Rinehart and Winston, 1978.

West, Guida, *The National Welfare Rights Movement: The Social Protest of Poor Women.* New York: Praeger, 1981.

Wiesner, Merry E. *Women and Gender in Early Modern Europe.* Cambridge: Cambridge University Press, 1993.

———. *Working Women in Renaissance Germany.* New Brunswick, N.J.: Rutgers University Press, 1986.

CHAPTER 5: ANTI-SEMITISM, EUROPEAN NATIONALISM, AND ZIONISM

American Friends Service Committee. *When the Rain Returns: Toward Justice and Reconciliation in Palestine and Israel.* Philadelphia: American Friends Service Committee, 2004.

Ateek, Naim, Cedar Duaybis, and Maurine Tobin, eds. *Challenging Christian Zionism: Theology, Politics and the Israel-Palestine Conflict.* London: Melisende, 2005.

Baer, Yitzhak. *The History of the Jews in Christian Spain: Volume 2. From the Fourteenth Century to the Expulsion.* Philadelphia: Jewish Publication Society, 1966.

Barrin, Philippe. *Nazi Anti-Semitism: From Prejudice to Holocaust.* Translated by Jannet Lloyd. New York: New Press, 2005.

Bergen, Doris. *War and Genocide: A Concise History of the Holocaust.* Lanham, Md.: Rowman & Littlefield, 2003.

Cohn, Norman. *Warrant for Genocide: The Myth of the Jewish World Conspiracy and the Protocols of the Elders of Zion.* New York: Harper and Row, 1969.

Cockburn, Alexander, and Jeffrey St. Clair, eds. *The Politics of Anti-Semitism.* Oakland, Calif.: AK Press, 2003.

Ellis, Marc. *Beyond Innocence and Redemption: Confronting the Holocaust and Jewish Power*. San Francisco: Harper and Row, 1990.

———. *O Jerusalem: The Contested Future of the Jewish Covenant*. Minneapolis: Fortress Press, 1999.

Feingold, Henry. *The Politics of Rescue*. New Brunswick, N.J.: Rutgers University Press, 1970.

Finkelstein, Louis, ed. *The Jews: Their History, Culture and Religion*. New York: Harper and Row, 1960.

Finkelstein, Norman G. *Beyond Chutzpah: On the Misuse of Anti-Semitism and the Abuse of History*. Berkeley: University of California Press, 2005.

Gregorovius, Ferdinand. *The Ghetto and the Jews of Rome*. New York: Schocken Books, 1966.

Hertzberg, Arthur. *The Zionist Idea: A Historical Analysis and Reader*. New York: Meridian Books, 1960.

Katz, Jacob. *Out of the Ghetto: The Social Background of Jewish Emancipation, 1770–1870*. Cambridge, Mass.: Harvard University Press, 1973.

Lustick, Ian. *The Palestinians in Israel: Israel's Control of a National Minority*. Austin: University of Texas Press, 1980.

Mosse, George. *The Crisis of German Ideology: Intellectual Origins of the Third Reich*. New York: Grosset and Dunlap, 1964.

Palumbo, Michael. *The Palestinian Catastrophe: The 1948 Expulsion of a People from Their Homeland*. London: Faber and Faber, 1987.

Parkes, James. *The Conflict of the Church and the Synagogue*. London: Socino, 1934.

———. *The Jew in the Medieval Community*. London: Socino, 1938.

Poliakov, Leon. *The History of Anti-Semitism: From Voltaire to Wagner*. New York: Vanguard Press, 1968.

Roth, Cecil. *A History of the Marranos*. Philadelphia: Jewish Publication Society, 1947.

Ruether, Rosemary. *Faith and Fratricide: The Theological Roots of Anti-Semitism*. Eugene, Ore.: Wipf and Stock, 1996.

Ruether, Rosemary, and Herman Ruether. *The Wrath of Jonah: The Crisis of Religious Nationalism in the Israeli-Palestinian Conflict*. 2nd ed. Minneapolis: Fortress Press, 2002.

Selzer, Michael, ed. *Zionism Reconsidered: The Rejection of Jewish Normalcy*. London: Macmillan, 1970.

Sharif, Regina. *Non-Jewish Zionism: Its Roots in Western History*. London: Zed Books, 1983.

Wells, Leon W. *Who Speaks for the Vanquished? American Judaism and the Holocaust*. New York: Peter Lang Press, 1987.

CHAPTER 6: RACISM IN THE UNITED STATES

Adam, David Wallace. *Education for Extinction*. Topeka: University Press of Kansas, 1995.

Bauer, J. Jack. *The Mexican War, 1846–8*. New York: Macmillan, 1974.

Brown, Dee. *Bury My Heart at Wounded Knee: An Indian History of the West.* New York: Holt, Rinehart and Winston, 1970.
Churchill, Ward. *A Little Matter of Genocide.* San Francisco: City Lights Books, 1997.
Cumings, Bruce. *Korea's Place in the Sun: A Modern History.* New York: Norton, 1997.
Daniels, Roger, and Harry H. I. Kitano. *American Racism: Exploration of the Nature of Prejudice.* Englewood Cliffs, N.J.: Prentice Hall, 1970.
Davis, F. James. *Who Is Black: One Nation's Definition.* University Park: Pennsylvania State University Press, 2001
Feldberg, Michael. *The Philadelphia Riots of 1844: A Study of Ethnic Conflict.* Westport, Conn.: Greenwood Press, 1975.
Fuller, John D. P. *The Movement for the Acquisition of all Mexico.* Baltimore: Johns Hopkins University Press, 1936.
Gossett, Thomas F. *Race: The History of an Idea in America.* New York: Oxford University Press, 1997.
Grodzins, Morton. *Americans Betrayed.* Chicago: University of Chicago Press, 1949.
Hagan, William T. *American Indians.* Chicago: University of Chicago Press, 1993.
Heizer, Robert F., and Alan J. Almquist. *The Other Californians: Prejudice and Discrimination under Spain, Mexico and the United States.* Berkeley: University of California Press, 1971.
Horsman, Reginald. *Expansion and American Indian Policy, 1783–1812.* East Lansing: Michigan State University Press, 1967.
Ignatiev, Noel. *How the Irish Became White.* New York: Routledge, 1995.
Jacobson, Matthew Frye. *Whiteness of a Different Color: European Immigrants and the Alchemy of Race.* Cambridge, Mass.: Harvard University Press, 1998.
McDonnell, Janet A. *The Dispossession of the American Indian, 1883–1934.* Bloomington: Indiana University Press, 1991.
Pitt, Leonard. *The Decline of the Californios: A Social History of the Spanish-Speaking Californians, 1846–1890.* Berkeley: University of California Press, 1998.
Staudenraus, Philip J. *The African Colonization Movement, 1816–1865.* New York: Columbia University Press, 1961.
Weinberg, Albert K. *Manifest Destiny: A Study of Expansionism in American History.* Chicago: Quadrangle Books, 1935.
Winthrop, Jordan D., *White over Black: American Attitudes toward the Negro, 1550–1812.* Chapel Hill: University of North Carolina Press, 1968.
Wolff, Leon. *Little Brown Brother: How the United States Purchased and Pacified the Philippine Islands at the Century's Turn.* New York: History Books Club Edition, 2006.
Woodward, C. Vann. *The Strange Career of Jim Crow.* New York: Oxford University Press, 1986.

CHAPTER 7: SOCIAL IDEOLOGIES

Barker-Benfield, G. J. *The Horrors of the Half-Known Life: Male Attitudes toward Women and Sexuality in Nineteenth Century America.* New York: Harper, 1976.

Borresen, Kari. *Subordination and Equivalence: The Nature and Role of Women in Augustine and Thomas Aquinas.* Washington, D.C.: University Press of America, 1981.
Freud, Sigmund. *Complete Psychological Works.* London: Hogath Press, 1961.
Garnsey, Peter. *Ideas of Slavery from Aristotle to Augustine.* Cambridge: Cambridge University Press, 1996.
Hanke, Lewis. *Aristotle and the American Indians: A Study of Race Prejudice in the Modern World.* Chicago: H. Regnery Press, 1959.
Kors, Alan C., and Edward Peters, eds. *Witchcraft in Europe, 1100–1700: A Documentary History.* Philadelphia: University of Pennsylvania Press, 1972.
Macdonald, Dennis. *The Legend and the Apostle: The Battle for Paul in Story and Canon.* Philadelphia: Westminster Press, 1983.
Ruether, Rosemary. *Goddesses and the Divine Feminine: A Western Religious History.* Berkeley: University of California Press, 2005.
———. *New Woman, New Earth.* Boston: Beacon Press, 1995.

CHAPTER 8: POLITICAL-ECONOMIC IDEOLOGIES

Bernstein, Eduard. *Evolutionary Socialism.* New York: Schocken Books, 1965.
Buber, Martin. *Paths in Utopia.* Boston: Beacon Press, 1958.
Chan, Adan. *Chinese Marxism.* New York: Continuum, 2003.
Chomsky, Noam. *Deterring Democracy.* New York: Verso Press, 1991.
———. *Hegemony or Survival: America's Quest for Global Dominance* New York: Metropolitan Books, 2003.
Danahern, Kevin. *Fifty Years Is Enough: The Case against the World Bank and the International Monetary Fund.* Cambridge, Mass.: South End Press, 1994.
Dijkstra, Geske. *Industrialization in Sandinista Nicaragua: Policy and Practice in a Mixed Economy.* Boulder, Colo.: Westview Press, 1992.
Djilas, Milovan. *The New Class: An Analysis of the Communist System.* New York: Praeger, 1957.
Engels, Friedrich. *Socialism: Utopian and Scientific.* 1882. Reprint, New York: International Publishers, 1935.
Fukuyama, Francis. *The End of History and the Last Man.* New York: Free Press, 1992.
Gray, John. *Liberalism.* 2nd ed. Minneapolis: University of Minnesota Press, 1995.
Grey, Stephen. *Ghost Plane: The True Story of the CIA Torture Program.* New York: St. Martin's Press, 2006.
Hayek, Friedrich. *The Road to Serfdom.* Chicago: University of Chicago Press, 1949.
Heilbroner, Robert L. *The Worldly Philosophers: The Lives, Times and Ideas of the Great Economic Thinkers.* 7th ed. New York: Simon and Schuster, 1999.
Hofstadter, Richard. *Social Darwinism in American Thought.* New York: George Braziller, 1959.
Keynes, John Maynard. *General Theory on Employment, Interest and Money.* New York: Harcourt and Brace, 1936.
Mill, John Stuart. *On Liberty.* New York: Bobbs-Merrill, 1956.

Pitzer, Donald E. *America's Communal Utopias*. Chapel Hill: University of North Carolina Press, 1997.
Ruether, Rosemary. *The Radical Kingdom: The Western Experience of Messianic Hope*. New York: Paulist Press, 1970.
Spencer, Herbert. *First Principles* 1864. Reprint, London: William and Norgate, 1884.
———. *Man versus State*. London: William and Norgate, 1884.
———. *Principles of Ethics*. 2 vols. New York: D. Appleton and Company, 1892–1893.
———. *Principles of Sociology*. 3 vols. New York: D. Appleton and Company, 1899–1900.
Taylor, Barbara. *Eve and the New Jerusalem: Socialism and Feminism in the Nineteenth Century*. New York: Pantheon Books, 1983.
Tutor, Henry, and J. M. Tutor. *Marxism and Social Democracy: The Revisionist Debate, 1896–98*. New York: Cambridge University Press, 1988.

CHAPTER 9: ECONOMIC CLASS IN THE UNITED STATES

Collins, Chuck, and Felice Yeskel. *Economic Apartheid in America: A Primer on Economic Inequality and Insecurity*. New York: New Press, 2000.
Cook, Blanche W. *Eleanor Roosevelt: Volume 2. 1933–38*. New York: Viking, 1999.
Domhoff, G. William. *Who Rules America? Power and Politics*. 4th ed. New York: McGraw-Hill, 2002.
———. *Who Rules America Now? A View for the '80s*. Englewood Cliffs, N.J.: Prentice Hall, 1983.
Foner, Eric. *Tom Paine and Revolutionary America*. New York: Oxford University Press, 1976.
Heintz James, Nancy Folbre, and the Center for Popular Economics. *Field Guide to the U.S. Economy*. New York: New Press, 2000.
Philips, Kevin. *Wealth and Democracy: A Political History of the American Rich*. New York: Broadway Books, 2002.

CHAPTER 10: EUROPEAN COLONIALISM, 1492–1965

Blum, William. *Killing Hope: U.S. Military and C.I.A. Interventions since World War II*. Monroe, Me.: Common Courage Press, 1995.
Chamberlain, Muriel E. *European Decolonization in the Twentieth Century*. New York: Longman, 1998.
———. *The Scramble for Africa*. London: Longman, 1999.
Fall, Bernard. *Hell in a Very Small Place: The Siege of Dien Bien Phu*. Philadelphia: Lippincott, 1967.
Galeano, Eduardo. *The Open Veins of Latin America: Five Centuries of the Pillage of a Continent*. New York: Monthly Review Press, 1973.

Johnson, Chalmers. *Nemesis: The Last Days of the American Republic.* New York: Henry Holt, 2006.
———. *The Sorrows of Empire: Militarism, Secrecy and the End of the Republic.* New York: Henry Holt, 2004.
Pakenham, Thomas. *The Scramble for Africa, 1976–1912.* New York: Random House, 1991
Porter, Gareth. *Perils of Dominance: Imbalance of Power and the Road to Vietnam.* Berkeley: University of California Press, 2005.

CHAPTER 11: THE GLOBAL ECONOMY

Barlow, Maude, and Tony Clarke. *Blue Gold: The Battle against Corporate Theft of the World's Water.* New York: New Press, 2002.
Bello, Walden. *The Future in Balance: Essays on Globalization and Resistance.* Oakland, Calif.: Food First and Focus on the Global South, 2001.
———. *The United States, Structural Adjustment and Global Poverty.* London: Pluto Press, 1994.
Bello, Walden, and Stephanie Rosenfeld. *Dragons in Distress: Asia's Miracle Economies in Crisis.* San Francisco: Institute for Food and Development Policy, 1992.
Cobb, John. *The Earthist Challenge to Economism: The Theological Critique of the World Bank.* New York: St. Martin's Press, 1999.
George, Susan, and Fabrizio Sabelli. *Faith and Credit: The World Bank's Secular Empire.* Boulder, Colo.: Westview Press, 1994.
Hostetler, Sharon, et al. *A High Price to Pay: Structural Adjustment and Women in Nicaragua.* Washington, D.C.: Witness for Peace, 1995.
Rich, Bruce. *Mortgaging the Earth: The World Bank, Environmental Impoverishment and the Crisis of Development.* Boston: Beacon Press, 1994.
Ruether, Rosemary. *Integrating Ecofeminism, Globalization and World Religions.* Lanham, Md.: Rowman & Littlefield, 2004.
Shiva, Vandana. *Biopiracy: The Plunder of Nature and Knowledge.* Boston: South End Press, 1997.
———. *Stolen Harvest: The Hijacking of the Global Food Supply.* Boston: South End Press, 1999.
Steger, Manfred B. *Globalism: The New Market Ideology.* Lanham, Md.: Rowman & Littlefield, 2002.
Sutcliffe, Bob. *100 Ways of Seeing an Unequal World.* London: Zed Books, 2002.

CHAPTER 12: U.S. AND GLOBAL MILITARISM

Alperovitz, Gar. *The Decision to Use the Atomic Bomb and the Architecture of an American Myth.* New York: Knopf, 1995.

Bacevich, Andrew J. *American Empire: The Reality and Consequences of U.S. Diplomacy.* Cambridge, Mass.: Harvard University Press, 2002.

———. *The New American Militarism: How Americans Are Seduced by War.* New York: Oxford University Press, 2005.

Berrigan, Frita. "A Nation of Firsts Arms the World." http://www.tomdispatch.com/index.mhtml?pid=196017.

Chatterje, Pratap. *Iraq, Inc: A Profitable Occupation.* New York: Seven Stories Press, 2004.

Cumings, Bruce. *Korea's Place in the Sun: A Modern History.* New York: Norton, 1997.

Fall, Bernard F. *Hell in a Very Small Place: The Siege of Dien Bien Phu.* New York: Lippincott, 1967.

Grey, Stephen, *Ghost Plane: The True Story of the CIA Torture Program.* New York: St. Martin's Press, 2006.

Griffin, David Ray. *The New Pearl Harbor: Disturbing Questions about the Bush Administration and 9/11.* Northampton, Mass.: Olive Branch Press, 2004.

Heizer, Robert F., and Alan J. Almquist. *The Other Californians: Prejudice and Discrimination under Spain, Mexico and the United States to 1920.* Berkeley: University of California Press, 1971.

Johnson, Chalmers, *Nemesis: The Last Days of the American Republic.* New York: Henry Holt, 2006.

———. *Sorrows of Empire: Militarism, Secrecy and the End of the Republic.* New York: Henry Holt, 2004.

Leitenberg, Milton. "Deaths in Wars and Conflicts, 1945 to 2000." http://www.pcr.uu.se/conferences/Euroconference/Leitenberg_paper_pdf.

Mann, James. *The Rise of the Vulcans: A History of the Bush War Cabinet.* New York: Viking Press, 2004.

Marola, Edward J., ed. *Theodore Roosevelt, the U.S. Navy and the Spanish-American War.* New York: Palgrave, 2001.

Melman, Seymour. *Pentagon Capitalism: The Political Economy of War.* New York: McGraw-Hill, 1970.

Physicians for Social Responsibility. "Medical Consequences of a Nuclear Attack on Iran: Fact Sheet." http://www.psr.org/suite/PageServer?pagename=security_main_iranfactsheet.

Scahill, Jeremy. *Blackwater: The Rise of the World's Most Powerful Mercenary Army.* New York: Nation Books, 2007.

Schoonover, Thomas. *Uncle Sam's War of 1898 and the Origins of Globalization.* Lexington: University Press of Kentucky, 2003.

CHAPTER 13: NICARAGUA IN THE CARIBBEAN AND CENTRAL AMERICAN CONTEXT

Baltodano, Monica. "From Sandinismo to 'Danielismo.'" *International Socialist Review*, November–December 2006, 31–35.

Berryman, Philip. *Liberation Theology.* Philadelphia: Temple University Press, 1987.
——. *Religious Roots of Rebellion: Christians in the Central America Revolution.* Maryknoll, N.Y.: Orbis Books, 1984.
Blum, Leonor. "The Literacy Campaign, Nicaraguan Style." *Caribbean Review* 10 (winter 1981): 18–21.
Blum, William. *Killing Hope: U.S. Military and CIA Interventions since World War II.* Monroe, Me.: Common Courage Press, 1995.
Blumenthal, Max. "The Kinder, Gentler Daniel Ortega." *The Nation* (February 5, 2007) www.thenation.com/doc/20070205/Blumenthal.
Bonner, Raymond. *Weakness and Deceit: U.S. Policy and El Salvador.* New York: Times Books, 1984.
Booth, John A. *The End and the Beginning: The Nicaraguan Revolution.* Boulder, Colo.: Westview Press, 1985.
Cardenal, Ernesto. *The Gospel of Solentiname.* Maryknoll, N.Y.: Orbis Books, 1976.
Galeano, Eduardo. *Guatemala: Occupied Country.* New York: Monthly Review Press, 1969.
Jonas, Suzanne. *The Battle for Guatemala.* Boulder, Colo.: Westview Press, 1991.
Kraus, Clifford. *Inside Central America: Its People, Politics and History.* New York: Summit Books, 1991.
Lanusa, Magna. "Nicaragua: Ecological Debt and the Model of Indebtedness, Impoverishment and Predatory Destruction." In *Jubilee South,* 7 http://www.Jubileesouth.org/journal/Nicaragua.htm.
McCann, Thomas P. *An American Company: The Tragedy of United Fruit.* New York: Crown, 1976.
Pearce, Jenny. *Under the Eagle: U.S. Intervention in Central America and the Caribbean.* Boston: South End Press, 1982.
Romero, Arnulfo. *Voice of the Voiceless: Four Pastor Letters and Other Statements.* Introduced by Ignacio Martin-Baro and Jon Sobrino. Maryknoll, N.Y.: Orbis Books, 1985.
Roosevelt, Theodore. *Autobiography.* New York: Charles Scribner and Sons, 1925.
Schlesinger, Stephen, and Stephen Kinzer. *Bitter Fruit: The Untold Story of the American Coup in Guatemala.* New York: Doubleday, 1982.
Scott, Pater Dale, and Jane Hunter. *The Iran Contra Connection: Secret Teams and Covert Operations in the Reagan Era.* Boston: South End Press, 1987.
Trouillot, Rolph. *Haiti: State against Nation: The Origins and Legacy of Duvalierism.* New York: Monthly Review Press, 1990.
Walsh, Lawrence. *Firewall: The Iran Contra Conspiracy and Cover-Up.* New York: Norton, 1997.
Wiarda, Howard J., and Michael J. Kryanek. *The Dominican Republic: A Caribbean Crucible.* Boulder, Colo.: Westview Press, 1992.

CHAPTER 14: THE TWO KOREAS

Commission on Theological Concerns of the Christian Conference of Asia, ed. *Minjung Theology: People as the Subjects of History.* Maryknoll, N.Y.: Orbis Books, 1983.

Cumings, Bruce. *Divided Korea: United Future?* Headline Series no. 306. New York: Foreign Policy Association, 1995.
———. *Korea's Place in the Sun: A Modern History*. New York: Norton, 1997.
———. *North Korea: A Different Country*. New York: New Press, 2004.
———. *The Origins of the Korean War*. 2 vols. Princeton, N.J.: Princeton University Press, 1981, 1990.
Foot, Rosemary. *The Wrong War: American Policy and the Dimensions of the Korean Conflict, 1950–1953*. New York: Cornell University Press, 1985.
Hicks, George. *The Comfort Women: Japan's Brutal Regime of Enforced Prostitution in the Second World War*. New York: Norton, 1995.
Kim, Key-Hink. *The Last Phase of the East Asian Order: Korea, Japan and the Chinese Empire, 1860–1882*. Berkeley: University of California Press, 1980.
Woo, Jung-en. *Race to the Swift: State and Finance in Korean Industrialization*. New York: Columbia University Press, 1991.

CHAPTER 15: SOUTH AFRICA

Adams, Hettie, and Hermione Sutter. *William Street, District Six*. Diep River, South Africa: Chameleon Press, 1988.
Biko, Steve. *I Write What I Like*. Harmondsworth: Penguin, 1988.
Boezak, Allan. *Farewell to Innocence: A Socio-Ethical Study of Black Theology and Black Power*. Maryknoll, N.Y.: Orbis Books, 1977.
Cock, Jacklyn. *Maids and Madams: Domestic Workers under Apartheid*. Johannesburg: Ravan Press, 1980.
Huttenbach, Robert A. *Gandhi in South Africa: British Imperialism and the Indian Question, 1860–1914*. Ithaca, N.Y.: Cornell University Press, 1971.
Itumeleng, Mosala, and Buti Tihagalo. *The Unquestionable Right to Be Free: Black Theology from South Africa*. Maryknoll, N.Y.: Orbis Books, 1986.
Johnson, R. W., and Lawrence Schlemmer. *Launching Democracy in South Africa: The First Open Election, April, 1994*. New Haven, Conn.: Yale University Press, 1996.
Kairos Theologians. *Challenge to the Church: A Theological Comment on the Political Crisis in South Africa: The Kairos Document and Commentaries*. Geneva: World Council of Churches, 1985.
Louw, P. Eric. *The Rise, Fall and Legacy of Apartheid*. Westport, Conn.: Praeger, 2004.
Mandela, Nelson. *Long Walk to Freedom: The Autobiography of Nelson Mandela*. London: Little, Brown, 1994.
Mattera, Don. *Gone with the Twilight: The Story of Sophiatown*. London: Zed Books, 1987.
Ross, Robert. *A Concise History of South Africa*. Cambridge: Cambridge University Press, 1999.
Waldmeir, Patti. *Anatomy of a Miracle: The End of Apartheid and the Birth of a New South Africa*. New York: Norton, 1997.

Worger, William H. *South Africa's City of Diamonds: Mine Workers and Monopoly Capitalism in Kimberley, 1867–1895*. New Haven, Conn.: Yale University Press, 1987.
Zegeye, Abebe, Richard L. Harris, and Pat Lauderdale, *Globalization and Post-Apartheid South Africa*. Toronto, Calif.: de Sitter Publications, 2005.

CHAPTER 16: ECOLOGY

Brown, Lester. *Changing the World's Food Prospect: The Nineties and Beyond*. Worldwatch Paper no. 85. Washington, D.C.: Worldwatch Institute, 1986.
———. *Population Policies for a New Economic Era*. Worldwatch Paper no. 53. Washington, D.C.: Worldwatch Institute, 1983.
Cass, Loren R. *The Failure of American and European Climate Policy: International Norms, Domestic Politics and Unachievable Commitments*. Albany: State University of New York Press, 2006.
Eaton, Heather. "The Revolution of Evolution." *Worldviews: Environment, Culture, Religion* 11, no. 1 (2007): 6–31.
Ehrlich, Paul R., and Anne H. Ehrlich. *Extinction: The Causes and Consequences of Disappearance of Species*. New York: Random House, 1981.
Ehrlich, Paul R., Anne H. Ehrlich, and John P. Holdren, *Human Ecology: Problems and Solutions*. San Francisco: Freeman, 1973.
Kennedy, Robert, Jr. *Crimes against Nature: How George W. Bush and His Corporate Pals Are Plundering the Country and Hijacking Our Democracy*. New York: HarperCollins, 2004.
Ruether, Rosemary R., and Dieter T. Hessel, eds. *Christianity and Ecology: Seeking the Well-Being of Earth and Humans*. Cambridge, Mass.: Harvard University Press, 2000.
Ruether, Rosemary R. *Gaia and God: An Ecofeminist Theology of Earth Healing*. San Francisco: HarperSanFrancisco, 1992.
———. *Integrating Ecofeminism, Globalization and World Religions*. Lanham, Md.: Rowman & Littlefield, 2004.
Shiva, Vandana. *The Violence of the Green Revolution: Third World Agriculture, Ecology and Politics*. London: Zed Books, 1991.
Wolf, Edward C. *On the Brink of Extinction: Conserving the Diversity of Life*. Worldwatch Paper no. 78. Washington, D.C.: Worldwatch Institute, 1987.

CHAPTER 17: SOCIAL SYSTEMS AND THE CHURCH'S MISSION

Bouma-Prediger, Steven. *For the Beauty of the Earth: A Christian Vision for Creation Care*. Grand Rapids, Mich.: Baker Academic, 2001.

Diamond, Sara. *Roads to Dominion: Right-Wing Movements and Political Power in the United States.* New York: Guilford Press, 1995.

Dorrien, Gary J. *Imperial Designs: Neoconservatives and the New Pax Americana.* New York: Routledge, 2004.

Haller, William. *The Elect Nation: The Meaning and Relevance of Foxe's Book of Martyrs.* New York: Harper and Row, 1963.

Horsley, Paul, A. ed. *Paul and Empire: Religion and Power in Roman Imperial Society.* Harrisburg, Pa.: Trinity Press International, 1997.

Horsley, Richard A. *Jesus and Empire: The Kingdom of God and the New World Disorder.* Minneapolis: Fortress Press, 2003.

Keller, Catherine. *God and Power: Counter-Apocalyptic Journeys.* Minneapolis: Fortress Press, 2005.

King, Martin Luther. *A Triumph of Conscience.* New York: Harper and Row, 1967.

Marsten, George. *Fundamentalism and American Culture: The Shaping of Twentieth-Century Evangelism, 1870–1925.* New York: Oxford University Press, 1980.

Niebuhr, Reinhold. *The Irony of American History.* New York: Charles Scribner and Sons, 1954.

Rauschenbusch, Walter. *Theology for the Social Gospel.* New York: Macmillan, 1918.

Robertson, Pat. *The New World Order.* Dallas: Word Press, 1991.

Ruether, Rosemary R. *Christianity and the Making of the Modern Family: Ruling Ideologies, Diverse Realities.* Boston: Beacon Press, 2000.

Strong, Josiah. *Our Country: Its Possible Future and Present Crisis.* New York: Baker and Taylor, 1885.

Wallis, Jim, *God's Politics: Why the Right Gets It Wrong and the Left Doesn't Get It.* San Francisco: HarperSanFrancisco, 2005.

Washington, James Melvin, ed. *A Testament of Hope: The Essential Writings of Martin Luther King.* San Francisco: HarperSanFrancisco, 1991.

Weaver, Mary Jo, and R. Scott Appleby, eds. *Being Right: Conservative Catholics in America.* Bloomington: Indiana University Press, 1995.

Index

abortion, 49, 249–50
acid rain, 230
acquired immunodeficiency syndrome (AIDS), 161, 223
Adams, John, 126–27
Addams, Jane, 46
Adversus Judaeus literature, 61
Africa: colonization of, 135–38, 143; decolonization of, 149–51; female cleanliness and, 92; Jews and, 67; slave trade and, 51, 53
African Americans: civil rights movement and, 48–49; industrialism and, 46; post-slavery, 53; racism toward, 79–81; Rauschenbusch and, 247; segregation of, 80; voting rights and, 46; welfare and, 49
African National Congress (ANC), 215, 217, 219–22
Afrikaans Medium Decree (South Africa), 216
Afrikaner nationalism, 215
AIDS (acquired immunodeficiency syndrome), 161, 223
Alemán, Arnaldo, 190
Algeria, 150–51
All-India Congress, 148
Amador, Carlos Fonseca, 186
Ambedkar, B. R., 148

Ambrose of Milan, 13, 64
American Colonization Society, 79
American Friends Service Committee, 71
American Home Missionary Society, 247
American Indians: activism by, 249; assimilation of, 82; colonists and, 20; conceptions of "other" and, 102; racism toward, 81–83; removal of, 81–82; slave trade and, 51–52
American Revolution, 126–27, 135, 141, 245
Amos, book of, 248–49
Anabaptists, 18
ANC (African National Congress), 215, 217, 219–22
Anglicans, 21, 218, 245–46
Anglo-Saxons, 76–77, 96, 100, 245, 247
Angola, 150
anthropology, 25, 87
Antichrist, 66, 101
anti-Semitism: Arab Palestinians and, 70–71; conversion and, 65; Crusades and, 64; emancipation and, 65–66; European nationalism and, 66–67; expulsion from Europe and, 64–65; ideological differences and, 60, 61–62; Nazi Germany and, 69;

Pharisees and, 61; revolutionary tensions and, 66; in Roman Empire, 62–64; roots of, 59–60; Zionism and, 67–71
apartheid: aftermath of, 220–23; construction of, 215–17; dismantling of, 220; features of, 216–17; roots of, 215; struggle against, 217–20; World Alliance of Reformed Churches and, 21
Aquinas, Thomas, 94
Arab-Israeli wars, 137
Arab Palestinians, 69–71, 137
Arbenz, Jacobo, 191–92
ARENA (Nationalist Republican Alliance Party), 194
Aristotle, 94–96, 98
Armas, Carlos Castillo, 191–92
Armstrong, George, 99
Asia: colonization of, 135–36, 138, 142–43; decolonization of, 147–49; financial crisis in, 157–58. *See also specific countries*
Augustine, St., 34, 93–94, 97–99
Austro-Hungarian Empire, 4, 136
authoritarian paternalism, 208

Balfour, Arthur, 68
Bantu Authorities Act (South Africa), 216
Bantu Education Act (South Africa), 216
baptism, 18
Baptists, 245
Belgium, 145–46
Berlin Conference, 143
Bidault, Georges, 178
Biko, Steve, 217–18
Bill of Rights (American), 107, 245
Bill of Rights (South African), 220–21
biological essentialism, 3
birth control, 46, 232
bishops, 14
Black Codes, 76, 80
Black Consciousness Movement, 217–18

Black Economic Empowerment policy, 222
Black Homeland Citizenship Act (South Africa), 216
blacks, 45, 52, 75, 102, 139. *See also* African Americans
Blair, Tony, 156
Boas, Franz, 87
Boers, 144, 214
Bonesteel, Charles, 203
Boniface VIII (pope), 15–16
Brazil, 142
Bretton Woods institutions, 156–57, 164
British East India Company, 143
British Mandate for Palestine, 68
Buddhism, 20, 199–200
Burma, 147
Bush, George H. W., 170, 189
Bush, George W.: blacks and, 81; Christian fundamentalism and, 251; classism and, 121; environment and, 232, 237, 238; equal rights movements and, 249; fascism and, 117; imperial messianism and, 20, 252; Korea and, 207, 209; military waste and, 174; nuclear weapons and, 178; terrorist threat and, 171
Byzantine world, 14, 64

Cabreza, Manuel Estrada, 191
California, 84–86
Calvin, John, 16, 94
Calvinists, 5–6, 16–18, 65, 94
Cape Colony, South Africa, 144, 215
Cape Town, South Africa, 217
capitalism: communism and, 115; liberalism and, 110; neocolonialism and, 156; socialism and, 111, 112, 113, 118; U.S. military spending and, 173–74
carbon dioxide, 230
Cardenal, Ernest, 187
Cardenal, Fernando, 187
Caribbean, 139–41

Carter, Jimmy, 184, 186, 188, 193
Catholics/Catholicism: Charles I and, 17; "chosen people" ideology and, 246, 247; civil rights movement and, 248; contraception and, 46; El Salvador and, 193, 194; Great Schism and, 16; Guatemala and, 192; in Korea, 200, 207; Mexico and, 19; Napoleon and, 19; Nicaragua and, 187–88, 190; schisms among, 250; in South Africa, 218; twentieth-century America and, 20, 21; in twenty-first-century Latin America, 22; women's labor and, 42
celibacy, 42
Cenozoic era, 227–28
Center for Economic and Policy Research, 160
Center for Neighborhood Technology, 236
Central America, 139, 141, 142, 183, 184, 195. *See also specific countries*
Central American Free Trade Agreement, 194
Central American Peace Accord, 189
Central Intelligence Agency (CIA), 138, 176, 188, 205
Centro Ecuménico Antonio Valdivieso, 187–88
Chamorro, Violeta, 189
Charlemagne, 14
Chatterjee, Pratap, 174–76
chemical weapons, 178, 205
Cheney, Dick, 170–71, 174
Cherokees, 81–82
Chicago, Illinois, 46, 236–37
Chicano movement, 249
children: as economic liability, 47–48; household economy and, 41, 42, 43; labor by, 43–44, 47, 110, 129; Social Security Act and, 47
Children's Crusade, 51
China: communism and, 114; decolonization of Asia and, 147; Japan and, 201; Korea and, 199, 201, 204;

Marxism and, 19; nuclear weapons and, 177, 179; slavery and, 53–54; United Nations and, 5; U.S. national debt and, 174; Vietnam and, 148
Chinese persons in America, 78, 85
Choson dynasty (Korea), 199–200
Christ. *See* Jesus Christ
The Christian Doctrine of Slavery (George Armstrong), 99
Christians/Christianity: anti-imperial, 252–53; apartheid and, 218; birth of, 11; Constantine and, 62; ecological crisis and, 235–36; empires and, 5, 244; in Korea, 200, 207; progressive, 251, 253; schisms among American, 250–51; slavery and, 36; as social system, 243–44; universal identity by, 3–4. *See also* Catholics/Catholicism; church-state relations; New Testament; Protestants/Protestantism
Chun Doo Hwan, 206–7
Churchill, Winston, 147
Church of England, 19, 22
church-state relations: Ambrose and, 13; Anabaptists and, 18; Byzantine world and, 14; church superiority and, 13–14; colonial America and, 19–20; colonial nation-states and, 15–16; Constantine and, 12–13; disestablishment of churches and, 19–21; French Revolution and, 19; Gnostics and, 12; Lutheranism and, 16–17; Marxism and, 19; morality and, 22; papal power and, 15–16; Paul and, 11–12; Puritan separatists and, 17–18; Quakers and, 19; Roman Empire and, 11–12; separation of power and, 14–15; in twenty-first century, 22; U.S. Constitution and, 19
CIA (Central Intelligence Agency), 138, 176, 188, 205
Civil Rights Act (United States), 80
civil rights movement, 48–49, 83, 248–49. *See also* racism

civil wars: American, 53, 76, 80, 99, 127; in Angola, 150; colonialism and, 4; in El Salvador, 193–94; English, 52; in Guatemala, 192; Korean War as, 204; in South Africa, 150; in Spain, 116
classical liberalism, 107
Clermont-Tonnerre, Stanislas Marie, 66
Clinton, Bill, 49, 129, 170
Cold War: capitalism/socialism and, 118; decolonization of Asia and, 147, 148; fascism and, 117; neocolonialism and, 156; Russian military budget and, 172; U.S. military depth and, 168–69
Colombia, 184
colonialism, European: in Africa, 143–46; in Caribbean, 183; church-state relations and, 15–16; decolonization and global hegemony, 151–52; decolonization and neocolonialism, 138, 155; decolonization of Africa, 149–51; decolonization of Americas, 141–42; decolonization of Asia, 147–49; expanse of, 135; expansion of, 5; first waves of, 139–42; indigenous populace and, 141; land exploitation and, 141; nation-states and, 4; Ottoman Empire and, 136–37; overview of, 135–36; second wave of, 142–46; South Africa and, 213, 214; trade and, 141; universal identity and, 3–4
Coloreds, 215–16, 219, 221
Colossians, letter to, 6–7
Committee for Economic Development, 123
communism: anticommunist ideology and, 156; El Salvador and, 193–94; fascism and, 117; Guatemala and, 191–92; messianic zealotry and, 248; neocolonialism and, 155–56; Nicaragua and, 189; socialism and, 112–13, 114; South Africa and, 216
Confucianism, 91, 199–200

Congregationalists, 19, 246
Congress, U.S., 81, 83–84, 168, 189
conservative evangelism, 249–50
Constans, 13
Constantine (emperor of Rome), 5, 12–13, 62
Constantius, 13
Constitution, U.S.: corporations and, 163; freedom rights and, 106; Jews and, 65; religious freedom and, 19; shapers of, 126–27; slavery and, 53, 76; standing armies and, 167; voting rights and, 46, 107
contraception, 46, 232
Convention for a Democratic South Africa, 220
Corinthians, letters to, 1, 12
corporate mergers, 130
corporations, 2, 3, 108, 158–59, 162–63, 261
cotton, 52–53
Council on Foreign Relations, 123
Creation, orders of, 5–6
Creoles, 139
Cretaceous period, 228
Cromwell, Oliver, 52, 65
Crusades, 64
Cuba: communism and, 114; Marxism and, 19; military budget of, 172; nuclear weapons and, 178; slavery and, 51, 53; Soviet Union and, 188; Spanish-American War and, 168; structural adjustments and, 162; U.S. control of, 135, 141, 183, 201; U.S. military expansion and, 138, 175; U.S. military spending and, 169–70
currency trading, 157–58

Darwinism, 76, 99, 108–9
Dawes-Severalty Act (United States), 82
debt crisis, 159
Declaration of Independence (United States), 81, 167
Defiance Campaign (South Africa), 217

deforestation, 231
De Klerk, F. W., 219
Delgado, Sharon, 236
democracy: anticommunist ideology and, 156; "chosen people" ideology and, 4, 20, 101, 245, 246; Earth Charter and, 239, 259, 262; El Salvador and, 193–94; Guatemala and, 191; Korea and, 203, 205, 206–7; Pennsylvania constitution and, 127; revolution and, 113; Sandinistas and, 188, 189; socialism and, 112, 113, 114, 115, 118; South Africa and, 221–22; U.S. hidden agenda and, 156, 195
Democratic People's Republic of Korea. *See* North Korea
D'Escoto, Miguel, 187
despotism, 106–7
Deuteronomy, book of, 3
Diaspora Jews, 70
Dictate (Pope Gregory VII), 15
dictatorship, 114, 184–86, 191, 193
Dien Bien Phu, 148, 177–78
divorce, 16
dominator systems, 6–10, 243
Dominican Republic, 184
Dreyfus case, 67
Dulles, Allan, 191
Dulles, John Foster, 178, 191
Dutch Reform churches, 218

earth, 227, 257
Earth Charter: challenges ahead and, 258; democracy and, 262; ecological integrity and, 259–61; global situation and, 258; launching of, 238; nonviolence and, 263; objectives of, 239; origin of, 264–65; participants in, 238–39; peace and, 263–64; preamble of, 257; principles of, 259–64; progressive Christians and, 253; social/economic justice and, 261–62; universal responsibility and, 258; way forward and, 264

Earth Charter Commission, 239, 264–65
Eastern Europe, 4, 65–67, 157
East India Company, 143
East Indies, 143, 147, 149
ecological crisis: affluence/poverty and, 229–30; causes of, 257; Christian schisms and, 251; consumption rates and, 229, 230; deforestation and, 231; energy sources and, 230–31; food production and, 231; natural resources and, 228; pollution and, 234; population growth and, 227–29; remedies for, 232–35; technology and, 229, 230
ecological societies, 235–39
economic class in United States: colonial era and, 126–27; Constitution and corporate elite, 126–27; corporate community of elite and, 122; debt and, 132–33; Depression and, 128; expansion and, 127; Gilded Age and, 127–28; global trade and, 129, 130; government control by corporate elite, 123–24, 133; government subsidies and, 128; industrialization and, 127; media control by corporate elite, 124–25; New Deal and, 129; poverty prevalence and, 130, 132; Reagan and, 130; social cohesion of corporate elite, 125; tax burden and, 130; technology and, 128, 129; work benefits and, 130; work hours and, 130; World War II and, 129
economic liberalism, 108–11
"An Ecumenical Faith Stance against Global Empire for a Liberated Earth Community" (World Alliance of Reformed Churches study document), 252–53
education: ancient Romans and, 33, 34; communism and, 19; Earth Charter and, 261, 263; feminism and, 46, 49, 96; gender roles in, 42; globalization

period and, 106; Malawi and, 145; Mill and, 106; in Nicaragua, 187, 188, 190; population control and, 232; post–World War II and, 48; in South Africa, 216, 221, 222; truancy laws and, 47
Egypt, 59, 137
Eisenhower, Dwight, 204–5
Ellacuría, Ignacio, 194
Ellis, Marc, 71
El Salvador, 193–95
Emergency Detention Act (United States), 87
emperor worship, 11
empires, 5
empiricism, 105
encomienda system, 52
Engels, Friedrich, 112
English Civil War, 52
Enlightenment, 142
Ephesians, letter to, 76, 92
Episcopal Church, 251
Equal Rights Amendment (United States), 49
Europe: Eastern, 4, 65–67, 157; Jewish expulsion from, 64–65; slave trade and, 51; socialism in, 113; worldview transformation in, 105–6. *See also* colonialism, European; *specific countries*
European Economic Union, 156
Evangelicals, 53
Eve, 93, 101
Extension of University Education Act (South Africa), 216

factory economy, 43–44
factory farming, 233
Fair Labor Relations Act (United States), 47
Fair Labor Standards Act (United States), 110, 129
Faribundo Martí Front for National Liberation (FMLN), 193–95
fascism, 115–17, 164

feminism, 45–46, 49–50, 244
Fifteenth Amendment, 53, 76
First, Ruth, 218
First Amendment, 19, 106
FMLN (Faribundo Martí Front for National Liberation), 193–95
food production, 231, 233–34
foraging societies, 26
forced labor camps, 53–54
Ford Foundation, 123
forest preservation, 234–35
fossil fuels, 230, 232–33, 234, 237, 260
foundations, 123
Fourier, Charles, 112
Fourteenth Amendment, 46, 53, 76, 163
France: "chosen people" ideology and, 100, 244–45; colonial empire expanse of, 135; colonial empire in Africa, 144, 145, 150–51; colonial empire in Asia, 143; colonial empire in Caribbean, 141, 142, 183; colonial empire in North America, 139; Haiti and, 142, 183; Indochina and, 148; Jews and, 64, 65–66; Middle East and, 68; military budget of, 172; neocolonialism and, 138; nuclear weapons and, 177, 179; Ottoman Empire and, 137; papal power and, 15–16; Portugal and, 142; Reformation and, 16; slave trade and, 51; Spain and, 142; United Nations and, 5; World Bank/IMF and, 157
Franco, Francisco, 116
Franco-Prussian War, 67
free market, 108–11
FRELIMO, 150
French Revolution, 19, 65, 142
Freud, Sigmund, 96
Frey, Gerard, 164
Full Labor Standards Act (United States), 47

Galatians, letter to, 92
Gandhi, Mohandas K., 148, 215
gardening societies, 26, 29

Gates, Bill, 126, 129–30
GATT (General Agreement on Tariffs and Trade), 157–58
gay rights movement, 249
Gelasius (emperor of Rome), 13
gender roles/discrimination: in foraging societies, 26; in gardening societies, 26, 29; in herding societies, 29; hierarchy of power and, 29–30; household economy and, 41, 43; industrialization and, 43–45; Iroquoian society and, 27–28; middle-class ideal and, 44–45; Minangkabau and, 28–29; Roman family and, 32–33; seclusion of women and, 31; utopian socialism and, 112; work force and, 47; World War II and, 48. *See also* sexism
General Agreement on Tariffs and Trade (GATT), 157–58
Gentiles, 61–62, 97
German People's Union, 164
Germany: colonial empire of, 136, 145; Jewish emancipation and, 66; Jewish expulsion from, 64; Korea and, 200; military budget of, 172; Nazi, 67, 69, 102, 116; Nicaragua and, 185; Reformation and, 16; Roman Empire and, 14–15; slavery and, 53–54; technological competitiveness and, 174; U.S. military expansion and, 138, 169; work hours and, 130; World Bank/IMF and, 157
Gilded Age, 125, 127–28
globalization: bottom-up, 164–65; Bretton Woods system and, 156–57; development loans and, 158–62; financial markets and, 157–58; multinationals and, 108, 158, 159, 162–63, 261. *See also* neocolonialism
global warming, 230, 234
Gnosticism, 12, 60
gold rush, 84
gold standard, 157
Gossett, Thomas F., 77

Government of India Act, 143
Grande, Rutilio, 193
Great Britain: "chosen people" ideology and, 100, 244–45; colonial empire expanse of, 135; colonial empire in Africa, 5, 144–45, 150; colonial empire in Asia, 5, 142–43; colonial empire in Caribbean, 141, 183; colonial empire in Middle East, 5; colonial empire in North America, 139; colonial empire in South Africa and, 214; Iraq and, 4; Japan and, 201; Jews and, 64, 65, 68, 69; Korea and, 200, 201, 203; Middle East and, 68; military budget of, 172; nation-state concept and, 4; neocolonialism and, 138, 156; neoliberalism in, 110; nuclear weapons and, 177; Ottoman Empire and, 137; papal power and, 15; Reformation and, 16; slavery and, 51, 53; United Nations and, 5; U.S. military expansion and, 138, 169, 175; World Bank/IMF and, 157
Great Depression, 46–47, 109–10, 128
Greater Asia Co-Prosperity Sphere, 202
Great Schism, 16
Greece, 59–60, 75, 98, 136
green communities, 236
Green Cross International, 238
Green Revolution, 231
Greenslade, S. L., 14
Gregory VII (pope), 14–15
Group Areas Act (South Africa), 216
Guatemala, 191–92
guild system, 42

Haiti, 141–42, 168, 183–84
Ham, 75
Hamilton, Alexander, 126–27
Hammurabi, Code of, 30
Hasidic movements, 67
Hayek, Friedrich, 110
health insurance, 130
Henry IV (Holy Roman emperor), 14–15

288   Index

Henry VIII (king of England), 16
Henry the Navigator (prince of Portugal), 51
herding societies, 29
Hersh, Seymour, 178
Herzl, Theodor, 67–68
Hidalgo, Miguel, 142
Higgs, Robert, 176
High Commission Territories, 145
Hinduism, 91
Hindu-Muslim riots, 148
Hitler, Adolf, 69
Hizbollah, 8
Holmes, Oliver Wendell, 82
Holocaust, 67, 69–70
Holy Roman emperors, 14
Holy See, 21
Home Missionary Movement, 247–48
homoiousian formula, 13
homoousian formula, 13
homosexuality, 102, 249–51, 253
Hong Kong, China, 147, 161
Hope for the Earth (Sharon Delgado), 236
household economy, 41–43
Hovevei Zion movement, 67
human beings, 7, 227

Illinois, 81
IMF (International Monetary Fund), 111, 138, 156–58, 161, 190, 222
Immigration Act (United States), 77–78, 86
Immorality Act (South Africa), 216
India: British colonization of, 142–43; caste system and, 91; female cleanliness and, 92; Greeks and, 60; independence of, 148; nuclear weapons and, 177; political system in, 114; slavery and, 51, 53–54; socialism and, 114; South Africa and, 214; U.S. military spending and, 175
Indian National Congress, 148
Indian Removal Act (United States), 81
Indochina, 135, 143, 147–48

Indochinese Union, 143
Indonesia, 28, 135, 147, 149
Industrial Conciliation Act (South Africa), 216
industrialism, 43–45
Innocent III (pope), 15
Inquisition, 65
Internal Security Act (South Africa), 219
International Monetary Fund (IMF), 111, 138, 156–58, 161, 190, 222
Interreligious Sustainability Project of Greater Chicago, 53–54, 236–37
Iran, 169–70, 177–79
Iraq, 4, 137–38, 169–72, 175, 177
Iraq, Inc: A Profitable Occupation (Pratap Chatterjee), 174–75
Irish in United States, 77
Iroquois, 27–28
Islam/Muslims, 7, 20, 64, 246
Israel: anti-Semitism and, 62; citizenship in, 70; Hasidic movements and, 67; Hizbollah war and, 8; Jewish majority in, 70; nuclear weapons and, 177, 179; Palestine and, 69, 137; socialism in, 112; U.S. military bases in, 175; Zionism and, 65, 67
Italian nationalist movement, 116
Italy, 136, 138, 146, 157, 169

Jackson, Andrew, 81
Japan: atom bomb and, 176; China and, 201; European colonialism and, 147; financial crisis in, 158; IMF and, 157; Indonesia and, 149; Korea and, 199, 200, 201–3; Russia and, 201; slavery and, 53–54; technological competitiveness and, 174; U.S. military bases in, 169; World Bank and, 157, 161
Japanese in United States, 78, 85–87
Japheth, 75
Jefferson, Thomas, 52, 79–81, 126–27, 167
Jerome, St., 33

Jesus Christ: church-state relations and, 12; creation and, 6; deliverance at end by, 1, 6; empire and, 252; Judaism and, 60; male body of, 94; power relationships and, 7; scriptural subjugation codes and, 92
Jewish Enlightenment, 67
Jewish Exodus, 59
The Jewish State (Theodor Herzl), 67–68
Jewish wars, 62
Jews/Judaism: Byzantine Empire and, 64; civil rights movement and, 248; conceptions of "other" and, 101; moneylender stereotype of, 64; patriarchy and, 91–92; slavery and, 97; twentieth-century America and, 20; universal identity by, 3; WASP culture and, 246. *See also* anti-Semitism
Jim Crow laws: civil rights movement and, 53; Civil War aftermath and, 76; corporations and, 163; King and, 249; New Deal and, 129; Rauschenbusch and, 247; revolt against, 48; segregation and, 80; voting rights and, 46
Jinnah, Mohammed Ali, 148
Joao IV (king of Portugal), 142
Johannesburg, South Africa, 217
John, Gospel of, 61
John Paul II (pope), 250
Johnson, Chalmers, 138, 175
Josephus, 59
Jubilee, 97
Julian, 60
Justinian, Code of, 64

Kairos document, 218
KCIA (Korean Central Intelligence Agency), 205–7
Keynes, John Maynard, 110
Khrushchev, Nikita, 178
kibbutz, 112
Kim Dae Jung, 206–7, 210
Kim Il Sung, 202–4, 208

Kim Jae Kyu, 205
Kim Jong-Il, 207–8
Kim Young Sam, 206
King, Martin Luther, Jr., 248–49
Kook, Abraham Isaac, 68
Korea: civil war in, 204–5; division of, 199, 203–4; foreign powers and, 147, 200–203; history of, 199–201; Japan and, 85, 147, 201–3; religion in, 199–200; social classes in, 200; trade barriers and, 162; unification of, 199, 209–10; U.S. military expansion and, 138; World War II aftermath and, 203–4. *See also* North Korea; South Korea
Korean Central Intelligence Agency (KCIA), 205–7
Korean War, 169, 177, 204–5, 207, 209
Korten, David, 162–63
Koryo dynasty (Korea), 199
Kristol, Irving, 170–71
Ku Klux Klan, 80
Kyoto Protocol, 237–38

Land Act (South Africa), 215
Lateran Council, 64
Latin America: fascism in, 117; neocolonialism and, 156; socialism and, 114, 115; Spain and, 135; Spanish conquest of, 139; state-church residuals and, 22. *See also specific countries*
League of Nations, 4
Lebanon, 8
Leopold II (king of Belgium), 145
Leviticus, book of, 92, 97
liberalism, 106–11
liberation theology, 187, 207, 218, 244
Liberia, 79
libertarianism, 109
Lincoln, Abraham, 53
Lord's Prayer, 243
Louisiana Purchase, 127, 139
L'Ouverture, Toussaint, 142
Lula da Silva, Luiz Inacio, 115

Luther, Martin, 16–17, 94
Lutheran School of Theology, 236

Macao, China, 147
MacArthur, Douglas, 177, 203, 204
Maccabees, 60
Madison, James, 167
Malaysia, 143
malnutrition, 231
Manchuria, 147, 199, 200, 202, 204
Mandela, Nelson, 217, 220, 221, 223
Maoist revolution, 117
Marcion, 60
Marcos, Ferdinand, 158
Marine Corps, U.S., 168
Marshall, John, 81
Martí, Farabundo, 193
Martínez, Maximiliano Hernández, 193
Martinique, 141
Marx, Karl, 112
Marxism, 19, 112, 200. *See also* communism; socialism
Massachusetts Bay Colony, 18, 19, 126, 245
matriarchy, 25, 26–29
Matthew, Gospel of, 61
Mbeki, Thabo, 223
McClatchy, Valentine S., 86
McCloy, John J., 203
McKinley, William, 168
McNamara, Robert, 158
Meadville-Lombard school, 236
meat eating, 233–34
media, 124–25
Medicare/Medicaid, 130
Mellon family, 129
Melman, Seymour, 173–74
Mennonites, 19
Mesozoic era, 227
Methodists, 218, 236, 246
Mexican-American War, 83–84, 127, 142, 167, 183
Mexico, 19, 51, 83–84, 139, 142, 158, 189
Michigan, 81

Middle Ages, 51
Middle East, 53, 68, 136–37, 138, 150, 179. *See also specific countries*
Mill, John Stuart, 106–7
Minangkabau society, 28–29
Minh, Ho Chi, 148
Minjung theology, 207
Mississippi, 52–53
mixed economy, 114, 115, 187
mob spirit, 2
Monroe, James, 183
Monroe Doctrine, 183
Montreal Protocol on the Protection of the Ozone Layer, 237
Morales, Evo, 115, 190
morality, 22
Morelos, José María, 142
Mormonism, 247
Morocco, 135, 145
Moses, 60
Moshave, 112
Mozambican National Resistance, 218
Mozambique, 145, 150
Multilateral Agreement on Investment, 163
multilateral trade agreements, 157
multinational corporations, 108, 158, 159, 162–63, 261
Muslim League, 148
Mussolini, Benito, 115–16, 146

Nagasaki, Japan, 176
Namibia, 215, 218, 220
Naming the Powers (Walter Wink), 1
Napoleon (king of France), 19, 66
Napoleonic Wars, 142, 143, 144
Natal region (South Africa), 214–15
National Guard (Nicaraguan), 185–86
National Industrial Recovery Act, 47
nationalism, 66–67, 70, 215
Nationalist Party, 215
nationalist-protectionist movements, 164
Nationalist Republican Alliance Party (ARENA), 194

nations, 3
nation-states, 4, 15–16, 164
nature, 7, 28. *See also* ecological crisis
Nazi Germany, 67, 69, 102, 116
Nazism, 17
neocolonialism: control mechanisms of, 138; debt-payback lending and, 161–62; development loans and, 158–60, 162; enforcement of, 155; Indochina and, 148; mechanisms of, 156–57; military bases and, 175; nation-states and, 164; progress evaluation and, 160–61; resistance to, 155–56; structural adjustments and, 159–62; wealth distribution and, 164
neoliberalism: foreign policy and, 110–11; Latin America and, 115; progress evaluation and, 160; rise of, 157; socialism and, 113, 115; South Africa and, 222; structural adjustments and, 162
Netherlands: colonial empire in 1945, 135; colonial empire in Asia, 143, 149; colonial empire in Caribbean, 141, 183; colonial empire in North America, 139; Jews and, 66; slave trade and, 51; South Africa and colonial empire of, 214
Nevada, 83
New Covenant, 62, 65
New Deal, 47, 49, 83, 110, 113, 129, 191
New Guinea, 149
New Mexico, 83, 84
New Testament: anti-imperialism in, 252, 253; church-state relations and, 11; "household codes" in, 92, 99; powers of, 1–2; sexism in, 92–93; slavery and, 36, 76, 97, 99
New York, 127, 139
New Yorker magazine, 178
Nicaragua: Atlantic-Pacific canal and, 184, 185; earthquake in, 186; faction rivalries in, 185; reformation of, 187; Samoza and, 185–86; Sandinistas and, 114–15, 186–91; structural adjustments in, 160, 162; U.S. military presence in, 168
Niebuhr, Reinhold, 248
Nigeria, 144, 219
Noah, 75
North America, 139, 141. *See also specific countries*
North Korea: agriculture in, 208; economy of, 208–9; Kim Dae Jung and, 207; military budget of, 172; military might of, 209; nuclear weapons and, 177, 179; political system in, 208; reconstruction of, 207–8; U.S. military spending and, 169–70
nuclear energy, 209
Nuclear Non-Proliferation Treaty, 177–78
nuclear weapons: disarmament and, 177, 178–79; Japan and, 176; Korea and, 204–5, 209; nations possessing, 177; U.S. contemplation of using, 177–78, 204–5; U.S. military expansion and, 169; U.S. monopoly on, 176–77
Nyasaland, 145

oil, 138, 158, 230–31
"One Creation, One People, One Place" (Interreligious Sustainability Project of Greater Chicago), 53–54, 236–37
On Liberty (John Stuart Mill), 106–7
Orange Free State, 214
Organization for Economic Cooperation and Development, 163
Ortega, Daniel, 115, 189–91
Ortega, Humberto, 189
Ottoman Empire, 136–37
Our Country: Its Possible Future and Present Crisis (Josiah Strong), 247
Owen, Robert, 112

PAC (Pan-Africanist Congress), 217, 219
Pakistan, 53–54, 148, 177

Palestine, 60, 65, 67–69, 137
Pan-Africanist Congress (PAC), 217, 219
Panama, 184, 189
Panama Canal, 184
papacy, 14–17, 21
Papal States, 66
Paraguay, 142
Park Chung Hee, 205, 206–7
pastoral power, 17
patriarchy: anthropological studies on, 25–27; Christian schisms and, 250; civil rights movement and, 48–49; as divine ordinance, 6; education and, 42; feminism and, 45–46, 49–50; hierarchy of power and, 29–30; household economy and, 41–42; income data and, 50; industrialism and, 43–45; labor and, 42, 43–44, 46–47; middle-class ideal and, 44–45; nature and, 28; plow agriculture and, 29; professional opportunities and, 46–47; in Roman society, 31–37; seclusion of women and, 31; slavery and, 34–37, 99; women's power in, 32, 33; women's writings and, 33. *See also* sexism
Patriot Act, 117
Patronato, 16
Paul, St., 11–12, 36
Paulinism, 60
Pax Americana, 170
Pennsylvania, 126–27
Pentagon, 173
Pentagon Capitalism: The Political Economy of War (Seymour Melman), 173–74
permaculture, 7, 9
Peter, book of, 92
Pharisees, 61
Philadelphia, Pennsylvania, 126–27
Philippines, 87
Philip the Fair (king of France), 15–16
Physicians for Social Responsibility, 178
Pixley, F. M., 85

Plato, 95
Platonism, 60
Political and Social Doctrine of Fascism (Benito Mussolini), 115–16
political liberalism, 107
Polk, James, 83
pollution, 221, 228, 230–31, 234, 260
Poor People's Campaign, 249
popes, 14–17, 21
population growth, 227–29
Population Registration Act (South Africa), 216
Portugal: Brazil and, 142; colonial empire of, 135–36, 142, 145, 150; fascism and, 116; Jews and, 64–65; papal power and, 16; slave trade and, 51; South Africa and, 213–14
Portuguese Revolution, 150
power relations, 6–10, 17. *See also* church-state relations
Presbyterians, 17, 246, 252
Prevention of Illegal Squatting Act (South Africa), 216
Progressive movement, 113, 128
progressivism, 109
Prohibition of Mixed Marriages Act (South Africa), 216
Project for the New American Century, 170
Promotion of Black Self-Government Act (South Africa), 216
Protestants/Protestantism: American monopoly by, 20; "chosen people" ideology and, 100, 245, 246–48; contraception and, 46; denominational institutions in, 21; feminism and, 244; fundamental "dominionists" and, 20–21; in Korea, 200, 207; liberalism and, 249–50; in Nicaragua, 187–88; patriarchy and, 6, 42; Reformation and, 16; schisms among, 250; working class and, 246
Protocols of the Elders of Zion tract, 66
protoindustrialism, 43
Puritans, 17–18, 245

Quakers, 18–19

race, 75
Race: The History of an Idea in America (Thomas F. Gossett), 77
racism: conceptions of other and, 101–2; Earth Charter and, 262; European diversity and, 77; income and, 50; industrialism and, 46; language of, 78; marriage and, 77; Nazism and, 116; origin of man and, 75, 76; religious conversion and, 76, 100; settlement house movement and, 46; slavery and, 97; voting and, 46. *See also* anti-Semitism; apartheid
racism in United States: "chosen people" ideology and, 99–100, 247; current trends and, 87–88; Darwinism and, 76–77; Emergency Detention Act and, 87; gender stereotypes and, 78; King and, 248–49; "melting pot" and, 78–79, 88; mixed races and, 78–79; segregation and, 80; slavery and, 76, 79–80, 99; toward blacks, 79–81; toward Chinese, 85; toward European immigrants, 77–78; toward Japanese, 85–87; toward Mexicans, 83–84; toward Native Americans, 81–83
Rauschenbusch, Walter, 246–47
Reagan, Ronald: apartheid and, 219; defense budget and, 169; El Salvador and, 193–94; equal rights movements and, 249; Japanese internment and, 86; national debt and, 174; neoliberalism and, 110, 157; Nicaragua and, 188, 189; wealth distribution and, 130
Rebuilding American Defenses (Project for the New American Century), 170–71
Reconstruction, 80
recycling, 234–35
redemption, orders of, 5
Reformation, 16–17, 65, 94, 244–45
reform church, 252
reincarnation, 95
Republic (Plato), 95
Republicans, 80, 250
Reservation of Separate Amenities Act (South Africa), 216
Resolution Trust Corporation, 130
Revelation, book of, 11
Rhee, Syngman, 203–5
Rhodes, Cecil, 144–45
Rhodesia, 150
Roh Tae Woo, 206
Roman Empire: Christianity in, 5, 11–13, 62; human diversity, 75; Jews and, 59–60, 62; marriage, 33–34; patriarchy, 31–34; punishment, 34; slavery, 34–37
Romero, Oscar Arnulfo, 193
Roosevelt, Franklin D., 86
Roosevelt, Theodore, 82–83, 168, 184, 201
Ross, Frederick, 99
Rusk, Dean, 203
Russia: arms sales by, 173; communism and, 113; Jews and, 66; Korea and, 200, 201; military budget of, 172; nuclear weapons and, 179; United Nations and, 5; World Bank/IMF and, 157. *See also* Soviet Union
Russian Orthodox Church, 14
Russo-Japanese War, 201

San, Aung, 147
Sandinista Liberation Movement, 186–91
Sandinista Renewal Movement Party, 190–91
Sandinistas, 114–15, 162
Sandino, Augusto César, 185
Sanger, Margaret, 46
San Martin, 142
Satyricon satire, 36
school spirit, 2–3
science, 105
Scott, Winfield, 81–82

Seoul, Korea, 203–4
September 11, 2001, terrorist attacks, 171
settlement house movement, 46
sexism: Aquinas and, 94; Aristotle and, 95–96; Augustine and, 93–94; conceptions of "other" and, 101; Earth Charter and, 262; education and, 96; Freud and, 96; in Hebrew society, 91–92; in New Testament, 92–93; Plato and, 95; post-apartheid laws and, 220; Rauschenbusch and, 247; Reformation and, 94. *See also* patriarchy
shamanism (Korean), 200
Shem, 75
Sierra Leone, 144
Silla state (Korea), 199
slavery: abolishment of, 52–53, 54; Augustine and, 97–98, 99; in Caribbean, 139; child labor, 44; conceptions of "other" and, 102; Darwinism and, 99; de facto, 53–54; Greek philosophers and, 98–99; Haitian independence and, 142; household economy and, 41–42; illegal, 53; Jews and, 63; Korea and, 200; in Middle Ages, 51; New Testament and, 92, 97; patriarchy and, 99; racism and, 76, 79–80, 97, 99; redemption and, 97; revival of, 50–52; Romans and, 34–37; Spanish colonialism and, 139, 141; Texas and, 83
Slavery Ordained of God (Frederick Ross), 99
Smith, Adam, 108
social Darwinism, 76, 99, 108–9
Social Gospel, 77, 247–48
socialism: anticommunist ideology and, 156; capitalism and, 111, 112, 113, 118; communism and, 112–13, 114; democracy and, 113; fascism and, 117; gradual reform and, 113; mixed economy and, 114; neocolonialism and, 155; productive property ownership and, 111–12; Roosevelt and, 110; Third World and, 114; utopian, 112
Social Security Act (United States), 47, 110, 129
social systems: Christian churches as, 243–44; necessity of, 9; theological status of empires and, 5; theological status of nations and, 3–5; theological status of orders of creation and, 5–6; theological status of power with/over concept and, 7–10; theological status of questions on, 1, 5; Wink and 1–2, 6. *See also* patriarchy
Somoza, Anastasio, 185–86, 192
soul, 1–2
South Africa, 150, 213–14. *See also* apartheid
South African Students' Organization, 217–18
South Korea, 158, 161, 169, 179, 205–7
Soviet Union: anticommunist ideology and, 156; collapse of, 115, 156, 169; Cuba and, 188; El Salvador and, 194; Guatemala and, 191–92; Korea and, 203, 204; neocolonialism, 155, 156; nuclear weapons, 176, 178; rise of Marxism, 19; slavery, 53–54; Third World and, 147; Vietnam and, 148
Spain: "chosen people" ideology, 100, 244–45; colonial empire, 5, 135, 139, 142, 183–84; Dominican Republic and, 184; fascism, 116; Jews and, 64–65, 66; papal power, 16
Spanish-American War, 167, 183
Spencer, Herbert, 109
Starhawk, 7
Stegner, Manfred, 157
stock market, 128
Stoic tradition, 98–99
Strong, Josiah, 77, 247–48
Strong, Maurice, 238
structural adjustment programs, 159–62

Sukarno, Ahmed, 149
Sumatra, 28
Suppression of Communism Act (South Africa), 216
Supreme Court, U.S., 49–50, 80, 124, 249

Taft-Katsura Agreement, 85, 201
tar sands, 230
technology, 105, 125–26, 128, 163, 170, 208, 229
terrorism, 117, 171, 176
Texas, 83–84
Thatcher, Margaret, 219
Theodosian Code, 63
Theodosius (emperor of Rome), 13, 62, 64
think tanks, 123
Timaeus (Plato), 95
Timothy, book of, 92–93
totalitarianism: communism and, 156; economic intervention and, 110; fascism and, 116, 117; messianic zealotry and, 248; Nicaragua and, 189; slavery and, 53–54; U.S. military depth and, 168–69
trade barriers, 159, 162
trade-related intellectual property laws (TRIPS), 162–63
trade-related investment measures (TRIMS), 162–63
transnational corporations, 108, 158–59, 162–63, 261
Transvaal, 214–15
Treaty of Guadalupe-Hidalgo, 84
TRIMS (trade-related investment measures), 162–63
TRIPS (trade-related intellectual property laws), 162–63
Trujillo, Raphael, 184
Truman, Harry, 168–69
trust-busting, 128
Turkey, 137

Ubico, Jorge, 191
United Fruit Company, 191–92

United Nations: apartheid, 218; Catholic Church and, 21; Earth Charter, 239, 264; El Salvador, 194; environment, 237, 238; equality, 5; Holy See, 4; Palestine, 69, 137; slavery, 53; Vietnam, 148–49
United Nations Supplementary Convention on the Abolition of Slavery, 53
United Nicaraguan Opposition (UNO), 189
United States: anti-imperial Christianity and, 252–53; anti-Semitism in, 71; arms sales by, 173; "backyard" of, 141, 183; Caribbean and, 183, 184–85, 195; Central American agenda of, 195; child labor in, 47; "chosen people" ideology and, 245–53; Christian fundamentalism and, 251; church-state separation and, 246; civil rights movement and, 248–49; class and, 121; colonial era and, 245; communism and, 114; critics of, 246–47, 248; democracy and, 101, 245; disestablishment of churches and, 19–20; ecological crisis and, 230, 237, 238; economic depression in, 46–47, 109–10, 128; economic polarization in, 50; economic reform in, 45; El Salvador and, 193–94; empires and, 5; expansion of, 139, 167; fascism and, 117; global currency markets and, 157; government subsidies by, 162; Guatemala and, 191–92; Holocaust and, 69; homosexuals in, 102; immigrants to, 127; independence of, 141–42; industrialization in, 108; Iraq and, 4; Japan and, 201; Jews and, 65, 68–69; Korea and, 200, 201, 203–5, 209–10; Mexico and, 83–84, 127, 142, 167, 183; national debt of, 174; neoliberalism in, 110, 111; Nicaragua and, 114–15, 185, 188–90; power blocs in, 124; progressivism in, 109;

race and, 100; religious pluralism in, 20–21; slavery in, 52–53; socialism in, 113; social reform and, 251; South Africa and, 150; United Nations and, 5; Vietnam and, 148; World Alliance of Reformed Churches and, 252–53; wealthy in, 127; World Bank/IMF and, 157. *See also* Constitution, U.S.; economic class in United States; neocolonialism; racism in United States

United States military: budget for, 169–72; expansion of, 138, 167–71, 175–76; expenditure by, 173; foreign training by, 173; founding fathers and, 167–68; imperial rule and, 170; Korea and, 203–5; national debt and, 174; nuclear weapons and, 176–79; public service economy and, 174; terrorist threat and, 171; waste by, 173–76

UNO (United Nicaraguan Opposition), 189

Vietnam, 114, 147–49, 177–78
voting rights, 46, 84, 107, 216

Walker, William, 185
Wall Street Journal, 174
war, 173, 179. *See also specific wars*
WARC (World Alliance of Reformed Churches), 21–22, 219, 252
Washington, George, 126–27
Weizmann, Chaim, 68
welfare liberalism, 111
welfare state, 113, 118, 157, 160
When Corporations Rule the World (David Korten), 163
Williams, Roger, 18
Wink, Walter, 1–2, 6–8, 243
The Winning of the West (Theodore Roosevelt), 82–83
Winthrop, John, 126
Wolfowitz, Paul, 170–71
women's rights, 45–46, 49–50, 244, 251, 253, 262
World Alliance of Reformed Churches (WARC), 21–22, 219, 252
World Bank: development loans and, 158, 159; establishment of, 157; funding/control of, 157; Guatemala and, 192; Korea and, 206; neocolonialism and, 138; neoliberalism and, 111, 162; Nicaragua and, 190; progress evaluation and, 160, 161; protective practices and, 161; South Africa and, 222; wealth distribution figures and, 164; world system and, 156–57
World Charter for Nature, 238
World Social Forum, 165
World Trade Organization (WTO), 111, 156–58, 161–63
World War I, 4, 68, 128, 136–37, 168, 215
World War II: decolonization of Asia and, 147; European colonialism and, 136; female employment and, 48; Indian independence and, 148; Japanese and, 86; Koreans and, 202; nation-states and, 4; United Nations and, 5; U.S. military depth and, 168; U.S. wealthy and, 129
World Zionist Movement, 67–68
WTO (World Trade Organization), 111, 156–58, 161–63

Yi dynasty (Korea), 199

Zelaya, José Santos, 185
Zimbabwe, 150
Zionism, 65, 67–71
Zulus, 214